The Book of Psalms

A COMMENTARY

THE BIBLE COMMENTARIES FUND

This book IS PUBLISHED FROM
A FUND CREATED BY THE WILL OF

BENJAMIN BLUMAUER

AND ADMINISTERED BY THE TRUSTEES
OF TEMPLE BETH ISRAEL OF
PORTLAND, OREGON

THE JEWISH
COMMENTARY FOR BIBLE READERS

The Book of Psalms

A COMMENTARY

BY

SOLOMON B. FREEHOF, D. D.

CINCINNATI
UNION OF AMERICAN HEBREW CONGREGATIONS
mcmxxxviii

TO

L. S. F.

Foreword

THE Committee in charge of the series of books issued by the Union of American Hebrew Congregations, through the Committee on Bible Commentaries of the Commission on Jewish Education, herewith present the Commentary on the Psalms by Reverend Doctor Solomon B. Freehof as the first of the series which are to be known as "A Jewish Commentary for Bible Readers."

In 1927 Dr. Emanuel Gamoran, the Educational Director of the Commission, suggested in his annual report that a series of Commentaries on the most important books of the Bible be published. The Commission favored the suggestion, and appointed a Committee on Commentaries with Dr. Samuel Schulman as Chairman. In 1930 the Chairman of this Committee presented a report which covered the scope, plan, and rules for the carrying out of the project. This report was adopted by the Commission. Writers of the Commentaries are governed by the rules as thus adopted.

The Commentaries are intended to meet the needs of readers of the Bible. The Committee does not aim at Commentaries for scholars. It does not seek to compete with any other organizations that may desire to publish Commentaries of a more scientific and scholarly nature for students. While the Commentaries as the Committee conceives them are to be based upon sound learning, the main purpose is to reach the masses of the people. It was felt, therefore, that the less technical discussion in such a Commentary for the people, the better. Whatever critical problems an author may feel the need of discussing should be dealt with in Preface or in Introduction and in as brief and as condensed a form as possible. They should not burden the text of the Commentary.

The Commentary should give a simple, clear, and intelligible explanation of words where this may be necessary. It should very briefly explain the historical background which may be necessary for the understanding of any passage. While thoroughly abreast of modern research, the writer is instructed to utilize especially the Jewish tradition as it speaks in the works of the great classical commentators and in the Midrashic literature. The writer is required to bring out the ethical and religious significance of the book wherever possible. This Commentary while aiming to increase knowledge, also aims at edification, so that a reader will be helped by it ethically and religiously. The Commentary should also call attention to literary beauty. The purpose of the Commentator should be to bring out the meaning of the content of the book as a literary religious classic, irrespective of time.

The Commentary is to be based on the English text of the Bible as presented in the translation made by the Jewish Publication Society of America, whose representatives worked together with representatives of the Central Conference of American Rabbis in the preparation of this text.

The Chairman of the Committee on Commentaries appoints sub-committees who read and study the manuscript presented by an author and make whatever comments and suggestions they think necessary. While the author retains perfect freedom and makes his own decisions and is alone responsible for his work, he is expected to accept important suggestions inas- much as the Committee on Commentaries acts in the capacity of an Editorial Board.

The Committee are happy in presenting this first Commentary of the series and hope to be able to present more Commentaries in the future.

SAMUEL SCHULMAN, *Chairman,*

Committee on Bible Commentaries

Acknowledgments

THE author desires to express his great appreciation for the many valuable suggestions made by his colleagues, Rabbis Samuel Schulman, Chairman of the Committee on Bible Commentaries, William Rosenau, and Henry Englander, who were kind enough to study the manuscript; and also his gratitude to Dr. Emanuel Gamoran, without whose repeated encouragement this work might not have been undertaken; and to Rabbi Louis I. Egelson and Mr. M. Myer Singer for their devotion to the difficult task of seeing this rather complicated manuscript through the press.

Contents

Book of Psalms

Introduction

~

THE Book of Psalms contains almost every great religious idea which grew up in Israel. Some of the psalms are epic poetry of the type of the Song of Deborah (Judges 5) and the Song of Moses at the Red Sea (Exodus 15). See Psalm 18. There are psalms which express the ethical idealism of the prophets (Psalm 15). Some psalms express the mood of study and a love of wisdom characteristic of the Book of Proverbs. Other psalms echo the great historical vision with its idea of the role of God as the Guide of human destiny as expressed in Deuteronomy and in the historical books. The Book of Psalms is an epitome of all the nobler religious ideas developed in Israel.

Besides the fact that the Psalms embody the highest ideas of biblical literature they also possess a uniqueness of mood and expression, a spirit which was bound to give them a universal appeal. Although many of the psalms were often understood as describing the vicissitudes of the whole people of Israel, yet they are essentially personal in mood. They describe the inner life, tenderly and vividly. For pure lyrical poetry, for the emotional aspect of the spiritual life, the Psalms are unique in literature. "The Book of Psalms contains the whole music of the heart of man, swept by the hand of his Maker. In it are gathered the lyrical burst of his tenderness, the moan of his penitence, the pathos of his sorrow, the triumph of his victory, the despair of his defeat, the firmness of his confidence, the rapture of his assured hope. In it is presented the anatomy of all parts of the human soul; in it, as Heine says, are collected 'sunrise and sun-

3

Introduction set, birth and death, promise and fulfillment—the whole drama of humanity.'" (*The Psalms in Human Life* by Rowland E. Prothero, p. 1.)

The literature of antiquity was rich in many types of expression, but it was poorest in voicing the language of the heart. The Hebrew Psalms were the first to give expression to the conversation of the human heart with God, in purer lyric language than ever before uttered. "David is the first of the poets of feeling—the king of lyrists. Never has the thought of poet risen so high and pure. Never has the soul opened before man and God in language so tender, so sympathetic and moving. All the secret cries of the human heart have found a voice through his life." (Lamartine.)

It is not surprising, therefore, that the Book of Psalms is the most widely read of all the biblical books. It was largely due to the Psalms that the Bible became one of the most influential books in the world. When Christianity emerged from Palestine and began to spread westward the Psalter was its hymn book and of all of the "Old Testament" books its greatest inspiration. The early Church made constant use of it. "It was the first book which the early Church put into the hands of her young converts, the primer of her religious teaching; and no man could be admitted to the highest order of the clergy unless he knew the Psalter by heart. It was used for singing in the first assemblies for Christian worship and it has ever continued to be used, sometimes as the sole book of praise, and always as the best and most enduring of all." (James Robertson, D.D., *The Poetry and the Religion of the Psalms*, pp. 7-8.)

When the New Testament was published apart from the "Old" Testament, the Book of Psalms was usually printed with it. It was used as frequently as the Gospel itself. In many denominations the Psalms are printed together with the prayer-book. There is hardly a festival or saint's day that does not have a specific psalm assigned to it.

Not only has the Psalm Book been used officially by the Church since the beginnings of Christianity, but its influence in personal life has been incalculably great. Soldiers, explorers,

4

statesmen, and philosophers, the great of the earth and the humble, have found religious inspiration and personal strength in the reading of the Psalms. Prothero, in his book, *The Psalms in Human Life,* tells of the great Christians in world history whose lives were constantly guided by the Psalms. It is perhaps correct to say that through Christianity the Psalms have become the most influential book in all of world literature.

In the life and thought of the people of Israel the Psalms have continually exerted a profound influence. The influence of the Psalms is conspicuous in the development of the prayerbook. The Jewish prayerbook, the first text for purely spiritual worship in the history of religion, is almost an echo of the Book of Psalms. In the earliest religious service the Torah and the Prophets were read and interpreted for the purpose of instruction, but the spiritual and emotional part of the service, that which became the actual text of the prayerbook itself, came almost entirely from the Book of Psalms. Many of the psalms were simply embodied in the service, or perhaps were the bulk of the original content of the service. To this day the regular synagogue services consist largely of psalms or psalm verses. In the daily services, Psalms 145-150 are read. Among those psalms recited on the Sabbath are Psalm 19, "The Heavens declare the glory of God"; Psalm 90, "Lord, Thou has been our dwelling-place in all generations"; Psalm 136, "Give thanks unto the Lord for He is good, for His mercy endureth forever"; Psalm 33, "Rejoice in the Lord, O ye righteous, praise is comely for the upright"; Psalm 92, "It is a good thing to give thanks unto the Lord, and to sing praises unto Thy name, O Most High." For the holidays, the regular psalm reading consists of Psalms 113-118, all of which are songs of rejoicing in the divine deliverance, and are subsumed under the general heading of "Hallel," meaning "praise." (See "The Jewish Prayerbook," Jewish Tracts, No. 10.)

Not only were whole psalms and psalm quotations taken over into the prayerbook until the bulk of the prayerbook consisted largely of psalm material, but even the original prayers in the prayerbook were (the earlier ones among them) under

5

the influence of the Psalms. This is evident even in the comparatively superficial fact of literary style. Many of the prayers are mere mosaics of psalm verses. Others, more original, are written in the poetic style characteristic of all biblical poetry, particularly that of the Psalms. As late as the middle of the talmudic epoch we find prayers still written in the couplet style of the Psalms. An examination of the older prayers will reveal the fact that in many of them (that is to say, those which are not in the fixed form of a "Berakah," a "blessing") each separate thought is expressed twice in the manner of the poetic style of biblical poetry. A few examples from Tract No. 10 (pp. 10 and 11), will suffice to make this evident.

> The help of our fathers hast Thou been forever,
> In all generations a Shield and Savior to their sons.
> > Happy the man who hearkens to Thy commands,
> > And the word of Thy law he taketh to heart . . .
> Let us adore the LORD of all
> And honor give to the world's Creator.
> The seat of His glory is in heaven above,
> The place of His power in the Highest heights . . .

The medieval Jewish poetry which embellished the prayerbook for Sabbath and holidays was likewise influenced by the poetry of the Psalms. The very idea that the prayerbook should be poetic and that worship can find its best expression in poetry was firmly established by the presence of the Psalms as part of the prayerbook.

In addition to this public use of the Psalms it would be impossible to estimate what the Psalms meant in the private life of the Jew. Regularly as a spiritual exercise, or especially in times of sorrow or joy, the reading of Psalms was the chief mode of religious self-expression.

THE Psalms are generally referred to as the Psalms of David and it is usually assumed that the author was the King of Israel, "the sweet singer of Israel." However, the critical studies of the Bible have produced many opinions as to the authorship of the psalms, some critical scholars going so far as to say that none of the psalms were written before the exile, either by David or by any of the earlier prophets. But this extreme view is not generally held. There is no doubt that some of the psalms were written centuries after the return from the exile but many of them have undoubtedly been written at an early date.

It is to be noted that Jewish tradition did not assert that the psalms were all written by David. In fact, in the Psalm Book itself many of the psalms are ascribed to other authors. Thus, Psalm 90 is ascribed to Moses; Psalms 72 and 127 to Solomon; twelve, Psalms 50, 73-83 to Asaph; Psalm 88 to Heman; eleven psalms to Korach, etc. The Babylonian Talmud (Baba Bathra, 15 a) which says that David wrote the Psalms with the help of ten elders, evidently looked upon him as the editor rather than the author of the whole book, although he has seventy-three individual psalms specifically assigned to him as author.

The Book of Psalms is divided into five books corresponding to the five books of the Pentateuch. "Moses gave the Five Books of the Torah and similarly David gave the Five Books of the Psalms" (Midrash Tehillim to Psalm 1). It is evident that the five books represented separate collections since three of them and possibly four end with a special sentence of praise, a concluding doxology. Also within these five books there is evidence of earlier and therefore smaller collections. For example, Songs of Ascent (Psalms 120-134) and also the psalms ascribed to Asaph, 73-83, very likely belong to a complete collection. The psalms at the end of Book Five, the Hallelujah psalms, must likewise have been part of an original collection. These various collections, many of them containing ancient psalms, gradually were brought together during the period of the second Temple. Certain of these psalms were sung by the Levites in the Temple of Mount Zion during the sacrificial service (m. Sukkah IV, 5). Many of them were, in all likelihood, used only in the synagogues throughout the land. Some were individual outpourings of the heart, written as a poet writes any poem, serving as personal devotion for those who read it. From these

7

various sources the collections were built up into the present book.

Considering the large number of authors and the number of anonymous psalms, the different types of religious mood expressed, the gradual way in which the various collections were built up and merged, it was inevitable that the psalms should express the emerging spirituality of the people of Israel. It was Israel's hymn book built up in the great creative period of the second Temple when the Synagogue arose, when the schools developed. The people of Israel was the real author of the Book of Psalms.

$\mathcal{H}$EBREW poetry, in its biblical form, does not make use of rhyme as does modern poetry although, of course, owing to the grammatical construction of the Hebrew language occasional rhymes may occur; nor does it make use of metre which is the basis of the poetry of Greece and of Rome, although certain scholars have tried to discover a metrical system in certain of the psalms. The psalm poetry is, generally, a succession of double clauses. The thought is stated in the first clause and then is repeated with different phraseology in the second clause. Thus, the thought is expressed twice in each couplet, and two by two the lines march on through the poem. This parallelism is frequently a synonymous parallelism, that is to say, the thought of the first line is repeated with slight variation in the second line of the couplet. For example, Psalm 18, verse 17:

> (a) He sent from on high, He took me;
> (b) He drew me out of many waters.
> (a) He delivered me from mine enemy most strong,
> (b) And from them that hated me, for they were
> too mighty for me.

Sometimes the couplet is *antithetic*, the second line expressing a thought opposite to that of the first line of the couplet. Thus, in the very first psalm, verse 6:

> (a) For the LORD regardeth the way of the righteous;
> (b) But the way of the wicked shall perish.

8

There are many variations of this style and sometimes they are used within one psalm. Sometimes the lines are built up into groups of three or four. Generally speaking, the method of Psalm (and other biblical) poetry is the use of successive clauses related to each other closely in thought and generally written in couplets. Therefore, the psalms were admirably suited for responsive readings or responsive singing by choirs or by congregations. The reader or the choir master would recite or sing one line, and the second line of the couplet would be spoken or chanted by the congregation or the choir.

The Psalms use many different technical terms as headings. These terms refer either to the style or the thought of the poem or to the instrument used when that particular psalm was given by the Levites in the Temple or the melody used when the psalm was sung. Fifty-seven of the psalms are described as *Mizmor*, a melody. Thirty of them are described as *Shir*, a song. Thirteen are marked as *Maschil*. Six are described as *Michtam*. The term *Neginoth* (used as heading for Psalms 4, 6, 54, 55, 61, 67, 76), very likely means a stringed instrument. *Nehiloth* used in Psalm 5, may mean a flute. Other musical terms are *Alamoth* (Psalm 46), may mean maidens' voices or soprano; *Sheminith* (Psalms 6 and 12), which probably means the eighth, may refer to octaves; *Gittith* (Psalms 8, 81, 84), may refer to some instrument that came from Gath or a melody from Gath sung by the Gittite guards. Some of the titles may refer to a well-known melody, now, of course, forgotten. Thus, for example, Psalm 9 *Muth-labben*, "The Death of the Son"; Psalm 22, *Aijeleth ha-Shahar*, "The Hind of the Morning"; Psalm 45, *Shoshannim,* "The Lilies"; Psalm 56, *Yonath elem rechokim*; Psalms 57-59, 75, set to the melody *Al-tashheth*. (For fuller discussion of the question see Chapter III in the Introduction of the Psalms by Kirkpatrick in the Cambridge Bible.)

Thus it is evident that many of the psalms were songs sung by choir with certain specified instrumental accompaniment to certain well known melodies. Others were recited as poetry. Others were read as silent meditations. The Psalm Book was hymn book, poetry book, prayerbook all in one.

9

Introduction This commentary is not written as a contribution to the scientific study of the Psalms. It is intended for the general reader with the purpose of simplifying the thought and interpreting the more difficult passages. It does not aim at completeness. While there will be some comment made on every psalm, these comments will be confined to such verses as are not readily understandable.

The commentary on each psalm will begin with a statement setting forth the thought or purpose of the poem and then there will follow a series of brief notes to those verses which require explanation.

The translations and commentaries which will be most frequently referred to are:

1. THE TARGUM: the Aramaic translation. For the description of the various Aramaic translations see *Jewish Encyclopedia*, Vol. XII, pp. 57 ff.

2. THE SEPTUAGINT: the Greek translation of the Bible (begun in the third pre-Christian century).

3. RASHI (Solomon bar Isaac, 1040-1105): French talmudic and biblical commentator.

4. IBN EZRA (Abraham ibn Ezra, 11th century): Spanish philosopher, poet and biblical commentator.

5. KIMCHI (David, 1160-1235): French grammarian and biblical commentator.

Book One

~~

THE first of the five books contains forty-one psalms. All of them, except four, have the name "David" in the title. The four exceptions are Psalms 1 and 2, which may be considered introductory to the book; Psalm 10, which may be a continuation of Psalm 9 and therefore needs no separate heading; and Psalm 33. This last psalm, however, has the heading "Of David" in the Greek Version (the Septuagint). These references to David are sometimes given simply "Of David" or "A Psalm of David," or "For the leader with string instrument, a Psalm of David," etc. The verse at the end of the forty-first psalm reads: "Blessed be the Lord, the God of Israel, from everlasting to everlasting, Amen and Amen." This verse does not belong to Psalm 41 but is the doxology closing the entire first book.

Psalm 1

1

1. Happy is the man that hath not walked in the counsel
     of the wicked,
  Nor stood in the way of sinners,
  Nor sat in the seat of the scornful.
2. But his delight is in the law of the LORD;
  And in His law doth he meditate day and night.
3. And he shall be like a tree planted by streams of water,
  That bringeth forth its fruit in its season,

THE theme of the psalm is fully stated in verses one and
two. Happiness is to be found in avoiding the counsel of the
wicked and in meditating on the Divine Law. The Law of God
is the source not only of knowledge but also of moral excellence
and of human happiness. (See introduction to Psalm 119.)
Hence the Law is contrasted with the counsel of the wicked,
and the happiness of him who constantly meditates on the Law
is contrasted with the miseries of the scorner. This is the
thought that runs through the entire biblical Book of Proverbs
and is the dominant attitude of the rabbis.

1. HAPPY IS THE MAN. The Hebrew word *ashre*, used as in
description of the spiritual result of righteousness and trust in
God, occurs frequently in the Psalms and occasionally in other
books of the Bible. Thus, "Happy are all they that take refuge
in Him," Psalm 2:12; "Happy is the nation whose God is the
Lord," Psalm 33:12; "Happy is the man whom Thou instructest, O Lord," Psalm 94:12; "Happy are they that are upright
in the way," Psalm 119:1. The well-known beatitudes in the
New Testament (Matthew 5:3-11) are a succession of phrases
beginning with *ashre*, i. e. "happy (or blessed) are," etc.

WALKED . . . STOOD . . . SAT. The verbs work to a climax.
Happy is he who does not walk with the wicked, who does not
remain in their company, and certainly does not participate in
their councils.

2. MEDITATE DAY AND NIGHT. Compare Deuteronomy 6:6-7,
"These words, which I command thee . . . thou shalt talk of
them . . . when thou liest down, and when thou risest up."

3. LIKE A TREE PLANTED BY STREAMS. The same metaphor is

12

And whose leaf doth not wither;
And in whatsoever he doeth he shall prosper.
4. Not so the wicked;
But they are like the chaff which the wind driveth away.
5. Therefore the wicked shall not stand in the judgment,
Nor sinners in the congregation of the righteous;
6. For the LORD regardeth the way of the righteous;
But the way of the wicked shall perish.

used in Jeremiah 17:8, "He shall be as a tree planted by the waters," etc. This passage in Jeremiah likewise begins with a "blessed" or "happy": "Blessed is the man that trusteth in the Lord, he shall be as a tree," etc. The Law itself is described as a tree of life (Proverbs 3:18).

4. NOT SO THE WICKED . . . LIKE CHAFF. The metaphor continues. The righteous are like a firmly rooted tree, but the wicked like wind-driven chaff.

5. SHALL NOT STAND IN THE JUDGMENT. According to the Targum and the medieval commentators this means the final judgment, but the whole psalm indicates that the meaning is that in our earthly life wickedness leads to condemnation and destruction, and righteousness to growth and permanence. Compare Proverbs 14:11, "The house of the wicked shall be overthrown; but the tent of the upright shall flourish."

PSALM 2 is based upon a specific historical event, now no longer definitely identifiable. It describes a rebellion of subject peoples against the King of Israel. The rebellion, therefore, is looked upon as a rebellion against God because in the first place, Israel is, in biblical metaphor, God's child (see Exodus 4:22, "Thus saith the Lord: Israel is My son, My first-born"); and the anointed King of Israel is God's chosen son. Thus David is assured in II Samuel 7:14, that Solomon, his son, who would succeed him as king, would be looked upon as God's own son: "I will be to him for a father, and he shall be to Me for a son." Perhaps, therefore, this rebellion was one which

13

Psalm 2
1

2. Why are the nations in an uproar?
   And why do the peoples mutter in vain?
2. The kings of the earth stand up,
   And the rulers take counsel together,
   Against the LORD, and against His anointed:
3. 'Let us break their bands asunder,
   And cast away their cords from us.'
4. He that sitteth in heaven laugheth,
   The LORD hath them in derision.
5. Then will He speak unto them in His wrath,
   And affright them in His sore displeasure:
6. 'Truly it is I that have established My king
   Upon Zion, My holy mountain.'
7. I will tell of the decree;

threatened at the time King Solomon was crowned as King. Out of this incident the psalmist draws a general conclusion, addressed to the rulers of the earth not to rebel against God's Law but to serve Him in purity, since the stability of nations depends upon their adherence to the higher Law. The Psalm ends: "Happy are all they that take refuge in Him," thus connecting the close of Psalm 2 with the beginning of Psalm 1 and binding them into a unity. Psalm 1 deals with the individual happiness based upon obedience to the Divine Law, and in Psalm 2 the stability of nations is based upon the same foundation.

1. WHY ARE THE NATIONS, ETC. The translation in the King James version is not as correct but is more famous: "Why do the heathen rage." Note the complete parallelism of the first and second phrases of each couplet throughout the psalm.

7. THOU ART MY SON. Addressed to the king, very likely Solomon, in fulfillment of the promise to David in II Samuel 7:14. "This day have I begotten thee." That is to say: "This day thou hast been anointed king."

10. From here the historical incident dramatized above is generalized into the principle that stability of nations is based upon obedience to the Divine Law.

11. SERVE THE LORD WITH FEAR. The Hebrew word for "fear," used in connection with serving God, means not abject

14

The Lord said unto me: 'Thou art My son,
This day have I begotten thee.
8. Ask of Me, and I will give the nations for thine inheritance,
And the ends of the earth for thy possession.
9. Thou shalt break them with a rod of iron;
Thou shalt dash them in pieces like a potter's vessel.'
10. Now therefore, O ye kings, be wise;
Be admonished, ye judges of the earth.
11. Serve the Lord with fear,
And rejoice with trembling.
12. Do homage in purity, lest He be angry, and ye perish
in the way,
When suddenly His wrath is kindled.
Happy are all they that take refuge in Him.

terror but reverential awe. The complete Hebrew phrase
yirath adonoi, means virtually "worship," "religion," or, in general, "reverence." Thus, Psalm 19:10, "The fear of the Lord is
clean" means "the worship of the Lord" or "reverence for the
Lord."

12. DO HOMAGE IN PURITY. Mistranslated in the King James
version as "kiss the son." Neither the Targum nor even the
earlier Christian commentators give the translation "kiss the
son" which is referred by many Christians to Jesus. *Bar* is
Aramaic for "son" but Hebrew for "purity." The word *bar* is
used once in the Bible for "son," namely, in Proverbs 31:2. But
the passage in Proverbs is late Hebrew which is influenced by
Aramaic. Since this psalm is not late Aramaized Hebrew, it uses
the regular Hebrew word *ben* for "son." The correct translation
is as given: "Do homage in purity." Some scholars take the word
bar to mean "earth," and translate the phrase, "kiss the earth,"
i. e., bow down in homage.

SOME historical incident is the basis of Psalm 3, also. The
heading refers to the rebellion of Absalom against his father,
David (compare II Samuel 15-18). In the psalm itself the description is given of the increasing number of adversaries
(verses 2, 7), and of David remaining quite confident. All this

15

Psalm 3
1

3. A PSALM OF DAVID, WHEN HE FLED FROM ABSALOM HIS SON.

2. LORD, how many are mine adversaries become!
   Many are they that rise up against me.
3. Many there are that say of my soul:
   'There is no salvation for him in God.'   Selah
4. But Thou, O LORD, art a shield about me;
   My glory, and the lifter up of my head.
5. With my voice I call unto the LORD,
   And He answereth me out of His holy mountain.   Selah
6. I lay me down, and I sleep;
   I awake, for the LORD sustaineth me.

reflects the narrative as given in the Book of Samuel. As in the preceding psalm, this one incident becomes the basis of a general religious principle, stated in verse 9, that numbers and physical might do not determine history; deliverance comes from God alone; thus expressing the view of the verse in Zechariah 4:6, "Not by might, nor by power but by My spirit" [does deliverance come]. Psalm 2 ended with the thought that obedience to God's Law is the source of a nation's stability; Psalm 3 asserts that in national crises God alone is the source of strength.

3. SALVATION. The Hebrew word *yeshuah* means "deliverance" or "help." The term is frequently used in the Bible. The Christian use of "transformation of the soul" is not the Old Testament meaning at all.

SELAH is used three times in this psalm, each time at a division of a thought. It is found seventy-one times in the Book of Psalms, also in the third chapter of the prophet, Habakkuk. The Targum and older commentators translate the word as meaning "forever." But such a meaning does not fit in with the context. The term is evidently not a part of the text at all, but marks the close of a stanza. Since twenty-eight of the thirty-nine psalms in which it is found have the heading, "For the Chief Musician," the word is in all likelihood of musical significance. Etymologically it may come from the root "solal" which means "to raise," "to raise the voice." Since it is evidently a musical

16

7. I am not afraid of ten thousands of people,
  That have set themselves against me round about.
8. Arise, O Lord; save me, O my God;
  For Thou hast smitten all mine enemies upon the cheek,
  Thou hast broken the teeth of the wicked.
9. Salvation belongeth unto the Lord;
  Thy blessing be upon Thy people.   Selah

4. FOR THE LEADER; WITH STRING-MUSIC. A PSALM OF DAVID.

2. Answer me when I call, O God of my righteousness,
  Thou who didst set me free when I was in distress;
  Be gracious unto me, and hear my prayer.

notation marking a pause, it is better simply to use the word
selah without translation.

4. THOU ART A SHIELD, a soldier's metaphor. "God is my protection and strength."

5. HIS HOLY MOUNTAIN, Mount Zion.

6. I LAY ME DOWN, etc. Though surrounded by enemies I
trust in God and sleep in peace.

8. THOU HAST SMITTEN. In the past "thou hast defeated mine
enemies," hence, "save me, Oh Lord," now.

THIS psalm is closely related to the preceding one. Verse 3,
"O ye sons of men," addresses the rebels and appeals to them to
abandon their rebellion. Verse 9, "In peace I lay me down to
sleep," echoes the thought of verse 6 in the preceding psalm:
"I lay me down and sleep . . ." Upon the basis of the same experience a more personal note is struck than in Psalm 3. Psalm
3 concludes that from God alone can a people's deliverance
come. This psalm stresses the *personal* confidence and peace of
heart of those who trust in God.

2. SET ME FREE WHEN I WAS IN DISTRESS. The word "distress,"
zar, means literally, "in a tight place," and "set me free" literally means, "Thou hast given me space." Thus in Psalm 118:5,
the same phrase is used "out of my straits I called upon the
Lord; He answered me with great enlargement."

17

3. O ye sons of men, how long shall my glory be put to shame,
   In that ye love vanity, and seek after falsehood? Selah
4. But know that the Lord hath set apart the godly man
   as His own;
   The Lord will hear when I call unto Him.
5. Tremble, and sin not;
   Commune with your own heart upon your bed,
   and be still.   Selah

3. MY GLORY. My status as king.

LOVE VANITY. Vain delusion that your rebellion will succeed. As in Psalm 2:1, the rebelling peoples "mutter in vain."

5. COMMUNE WITH YOUR HEART AND BE STILL. Consult your conscience and cease your rebellion. In a more general sense the verse means: The wicked are always restless and in an uproar: "The wicked are like the troubled sea," Isaiah 57:20; and the righteous learn to be serene and confident: "Keep calm, and be quiet; fear not," Isaiah 7:4.

6. SACRIFICES OF RIGHTEOUSNESS. The Targum and the commentators take this phrase in the prophetic spirit: Live righteously and your conduct will be as acceptable as an offering.

7. MANY THAT SAY, etc. The faint-hearted say: Would that God would bless us with His gifts, then we, too, could be confident and trust in Him.

LIFT UP THE LIGHT. As in the priestly blessing, "The Lord lift up His countenance upon thee, and give thee peace" (Numbers 6:26).

8, 9. THOU HAST PUT, etc. I do not envy the prosperity of the wicked. Thou hast given me an inner gladness; trusting in Thee my heart is at peace and I dwell in safety.

ALTHOUGH Psalm 5 is headed "A Psalm of David," it may well have been written after David's time. The reference in verse 8: "I come into Thy house; I will bow down toward Thy holy temple," evidently visualizes a permanent sanctuary and describes the custom of facing the Temple during prayer, a custom which was not prevalent until the period of the second Temple.

6. Offer the sacrifices of righteousness,
   And put your trust in the LORD.
7. Many there are that say: 'Oh that we could see some good!'
   LORD, lift Thou up the light of Thy countenance upon us.
8. Thou hast put gladness in my heart,
   More than when their corn and their wine increase.
9. In peace will I both lay me down and sleep;
   For Thou, LORD, makest me dwell alone in safety.

It was during the time of the second Temple that the custom
of regular public prayer arose in connection with the sacrificial
ritual in the Temple on Mount Zion. As part of the democratiz-
ing of Jewish worship, committees of the people stood beside
the priests during the offering of the regular sacrifice (the
tamid). The country was divided into twenty-four districts and
from each district a committee (*ma'amod*) came in its turn to
Jerusalem to stand beside the priest during the sacrifice. During
the week when the committee of a particular district would be
in Jerusalem, the people of that district gathered in their synagogues for prayer at the same hour of the day when the sacrifices
were being offered in Jerusalem. Thus it came about that they
naturally faced Jerusalem during their prayers and the synagogues all were built facing Jerusalem, and thus, also, it came
about that the *time* for Jewish services corresponded to the time
of the sacrifices, the morning prayer at the time of the morning
sacrifice, the afternoon prayer at the time of the afternoon sacrifice.

This psalm is a prayer of deep devotional feeling and of
high ethical sincerity. The prophets taught that the sacrifices
could not be properly offered by people who were unrighteous.
(See Isaiah 1:10-17, "To what purpose is the multitude of your
sacrifices unto Me? . . . your hands are full of blood. Wash
you, make you clean, put away the evil of your doings from before Mine eyes.") The psalmist lived at a later age when prayer
began to be an accompaniment of the sacrifices and soon to be
a *substitute* for them. He therefore applied to prayer the same
ethical standard which the prophets gave to sacrifice. Thus, the
essential thought of this psalm is that the wicked and the hypo-

Psalm 5

1

FOR THE LEADER; UPON THE NEHILOTH. A PSALM OF DAVID.

2. Give ear to my words, O LORD,
Consider my meditation.
3. Hearken unto the voice of my cry, my King, and my God;
For unto Thee do I pray.
4. O LORD, in the morning shalt Thou hear my voice;
In the morning will I order my prayer unto Thee, and will
look forward.
5. For Thou art not a God that hath pleasure in wickedness;
Evil shall not sojourn with Thee.
6. The boasters shall not stand in Thy sight;
Thou hatest all workers of iniquity.
7. Thou destroyest them that speak falsehood;
The LORD abhorreth the man of blood and of deceit.
8. But as for me, in the abundance of Thy lovingkindness
will I come into Thy house;
I will bow down toward Thy holy temple in the fear of Thee.

critical cannot stand in God's presence, whereas the psalmist
hopes that his own prayer will be acceptable and that God will
protect him against the schemings of the insincere and the unrighteous.

1. UPON NEHILOTH. Probably a wind instrument.

2. MY WORDS . . . MY MEDITATION. Prayer consists not only of
spoken words but also of unspoken thoughts. Thus, Psalm
19:15, "Let the words of my mouth and the meditation of my
heart be acceptable before Thee."

4. IN THE MORNING WILL I ORDER MY PRAYER UNTO THEE. The
Hebrew word *aroch*, "to order" or "arrange," is used with reference to arranging the wood on the altar for the sacrifice,
(Genesis 22:9); and because those who pray, facing Jerusalem,
visualize the services in the Temple, the psalmist uses the same
verb which therefore means: "I will arrange my prayer as a sacrifice before Thee."

5-7. NOT A GOD THAT HATH PLEASURE IN WICKEDNESS. The
whole passage is reminiscent of God's denunciation of wickedness in Isaiah 1:15-17.

8. I WILL BOW TOWARD THY HOLY TEMPLE. The custom of facing Jerusalem during prayer arose during the time of the second

20

9. O Lord, lead me in Thy righteousness because of
    them that lie in wait for me;
  Make Thy way straight before my face.
10. For there is no sincerity in their mouth;
  Their inward part is a yawning gulf,
  Their throat is an open sepulchre;
  They make smooth their tongue.
11. Hold them guilty, O God,
  Let them fall by their own counsels;
  Cast them down in the multitude of their transgressions;
  For they have rebelled against Thee.
12. So shall all those that take refuge in Thee rejoice,
  They shall ever shout for joy,
  And Thou shalt shelter them;
  Let them also that love Thy name exult in Thee.
13. For Thou dost bless the righteous;
  O Lord, Thou dost encompass him with favour as
    with a shield.

Temple and is referred to in the Book of Daniel which was
written during that period, "His windows were open in his upper chamber toward Jerusalem—and he kneeled upon his knees
three times a day, and prayed, and gave thanks before his God"
(Daniel 6:11).

IN THE FEAR OF THEE. As always in the Psalms, this phrase
means "in awe and reverence before Thee."

9-11. His enemies are here described in two metaphors, one,
as an ambush, "them that lie in wait for me," and as an abyss or
an open grave, "their throat is an open sepulchre."

10. THEY MAKE SMOOTH THEIR TONGUE. Their smooth hypocrisy is an attempt to conceal their evil intention.

11. REBELLED AGAINST THEE. All violence is a rebellion against
God, as justice and mercy towards our fellowmen is a service of
God.

12. REFUGE IN THEE. God is frequently described in the metaphor of a citadel upon a high tower to which the persecuted
may flee for safety. Thus, for example, Psalm 18:2, "The Lord
is my rock, and my fortress."

13. WITH FAVOUR AS WITH A SHIELD. God's help protects him
as a soldier is protected by his shield.

6. FOR THE LEADER; WITH STRING-MUSIC; ON THE SHEMINITH.
A PSALM OF DAVID.

2. O LORD, rebuke me not in Thine anger,
Neither chasten me in Thy wrath.
3. Be gracious unto me, O LORD, for I languish away;
Heal me, O LORD, for my bones are affrighted.
4. My soul also is sore affrighted;
And Thou, O LORD, how long?
5. Return, O LORD, deliver my soul;
Save me for Thy mercy's sake.
6. For in death there is no remembrance of Thee;

A PSALM written in a time of physical and spiritual misery. The psalmist is broken in body. He lies upon a bed of sickness. To his physical unhealth is added the consciousness of his own unworthiness. He asks God not to rebuke him. He is also aware of the scheming of his enemies who seek to do him harm. He prays for deliverance from them. This is a penitential psalm written in the midst of a multitude of sorrows.

1. SHEMINITH. Literally "the eighth," a musical term.

2. REBUKE . . . CHASTEN. Observe the parallelism of both lines of the couplet.

3. MY BONES ARE AFFRIGHTED. Bones, the framework of the body, are a symbol of the physical self.

4. MY SOUL IS AFFRIGHTED. His terror sweeps through the body and the mind. Bones and soul as body and mind are used in Proverbs 16:24, "Pleasant words are . . . sweet to the soul, and health to the bones."

5. RETURN, O LORD. In his anguish the psalmist feels that God has abandoned him, therefore, "Return, O Lord." The commentators suggest another explanation: "Return from Thine anger and forgive me."

6. IN DEATH THERE IS NO REMEMBRANCE OF THEE. In the psalms, as indeed in all biblical literature (with the exception of three late verses), there is no clear picture of life after death. The nether-world is a vague limbo in which there is no consciousness. See also Psalm 30:10, "What profit is there in my

In the nether-world who will give Thee thanks?
7. I am weary with my groaning;
    Every night make I my bed to swim;
    I melt away my couch with my tears.
8. Mine eye is dimmed because of vexation;
    It waxeth old because of all mine adversaries.
9. Depart from me, all ye workers of iniquity;
    For the LORD hath heard the voice of my weeping.
10. The LORD hath heard my supplication;
    The LORD receiveth my prayer.
11. All mine enemies shall be ashamed and sore affrighted;
    They shall turn back, they shall be ashamed suddenly.

blood, when I go down to the pit? Shall the dust praise Thee? Shall it declare Thy truth?" Psalm 88:12, "Shall Thy mercy be declared in the grave?" Psalm 115:17, "The dead praise not the Lord, neither any that go down into silence." It may be, of course, that the psalmist, because of his intense faith in God, has some *intimations* of immortality. A modern reader of the Psalms would get the impression of such intimations from certain passages, as for example: "Thou wilt guide me . . . and afterward receive me with glory" (Psalm 73:24). See also Psalm 116:6 ff. These passages at most can be interpreted as hopes. But the definite belief in a life after death arose in Maccabean times. It is important to note that the greatest products of biblical spiritual genius were created by a people who confined their attention to the duties and hopes of life on earth.

8. MINE EYE IS DIMMED . . . IT WAXETH OLD. In Deuteronomy 34:7, Moses is described: "His eye was not dim." That Moses retained his health to the day of his death was evidenced by his clear and undimmed vision. The psalmist is broken in health. His vision is dimmed because of his adversaries.

9-11. The psalmist changes the objects of address. He now speaks not to God but to his enemies. Confident that God will hear his prayer, he calls upon his enemies to depart from him for their plans are bound to fail. In verse 11 he refers to his enemies in the third person. Such shifting of grammatical "person" occurs frequently in biblical literature.

23

Psalm 7

7. SHIGGAION OF DAVID, WHICH HE SANG UNTO THE LORD,
   CONCERNING CUSH A BENJAMITE.

2. O LORD my God, in Thee have I taken refuge;
   Save me from all them that pursue me, and deliver me;
3. Lest he tear my soul like a lion,
   Rending it in pieces, while there is none to deliver.
4. O LORD my God, if I have done this;
   If there be iniquity in my hands;
5. If I have requited him that did evil unto me,
   Or spoiled mine adversary unto emptiness;
6. Let the enemy pursue my soul, and overtake it,

THIS psalm is clearly based upon an historic event. The heading which refers to Cush, a Benjamite, who is evidently a kinsman or a clansman of Saul, reflects the dispute between David and Saul in the last dark years of Saul's reign. (See I Samuel 22:6-10, where Doeg, the Edomite, insinuates that David planned to kill Saul.) The content of the psalm bears out this interpretation. The psalm is a prayer to God for protection against slander. David disavows any evil intention against Saul and pleads to God, who judges the heart, to vindicate him and to bring about the defeat of the slanderers.

1. SHIGGAION. A dubious word found in the plural as the description of a poem in Habakkuk 3:1. Many meanings are suggested. One possible meaning bases the word upon the root which means "to go astray" or "to reel," thus giving the meaning: "an irregular and emotional poem."

CUSH A BENJAMITE. This Benjamite is not mentioned elsewhere in the Bible. The older commentators tried to identify the name Cush with Saul, one saying that inasmuch as Cush means, "an Ethiopian" whose skin is different from other men, so Saul's behavior changed and became different from that of others. It is sufficient to say that this must have been some kinsman or intimate of Saul who brought reports to Saul that David was plotting against him.

2. FROM ALL THEM THAT PURSUE ME. Clearly reflecting the time when David and his followers were fugitives from Saul.

And tread my life down to the earth;
Yea, let him lay my glory in the dust. Selah
7. Arise, O LORD, in Thine anger,
  Lift up Thyself in indignation against mine adversaries;
  Yea, awake for me at the judgment which Thou hast com-
    manded.
8. And let the congregation of the peoples compass Thee about,
  And over them return Thou on high.
9. O LORD, who ministerest judgment to the peoples,
  Judge me, O LORD, according to my righteousness, and accord-
    ing to mine integrity that is in me.
10. Oh that a full measure of evil might come upon the wicked,

4-5. David disavows any evil intention against Saul, a dis-
avowal which he proves by refusing to take Saul's life when he
had an easy opportunity to do so. (I Samuel 24, the story of
David cutting off the corner of Saul's garment.)

5. SPOILED MINE ADVERSARY UNTO EMPTINESS. If I had de-
spoiled my enemy, Saul, then I would merit God's punishment.
However, the commentators, Ibn Ezra and Kimchi, translate this
verse to mean: I even *delivered* him (i. e. Saul) who, without
justification, was my enemy.

6. MY GLORY IN THE DUST. Glory means "the soul," "the life."
Psalm 16:9: "My heart is glad and my glory rejoiceth." Psalm
30:13, "So that my glory may sing praise to Thee."

SELAH. The phrase marks the end of a stanza. See comment
on Psalm 3.

7-8. A picture of God exercising judgment. The scene taken
from an earthly scene of judgment. The mass of people and the
judge rising above them to sit upon a throne. Hence: "Lift up
Thyself . . . let the congregation of the peoples compass Thee
about, and (therefore) return Thou on high."

9. JUDGE ME, O LORD. God judges not only nations but individuals. He knows the truth since he reads the heart of man.
Only He can know "mine integrity that is in me," for only He
is able to try "the hearts and reins" (verse 10).

10. THE REINS (i. e. the kidneys) were believed to be the seat
of the emotions. The phrase "heart and reins," i. e., will and

25

And that Thou wouldest establish the righteous;
For the righteous God trieth the hearts and reins.
11. My shield is with God,
Who saveth the upright in heart.
12. God is a righteous judge,
Yea, a God that hath indignation every day:
13. If a man turn not, He will whet His sword,
He hath bent His bow, and made it ready;
14. He hath also prepared for him the weapons of death,
Yea, His arrows which He made sharp.
15. Behold, he travaileth with iniquity;
Yea, he conceiveth mischief, and bringeth forth falsehood.
16. He hath digged a pit, and hollowed it,
And is fallen into the ditch which he made.
17. His mischief shall return upon his own head,
And his violence shall come down upon his own pate.

the emotion, is found frequently in the Bible. For example, Jeremiah 20:12, "O Lord, that triest the righteous, that seest the reins and the heart."

12-14. God's anger at the unrepentant; God being described as the warrior ready for battle.

12. INDIGNATION EVERY DAY. The Divine punishment for evil, never relaxing, unless man repents.

15. TRAVAILETH, CONCEIVETH, BRINGETH FORTH. Evil is described with the metaphor of a woman bearing a child.

16. Evil is described as a pit dug to trap the innocent into which the violent will himself fall.

18. HIS RIGHTEOUSNESS. God's vindication of the innocent proves that God is a just ruler whose righteous decisions will triumph.

A NATURE psalm describing God's glory in the universe but particularly in the soul of man. The theme of the psalm is that although God is the majestic Creator of the infinite heavens, yet man is given the privilege of mastery over the animal world and the glory of testifying to the Divine Presence.

1. GITTITH. The word is derived from the city of Gath, a city

18. I will give thanks unto the LORD according to His
    righteousness;
    And will sing praise to the name of the LORD Most High.

8. FOR THE LEADER; UPON THE GITTITH. A PSALM OF DAVID.

2. O LORD, our Lord,
   How glorious is Thy name in all the earth!
   Whose majesty is rehearsed above the heavens.
3. Out of the mouth of babes and sucklings hast Thou
     founded strength,
   Because of Thine adversaries;
   That Thou mightest still the enemy and the avenger.
4. When I behold Thy heavens, the work of Thy fingers,
   The moon and the stars, which Thou hast established;
5. What is man, that Thou art mindful of him?
   And the son of man, that Thou thinkest of him?

in Philistia. *Gittith* therefore means either the name of an instrument which comes from Gath or a melody known by the
name. Perhaps a song sung by Gittite guards of King David (II
Samuel 15:18 ff.).

2. O LORD, OUR LORD. For the first time in the Psalm Book
the plural is used: *"our* Lord" instead of *"my* Lord" or *"my*
God." Since the psalmist speaks of the status of all mankind in
the universe he speaks as it were in the name of mankind,
therefore uses the plural.

WHOSE MAJESTY IS REHEARSED. Thus Psalm 19, "The heavens
declare the glory of God."

3. OUT OF THE MOUTH OF BABES. God's boundless might is
revealed in the infinite heavens, yet even children and infants
are aware of His presence and testify to His greatness.

BECAUSE OF THINE ADVERSARIES. The wicked and the venge-
ful whose actions are in themselves a denial of God's existence
and justice are refuted by the testimony which the heart of
every child gives to the presence of the Divine.

4. THY HEAVENS, THE WORK OF THY FINGERS. The metaphor
visualizes God as an infinite artisan creating all nature with his
hands. Thus, too, in Psalm 19:2, "The firmament showeth His
handiwork."

27

6. Yet Thou hast made him but little lower than the angels,
   And hast crowned him with glory and honour.
7. Thou hast made him to have dominion over the works of
   Thy hands;
   Thou hast put all things under his feet:
8. Sheep and oxen, all of them,
   Yea, and the beasts of the field;
9. The fowl of the air, and the fish of the sea;
   Whatsoever passeth through the paths of the seas.
10. O LORD, our Lord,
   How glorious is Thy name in all the earth!

9. FOR THE LEADER; UPON MUTH-LABBEN. A PSALM OF DAVID.

2. I will give thanks unto the LORD with my whole heart;

6. YET THOU HAST MADE HIM BUT LITTLE LOWER THAN THE ANGELS. Although God is the great creator of the boundless heavens and in contrast with their immensity man seems small and insignificant, yet God had given man privilege and power.

THAN THE ANGELS. The people of Israel, as did many other peoples, believed in superhuman beings, the messengers of God, the angels. (Cf. article "Angelology," *Jewish Encyclopedia*, Vol. I.)

7. DOMINION OVER THE WORKS OF THY HANDS. Evidence of man's privilege in his mastery over all the living things on earth and in the sea and air.

10. The psalm ends with the opening verse repeated as a refrain.

A PRAYER written in acrostic form. This acrostic follows the alphabet, thus verses 2 and 3 begin with the letter *aleph*, verse 4 with *bays*, verse 6 with *gimmel*, and so with some irregularity through the first half of the alphabet. There are eight psalms written as acrostics, 25, 34, 37, 111, 112, 119 (an octuple alphabetical acrostic), and Psalm 145. As a prayer, this psalm follows the sequence of moods which has become classic in Jewish prayer, namely, first to praise God for His past favors and then to ask for further help. (One must first utter the praise of God and then voice his petition.—b Berachoth 32a) Thus

I will tell of all Thy marvellous works.
3. I will be glad and exult in Thee;
  I will sing praise to Thy name, O Most High:
4. When mine enemies are turned back,
  They stumble and perish at Thy presence;
5. For Thou hast maintained my right and my cause;
  Thou sattest upon the throne as the righteous Judge.
6. Thou hast rebuked the nations,
  Thou hast destroyed the wicked,
  Thou hast blotted out their name for ever and ever.
7. O thou enemy, the waste places are come to an end
    for ever;
  And the cities which thou didst uproot,
  Their very memorial is perished.

(verses 2-13), God is praised for His "marvelous works" in defeating the wicked and the violent, and from verse 14 on He is asked "to be gracious . . . behold mine affliction at the hands of them that hate me."

1. UPON MUTH-LABBEN. The commentators offer various explanations of this phrase. *Muth-labben* is perhaps the name of a melody well known at that time. The heading of the psalm instructs the chief musician to chant the psalm to that melody.

2. WITH MY WHOLE HEART. With complete sincerity and without reservations. Thus, Deuteronomy 6:5, "Thou shalt love the Lord thy God with *all* thy heart." Note the perfect parallelism between each of the two lines in every couplet throughout the psalm.

6. THOU HAST BLOTTED OUT THEIR NAME. The Hebrew metaphor refers to the idea that the names of nations and individuals are all written down in God's book of record. When Moses asks that God destroy him rather than destroy his people, he says: "Blot me out of Thy book which Thou hast written" (Exodus 32:32). So, "I shall blot out the remembrance of Amalek" (Exodus 17:14). Therefore here the phrase "Thou hast blotted out their name" is the parallel to the preceding line in the strophe: "Thou hast destroyed the wicked."

7. THE WASTE PLACES ARE COME TO AN END FOR EVER. This difficult verse is made clearer by the parallel verse of the

29

8. But the LORD is enthroned for ever;
   He hath established His throne for judgment.
9. And He will judge the world in righteousness,
   He will minister judgment to the peoples with equity.
10. The LORD also will be a high tower for the oppressed,
    A high tower in times of trouble;
11. And they that know Thy name will put their trust
      in Thee;
    For Thou, LORD, hast not forsaken them that seek Thee.
12. Sing praises to the LORD, who dwelleth in Zion;
    Declare among the peoples His doings.
13. For He that avengeth blood hath remembered them;
    He hath not forgotten the cry of the humble.
14. Be gracious unto me, O LORD,
    Behold mine affliction at the hands of them that
      hate me;
    Thou that liftest me up from the gates of death;

strophe, "the cities which thou didst uproot, their memorial is perished." The psalmist rebukes the enemy for the permanent destructions which his violence has caused.

8. BUT THE LORD IS ENTHRONED. The destructiveness of human violence would break our courage were it not for our confidence that God is enthroned and will "minister judgment to the peoples" (verse 9), and will be "a high tower for the oppressed" (verse 10).

13. HE THAT AVENGETH BLOOD HATH REMEMBERED THEM. Among the Semitic peoples the "avenger of the blood" was the closest relative who (before the state took over that function) exacted punishment for bloodshed and violence. The poor who have no protector can rely upon God as their protector, the "avenger of their blood," i. e. "the Vindicator of justice."

15. IN THE GATES OF THE DAUGHTER OF ZION. In the gates of the people of Zion. The city gates, the place of the busiest traffic during the day, was therefore also the place of assembly and judgment. Thus, wisdom crieth aloud, (Proverbs 8:3): "Beside the gates, at the entry of the city." The phrase here therefore, means: "I will tell Thy praise where all will hear."

16. THE PIT . . . THE NET. The metaphor for the destructive

30

15. That I may tell of all Thy praise in the gates of the
    daughter of Zion,
  That I may rejoice in Thy salvation.
16. The nations are sunk down in the pit that they made;
  In the net which they hid is their own foot taken.
17. The LORD hath made Himself known, He hath executed
    judgment,
  The wicked is snared in the work of his own hands.
    Higgaion.   Selah
18. The wicked shall return to the nether-world,
  Even all the nations that forget God.
19. For the needy shall not alway be forgotten,
  Nor the expectation of the poor perish for ever.
20. Arise, O LORD, let not man prevail;
  Let the nations be judged in Thy sight.
21. Set terror over them, O LORD;
  Let the nations know they are but men. Selah

plans of the wicked, compare Psalm 5:10, "a yawning gulf."

17. HIGGAION. SELAH. The musical notation marking the end of the thought. Possibly a triumphant flourish of music.

18. SHALL RETURN TO THE NETHER-WORLD. Death is a return to the earth from which man has sprung. Genesis 3:19, "Till thou return unto the ground; for out of it wast thou taken." The earth, to which the dead return, was extended into a limbo of forgetfulness, the shadowy nether-world.

19. THE NEEDY . . . THE POOR. The humble, the needy, and the poor are often referred to in the psalms in contrast to the proud and the violent.

IN all likelihood Psalm 10 forms a unity with Psalm 9. This conclusion is based upon a number of considerations: first, the acrostic in Psalm 9 goes only to the letter *lamed*, halfway through the alphabet, and while the acrostic in Psalm 10 is not perfect the psalm does end with the four final letters of the alphabet. Thus, verse 12 begins with *kof*, verse 14 with *resh*, verse 15 with *shin*, verse 17 with *tav*. Furthermore, this psalm has no heading of its own, whereas every psalm in Book One

10. Why standest Thou afar off, O LORD?
  Why hidest Thou Thyself in times of trouble?
2. Through the pride of the wicked the poor is hotly pursued,
  They are taken in the devices that they have imagined.
3. For the wicked boasteth of his heart's desire,
  And the covetous vaunteth himself, though he contemn the LORD.
4. The wicked, in the pride of his countenance [,saith]: 'He will
    not require';
  All his thoughts are: 'There is no God.'
5. His ways prosper at all times;
  Thy judgments are far above out of his sight;
  As for all his adversaries, he puffeth at them.
6. He saith in his heart: 'I shall not be moved,
  I who to all generations shall not be in adversity.'
7. His mouth is full of cursing and deceit and oppression;
  Under his tongue is mischief and iniquity.
8. He sitteth in the lurking-places of the villages;
  In secret places doth he slay the innocent;
  His eyes are on the watch for the helpless.
9. He lieth in wait in a secret place as a lion in his lair,
  He lieth in wait to catch the poor;

(except Psalm 1 and 2 and Psalm 33, and see Introduction to Book One) has a separate heading. Finally, the language of Psalm 10, resembles closely the language of Psalm 9. The phrase, "in times of trouble," an unusual phrase in 10:1, is also found in 9:10. Both psalms end with the thought that God will protect the humble by teaching the wicked that they are only mortal and cannot prevail against God's infinite justice.

1. WHY STANDEST THOU AFAR. A thought frequently voiced in psalms. God seems to have withdrawn from us and we plead for Him to return to our help. See Psalm 6:5, "Return, O Lord, deliver my soul."

2. THE WICKED . . . THEY ARE TAKEN IN THE DEVICES. Though the wicked persecute the poor the wicked are "taken" (i. e. caught) in their own snares.

4. THE WICKED SAITH HE WILL NOT REQUIRE . . . THERE IS NO GOD. The wicked, assuring themselves that there is no God, conclude therefore that there is no justice which can require them to make amends for their violence. Thus in Psalm 14:1, "The

He doth catch the poor, when he draweth him up in his net.
10. He croucheth, he boweth down,
And the helpless fall into his mighty claws.
11. He hath said in his heart: 'God hath forgotten;
He hideth His face; He will never see.'
12. Arise, O Lord; O God, lift up Thy hand;
Forget not the humble.
13. Wherefore doth the wicked contemn God,
And say in his heart: 'Thou wilt not require'?
14. Thou hast seen; for Thou beholdest trouble and vexation,
to requite them with Thy hand;
Unto Thee the helpless committeth himself;
Thou hast been the helper of the fatherless.
15. Break Thou the arm of the wicked;
And as for the evil man, search out his wickedness, till none
be found.
16. The Lord is King for ever and ever;
The nations are perished out of His land.
17. Lord, Thou hast heard the desire of the humble:
Thou wilt direct their heart, Thou wilt cause Thine ear
to attend;

fool hath said in his heart 'there is no God!' " (and therefore) "they have dealt corruptly."

5-6. HIS WAYS PROSPER . . . I SHALL NOT BE MOVED. The wicked assures himself that his prosperity will be permanent, there is none to punish him.

8-9. HE SITTETH IN THE LURKING-PLACES. The familiar figure of the ambushes and the nets of the wicked. See Psalm 9:16.

12. ARISE, O LORD. As the judge ascends the dais to pronounce judgment. See Psalm 3:8, "Arise; O Lord, save me O my God;" and Psalm 7:7.

LIFT UP THY HAND. Manifest Thy power. Raise Thy hand to help the humble.

14. THE HELPER OF THE FATHERLESS. In Psalm 68:6, God is described as "father of the fatherless," hence His command in Exodus 22:21, "Ye shall not afflict any widow, or fatherless child." See also Malachi 3:5.

17. THOU WILT DIRECT THEIR HEART. Thou wilt teach them to find strength in turning towards Thee in worship and "Thou

33

18. To right the fatherless and the oppressed,
    That man who is of the earth may be terrible no more.

11. FOR THE LEADER. [A PSALM] OF DAVID.
    In the LORD have I taken refuge;
    How say ye to my soul:
    'Flee thou! to your mountain, ye birds'?
2. For, lo, the wicked bend the bow,
    They have made ready their arrow upon the string,
    That they may shoot in darkness at the upright in heart.
3. When the foundations are destroyed,
    What hath the righteous wrought?
4. The LORD is in His holy temple,

wilt cause Thine ear to attend" their prayer and supplication.

18. THAT MAN . . . MAY BE TERRIBLE NO MORE. Parallels the last sentence of Psalm 9, namely, that when men learn that there is a Divine Law governing the world they will no longer terrify the humble and the weak.

THE psalmist is in peril. His friends advise him to flee. His answer is that he trusts in God's help to defend him. There was a period in the life of David in which this psalm might well have been written. David, at King Saul's court, was in increasing danger as the king's suspicions mounted against him. He is advised to flee for safety to the mountains.

1. IN THE LORD HAVE I TAKEN REFUGE. I do not need to fly away for safety; God is my rock and my salvation.

FLEE THOU. The more familiar translation is: "Flee as the bird to your mountain." When in danger Israel fled to the mountain fastness, thus I Samuel 14:22, "The men of Israel hid themselves in the hill-country of Ephraim."

2. THE WICKED BEND THE BOW. Continuing the metaphor of the bird aimed at by the archer.

3. WHEN THE FOUNDATIONS, ETC. When the security of life is destroyed by violence, righteousness seems so futile a defense. "What hath the righteous wrought?" A note of despair. The rest of the psalm gives the answer that God's justice will prevail.

34

The LORD, His throne is in heaven;
His eyes behold, His eyelids try, the children of men.
5. The LORD trieth the righteous;
But the wicked and him that loveth violence His soul hateth.
6. Upon the wicked He will cause to rain coals;
Fire and brimstone and burning wind shall be the portion
of their cup.
7. For the LORD is righteous, He loveth righteousness;
The upright shall behold His face.

12. FOR THE LEADER; ON THE SHEMINITH. A PSALM OF DAVID.

2. Help, LORD; for the godly man ceaseth;
For the faithful fail from among the children of men.

4. HIS THRONE IS IN HEAVEN . . . HIS EYES BEHOLD. Though God is enthroned on high His eyes behold the doings of the children of men. Thus "The Lord, our God, that is enthroned on high, that looketh down low upon heaven and upon the earth" (Psalm 113:5-6).

5. TRIETH THE RIGHTEOUS. God tests the courage and the patience of the righteous.

6. COALS, FIRE AND BRIMSTONE. This description recalls the destruction of the city of Sodom, "The Lord caused to rain upon Sodom brimstone and fire," Genesis 19:24.

7. THE UPRIGHT SHALL BEHOLD HIS FACE. Only those who are acceptable to the King are privileged to come into His presence. Thus, "The boasters shall not stand in Thy sight" (Psalm 5:6), and "I shall behold Thy face in righteousness" (Psalm 17:15).

ON Psalm 11 the psalmist is in danger of plotters who seek his life. In Psalm 12 he is surrounded by hypocrites who seek to overcome him by flattery. In this psalm he expresses his disgust at the insincerities and the hypocrisy of his time and turns to God whose words are pure as "silver seven times refined."

1. SHEMINITH. A musical term, possibly meaning an octave. See Psalm 6:1.

2. THE GODLY MAN CEASETH. There seems to be no one left who speaks the truth.

35

3. They speak falsehood every one with his neighbour;
   With flattering lip, and with a double heart, do they speak.
4. May the LORD cut off all flattering lips,
   The tongue that speaketh proud things!
5. Who have said: 'Our tongue will we make mighty;
   Our lips are with us: who is lord over us?'
6. 'For the oppression of the poor, for the sighing of the needy,
   Now will I arise,' saith the LORD;
   'I will set him in safety at whom they puff.'
7. The words of the LORD are pure words,
   As silver tried in a crucible on the earth, refined seven times.
8. Thou wilt keep them, O LORD;
   Thou wilt preserve us from this generation for ever.
9. The wicked walk on every side,
   When vileness is exalted among the sons of men.

13. FOR THE LEADER. A PSALM OF DAVID.

2. How long, O LORD, wilt Thou forget me for ever?

3. WITH A DOUBLE HEART. A vivid metaphor for hypocrisy.

5. OUR TONGUE WILL WE MAKE MIGHTY. They believe that their skill in flattery will bring them permanent power.

6. NOW WILL I ARISE. As judge in behalf of the deceived and the oppressed. See Psalm 7:7.

AT WHOM THEY PUFF. The Hebrew is difficult but seems to mean that the unfortunate at whom these flatterers scornfully puff will, through God's help, be brought to safety.

7. THE WORDS OF THE LORD ARE PURE. In contrast to the false words of the hypocrite.

9. THE WICKED WALK ON EVERY SIDE. This thought re-echoes the opening phrase of the psalm achieving a unity of thought as in Psalm 8.

A PLAINTIVE psalm written in time of despair. Its mood is consistent with that of the two preceding psalms. Psalm 11 describes violence and Psalm 12 the hypocrisy of men. Because of these depressing facts, the psalmist is saddened and discouraged.

2. WILT THOU HIDE THY FACE. How long wilt Thou deny me

How long wilt Thou hide Thy face from me?
3. How long shall I take counsel in my soul,
   Having sorrow in my heart by day?
   How long shall mine enemy be exalted over me?
4. Behold Thou, and answer me, O LORD my God;
   Lighten mine eyes, lest I sleep the sleep of death;
5. Lest mine enemy say: 'I have prevailed against him';
   Lest mine adversaries rejoice when I am moved.
6. But as for me, in Thy mercy do I trust;
   My heart shall rejoice in Thy salvation.
   I will sing unto the LORD,
   Because He hath dealt bountifully with me.

14. FOR THE LEADER. [A PSALM] OF DAVID.
   The fool hath said in his heart: 'There is no God';
   They have dealt corruptly, they have done
      abominably;
   There is none that doeth good.

Thy help? The Divine blessing (Numbers 6:25) is described: "God will cause the light of His countenance to shine upon thee." Therefore the psalmist in his sorrow feels that God has hidden His radiance from him.

3. COUNSEL IN MY SOUL . . . SORROW IN MY HEART. How long must I brood and find within me only anguished thoughts?

4. LIGHTEN MINE EYES. Sickness causes the eyes to be dimmed. Death darkens them entirely. Hence, the psalmist prays: Bring light to mine eyes lest I die.

5. WHEN I AM MOVED. When I am shaken. See Psalm 38:17, "Lest they rejoice over me; when my foot slippeth."

6. I WILL SING UNTO THE LORD. In my despair I find strength again when I recall God's bounty in the past.

As the three preceding psalms, this psalm also is a psalm of loneliness. In Psalm 11, the psalmist describes himself as surrounded by the violent; in Psalm 12 by the hypocritical; and in Psalm 14 by the corrupt.

1. THE FOOL HATH SAID IN HIS HEART. The psalmist concludes

2. The LORD looked forth from heaven upon the children of men,
   To see if there were any man of understanding, that did seek
   after God.
3. They are all corrupt, they are together become impure;
   There is none that doeth good, no, not one.
4. 'Shall not all the workers of iniquity know it,
   Who eat up My people as they eat bread,
   And call not upon the LORD?'
5. There are they in great fear;
   For God is with the righteous generation.
6. Ye would put to shame the counsel of the poor, but the LORD
   is his refuge.
7. Oh that the salvation of Israel were come out of Zion!
   When the LORD turneth the captivity of His people,

that the fool must surely disbelieve in the existence of God for
the fool's corrupt actions prove his doubt of a Divine justice.
The Hebrew word *Navval*, translated here "the fool," implies
both mental and moral folly.

3. THEY ARE ALL CORRUPT. The description recalls the con-
dition of mankind in the days of Noah. Genesis 6:12, "And God
saw the earth, and, behold, it was corrupt; for all flesh had corrupted their way upon the earth."

4. WHO EAT UP MY PEOPLE. A vivid description of the ex-
ploitation of the weak. A similar phrase is used in Micah 3:3,
"Who eat the flesh of my people."

5. THERE ARE THEY IN GREAT FEAR. But the violent will soon
be made afraid "for God is with the righteous," etc.

7. WHEN THE LORD TURNETH THE CAPTIVITY OF HIS PEOPLE.
If this verse is an integral part of the psalm then this psalm
must have been written after the exile. It may be that this verse
is a later addition to an older psalm or else that the phrase
"turneth the captivity" may mean "when God will restore the
prosperity of His people," as some modern commentators translate it.

A DESCRIPTIVE definition of ethical nobility. Since the preceding psalms spoke of the violent, the hypocritical, and the

15. A PSALM OF DAVID.

LORD, who shall sojourn in Thy tabernacle?
Who shall dwell upon Thy holy mountain?
2. He that walketh uprightly, and worketh righteousness,
And speaketh truth in his heart;
3. That hath no slander upon his tongue,
Nor doeth evil to his fellow,
Nor taketh up a reproach against his neighbour;
4. In whose eyes a vile person is despised,
But he honoureth them that fear the LORD;
He that sweareth to his own hurt, and changeth not;
5. He that putteth not out his money on interest,

corrupt whose sins remove them far from God, this psalm
speaks of the type of life that brings man to the Divine Presence. The psalm is closely parallelled in thought by Psalm 24.

1. THY TABERNACLE . . . THY HOLY MOUNTAIN. While literally
the psalm asks who shall dwell in God's temple on Mount Zion,
the introduction to Psalm 24 makes it clear that it is to be
understood in the wider sense; that the whole earth is the
Lord's and, therefore, the psalm really means, what sort of man
can dwell in the near presence of God?

2. UPRIGHTLY. The Hebrew word means "perfect," or "complete" (i. e. whole-hearted in allegiance to God). The phrase,
therefore, means, he who follows a noble rule of life.

TRUTH IN HIS HEART. Even his unspoken thoughts are sincere.

3. NOR TAKETH UP A REPROACH. He does not carry gossip to
shame his neighbor.

4. A VILE PERSON IS DESPISED. The commentator, Ibn Ezra,
takes this to mean that he is humble in his judgment of himself. But the second line of the couplet, which parallels the
thought, indicates that the translation, as given, is correct. He
despises the vile and honors the righteous.

4. HE THAT SWEARETH. Though he makes a promise to his
own disadvantage he keeps his word.

5. PUTTETH NOT OUT HIS MONEY ON INTEREST. According to

39

Nor taketh a bribe against the innocent.
He that doeth these things shall never be moved.

16. MICHTAM OF DAVID.

Keep me, O God; for I have taken refuge in Thee.
2. I have said unto the LORD: 'Thou art my Lord; I have no good
    but in Thee';
3. As for the holy that are in the earth,
    They are the excellent in whom is all my delight.
4. Let the idols of them be multiplied that make suit unto another;
    Their drink-offerings of blood will I not offer,
    Nor take their names upon my lips.

the Jewish law (taken over by the Church) it was wrong for an
Israelite to take interest for money loaned to a fellow-Israelite.
Leviticus 25:35-37, "If thy brother be waxen poor . . . take thou
no interest of him. Thou shalt not give him thy money upon
interest." Of course, if an Israelite would borrow money from a
non-Israelite, he would be compelled to pay interest on the
loan, therefore an Israelite may take interest from a non-
Israelite if he lends him money. "Unto a foreigner thou mayest
lend upon interest." (Deuteronomy 23:21.)

5. SHALL NEVER BE MOVED. Shall endure and live confident of
God's help. Thus in Psalm 16:8, "He is at my right hand, I shall
not be moved."

THE psalmist rejoices in his fellowship with God. When
he recalls the idol worship which he has seen he is glad that
"the Lord is the portion of mine inheritance." The thought of
the psalm may well reflect a period in the life of David. When
David was in exile he lived for a while among the idolatrous
Philistines. "For they have driven me out this day (from the
land of Israel) that I should not cleave unto the inheritance of
the Lord, saying: 'Go, serve other gods,'" I Samuel 26:19. Yet,
though a stranger and exiled from the land where God was
worshipped he maintained his loyalty to the God of Israel.

1. MICHTAM. A word of doubtful meaning, perhaps referred

5. O LORD, the portion of mine inheritance and of my cup,
   Thou maintainest my lot.
6. The lines are fallen unto me in pleasant places;
   Yea, I have a goodly heritage.
7. I will bless the LORD, who hath given me counsel;
   Yea, in the night seasons my reins instruct me.
8. I have set the LORD always before me;
   Surely He is at my right hand, I shall not be moved.
9. Therefore my heart is glad, and my glory rejoiceth;
   My flesh also dwelleth in safety;
10. For Thou wilt not abandon my soul to the nether-world;
    Neither wilt Thou suffer Thy godly one to see the pit.

to *kethem*, meaning "gold," hence "a golden hymn." Whatever its precise meaning may be, it is evidently a technical term descriptive of poetry or of music. The heading *Michtam* is found also in a group of psalms, 56-60.

2. I HAVE NO GOOD BUT IN THEE. Thou art the sole source of whatever happiness comes to me.

3. THE HOLY . . . IN WHOM IS ALL MY DELIGHT. My happiness comes not only from direct communion with God but also in the companionship of those who worship Him with a pure heart.

4. NOR TAKE THEIR NAMES UPON MY LIPS. To utter the name of a god was equivalent to invoking him. Hence it was considered wrong even to mention the names of idols. "And make no mention of the name of other gods, neither let it be heard out of thy mouth." Exodus 23:13.

5. THOU MAINTAINEST MY LOT. God is my lot and my inheritance. He helps me maintain my loyalty to Him. Or, Thou supportest me in the vicissitudes of life.

6. THE LINES. Continue the metaphor of God as an inheritance. The measuring lines marking out the land have allotted me a good heritage.

7. MY REINS, i. e., my emotions, my thoughts. (See Psalm 7:10.) Our meditations in the silence of the night turn us to God. The same idea is expressed in Psalm 4:5.

10. THOU WILT NOT ABANDON. If this means that after the

11. Thou makest me to know the path of life;
    In Thy presence is fulness of joy,
    In Thy right hand bliss for evermore.

17. A PRAYER OF DAVID.

    Hear the right, O Lord, attend unto my cry;
    Give ear unto my prayer from lips without deceit.
2. Let my judgment come forth from Thy presence;
    Let Thine eyes behold equity.
3. Thou hast tried my heart, Thou hast visited it in the night;
    Thou hast tested me, and Thou findest not
    That I had a thought which should not pass my mouth.
4. As for the doings of men, by the word of Thy lips
    I have kept me from the ways of the violent.
5. My steps have held fast to Thy paths,
    My feet have not slipped.
6. As for me, I call upon Thee, for Thou wilt answer me, O God;
    Incline Thine ear unto me, hear my speech.

death of the body his spirit will not die, that is to say, that he will be blessed with immortality, then the psalm must be very late. But there is no need for giving the verse this interpretation. The psalmist means God will not abandon him to an early death.

11. IN THY RIGHT HAND BLISS. A metaphorical description of God, the bestower of happiness. Thus, Psalm 145:16, "Thou openest Thy hand and satisfiest every living thing with favour."

A PRAYER to God for protection and vindication. Conscious of the sincerity of his prayer the psalmist calls upon God to "hide me in the shadow of Thy wings." The psalm is evidently a night prayer. It says, (verse 3) "Thou hast visited (my heart) in the night" and ends (verse 15), "I shall be satisfied, when I awake, with Thy likeness."

1. HEAR THE RIGHT . . . MY CRY. The consciousness of being in the right and the sense of complete sincerity, "lips without deceit," justifies the psalmist in crying to the Lord for His assistance.

42

7. Make passing great Thy mercies, O Thou that
     savest by Thy right hand
  From assailants them that take refuge in Thee.
8. Keep me as the apple of the eye,
  Hide me in the shadow of Thy wings,
9. From the wicked that oppress,
  My deadly enemies, that compass me about.
10. Their gross heart they have shut tight,
  With their mouth they speak proudly.
11. At our every step they have now encompassed us;
  They set their eyes to cast us down to the earth.
12. He is like a lion that is eager to tear in pieces,
  And like a young lion lurking in secret places.
13. Arise, O LORD, confront him, cast him down;
  Deliver my soul from the wicked, by Thy sword;
14. From men, by Thy hand, O LORD,
  From men of the world, whose portion is in this life,
  And whose belly Thou fillest with Thy treasure;

3-4. THOU FINDEST NOT . . . A THOUGHT . . . I HAVE KEPT ME FROM THE WAYS OF THE VIOLENT. In both thought and deed have I held fast to God's path, "my feet have not slipped."

8. THE APPLE OF THE EYE. As the apple of the eye is carefully protected, so guard Thou me.

THE SHADOW OF THY WINGS. A beautiful metaphor which is also found in other places of the Bible. It describes God's protection as that of a mother bird protecting her young. Thus, "the children of men take refuge in the shadow of Thy wings." (Psalm 36:8.)

10. THEIR GROSS HEART . . . THEY SPEAK PROUDLY. They are merciless and haughty.

12. HE IS LIKE A LION. The text describing the enemy changes from plural to singular. The meaning will be clearer if the words "he is" are omitted. Thus, "They set their eyes . . . like a lion."

14. FROM MEN. The word "men" is governed by the preceding verb: "Deliver my soul from men. . . ."

MEN OF THE WORLD. Though the wicked may be successful and powerful in the world, yet the psalmist is unafraid.

43

Who have children in plenty,
And leave their abundance to their babes.
15. As for me, I shall behold Thy face in righteousness;
I shall be satisfied, when I awake, with Thy likeness.

18. FOR THE LEADER. [A PSALM] OF DAVID THE SERVANT OF THE LORD, WHO SPOKE UNTO THE LORD THE WORDS OF THIS SONG IN THE DAY THAT THE LORD DELIVERED HIM FROM THE HAND OF ALL HIS ENEMIES, AND FROM THE HAND OF SAUL; 2. AND HE SAID:

3. I love Thee, O LORD, my strength.
The LORD is my rock, and my fortress, and my deliverer;
My God, my rock, in Him I take refuge;
My shield, and my horn of salvation, my high tower.
4. Praised, I cry, is the LORD,
And I am saved from mine enemies.
5. The cords of Death compassed me,
And the floods of Belial* assailed me.
6. The cords of Sheol* surrounded me;
The snares of Death confronted me.

15. AS FOR ME. The psalmist does not ask for material treasure. It is joy enough to be aware of the consciousness of God. "I shall be satisfied with Thy likeness."

AN ancient song described by the word *shirah* as are other ancient songs of victory in the Bible: the song by the sea, Exodus 15; the song of Moses before his death, Deuteronomy 32 and 33. This song of triumph sung by David when God had finally given him victory over his enemies is also found in the Book of Samuel, II Samuel 22. The texts in both versions are almost identical.

1. DAVID THE SERVANT OF THE LORD. The same description of David is given in the title to Psalm 36. In Deuteronomy 34:5, "Moses the servant of the Lord died." Many passages in Isaiah (especially Chapter 42) refer to the people of Israel as God's servant whose task it is to be "a light of the nations to open the blind eyes" (Isaiah 42:6-7).

* That is, the nether-world.

In my distress I called upon the LORD, and cried unto my God;
Out of His temple He heard my voice,
And my cry came before Him into His ears.
8. Then the earth did shake and quake,
The foundations also of the mountains did tremble;
They were shaken, because He was wroth.
9. Smoke arose up in His nostrils,
And fire out of His mouth did devour;
Coals flamed forth from Him.
10. He bowed the heavens also, and came down;
And thick darkness was under His feet.
11. And He rode upon a cherub, and did fly; .
Yea, He did swoop down upon the wings of the wind.
12. He made darkness His hiding-place, His pavilion round about
Him;
Darkness of waters, thick clouds of the skies.
13. At the brightness before Him, there passed through His thick
clouds hailstones and coals of fire.
14. The LORD also thundered in the heavens,

3. MY HORN OF SALVATION. This phrase is included among
the descriptions of God's strength, "rock," "refuge," "shield,"
"tower." It is frequently used in the Bible. It refers to the
strong horn of a stag.

5-6. BELIAL . . . SHEOL. Both refer to the nether-world, that
is, to death, as the parallel phrase in each couplet indicates.

CORDS. Carries out the metaphor of a net or snare.

7. OUT OF HIS TEMPLE. From heaven, God's dwelling place.

8-16. A vivid description: Earthquake and storm, symbolizing
the Divine Power manifesting itself on earth to destroy the
wicked and the violent.

9. HIS NOSTRILS . . . HIS MOUTH. These words were not understood by the psalmist literally, but as picturesque metaphors.

10. THE HEAVENS . . . THICK DARKNESS. A storm in which the
clouds are dark and low.

11. CHERUB. The cherubim were thought of as the angels of
the Divine Chariot or the bearers of the Divine Throne. Thus,
"The name of the Lord of hosts that sitteth upon the cherubim" (II Samuel 6:2 and Psalm 99:1).

And the Most High gave forth His voice;
Hailstones and coals of fire.
15. And He sent out His arrows, and scattered them;
And He shot forth lightnings, and discomfited them.
16. And the channels of waters appeared,
And the foundations of the world were laid bare ,
At Thy rebuke, O LORD,
At the blast of the breath of Thy nostrils.
17. He sent from on high, He took me;
He drew me out of many waters.
18. He delivered me from mine enemy most strong,
And from them that hated me, for they were too
mighty for me.
19. They confronted me in the day of my calamity;
But the LORD was a stay unto me.
20. He brought me forth also into a large place;
He delivered me, because He delighted in me.
21. The LORD rewarded me according to my righteousness;
According to the cleanness of my hands hath He
recompensed me.
22. For I have kept the ways of the LORD,
And have not wickedly departed from my God.
23. For all His ordinances were before me,
And I put not away His statutes from me.
24. And I was single-hearted with Him,
And I kept myself from mine iniquity.
25. Therefore hath the LORD recompensed me according
to my righteousness,
According to the cleanness of my hands in His eyes.

15. HIS ARROWS. Evidently the lightning, as is indicated by the parallel verse in the couplet and by the fact that the preceding verse refers to thunder.

17. The thought changes. In the midst of the storm and the flood, God "drew me out of many waters." The waters which threatened to drown him are explained in the next verse as the overwhelming forces of his enemies. So, too, in Psalm 124:2-4, "When men arose up against us . . . then the waters had overwhelmed us."

24. I WAS SINGLE-HEARTED. I was sincere. The opposite of "double-hearted" (Psalm 12:3) which means hypocritical.

26. With the merciful Thou dost show Thyself merciful,
With the upright man Thou dost show
Thyself upright;
27. With the pure Thou dost show Thyself pure;
And with the crooked Thou dost show Thyself subtle.
28. For Thou dost save the afflicted people;
But the haughty eyes Thou dost humble.
29. For Thou dost light my lamp;
The LORD my God doth lighten my darkness.
30. For by Thee I run upon a troop;
And by my God do I scale a wall.
31. As for God, His way is perfect;
The word of the LORD is tried;
He is a shield unto all them that take refuge
in Him.
32. For who is God, save the LORD?
And who is a Rock, except our God?
33. The God that girdeth me with strength,
And maketh my way straight;
34. Who maketh my feet like hinds',
And setteth me upon my high places;
35. Who traineth my hands for war,
So that mine arms do bend a bow of brass.
36. Thou hast also given me Thy shield of salvation,
And Thy right hand hath holden me up;
And Thy condescension hath made me great.
37. Thou hast enlarged my steps under me,
And my feet have not slipped.
38. I have pursued mine enemies, and overtaken them;

26-27. WITH THE MERCIFUL . . . MERCIFUL, WITH THE UPRIGHT . . . UPRIGHT. God deals with men as they deal with Him, as the Hebrew phrase describes it, "measure for measure." Or, we each find in God that which our own nature is capable of seeing.

29. LIGHT MY LAMP. The familiar biblical metaphor of light meaning life, and darkness, death. Thus "The spirit of man is the lamp of the Lord," Proverbs 20:27; and "The lamp of the wicked shall be put out," Proverbs 13:9.

33-37. All my skill and strength as a warrior is a gift of God.
38-46. All my victories are the gift of God.

47

Neither did I turn back till they were consumed.

39. I have smitten them through, so that they are not able to rise;
They are fallen under my feet.
40. For Thou hast girded me with strength unto the battle;
Thou hast subdued under me those that rose up against me.
41. Thou hast also made mine enemies turn their backs unto me,
And I did cut off them that hate me.
42. They cried, but there was none to save;
Even unto the Lord, but He answered them not.
43. Then did I beat them small as the dust before the wind;
I did cast them out as the mire of the streets.
44. Thou hast delivered me from the contentions of the people;
Thou hast made me the head of the nations;
A people whom I have not known serve me.
45. As soon as they hear of me, they obey me;
The sons of the stranger dwindle away before me.
46. The sons of the stranger fade away,
And come trembling out of their close places.

44. THE CONTENTIONS OF THE PEOPLE. Evidently refers to the victory in civil war, as "a people whom I have not known" refers to victory in foreign war.

51. GREAT SALVATION. The closing sentence of praise is chanted in the Jewish liturgy in the grace after meals.

A HYMN describing God's revelation to man. The heavens declare His glory; all of nature speaks of His presence; and in the soul of man the moral law reveals His governance of the universe.

Some of the modern commentators say that this psalm is a combination of two separate poems. The first, from 2-7 dealing with God's revelation in nature, is said to be of separate origin from the second half of the poem, 8-15, speaking of God's self-manifestation in the heart of man. The arguments offered are that the thought of one part of the psalm differs completely from that of the other part, and secondly that the first psalm uses *El* as the name of God and the second psalm uses *JHWH* as the Divine Name; and also, that the lines in the second part

47. The LORD liveth, and blessed be my Rock;
And exalted be the God of my salvation;
48. Even the God that executeth vengeance for me,
And subdueth peoples under me.
49. He delivereth me from mine enemies;
Yea, Thou liftest me up above them that rise up
against me;
Thou deliverest me from the violent man.
50. Therefore I will give thanks unto Thee, O LORD,
among the nations,
And will sing praises unto Thy name.
51. Great salvation giveth He to His king;
And showeth mercy to His anointed,
To David and to his seed, for evermore.

19. FOR THE LEADER. A PSALM OF DAVID.
2. The heavens declare the glory of God,
And the firmament showeth His handiwork;

of the psalm are longer and seem to reveal a different rhythm and therefore a different author.

The older Jewish commentators likewise seemed to feel the necessity of binding together the two halves of the psalm. Thus, Saadia (quoted by Ibn Ezra) understands the word "saying," before verse 8, implying: "The heavens declare God's glory *saying*, the Law of the Lord is perfect"; thus describing the second half of the psalm as the words which are uttered by nature in praise of God. Whereas, Ibn Ezra himself says that the word "saying" is not needed, that both parts of the psalm are an answer to the question as to where one can find evidence of God's revelation; we find such evidence first in nature itself, then in Divine Law. Ibn Ezra's explanation helps us see the psalm as a unit. Whether or not it was composed of two separate poems, both parts of the psalm nevertheless constitute a consistent unity. God is revealed to us both (to use the phrase of Immanuel Kant) "in the starry heavens above and in the moral law within." This psalm is recited in the Sabbath Morning Services.

2. THE FIRMAMENT. The word is parallel to the word

49

3. Day unto day uttereth speech,
   And night unto night revealeth knowledge;
4. There is no speech, there are no words,
   Neither is their voice heard.
5. Their line is gone out through all the earth,
   And their words to the end of the world.
   In them hath He set a tent for the sun,
6. Which is as a bridegroom coming out of his chamber,
   And rejoiceth as a strong man to run his course.
7. His going forth is from the end of the heaven,
   And his circuit unto the ends of it;
   And there is nothing hid from the heat thereof.
8. The law of the LORD is perfect, restoring the soul;
   The testimony of the LORD is sure, making wise the simple.
9. The precepts of the LORD are right, rejoicing the heart;
   The commandment of the LORD is pure, enlightening
      the eyes.

"heavens" in the first half of the couplet and means the expanse of the sky. Thus, Genesis 1:8, "And God called the firmament Heaven."

3. DAY UNTO DAY . . . NIGHT UNTO NIGHT. Each day gives its testimony to the following day and each night to the following night. Thus nature continuously "uttereth speech."

4. THERE IS NO SPEECH. The revelation of the heavens is not audible but its silent splendor speaks of God. This is well expressed in Addison's famous paraphrase of this psalm:

> What though nor real voice nor sound
> Amid their radiant orbs be found,
> In reason's ear they all rejoice
> And utter forth a glorious voice
> Forever singing as they shine:
> "The hand that made us is Divine."

5. THEIR LINE . . . TO THE END OF THE WORLD. Their course, or track.

IN THEM. In the heavens.

6. AS A BRIDEGROOM . . . AS A STRONG MAN. The sun appears in glory as a bridegroom attired in his splendid garments. It moves in strength as a hero running a race.

10. The fear of the LORD is clean, enduring for ever;
    The ordinances of the LORD are true, they are
      righteous altogether;
11. More to be desired are they than gold, yea, than much
      fine gold;
    Sweeter also than honey and the honeycomb.
12. Moreover by them is Thy servant warned;
    In keeping of them there is great reward.
13. Who can discern errors?
    Clear Thou me from hidden faults.
14. Keep back Thy servant also from presumptuous sins,
    That they may not have dominion over me; then shall
      I be faultless,
    And I shall be clear from great transgression.
15. Let the words of my mouth and the meditation of my
      heart be acceptable before Thee,
    O LORD, my Rock, and my Redeemer.

8. The thought changes to the revelation of God through the moral law. Various synonyms are used in this psalm: "Law," "testimony," "precepts," "commandments," "fear" (which, paralleling these nouns, clearly means "reverence" and "awe"), "ordinances."

10. FEAR OF THE LORD IS CLEAN. Reverence for God is pure and unselfish unlike homage which may be given to the mortal kings.

11. MORE TO BE DESIRED . . . THAN GOLD. The moral law within is a source of greater happiness than earthly treasures can give. Thus, "The law of Thy mouth is better unto me than thousands of gold and silver" (Psalm 119:72).

13-14. ERRORS . . . HIDDEN FAULTS . . . PRESUMPTUOUS SINS. Any one may err but we can help avoid error if we cherish no hidden faults within the heart and God guards us from presumptuousness and arrogance.

15. WORDS OF MY MOUTH . . . MEDITATION OF MY HEART. May my spoken and unspoken thoughts be as acceptable as an offering on an altar. This sentence is used in Jewish liturgy at the close of private devotion when we worship God with the unspoken thoughts of the heart.

51

20. FOR THE LEADER. A PSALM OF DAVID.

2. The LORD answer thee in the day of trouble;
The name of the God of Jacob set thee up on high;
3. Send forth thy help from the sanctuary,
And support thee out of Zion;
4. Receive the memorial of all thy meal-offerings,
And accept the fat of thy burnt-sacrifice;   Selah
5. Grant thee according to thine own heart,
And fulfil all thy counsel.
6. We will shout for joy in thy victory,
And in the name of our God we will set up our standards;
The LORD fulfil all thy petitions.
7. Now know I that the LORD saveth His anointed;
He will answer him from His holy heaven
With the mighty acts of His saving right hand.

EVIDENTLY a prayer in behalf of the king before he marches forth to war. The king has offered his sacrifices at the altar of the Temple, the people pray that these sacrifices be acceptable to God and that God aid him in battle.

2. SET THEE UP ON HIGH. Set thee on a high mountain place of safety from the attacks of the enemy.

4. MEMORIAL OF ALL THY MEAL-OFFERINGS. Part of every sacrifice was a cereal sacrifice or "meal" sacrifice. This was given either in the form of flour or baked into Matzoth. Part of the meal offering was given separately as a remembrance or memorial. "And the priest shall take off from the meal-offering the memorial-part thereof" (Leviticus 2:9).

THE FAT OF THY BURNT-SACRIFICE. The fat of the sacrifice is burnt as an especial gift to God. "And the priest shall make it (the fat) smoke upon the altar; it is the food of the offering made by fire unto the Lord" (Leviticus 3:11).

SELAH. Marks the end of the thought.

5-6. If God "fulfil thy council" then "we will shout for joy in thy victory."

7. FROM HIS HOLY HEAVEN. God sends His help not merely "from the sanctuary" (verse 3) but "from His holy heaven."

8. Some trust in chariots, and some in horses;
   But we will make mention of the name of the LORD our God.
9. They are bowed down and fallen;
   But we are risen, and stand upright.
10. Save, LORD;
    Let the King answer us in the day that we call.

21. FOR THE LEADER. A PSALM OF DAVID.

2. O LORD, in Thy strength the king rejoiceth;
   And in Thy salvation how greatly doth he exult!
3. Thou hast given him his heart's desire,
   And the request of his lips Thou hast not withholden.   Selah
4. For Thou meetest him with choicest blessings;
   Thou settest a crown of fine gold on his head.
5. He asked life of Thee, Thou gavest it him;
   Even length of days for ever and ever.

8. SOME TRUST IN CHARIOTS . . . BUT WE MENTION THE NAME OF THE LORD. This is almost exactly the expression used by David when, as a lad, he advanced to fight against Goliath, the Philistine. "Then said David to the Philistine: 'Thou comest to me with a sword, and with a spear, and with a javelin; but I come to thee in the name of the Lord of hosts'" (I Samuel 17:45).

THIS psalm is closely connected in thought with Psalm 20. Here too the people are praying in behalf of the king who must confront the enemy. Psalm 20 asked that God accept the king's sacrifice and help him. Psalm 21 voices the hope that just as God had given the king other blessings so now may He bless him with victory.

3. SELAH. Marks the end of the two introductory sentences. Thereafter follow the details of God's blessings bestowed upon the king: the crown, long life, glory, honor, etc.

5. LENGTH OF DAYS FOR EVER AND EVER. It can hardly mean that God has granted the king eternal life. The expression is based upon the formal phrase of greeting to a king. "And I

6. His glory is great through Thy salvation;
   Honour and majesty dost Thou lay upon him.
7. For Thou makest him most blessed for ever;
   Thou makest him glad with joy in Thy presence.
8. For the king trusteth in the LORD,
   Yea, in the mercy of the Most High; he shall not be moved.
9. Thy hand shall be equal to all thine enemies;
   Thy right hand shall overtake those that hate thee.
10. Thou shalt make them as a fiery furnace in the time
    of thine anger;
    The LORD shall swallow them up in His wrath,
    And the fire shall devour them.
11. Their fruit shalt thou destroy from the earth,
    And their seed from among the children of men.
12. For they intended evil against thee,

said unto the king: 'let the king live forever!' " (Nehemiah 2:3).

It also may mean that the king, through his descendants, will continue on the throne forever. His dynasty will endure.

7. GLAD WITH JOY IN THY PRESENCE. A familiar thought in the Psalms: that the sense of God's Presence is the source of happiness. Thus, "In Thy presence is fulness of joy" (Psalm 16:11).

9. WILL BE EQUAL TO. The word "overtake" in the parallel sentence of the couplet makes the meaning clear. "Thy hand will reach thine enemies."

11. THEIR FRUIT. Their children.

THE psalmist, surrounded by enemies who mock him and gloat over him, turns to God in Whom he has trusted all his life. The deliverance which God will send will be proclaimed amidst the people of Israel, and beyond the boundaries of the land of Israel. God's help will resound to the "end of the earth," and the "kindreds of the nations" shall come and worship Him.

In this psalm, as in many other psalms, the sorrows of the individual merge into the vicissitudes of the whole people of

54

They imagined a device, wherewith they shall not prevail.
13. For thou shalt make them turn their back,
Thou shalt make ready with thy bowstrings against the
face of them.
14. Be Thou exalted, O LORD, in Thy strength;
So will we sing and praise Thy power.

22. FOR THE LEADER; UPON AIJELETH HA-SHAHAR.
A PSALM OF DAVID.

2. My God, my God, why hast Thou forsaken me,
And art far from my help at the words of my cry?
3. O my God, I call by day, but Thou answerest not;
And at night, and there is no surcease for me.
4. Yet Thou art holy,
O Thou that art enthroned upon the praises of Israel.

Israel. The psalmist calls to all his brethren: "Ye that fear the
Lord, praise Him. Stand in awe of Him, all ye the seed of
Israel" (verse 24). Whether the psalm was written originally to
voice the grief of an individual or whether to describe the
sorrows of Israel, the psalm can be taken to express either idea.

1. AIJELETH HA-SHAHAR means literally the "hind of the
morning" and very likely was a well-known melody to which
this psalm was to be sung. See comment on *Muth-labben*
(Psalm 9:1).

2. WHY HAST THOU FORSAKEN ME? To the psalmist in his sorrow it appears as if God had abandoned him. The same thought
is expressed in Psalm 13:2. "How long, O Lord, wilt Thou forget me for ever?"

4. YET THOU ART HOLY. Although I sometimes fear that
Thou hast forsaken me yet I know that Thou art holy.

ENTHRONED UPON THE PRAISES OF ISRAEL. The usual biblical
phrase is that God is enthroned upon the cherubim, the angels
who support His throne. See Psalm 18:11, and Psalm 99:1: "He
is enthroned upon the cherubim." Here, the psalmist means to
say that just as the cherubim support the throne of God so do
the prayers of Israel rise up and surround His throne. This idea
is developed in the rabbinic literature which speaks of the
"gates of prayer" through which human supplications rise to

55

5. In Thee did our fathers trust;
   They trusted, and Thou didst deliver them.
6. Unto Thee they cried, and escaped;
   In Thee did they trust, and were not ashamed.
7. But I am a worm, and no man;
   A reproach of men, and despised of the people.
8. All they that see me laugh me to scorn;
   They shoot out the lip, they shake the head:
9. 'Let him commit himself unto the Lord! let Him rescue him;
   Let Him deliver him, seeing He delighteth in him.'
10. For Thou art He that took me out of the womb;
    Thou madest me trust when I was upon my mother's breasts.
11. Upon Thee I have been cast from my birth;
    Thou art my God from my mother's womb.
12. Be not far from me; for trouble is near;
    For there is none to help.
13. Many bulls have encompassed me;
    Strong bulls of Bashan have beset me round.
14. They open wide their mouth against me,
    As a ravening and a roaring lion.
15. I am poured out like water,
    And all my bones are out of joint;
    My heart is become like wax;
    It is melted in mine inmost parts.

God and expresses the idea that sincere prayers are no sooner uttered than they reach all through space to the very throne of God. (Pesikta Rabbati—ed. Friedmann, 185 a.)

5-9. IN THEE DID OUR FATHERS TRUST. But I feel broken down by the reproaches of men. "I am a worm, and no man."

9. LET HIM COMMIT HIMSELF. The enemies mockingly say: let him trust in God; God cannot deliver him.

10-12 parallels 5-7: "In Thee did our fathers trust" (5-7) is supplemented by the idea: *I have relied on Thee from the beginnings of my existence on earth* (10-11).

13. BULLS OF BASHAN. Bashan is the fertile land across the Jordan, north of Gilead. It was famous for its breed of strong cattle. The meaning here is: the enemies surround me like the fierce bulls of Bashan. The enemy is described throughout the psalm as a wild beast. Here as a bull; in verses 17 and 21 as a

16. My strength is dried up like a potsherd;
    And my tongue cleaveth to my throat;
    And thou layest me in the dust of death.
17. For dogs have encompassed me;
    A company of evil-doers have inclosed me;
    Like a lion, they are at my hands and my feet.
18. I may count all my bones;
    They look and gloat over me.
19. They part my garments among them,
    And for my vesture do they cast lots.
20. But Thou, O LORD, be not far off;
    O Thou my strength, hasten to help me.
21. Deliver my soul from the sword;
    Mine only one from the power of the dog.
22. Save me from the lion's mouth;
    Yea, from the horns of the wild-oxen do Thou answer me.
23. I will declare Thy name unto my brethren;
    In the midst of the congregation will I praise Thee:
24. 'Ye that fear the LORD, praise Him;
    All ye the seed of Jacob, glorify Him;
    And stand in awe of Him, all ye the seed of Israel.
25. For He hath not despised nor abhorred the lowliness
    of the poor;
    Neither hath He hid His face from him;

dog; in verses 14 and 22 as a lion; in verse 22 as wild oxen.

15. POURED OUT LIKE WATER, etc. There is no strength in me,
no powers of resistance.

16. LIKE A POTSHERD. As a piece of broken pottery dried up
in the sun; as a man dying of thirst in a desert.

21. MINE ONLY ONE. The meaning of the verse is made clear
from the parallel in the first half of the couplet, i. e., "my
soul": "Deliver my soul, mine only one." The same phrase is
used in Psalm 35:17, "Rescue my soul, . . . mine only one from
the lions."

23-24. I WILL DECLARE THY NAME. When you deliver me I
will testify of Thy help and call upon all the house of Israel to
glorify Thy name.

25. HE HATH NOT DESPISED THE POOR. God is not impressed
with the might of the violent nor is He contemptuous of the

But when he cried unto Him, He heard.'
26. From Thee cometh my praise in the great congregation;
   I will pay my vows before them that fear Him.
27. Let the humble eat and be satisfied;
   Let them praise the LORD that seek after Him;
   May your heart be quickened for ever!
28. All the ends of the earth shall remember and turn
      unto the LORD;
   And all the kindreds of the nations shall worship
      before Thee.
29. For the kingdom is the LORD's;
   And He is the ruler over the nations.
30. All the fat ones of the earth shall eat and worship;

"lowliness of the poor." The same thought is expressed in
Psalm 147:10-11, "He delighteth not in strength . . . the Lord
taketh pleasure in them . . . that wait for His mercy."

26. BEFORE THEM THAT FEAR HIM. Before them that worship
and revere His name.

27. LET THE HUMBLE EAT AND BE SATISFIED. The psalmist
means literally that the poor will partake of the meat of the
sacrifice and will eat and be satisfied. The commentator, Ibn
Ezra, suggests a more general interpretation, namely, that the
sight of his deliverance from his trouble will sustain the heart
of all the humble and give them hope and strength.

28-29. ALL THE ENDS OF THE EARTH. The psalmist enlarges
the scope of his vision. Not only will the humble of Israel be
encouraged by God's deliverance but "all the ends of the earth
will turn and worship God" and recognize that "He is the ruler
over the nations." This thought is frequently voiced in prophetic literature although, generally, the turning of all nations
to God is visualized as the ultimate attainment of human history which will come to pass "in the end of days." See Isaiah
2:1-4, "Many peoples shall go and say, 'let us go up to the
mountain of the Lord,'" etc.

30. ALL THE FAT ONES OF THE EARTH . . . EVEN HE, etc. The
verse is difficult. It seems to mean that in the days when men
will realize God's goodness not only will those who are con-

All they that go down to the dust shall kneel before Him,
Even he that cannot keep his soul alive.

31. A seed shall serve him;
It shall be told of the Lord unto the next generation.

32. They shall come and shall declare His righteousness
Unto a people that shall be born, that He hath done it.

23. A PSALM OF DAVID.

The LORD is my shepherd; I shall not want.

2. He maketh me to lie down in green pastures;
He leadeth me beside the still waters.

3. He restoreth my soul;
He guideth me in straight paths for His name's sake.

tented and comfortable ("the fat ones of the earth") turn to God in gratitude but also those who still are suffering ("that cannot keep his soul alive").

31. A SEED SHALL SERVE HIM. The vision proceeds. Not only will all the earth serve God but also all the future ages, the seed of man. The story of God's deliverance shall be related "unto a people that shall be born."

THE psalm speaks of God's kindly providence and constant protection. God is described first as a shepherd who tenderly guards His flock and then as a host who receives us hospitably.

1. MY SHEPHERD. The metaphor of God as a shepherd and Israel as His flock is frequently used in the Psalms. Thus, Psalm 74:1, "the flock of Thy pasture." And Psalm 100:3, "We are His . . . the flock of His pasture."

2. HE LEADETH ME. The shepherds of the east do not *drive* their flock as in the western lands; they *lead* them.

3. HE RESTORETH MY SOUL. With rest and refreshing water he restores my strength.

STRAIGHT PATHS. The Hebrew permits the translation "paths of righteousness."

FOR HIS NAME'S SAKE. By His guidance He teaches us to honor His name.

59

4. Yea, though I walk through the valley of the shadow
    of death,
I will fear no evil,
For Thou art with me;
Thy rod and Thy staff, they comfort me.
5. Thou preparest a table before me in the presence
    of mine enemies;
Thou hast anointed my head with oil; my cup runneth over.

4. VALLEY OF THE SHADOW OF DEATH. The mountain lands of Judea abound in dark valleys where dangerous beasts lurked but the shepherd with his "rod and staff" protects his flock.

THEY COMFORT ME. They assure me of my safety and still my fears.

5-6. The metaphor changes. God is no longer described as a shepherd but as a host. The psalmist sees himself walking upon a road where enemies lie in ambush. When he comes to God's house he is safe, protected against danger and honored as a guest.

5. A TABLE BEFORE ME. The host provides food for the famished wayfarer.

MY HEAD WITH OIL. At a banquet the guests were frequently anointed with precious oil. Thus Amos 6:6, the description of a banquet includes: "Anoint themselves with the chief ointments."

6. GOODNESS AND MERCY SHALL FOLLOW ME. Evil shall no longer dog my footsteps; happiness will accompany me on my path of life.

THE HOUSE OF THE LORD. It means literally the Temple. It is a joy to dwell in God's Holy house. Thus, Psalm 15:1, "Who shall sojourn in Thy tabernacle." The phrase also has a larger meaning of living in God's presence, everywhere. Thus, Psalm 90:1, "Lord, Thou hast been our dwelling-place in all generations."

FOR EVER. The Hebrew means "for length of days," i. e., for many years. Thus, Psalm 91:16, (using the same phrase): "With long life will I satisfy him."

6. Surely goodness and mercy shall follow me all the
    days of my life;
   And I shall dwell in the house of the LORD for ever.

24. A PSALM OF DAVID.
   The earth is the LORD's, and the fulness thereof;
   The world, and they that dwell therein.
2. For He hath founded it upon the seas,

A MAJESTIC psalm describing the procession which is
bringing the Ark of God into Jerusalem and to Mount Zion.
The psalm may have been written after David captured Jerusalem from the Jebusites or when the Ark was brought back
from the land of the Philistines. The first part of the psalm is
a series of questions and answers. It must have been sung re-
sponsively by two groups in the procession.

This psalm was recited by the Levites every Sunday in the
Temple. The Mishnah (Tamid VII, 4) lists the psalms which
were recited on each day of the week by the Levites in the
Temple. The same psalms are now recited in the synagogue on
the respective days of the week. Psalm 24 is recited on Sunday;
Psalm 48 on Monday; Psalm 82 on Tuesday; Psalm 94 on Wednesday; Psalm 81 on Thursday; Psalm 93 on Friday, and Psalm
92 on Saturday.

1. EARTH IS THE LORD'S. The idea is frequently expressed in
the Bible that all the earth belongs to God since He has created
it. Thus Psalm 50:12, "For the world is Mine, and the fullness
thereof." And Exodus 19:5, "For all the earth is Mine." The
significance of the statement is that although God's Ark is
brought into an earthly sanctuary yet He is omnipresent and
all the earth is His. Thus, in Isaiah 66:1, "Thus saith the
Lord: the heaven is My throne and the earth is My footstool.
Where is the house that ye may build unto Me?"

2. FOUNDED IT UPON THE SEAS. This is based upon the idea
that God created the earth by stretching it above the waters and
that therefore there are waters under the earth. This thought is
found in Psalm 136:6, "To Him that spread forth the earth

And established it upon the floods.

3. Who shall ascend into the mountain of the LORD?
   And who shall stand in His holy place?
4. He that hath clean hands, and a pure heart;
   Who hath not taken My name in vain,
   And hath not sworn deceitfully.
5. He shall receive a blessing from the LORD,
   And righteousness from the God of his salvation.
6. Such is the generation of them that seek after Him,
   That seek Thy face, even Jacob.   Selah
7. Lift up your heads, O ye gates,

above the waters"; Exodus 20:4, "The water under the earth."

3. WHO SHALL ASCEND INTO THE MOUNTAIN OF THE LORD. Verses 3-6 parallel the thought of Psalm 15. Both psalms ask the question as to who deserves to stand in the presence of the most High in His Holy Temple and both psalms give the same answer, namely, he whose actions are clean and whose heart is pure.

4. MY NAME IN VAIN. The Hebrew word for name is here pronounced *nafshi* although it is written *nafsho*. There are many cases in the Bible where a word is spelled in a certain way but read in another. The *spelling* is called the *kethib*, while the traditional *reading* of the word is called the *k'ri*. Some commentators follow the spelling (the *kethib*) and take the word to mean "his soul" and therefore translate the phrase, "He who hath not lifted up his soul to vanity." But the traditional reading (*k'ri*) takes it to mean "*My* soul" or "My presence" referring to God. Thus, following the *k'ri* and paralleling the thought of the next line of the couplet the verse is translated: "He who hath not taken My name in vain."

5. THE GOD OF HIS SALVATION. God who will deliver him. The phrase is frequently used in the Bible, e. g., Psalm 25:5, "God of my salvation."

6. THAT SEEK THY FACE, EVEN JACOB. The Greek version adds the word "God" before Jacob, understanding the phrase: "Who seek Thy presence, O God of Jacob." If, however, the word "God" is not inserted the meaning is as in the translation:

And be ye lifted up, ye everlasting doors;
That the King of glory may come in.

8. 'Who is the King of glory?'
'The LORD strong and mighty,
The LORD mighty in battle.'
9. Lift up your heads, O ye gates,
Yea, lift them up, ye everlasting doors;
That the King of glory may come in.
10. 'Who then is the King of glory?'
'The LORD of hosts;
He is the King of glory.'   Selah

"Such is the generation of them that seek Thy face," namely, the household of Jacob.

SELAH. The word marks the transition between one thought and another. The first part of the psalm, 1-6, visualizes the procession marching towards Jerusalem. In 7-10, it is described as standing outside of the gates demanding that the gates be opened. The marchers call upon the gatekeepers to open the gates in order that the King of Glory may enter. The sentries challenge: "Who is the king of glory?" and the procession answers: "The Lord, strong and mighty."

7. LIFT UP YOUR HEADS, O YE GATES. The idea is difficult to visualize. How can gates lift up their heads? It would seem that the psalmist should say: be opened up, ye gates. Because of this difficulty some of the commentators take the phrase in a metaphorical sense, namely, "be ye exalted, O ye gates at the glory which has come to you." The Midrash (Midrash Rabba II, Exodus 8:1) tells a legend about Solomon, that when he came to bring the ark into the Holy of Holies he found that the ark was ten cubits high and the door was ten cubits high. Since the Ark could not get through the door he called out: "Lift up your heads, O ye gates." But since it is fairly evident from the psalm that the gates referred to are the city gates it may mean, "Be ye lifted off the hinges in honor of the coming of the King."

The challenge and the answer of verses 7-8 are repeated in verses 9-10. But instead of the response of "The Lord strong

25. [A PSALM] OF DAVID.

Unto Thee, O LORD, do I lift up my soul.

2. O my God, in Thee have I trusted, let me not be ashamed;
Let not mine enemies triumph over me.

3. Yea, none that wait for Thee shall be ashamed,
They shall be ashamed that deal treacherously without cause.

4. Show me Thy ways, O LORD;
Teach me Thy paths.

5. Guide me in Thy truth, and teach me;
For Thou art the God of my salvation;
For Thee do I wait all the day.

6. Remember, O LORD, Thy compassions and Thy mercies;
For they have been from of old.

and mighty, the Lord mighty in battle" (verse 8), the response is *"The Lord of hosts."* The Lord of Hosts, used as description of God, must first have meant the Lord who guided the hosts of Israel and then came to mean the Lord of heavenly hosts. See I Samuel 17:45, "I come to thee in the name of the Lord of hosts, the God of the armies of Israel."

$\mathcal{A}$N acrostic psalm. See introduction to Psalm 9.

The psalm visualizes God as the Teacher and Guide (verses 8, 9) who instructs "sinners in the way and guideth the humble in justice." Thus, the psalm is a prayer to God for forgiveness, enlightenment, and protection.

1. I LIFT UP MY SOUL. The phrase may have originally meant to lift up the hand with a sacrifice. The gesture was used in prayer and was extended to the soul raising itself towards God. Thus, Lamentations 3:41, "Let us lift up our heart with our hands unto God in the heavens." Also Psalm 143:8, "For unto Thee have I lifted up my soul."

3. NONE THAT WAIT FOR THEE. The phrase "to wait for the Lord," meaning confidently to expect His help, is used a number of times in this psalm and throughout the Book of Psalms. Thus, for example, Psalm 37:7, "Wait patiently for Him."

7. Remember not the sins of my youth, nor my
transgressions;
According to Thy mercy remember Thou me,
For Thy goodness' sake, O Lord.
8. Good and upright is the Lord;
Therefore doth He instruct sinners in the way.
9. He guideth the humble in justice;
And He teacheth the humble His way.
10. All the paths of the Lord are mercy and truth
Unto such as keep His covenant and His testimonies.
11. For Thy name's sake, O Lord,
Pardon mine iniquity, for it is great.
12. What man is he that feareth the Lord?
Him will He instruct in the way that he should choose.

4. SHOW ME THY WAYS, O LORD. A prayer for guidance. Thus
in Psalm 27:11, "Teach me Thy way, O Lord, and lead me in
an even path." The psalmist asks for knowledge of the path of
righteousness, God's path, that he may follow it. Also, Moses
in his perplexity prays: "Show me now Thy ways, that I may
know Thee . . . and find grace in Thy sight" (Exodus 33:13).

7. FOR THY GOODNESS' SAKE. Because of Thy lovingkindness
forgive my sins.

8-10. God is the Teacher who instructs the humble, leading
them along the paths of "mercy and truth."

10. SUCH AS KEEP HIS COVENANT. Throughout biblical literature the human obligation to obey God's commandments is described as based upon a mutually binding agreement—a covenant. Thus, in Genesis 9 (in the story of Noah) God enters
into a covenant with the entire human race: If mankind would
refrain from bloodshed, etc., God would never again send a
flood to destroy the earth. God entered into a covenant with
Abraham (Genesis 17); and with the people of Israel at Mount
Sinai (Exodus 19:5-6): "Now if ye will keep My covenant . . .
ye shall be unto Me a kingdom of priests, and a holy nation."
In the task of "perfecting the world through the sovereignty of
God," man and his Maker are covenanted partners. Man is "a
co-worker with God."

65

13. His soul shall abide in prosperity;
    And his seed shall inherit the land.
14. The counsel of the LORD is with them that fear Him;
    And His covenant, to make them know it.
15. Mine eyes are ever toward the LORD;
    For He will bring forth my feet out of the net.
16. Turn Thee unto me, and be gracious unto me;
    For I am solitary and afflicted.
17. The troubles of my heart are enlarged;
    O bring Thou me out of my distresses.
18. See mine affliction and my travail;
    And forgive all my sins.
19. Consider how many are mine enemies,
    And the cruel hatred wherewith they hate me.
20. O keep my soul, and deliver me;
    Let me not be ashamed, for I have taken refuge in Thee.
21. Let integrity and uprightness preserve me,
    Because I wait for Thee.

13. HIS SOUL SHALL ABIDE IN PROSPERITY. Those who follow the Divine Laws of mercy and truth will find happiness in life. This thought is the theme of Psalm 1.

14. THE COUNSEL OF THE LORD IS WITH THEM THAT FEAR HIM. Those who revere God are guided by His wisdom. Thus: "The fear of the Lord is the beginning of wisdom" (Proverbs 9:10).

17. THE TROUBLES OF MY HEART ARE ENLARGED. Because of the "cruel hatred wherewith they hate me" (verse 19) and "mine iniquity, for it is great" (verse 11), my griefs trouble my heart.

21. LET INTEGRITY PRESERVE ME. If I hold to my integrity my heart will be glad and I will be strong enough to endure.

22. REDEEM ISRAEL, O GOD. The acrostic alphabet is finished with the preceding sentence. This sentence is therefore an additional prayer in behalf of all of Israel.

𝒜 PRAYER for Divine protection. It is difficult to fix upon a specific event in the life of David when this psalm might have been uttered. But evidently it was spoken in a time of general

26. [A PSALM] OF DAVID.

Judge me, O LORD, for I have walked in mine integrity,
And I have trusted in the LORD without wavering.
2. Examine me, O LORD, and try me;
Test my reins and my heart.
3. For Thy mercy is before mine eyes;
And I have walked in Thy truth.
4. I have not sat with men of falsehood:
Neither will I go in with dissemblers.
5. I hate the gathering of evil-doers,
And will not sit with the wicked.
6. I will wash my hands in innocency;
So will I compass Thine altar, O LORD,
7. That I may make the voice of thanksgiving to be heard,
And tell of all Thy wondrous works.

danger. The psalmist prays that God shall not gather his soul (to death) with the sinners but preserve him from danger because of his effort to live a life of integrity.

1. JUDGE ME. This thought is frequently expressed in the Psalms. The psalmist, conscious of his striving to live a life of righteousness, asks God to judge him and see what is in his heart. Almost the identical phrase is found in Psalm 35:24, "Judge me, O Lord my God, according to Thy righteousness."

WITHOUT WAVERING. The word for "wavering" literally means without stumbling or slipping on the road.

2. MY REINS. Literally, "my kidneys," considered to be the seat of the emotions. See the comment on Psalm 7:10, "God trieth the hearts and reins."

3. THY MERCY IS BEFORE MINE EYES. I know that God will forgive my errors because of His mercy.

4-5. I HAVE NOT SAT . . . NEITHER WILL I GO . . . I HATE THE GATHERING. This thought is expressed fully in Psalm 1. "Happy is the man who *walks* not with the wicked nor *sits* in the seats of the scornful."

6. I WILL WASH MY HANDS IN INNOCENCY . . . THINE ALTAR, O

67

8. Lord, I love the habitation of Thy house,
   And the place where Thy glory dwelleth.
9. Gather not my soul with sinners,
   Nor my life with men of blood;
10. In whose hands is craftiness,
   And their right hand is full of bribes.
11. But as for me, I will walk in mine integrity;
   Redeem me, and be gracious unto me.
12. My foot standeth in an even place;
   In the congregations will I bless the Lord.

27. [A PSALM] OF DAVID.

The Lord is my light and salvation; whom shall I fear?
The Lord is the stronghold of my life; of whom shall I be afraid?
2. When evil-doers came upon me to eat up my flesh,
   Even mine adversaries and my foes, they stumbled and fell.

Lord. The priests, before offering sacrifices, washed their hands as a symbol of purity. Also, among non-priests, washing of the hands was a symbol of purity. Thus, Deuteronomy 21:6, when a body of a slain man was found between two cities, the leaders of the cities, in order to indicate their innocence, ceremonially washed their hands.

8. I LOVE THE HABITATION OF THY HOUSE. It is a joy to come into God's presence. A familiar thought in the Psalms. See for example, Psalm 84:11, "For a day in Thy courts is better than a thousand (elsewhere)."

9. GATHER NOT MY SOUL WITH SINNERS. Do not let me perish as sinners, and "men of blood" for "I have walked in Thy truth" (verse 3).

12. MY FOOT STANDETH IN AN EVEN PLACE. Correlative with the thought with which the psalm began (verse 1), "I have trusted in the Lord without wavering," i. e., without stumbling.

AN EVEN PLACE. A level road equivalent to the expression in Psalm 23:3, "He guideth me in straight paths."

A PSALM of confidence in God's help. The psalmist pro-

3. Though a host should encamp against me,
   My heart shall not fear;
   Though war should rise up against me,
   Even then will I be confident.
4. One thing have I asked of the LORD, that will I seek after:
   That I may dwell in the house of the LORD all the days of my
      life,
   To behold the graciousness of the LORD, and to visit early in His
      temple.
5. For He concealeth me in His pavilion in the day of evil;
   He hideth me in the covert of His tent;
   He lifteth me up upon a rock.
6. And now shall my head be lifted up above mine enemies round
      about me;
   And I will offer in His tabernacle sacrifices with trumpet-sound;
   I will sing, yea, I will sing praises unto the LORD.

claims that God has been his "light and salvation," giving him courage to face all enemies. He, therefore, prays that now, too, God may protect him. The psalm ends with the same note of confidence with which it begins. He says unto his heart, "be strong, wait thou for the Lord."

1. THE LORD IS MY LIGHT. A favorite metaphor in the Bible; God, as radiance, illumining the path of life. Thus, Psalm 36:10, "In Thy light do we see light." Micah 7:8, "Though I sit in darkness, the Lord is a light unto me."

2. TO EAT UP MY FLESH. As in Psalm 22, where the enemy is compared to a ravening beast. Here the enemies come "to eat my flesh."

2-3. The figure is cumulative. Whether they come as a number of wild beasts or encamp as an army or actually join in battle "even then will I be confident."

4-6. A familiar thought in the Psalms: the joy of dwelling in God's presence. The metaphor contains a number of connotations. One is the joy of being in God's Temple and offering sacrifices of thanksgiving. Another, and a wider connotation, is that God is a host in Whose house we dwell and Whose presence protects us. This thought, expressed at the end of Psalm 23, is here repeated.

7. Hear, O LORD, when I call with my voice,
   And be gracious unto me, and answer me.
8. In Thy behalf my heart hath said: 'Seek ye My face';
   Thy face, LORD, will I seek.
9. Hide not Thy face from me;
   Put not Thy servant away in anger;
   Thou hast been my help;
   Cast me not off, neither forsake me, O God of my
     salvation.
10. For though my father and my mother have forsaken me,
    The LORD will take me up.
11. Teach me Thy way, O LORD;
    And lead me in an even path,
    Because of them that lie in wait for me.
12. Deliver me not over unto the will of mine adversaries;

4. THE GRACIOUSNFSS OF THE LORD. The kindly lovableness of the gracious host. The phrase is used also in Psalm 90:17, "Let the graciousness of the Lord our God be upon us."

5. CONCEALETH ME . . . HIDETH ME. The host protects me against pursuing enemies. Thus, in Psalm 23 God, the host, gives me hospitality "in the presence of mine enemies."

6. MY HEAD SHALL BE LIFTED UP. I shall walk erectly, proudly, and unafraid, because of God's protection. The same phrase is used in Psalm 3:4, "Thou, O Lord, art a shield about me . . . the lifter up of my head."

SACRIFICES WITH TRUMPET-SOUND . . . I WILL SING. The sacrifices on joyous occasions were offered among the sound of the trumpet and song. "In the day of your gladness . . . ye shall blow with trumpets over your burnt-offerings and peace-offerings." (Numbers 10:10.)

8-9. MY HEART HATH SAID, SEEK YE, etc. The psalmist speaks with his own heart. His heart recalls God's command: "Seek ye my face," and he answers: "Thy face, Lord, will I seek." When I will seek thee "hide not Thy face from me."

10. THOUGH MY FATHER, etc. The commentator, Ibn Ezra, explains this as follows: though father and mother die and I am orphaned, God is still father to me. It may be taken in a more general sense: though no human love is left to me, God's

For false witnesses are risen up against me, and such as
    breathe out violence.
13. If I had not believed to look upon the goodness of the LORD
    In the land of the living!—
14. Wait for the LORD;
    Be strong, and let thy heart take courage;
    Yea, wait thou for the LORD.

28. [A PSALM] OF DAVID.

    Unto Thee, O LORD, do I call;
    My Rock, be not Thou deaf unto me;
    Lest, if Thou be silent unto me,
    I become like them that go down into the pit.
2. Hear the voice of my supplications, when I cry unto Thee,
    When I lift up my hands toward Thy Holy Sanctuary.

fatherly love remains. See Psalm 103:13, "Like as a father hath
compassion upon his children, so hath the Lord compassion
upon them that fear Him." See also Isaiah 66:13, "As one
whom his mother comforteth, so will I comfort you."

13. IF I HAD NOT BELIEVED. Ibn Ezra connects this sentence
with the preceding verse, giving the following meaning: when
false witnesses rise against me (I would not have had the
strength to resist) if I had not believed, etc. Therefore, "wait
for the Lord; be strong."

A PRAYER for help in time of danger. The structure of this
psalm is the reverse of that of the preceding psalm. Psalm 27
begins with an assurance of God's help: "The Lord is my light
and my salvation" (27:1). Based upon that assurance the
psalmist continues with the prayer: "Hear, O Lord" (27:7 ff.).
This psalm begins with petition: "Unto Thee, do I call . . .
hear the voice of my supplications" (28:1-2), and ends with
assurance: "The Lord is a strength" (28:8).

1. THAT GO DOWN INTO THE PIT. The nether-world, death.
Thus, Psalm 30:4, "Thou didst keep me alive, that I should not
go down to the pit."

2. WHEN I LIFT UP MY HANDS. In prayer.

3. Draw me not away with the wicked,
   And with the workers of iniquity;
   Who speak peace with their neighbours,
   But evil is in their hearts.
4. Give them according to their deeds, and according to
      the evil of their endeavours;
   Give them after the work of their hands;
   Render to them their desert.
5. Because they give no heed to the works of the LORD,
   Nor to the operation of His hands;
   He will break them down and not build them up.
6. Blessed be the LORD,
   Because He hath heard the voice of my supplications.
7. The LORD is my strength and my shield,

3. DRAW ME NOT AWAY WITH THE WICKED. Let me not die prematurely as do the wicked. This thought was expressed in Psalm 26:9, "Gather not my soul with sinners nor my life with men of blood."

WHO SPEAK . . . BUT EVIL IS IN THEIR HEARTS. The description of the wicked as hypocrites is found frequently in the Psalms. Thus, for example: "With flattering lip, and with a double heart, do they speak." (Psalm 12:3.)

5. This sentence is an aside. It does not address God but speaks to the listener and refers to God and His punishment for the wicked.

6-9. These verses express the strong assurance that God has heard "the voice of my supplications," and that He is "my strength and my shield."

8. This verse, like verse 5, is also an aside. It does not address God but refers to God in the third person and addresses the listener.

A STRONGHOLD OF SALVATION TO HIS ANOINTED. To the king, as in Psalm 18:51, "Great salvation giveth He to his king; and showeth mercy to his anointed."

9. THE PEOPLE . . . THINE INHERITANCE. Israel is described as God's inheritance. Thus, "Happy . . . the people whom He hath chosen for His own inheritance." (Psalm 33:12.)

In Him hath my heart trusted,
And I am helped;
Therefore my heart greatly rejoiceth,
And with my song will I praise Him.
8. The LORD is a strength unto them;
And He is a stronghold of salvation to His anointed.
9. Save Thy people, and bless Thine inheritance;
And tend them, and carry them for ever.

29. A PSALM OF DAVID.

Ascribe unto the LORD, O ye sons of might,
Ascribe unto the LORD glory and strength.
2. Ascribe unto the LORD the glory due unto His name;
Worship the LORD in the beauty of holiness.

A NATURE psalm. Specifically it is a declaration of God's might as manifested in the storm. The storm is vividly described as beginning in the northwest over the Mediterranean ("The voice of the Lord is upon the waters," verse 3), reaching the land to strike the cedar-clad mountains in the north ("Lebanon and Sirion," verse 6), and moving on southward over Palestine to the wilderness of Kadesh to the southeast (verse 8). According to tradition (b. Berachoth 29b), the fact that there are eighteen benedictions in *Shemone Esreh* (the *Tefillah* of the daily prayers) is derived from the use of God's name eighteen times in this psalm. The psalm is now recited in the Synagogue on Friday evening at the services ushering in the Sabbath.

1. YE SONS OF MIGHT. The angels. The Targum (the Aramaic translation) paraphrases this sentence: "Utter praises in the presence of God, ye companies of angels, sons of might." The vision of angels praising God is described dramatically by Isaiah (Chapter 6) where the angels surrounding God's throne chant, "Holy, holy, holy, . . . the earth is full of His glory." Thus, here also, in verse 2, the angels' praise includes God's glory and holiness.

Verses 1 and 2 are the introduction to the description of God's majesty in the storm.

73

3. The voice of the LORD is upon the waters;
   The God of glory thundereth,
   Even the LORD upon many waters.
4. The voice of the LORD is powerful;
   The voice of the LORD is full of majesty.
5. The voice of the LORD breaketh the cedars;
   Yea, the LORD breaketh in pieces the cedars of Lebanon.
6. He maketh them also to skip like a calf;
   Lebanon and Sirion like a young wild-ox.
7. The voice of the LORD heweth out flames of fire.
8. The voice of the LORD shaketh the wilderness;
   The LORD shaketh the wilderness of Kadesh.
9. The voice of the LORD maketh the hinds to calve,
   And strippeth the forests bare;
   And in His temple all say: 'Glory.'
10. The LORD sat enthroned at the flood;

3-9. Describe the storm moving from the sea over the mountains across Palestine to the desert beyond.

3. UPON THE WATERS . . . THUNDERETH. The thunder of the distant storm.

5. BREAKETH THE CEDARS OF LEBANON. The two highest mountains in Palestine, Lebanon and Hermon, were crowned with great cedars. As soon as the storm strikes them these powerful trees are broken.

6. SIRION. Mount Hermon. "Which Hermon the Sidonians call Sirion" (Deuteronomy 3:9).

8. THE WILDERNESS OF KADESH. Southeast of Palestine.

9. MAKETH THE HINDS TO CALVE. Prematurely in terror.

IN HIS TEMPLE ALL SAY "GLORY." As the Targum translates it, "in His heavenly temple." Thus interpreted, this sentence parallels the opening sentence. The storm begins with the angels' praise; and at the end of the storm the voices of the angels are again heard proclaiming God's glory.

10. ENTHRONED AT THE FLOOD . . . KING FOR EVER. The storm is a passing phenomenon but God's majesty revealed in it, is an eternal fact. God was enthroned in ancient days (in days of the flood), and will be enthroned forever.

11. STRENGTH . . . PEACE. God's crowning blessing of peace

Yea, the LORD sitteth as King for ever.
11. The LORD will give strength unto His people;
The LORD will bless His people with peace.

30. A PSALM; A SONG AT THE DEDICATION OF THE HOUSE; OF DAVID.

2. I will extol Thee, O LORD, for Thou hast raised me up,
And hast not suffered mine enemies to rejoice over me.
3. O LORD my God,
I cried unto Thee, and Thou didst heal me;
4. O LORD, Thou broughtest up my soul from the nether-world;
Thou didst keep me alive, that I should not go down to the pit.
5. Sing praise unto the LORD, O ye His godly ones,
And give thanks to His holy name.
6. For His anger is but for a moment,
His favour is for a life-time;
Weeping may tarry for the night,

comes as His final benediction after the storm has ceased.

SONG of praise to God for having delivered the psalmist from dangerous sickness, "I cried unto Thee, and Thou didst heal me" (verse 3). The psalm is headed, "A Song at the Dedication of the House." There is nothing in the psalm which points specifically to an occasion such as is indicated in this heading. Nevertheless the psalm is assigned for reading on the Feast of Dedication, Hanukkah. (Soferim 18, 2.) If the deliverance of the psalmist from sickness is understood to apply to all of Israel then the assigning it for Hanukkah is quite suitable. Israel is in danger and on the verge of destruction by his Syrian enemies. He is rescued from danger and, being delivered, he rededicated the Temple.

2. EXTOL THEE. Exalt Thee with my praise.

RAISED ME UP. From the pit of destruction, from the danger of death. Thus, in Psalm 9:14, "Thou that liftest me up from the gates of death."

4. NETHER-WORLD . . . PIT. See comment on Psalm 6:6.

6. ANGER BUT FOR A MOMENT. God's punishment is but for a moment. It is greatly exceeded by His kindness.

75

But joy cometh in the morning.

7. Now I had said in my security: 'I shall never be moved.'
8. Thou hadst established, O Lord, in Thy favour my mountain
    as a stronghold—
Thou didst hide Thy face; I was affrighted.
9. Unto Thee, O Lord, did I call,
    And unto the Lord I made supplication:
10. 'What profit is there in my blood, when I go down to the pit?
    Shall the dust praise Thee? shall it declare Thy truth?
11. Hear, O Lord, and be gracious unto me;
    Lord, be Thou my helper.'
12. Thou didst turn for me my mourning into dancing;
    Thou didst loose my sackcloth, and gird me with gladness;
13. So that my glory may sing praise to Thee, and not be silent;
    O Lord my God, I will give thanks unto Thee for ever.

NIGHT . . . MORNING. The psalmist frequently refers to night as the time of sorrow and weeping, and to morning as the time of strength and hope returned. Thus, Psalm 143:8, "Cause me to hear Thy loving-kindness in the morning."

7. I HAD SAID IN MY SECURITY. When I was in health I was boastful of my strength not realizing that my strength came from Thee and that Thou "hadst established my mountain as a stronghold," (verse 8). But when God hid His face from me my health departed and "I was affrighted."

10-11. His prayer in time of sickness.

10. WHAT PROFIT . . . WHEN I GO DOWN. The same thought as is expressed in Psalm 6:6, that "In death there is no remembrance of Thee; in the nether-world who will give Thee thanks?"

12. MOURNING . . . DANCING; SACK-CLOTH . . . GLADNESS. The contrasts are sharp. Mourning which is expressed by gestures of sorrow, such as beating the breast, will be supplanted by the gesture of joy, the dance. Sack-cloth, the ugly garment of sorrow, will be supplanted with gladness as a garment, thus "Gird me with gladness."

13. MY GLORY MAY SING PRAISE. "My glory" means "my soul" as is clear from the couplet in Psalm 7:6, "And tread my life down to the earth; yea, let him lay my glory in the dust."

31. FOR THE LEADER. A PSALM OF DAVID.

2. In Thee, O Lord, have I taken refuge; let me never be ashamed;
Deliver me in Thy righteousness.
3. Incline Thine ear unto me, deliver me speedily;
Be Thou to me a rock of refuge, even a fortress of defence,
to save me.
4. For Thou art my rock and my fortress;
Therefore for Thy name's sake lead me and guide me.
5. Bring me forth out of the net that they have hidden for me;
For Thou art my stronghold.
6. Into Thy hand I commit my spirit;
Thou hast redeemed me, O Lord, Thou God of truth.
7. I hate them that regard lying vanities;
But I trust in the Lord.

THE thought of this psalm is quite similar to that of Psalms 22 and 28. Its phraseology parallels a number of other psalms and passages in the books of Jeremiah, Jonah, and Job. The thought is the familiar prayer of the psalmist when troubled by physical sickness and dejection of mind. Beset by enemies and haunted by fears, he turns to God whose "wondrous loving kindness" gives him courage and strength.

2. LET ME NEVER BE ASHAMED. Let me not be disappointed when I trust in Thy help. Thus, Psalm 25:2, "In Thee have I trusted, let me not be ashamed."

3. A REFUGE . . . FORTRESS OF DEFENCE. The phrase is similar to that in Psalm 18:3, "The Lord is my rock, and my fortress."

5. THE NET THAT THEY HAVE HIDDEN FOR ME. See Psalm 9:16, "The net which they hid."

6. INTO THY HAND I COMMIT MY SPIRIT. I confidently entrust my life to Thy keeping for in the past "Thou hast redeemed me." This verse, expressing man's complete trust in God, has become part of the last prayer at night when man entrusts his soul into God's keeping. It also is used in the last prayer of the dying.

7. LYING VANITIES. This phrase is also found in the psalm given in Jonah 2:9, "they that regard lying vanities."

8. I will be glad and rejoice in Thy lovingkindness;
    For Thou hast seen mine affliction,
    Thou hast taken cognizance of the troubles of my soul,
9. And Thou hast not given me over into the hand of the enemy;
    Thou hast set my feet in a broad place.
10. Be gracious unto me, O LORD, for I am in distress;
    Mine eye wasteth away with vexation, yea, my soul and my body.
11. For my life is spent in sorrow, and my years in sighing;
    My strength faileth because of mine iniquity, and my bones
      are wasted away.
12. Because of all mine adversaries I am become a reproach,
    Yea, unto my neighbours exceedingly, and a dread to mine
      acquaintance;
    They that see me without flee from me.
13. I am forgotten as a dead man out of mind;
    I am like a useless vessel.
14. For I have heard the whispering of many,
    Terror on every side;
    While they took counsel together against me,
    They devised to take away my life.
15. But as for me, I have trusted in Thee, O LORD;
    I have said: 'Thou art my God.'
16. My times are in Thy hand;
    Deliver me from the hand of mine enemies, and from them
      that persecute me.

9. SET MY FEET IN A BROAD PLACE. Sorrow and trouble are visualized as a narrow ravine and God's deliverance as a broad and open place. Thus, "He brought me forth into a large place." (Psalm 18:20.)

10. MINE EYE WASTETH AWAY WITH VEXATION. Compare with Psalm 6:8, "Mine eye is dimmed because of vexation."

12. I AM BECOME A REPROACH. A mockery.

A DREAD TO MINE ACQUAINTANCE. My enemies mock me and my neighbors are afraid to associate with me. My miseries are so great that they terrify them.

13. LIKE A USELESS VESSEL. No one considers me worthy of notice. I am cast aside like a broken piece of pottery.

14. TERROR ON EVERY SIDE. This phrase is used frequently by the prophet Jeremiah to describe the dangers which surround

17. Make Thy face to shine upon Thy servant;
Save me in Thy lovingkindness.
18. O Lord, let me not be ashamed, for I have called upon Thee;
Let the wicked be ashamed, let them be put to silence in the
nether-world.
19. Let the lying lips be dumb,
Which speak arrogantly against the righteous,
With pride and contempt.
20. Oh how abundant is Thy goodness, which Thou hast laid up
for them that fear Thee;
Which Thou hast wrought for them that take their refuge in
Thee, in the sight of the sons of men!
21. Thou hidest them in the covert of Thy presence from the
plottings of man;
Thou concealest them in a pavilion from the strife of tongues.
22. Blessed be the Lord;
For He hath shown me His wondrous lovingkindness in an
entrenched city.
23. As for me, I said in my haste: 'I am cut off from before Thine
eyes';
Nevertheless Thou heardest the voice of my supplications when
I cried unto Thee.
24. O love the Lord, all ye His godly ones;
The Lord preserveth the faithful,
And plentifully repayeth him that acteth haughtily.

him and the people of Israel. Thus, Jeremiah 6:25, "The sword of the enemy, and terror on every side."

17. MAKE THY FACE TO SHINE. As a radiant sign of Thy blessing. So in the priestly benediction, "The Lord make His face to shine upon thee." (Numbers 6:25.)

20. THY GOODNESS, WHICH THOU HAST LAID UP. God's loving kindness is inexhaustible. It is like a vast treasure stored up for those who seek His help.

21. THOU HIDEST THEM IN THE COVERT . . . IN A PAVILION. In God's house and in His presence we are protected from all hostility. Almost the identical phrase is used in Psalm 27:5, "He concealeth me in His pavilion . . . in the covert of His tent."

22. IN AN ENTRENCHED CITY. God's lovingkindness is like a strong fortress.

79

25. Be strong, and let your heart take courage,
      All ye that wait for the LORD.

32. [A PSALM] OF DAVID. MASCHIL.

Happy is he whose transgression is forgiven, whose
    sin is pardoned.
2. Happy is the man unto whom the LORD counteth
    not iniquity,
And in whose spirit there is no guile.
3. When I kept silence, my bones wore away
    Through my groaning all the day long.

25. BE STRONG . . . YE THAT WAIT. The same confident ending
as in Psalm 27:14, "Be strong, wait thou for the Lord."

THE spiritual joy of confession and forgiveness. In this
psalm the author rises above the mood heretofore expressed,
namely, that he is surrounded by sinful enemies from whose
violence he asks God to deliver him. Here he confronts his own
unworthiness and prays for forgiveness, knowing that once his
own conscience is clear he will have inner happiness.

The word *selah*, occurring three times in the psalm, divides
the psalm into its three logical divisions. In verses 1-4, the
psalmist begins with a general statement of the joy of being
forgiven and describes his misery as long as his sin remained
unconfessed. Verse 5 gives his frank confession. Verses 6 and 7
address both the listener and God, and voice the assurance that
God will pardon. The psalm ends (8-11) with a description of
God's guidance, with a final appeal to full confession, and with
a reiteration of the joy of him whose heart is purified.

1. MASCHIL. A technical term describing the psalm. Its meaning is doubtful. The commentator, Ibn Ezra, connects it with
the word in verse 8 (a word of the same root), which means:
"he will instruct thee," hence he takes *Maschil* to mean, a
psalm of instruction.

HAPPY IS HE. Psalm 1 which begins with a description of the
way to happiness says: Happy is he who does not associate with

4. For day and night Thy hand was heavy upon me;
   My sap was turned as in the droughts of summer.   Selah
5. I acknowledged my sin unto Thee, and mine iniquity have
   I not hid;
   I said: 'I will make confession concerning my transgressions
   unto the LORD'—
   And Thou, Thou forgavest the iniquity of my sin.   Selah
6. For this let every one that is godly pray unto Thee in a time
   when Thou mayest be found;
   Surely, when the great waters overflow, they will not reach
   unto him.

the wicked. This psalm is more personal and intimate and says:
Happy is he whose own *inner* wickedness is overcome.

1-2. TRANSGRESSION . . . SIN . . . INIQUITY. These three types
of sin are mentioned in Exodus 34:7, in the sentence which
God speaks to Moses, "forgiving iniquity and transgression and
sin." These three terms are also used in the confession of the
high priest on the Day of Atonement in the Temple (Mishnah
Yoma III, 8). Transgression (*pesha*) means rebellion. Sin
(*chet*) means error. Iniquity (*avon*) means perversion of God's
Law.

2. THERE IS NO GUILE. Happy is he who attempts no hypocritical concealment of his sin but frankly searches it out.

3-4. His mental and bodily discomfort due to a troubled
conscience.

MY BONES WORE AWAY. I seemed broken in body.

4. MY SAP WAS TURNED AS IN THE DROUGHTS OF SUMMER. A
familiar expression in the Psalms. As a tree is dried up in the
heat of summer or as a broken piece of pottery is burned up by
a blazing sun so is my body shrivelled up by my sinfulness. The
same description of grief leaving the body parched and dry is to
be found in Psalm 22:16, "My strength is dried up like a
potsherd."

6. WHEN THOU MAYEST BE FOUND. The commentator, Ibn
Ezra, suggests that it means: Pray to God for forgiveness at a
time when the mind is not distracted by other affairs. But it
may mean simply: Pray to God before your sin becomes so

81

7. Thou art my hiding-place; Thou wilt preserve me from the
   adversary;
   With songs of deliverance Thou wilt compass me about.   Selah
8. 'I will instruct thee and teach thee in the way which thou
   shalt go;
   I will give counsel, Mine eye being upon thee.'
9. Be ye not as the horse, or as the mule, which have no
   understanding;
   Whose mouth must be held in with bit and bridle,
   That they come not near unto thee.
10. Many are the sorrows of the wicked;
    But he that trusteth in the LORD, mercy compasseth
    him about.
11. Be glad in the LORD, and rejoice, ye righteous;
    And shout for joy, all ye that are upright in heart.

habitual you can no longer find Him. Thus, Isaiah 55:6, "Seek
ye the Lord while He may be found, call ye upon Him while
He is near."

WHEN THE GREAT WATERS OVERFLOW. When trouble arises to
overwhelm you. The same metaphor is used in Psalm 18:17,
"He drew me out of many waters."

7. MY HIDING-PLACE. The phrase is a familiar one in the
Psalms. God, the Host, conceals us in His tent, protecting us
from danger. Thus, Psalm 31:21, "Thou hidest them in the
covert of Thy presence."

9. AS THE HORSE OR AS THE MULE. Brute beasts need physical
restraint to keep them from doing harm. "Be ye not as the
horse," etc. Let your restraint and discipline come from within.

11. BE GLAD IN THE LORD, . . . YE RIGHTEOUS. Those whose
hearts are cleansed of sin will find inner joy and strength to resist every misfortune.

*T*HIS psalm is one of the four psalms in Book I, which do
not have the heading "of David." However, in the Septuagint
(the Greek version), the heading "of David" is found. (See introductory note to Book I.)

A hymn of praise to God for His Laws of righteousness and

7

33. Rejoice in the Lord, O ye righteous,
   Praise is comely for the upright.
2. Give thanks unto the Lord with harp,
   Sing praises unto Him with the psaltery of ten strings.
3. Sing unto Him a new song;
   Play skilfully amid shouts of joy.
4. For the word of the Lord is upright;
   And all His work is done in faithfulness.
5. He loveth righteousness and justice;
   The earth is full of the lovingkindness
      of the Lord.
6. By the word of the Lord were the heavens made;
   And all the host of them by the breath of His mouth.
7. He gathereth the waters of the sea together as a heap;
   He layeth up the deeps in store-houses.

His governance of human history. This psalm is recited on Sabbath mornings.

1. REJOICE IN THE LORD. The command given in the closing verse of the preceding psalm, that the righteous rejoice in God, is echoed here at the opening of this psalm.

PRAISE IS COMELY. It behooves the righteous to praise God for His kindness.

3. A NEW SONG. Since God's mercies are constantly renewed, our prayers of praise must never become mere routine but must be recreated constantly. The same idea is expressed in Psalm 98:1, "O sing unto the Lord a new song; for He hath done marvelous things."

4-11. After the first three verses which constitute an introductory call to the righteous to praise God, verses 4-11 set forth the reason why God is to be praised. Verses 4 and 5 speak of the righteousness of God's actions. Verses 6 to 9 describe His creation of the world. Verses 10-11, God's mastery over history.

4. IN FAITHFULNESS. God's actions in human life are faithful and trustworthy. They can be relied upon.

7. HE GATHERETH THE WATERS . . . AS A HEAP. This description follows that of Genesis 1:9, "Let the waters be gathered together unto one place."

LAYETH UP THE DEEPS IN STORE-HOUSES. As grain is poured

83

8. Let all the earth fear the LORD;
   Let all the inhabitants of the world stand in awe of Him.
9. For He spoke, and it was;
   He commanded, and it stood.
10. The LORD bringeth the counsel of the nations to nought;
    He maketh the thoughts of the peoples to be of no effect.
11. The counsel of the LORD standeth for ever,
    The thoughts of His heart to all generations.
12. Happy is the nation whose God is the LORD;
    The people whom He hath chosen for His own inheritance.
13. The LORD looketh from heaven;
    He beholdeth all the sons of men;
14. From the place of His habitation He looketh intently
    Upon all the inhabitants of the earth;
15. He that fashioneth the hearts of them all,
    That considereth all their doings.
16. A king is not saved by the multitude of a host;
    A mighty man is not delivered by great strength.

into a store-house so God fills the abysses of the sea with water.

10. THE COUNSEL OF THE NATIONS TO NOUGHT. Since God is the Creator of the world, His Law alone can govern it. All plans contrary to His Law will come to naught. Thus, Proverbs 21:30, "There is no wisdom . . . nor counsel against the Lord."

12-19. Since God alone rules the world, happy is the nation which relies upon Him for its strength.

12. THE PEOPLE . . . CHOSEN FOR HIS OWN INHERITANCE. Israel, God's inheritance. See comment to Psalm 28:9.

15. HE THAT FASHIONETH. Since God created man He knows all his thoughts. Therefore man can never prevail against God.

16-17. A KING IS NOT SAVED . . . BY GREAT STRENGTH. This thought was expressed in Psalm 20:8, "Some trust in chariots . . . but we will make mention of the Lord, our God."

18. THE EYE OF THE LORD. The same phrase is used in the preceding Psalm 32:8, "Mine eye being upon thee," God's watchfulness and care guide us in all our perplexities.

20-21. The conclusion of the psalm parallels the beginning. The psalm begins: "Rejoice in the Lord." It concludes with the thought: "In Him doth our heart rejoice."

17. A horse is a vain thing for safety;
    Neither doth it afford escape by its great strength.
18. Behold, the eye of the Lord is toward them that fear Him,
    Toward them that wait for His mercy;
19. To deliver their soul from death,
    And to keep them alive in famine.
20. Our soul hath waited for the Lord;
    He is our help and our shield.
21. For in Him doth our heart rejoice,
    Because we have trusted in His holy name.
22. Let Thy mercy, O Lord, be upon us,
    According as we have waited for Thee.

34. [A PSALM] OF DAVID; WHEN HE CHANGED HIS DEMEANOUR BE-
    FORE ABIMELECH, WHO DROVE HIM AWAY, AND HE DEPARTED.

2. I will bless the Lord at all times;
   His praise shall continually be in my mouth.
3. My soul shall glory in the Lord;

AN acrostic psalm. (See comment on Psalm 9.) It is closely related in thought and in phraseology with Psalm 25 which is also an acrostic psalm.

This psalm is a hymn of praise to God, beginning with three introductory verses, 2-4, in which the psalmist calls upon the people to join him in praise of God. Verse 5 speaks of God's deliverance; and 6-11 extends this personal fact to a general experience, describing God's help to all the humble. In 12-15 the psalmist becomes a teacher, instructing his listeners in the right path of life. In 16-22 he speaks again of God's help to the humble. Verse 23 is a concluding verse summing up the thought of the entire psalm.

The heading of the psalm connects it with a specific incident in the life of David related in I Samuel 21:11-16. David fled to Gath in the land of the Philistines; he feigned madness while there in order to save himself from being killed. According to the heading it was after this incident that David wrote this psalm. The same event is referred to in the heading of Psalm 56.

This psalm is recited in the Sabbath morning services.

85

The humble shall hear thereof, and be glad.
4. O magnify the LORD with me,
And let us exalt His name together.
5. I sought the LORD, and He answered me,
And delivered me from all my fears.
6. They looked unto Him, and were radiant;
And their faces shall never be abashed.
7. This poor man cried, and the LORD heard,
And saved him out of all his troubles.
8. The angel of the LORD encampeth round about
them that fear Him,
And delivereth them.
9. O consider and see that the LORD is good;
Happy is the man that taketh refuge in Him.
10. O fear the LORD, ye His holy ones;
For there is no want to them that fear Him.
11. The young lions do lack, and suffer hunger;
But they that seek the LORD want not any good thing.
12. Come, ye children, hearken unto me;
I will teach you the fear of the LORD.

4. MAGNIFY THE LORD . . . EXALT HIS NAME. The psalmist
calls upon the humble to glorify God's name. This verse is used
in the Torah service.

5-6. I SOUGHT . . . THEY LOOKED. The psalmist changes the
person of reference. He extends the thought from his own experience to that of all the righteous.

8. THE ANGEL OF THE LORD ENCAMPETH. God's angels are described as surrounding the righteous as a protecting army. The
prophet Zechariah (Chapter 9:8) speaks of God Himself as encamped around Israel, "And I will encamp about My house . . .
and no oppressor shall pass through."

12-15. COME, YE CHILDREN. The psalmist speaks as a teacher
pointing out the moral prerequisite for a true worship of God,
namely, to keep from speaking evil, from doing evil, and to
persist in seeking peace.

13. WHO IS THE MAN THAT DESIRETH LIFE. An analogous
question is asked in Psalm 25:12, "What man is he that feareth
the Lord? Him will He instruct," etc.

13. Who is the man that desireth life,
    And loveth days, that he may see good therein?
14. Keep thy tongue from evil,
    And thy lips from speaking guile.
15. Depart from evil, and do good;
    Seek peace, and pursue it.
16. The eyes of the LORD are toward the righteous,
    And His ears are open unto their cry.
17. The face of the LORD is against them that do evil,
    To cut off the remembrance of them from the earth.
18. They* cried, and the LORD heard,
    And delivered them out of all their troubles.
19. The LORD is nigh unto them that are of a broken heart,
    And saveth such as are of a contrite spirit.
20. Many are the ills of the righteous,
    But the LORD delivereth him out of them all.
21. He keepeth all his bones;
    Not one of them is broken.
22. Evil shall kill the wicked;
    And they that hate the righteous shall be held guilty.

16. THE EYES OF THE LORD ARE TOWARD THE RIGHTEOUS. God keeps watch of the righteous, protecting them. The same phrase is used in Psalm 33:18, "The eye of the Lord is toward them that fear Him."

17. THE FACE OF THE LORD IS AGAINST THEM THAT DO EVIL. The converse of the statement in the preceding verse; God turns His face in wrath against the wicked.

18. THEY CRIED. The antecedent is in verse 16. "The righteous cried and the Lord heard."

19. THE LORD IS NIGH. Those who are "of a broken heart" are near to God. Their sorrows save them from pride and vainglory and they turn to God for help.

20. MANY ARE THE ILLS. The righteous are not spared sorrow but their sufferings will not destroy them.

21-22. HE KEEPETH ALL HIS BONES. God preserves the righteous. They are never broken by their misfortunes. But "the evil" that is within the sinful "shall kill the wicked."

* That is, the righteous.

87

23. The LORD redeemeth the soul of His servants;
And none of them that take refuge in Him shall be desolate.

35. [A PSALM] OF DAVID.

Strive, O LORD, with them that strive with me;
Fight against them that fight against me.
2. Take hold of shield and buckler,
And rise up to my help.
3. Draw out also the spear, and the battle-axe, against them that
pursue me;
Say unto my soul: 'I am thy salvation.'
4. Let them be ashamed and brought to confusion that seek after
my soul;
Let them be turned back and be abashed that devise my hurt.
5. Let them be as chaff before the wind,
The angel of the LORD thrusting them.

23. A verse of praise, which is added to sum up the thought
of the entire Psalm. The alphabet is completed with verse 22.

A PRAYER for Divine help against unjustified hostility.
Describing his struggle against his enemies, the psalmist uses
two different metaphors. He uses the metaphor of a battle, asking God to march against his adversaries, and he also depicts a
scene in a law court, asking God to confound the false witnesses
who have risen against him. In both metaphors the psalmist
makes use of many phrases which occur frequently throughout
the Book of Psalms. His enemies "dig a pit," they "spread a
net," like lions they "gnash their teeth" seeking to destroy him.
Yet, although much of the phraseology of the psalm is familiar,
the psalm has considerable originality. The metaphor of the
law-suit and the false witnesses is vividly described and the dis-
tinction between his considerateness for his adversaries and
their cruelty to him is sharply delineated.

The psalm may well be assigned to a definite period in the
life of David, namely, when his enemies came to Saul and
maligned him.

1-3. A bold metaphor of God as a military champion taking

88

6. Let their way be dark and slippery,
   The angel of the LORD pursuing them.
7. For without cause have they hid for me the pit, even their net,
   Without cause have they digged for my soul.
8. Let destruction come upon him unawares;
   And let his net that he hath hid catch himself;
   With destruction let him fall therein.
9. And my soul shall be joyful in the LORD;
   It shall rejoice in His salvation.
10. All my bones shall say: 'LORD, who is like unto Thee,
    Who deliverest the poor from him that is too strong for him,
    Yea, the poor and the needy from him that spoileth him?'
11. Unrighteous witnesses rise up;
    They ask me of things that I know not.
12. They repay me evil for good;
    Bereavement is come to my soul.

up "shield and spear" to defend the psalmist against his foes. This soldierly picture of God is inherent in the biblical phrase, "The Lord of hosts," and is expressed specifically in the poem in Exodus 15:3, "The Lord is a man of war."

4-6. He prays that his enemies be driven back in confusion. He visualizes their headlong rout "as chaff before the wind." They are to find no foothold. "Let their way be dark and slippery."

7-8. The evil which his enemies have done. "Without cause have they hid for me the pit."

9-10. These verses close the first part of the prayer and anticipate his gratitude when God will have delivered him.

11-12. The metaphor changes from battle to a scene in a law court.

11. UNRIGHTEOUS WITNESSES . . . ASK ME OF THINGS THAT I KNOW NOT. They charge me with crimes of which I know nothing.

13-16. Their hostility is unjustified. When they were in trouble I sympathized with them, but now that I am in trouble they take advantage of my misfortunes to destroy me. "When they were sick . . . I afflicted my soul. But when I halt (i. e., stumble) . . . they gnash at me with their teeth."

89

13. But as for me, when they were sick, my clothing was sackcloth,
 I afflicted my soul with fasting;
 And my prayer, may it return into mine own bosom.

14. I went about as though it had been my friend or my brother;
 I bowed down mournful, as one that mourneth for his mother.

15. But when I halt they rejoice, and gather themselves together;
 The abjects gather themselves together against me, and those
  whom I know not;
 They tear me, and cease not;

16. With the profanest mockeries of backbiting
 They gnash at me with their teeth.

17. Lord, how long wilt Thou look on?
 Rescue my soul from their destructions,
 Mine only one from the lions.

18. I will give Thee thanks in the great congregation;
 I will praise Thee among a numerous people.

19. Let not them that are wrongfully mine enemies rejoice over me;
 Neither let them wink with the eye that hate me without a cause.

20. For they speak not peace;
 But they devise deceitful matters against them that are quiet in
  the land.

21. Yea, they open their mouth wide against me;
 They say: 'Aha, aha, our eye hath seen it.'

13. MY PRAYER, MAY IT RETURN INTO MINE OWN BOSOM. I
prayed in their behalf. May my good wishes for them redound
to my welfare.

15. THE ABJECTS GATHER THEMSELVES. The rabble.

17-18. Closes the second part of the prayer and parallels
verses 9-10, asking for God's help and anticipating the prayers
of gratitude for deliverance.

19. NEITHER LET THEM WINK WITH THE EYE. Knowingly,
scornfully at my misfortunes. See the same phrase in Proverbs
6:12-13, "A base person . . . that winketh with his eyes."

21. AHA, OUR EYE HATH SEEN IT. The enemies say: We now
rejoice at beholding his destruction.

22. THOU HAST SEEN, O LORD. In answer to the words of the
enemies "our eye hath seen it," the psalmist says, "Thou" hast
seen their evil. Therefore (verse 23), "Awake to my judgment."

27. LET THEM SHOUT FOR JOY . . . THAT DELIGHT IN MY RIGHT-

22. Thou hast seen, O LORD; keep not silence;
O Lord, be not far from me.
23. Rouse Thee, and awake to my judgment,
Even unto my cause, my God and my LORD.
24. Judge me, O LORD my God, according to Thy
righteousness;
And let them not rejoice over me.
25. Let them not say in their heart: 'Aha, we have our desire';
Let them not say: 'We have swallowed him up.'
26. Let them be ashamed and abashed together that rejoice
at my hurt;
Let them be clothed with shame and confusion that
magnify themselves against me.
27. Let them shout for joy, and be glad, that delight in my
righteousness;
Yea, let them say continually: 'Magnified be the LORD,
Who delighteth in the peace of His servant.'
28. And my tongue shall speak of Thy righteousness,
And of Thy praise all the day.

36. FOR THE LEADER. [A PSALM] OF DAVID THE SERVANT OF THE LORD.

2. Transgression speaketh to the wicked, methinks—
There is no fear of God before his eyes.

EOUSNESS. Let those rejoice who will be happy at my vindication.

28. The psalm ends with anticipated praise of God. "My tongue shall speak . . . Thy praise all the day."

𝒯HE psalmist describes those evil ones whose wickedness is cumulative. Transgression itself flatters them and keeps them from attaining that sound wisdom which could cure them of sin. Against the violence of such incorrigibles there is no protection except the boundless goodness of God, Whose "faithfulness reacheth unto the skies," and in the shadow of Whose wings "the children of men take refuge." He will not "let the hand of the wicked" drive me away.

1. DAVID, THE SERVANT OF GOD. See the comment to Psalm 18:1, where the same heading is used.

2. TRANSGRESSION SPEAKETH. Transgression is here personi-

Psalm 36

3

3. For it flattereth him in his eyes,
   Until his iniquity be found, and he be hated.
4. The words of his mouth are iniquity and deceit;
   He hath left off to be wise, to do good.
5. He deviseth iniquity upon his bed;
   He setteth himself in a way that is not good;
   He abhorreth not evil.
6. Thy lovingkindness, O LORD, is in the heavens;
   Thy faithfulness reacheth unto the skies.
7. Thy righteousness is like the mighty mountains;
   Thy judgments are like the great deep;
   Man and beast Thou preservest, O LORD.

fied, just as wisdom is personified in the Book of Proverbs.

THERE IS NO FEAR OF GOD. This is not the speech of transgression, but is the reasoning of the psalmist himself and is in the nature of an aside.

3. IT FLATTERETH HIM. Continues the thought of the first half of verse 2, thus: "Transgression speaketh to the wicked" and "flattereth him." It will continue to blind him with flattery until the day when "his iniquity (will) be found (out)."

4. HE HATH LEFT OFF TO BE WISE, TO DO GOOD. He has abandoned wisdom which might have led him to goodness.

6-10. Is in sharp contrast with verses 2-5. From a description of the self-deceiving wicked, the psalmist moves to a declaration of the inexhaustible goodness of God. The connection between the two ideas is that only the boundless mercies of God can protect us against the devices of the sinful.

6. THY LOVINGKINDNESS . . . UNTO THE SKIES. God's love is limitless.

7. THY RIGHTEOUSNESS IS LIKE THE MIGHTY MOUNTAINS. Unshakeable and imposing.

LIKE THE GREAT DEEP. Profound, unfathomable.

8. THE SHADOW OF THY WINGS. A familiar metaphor in the Psalms. Thus, Psalm 17:8, "Hide me in the shadow of Thy wings."

9. THE FATNESS OF THY HOUSE. God is our host Whose gracious hospitality satisfies the body and the soul.

8. How precious is Thy lovingkindness, O God!
And the children of men take refuge in the shadow of Thy wings.
9. They are abundantly satisfied with the fatness of Thy house;
And Thou makest them drink of the river of Thy pleasures.
10. For with Thee is the fountain of life;
In Thy light do we see light.
11. O continue Thy lovingkindness unto them that know Thee;
And Thy righteousness to the upright in heart.
12. Let not the foot of pride overtake me,
And let not the hand of the wicked drive me away.
13. There are the workers of iniquity fallen;
They are thrust down, and are not able to rise.

Psalm 36
13

10. THE FOUNTAIN OF LIFE. As a wayfarer refreshes himself at the bubbling waters of an inexhaustible fountain, so do we draw life from God, the endless fountain of life.

IN THY LIGHT DO WE SEE LIGHT. God, the Infinite Mind, is the source of all wisdom. Whatever enlightenment we attain comes from Him. Whatever beauty there is in our life is a reflection of the Divine Radiance. Thus, Isaiah 60:1, "Arise, shine, for thy light is come, and the glory of God is risen upon thee."

11-13. The thought returns to the contemplation of the wicked and voices the prayer that God may "continue Thy lovingkindness" so as to protect us against "the foot of pride" and "the hand of the wicked."

13. THE WORKERS OF INIQUITY . . . FALLEN. Not only will their evil devices fail to harm me but they themselves will be overthrown.

AN acrostic psalm. See comment on the acrostic Psalm 9.
The psalmist deals with the problem of the prosperity of the wicked and the suffering of the righteous. In a later period in the history of Judaism when the belief in life after death was firmly established, this problem could receive a rather simple solution, namely, that in the life beyond the grave all the apparent injustices of earthly life would be remedied, the

93

37. [A PSALM] OF DAVID.
　Fret not thyself because of evil-doers,
　Neither be thou envious against them that work
　　unrighteousness.
2. For they shall soon wither like the grass,
　And fade as the green herb.
3. Trust in the LORD, and do good;
　Dwell in the land, and cherish faithfulness.
4. So shalt thou delight thyself in the LORD;
　And He shall give thee the petitions of thy heart.
5. Commit thy way unto the LORD;

righteous being recompensed for their earthly sorrows and the
wicked requited according to their deserts. But in the time of
the psalmist there was no definite belief in life after death and
such an answer to the problem was therefore impossible. The
answer which the psalmist gives is, indeed, based upon the
events of the future but it is an earthly future which the psalmist has in mind, namely, that the posterity of the righteous will
flourish but the future of the wicked will be destroyed. From
the larger point of view of history this solution has in it much
that is sound, namely, that violence and hypocrisy destroy themselves ultimately, and truth and justice make for a stable society. This thought was used in the psalm which opened the
entire Book of Psalms, namely, that the wicked are like "chaff
which the wind driveth away" and the righteous like "a tree
. . . whose leaf does not wither."

　Psalm 37 adds to this confident assertion of Psalm 1 the
plea to the righteous not to fret or be envious of the evildoers
but to have faith that their future and the future of their children will be blessed.

　The answer of the psalmist is perhaps less satisfying to modern people than it was to those who lived at the time when the
psalm was written. In modern days where the sense of individuality is stronger than the family sense, it often seems a scant
comfort to be assured that the family of the righteous, though
it suffers, will grow strong through its suffering, and will be es-

Trust also in Him, and He will bring it to pass.
6. And He will make thy righteousness to go forth as the light,
And thy right as the noonday.
7. Resign thyself unto the Lord, and wait patiently for Him;
Fret not thyself because of him who prospereth in his way,
Because of the man who bringeth wicked devices to pass.
8. Cease from anger, and forsake wrath;
Fret not thyself, it tendeth only to evil-doing.
9. For evil-doers shall be cut off;
But those that wait for the Lord, they shall inherit the land.
10. And yet a little while, and the wicked is no more;
Yea, thou shalt look well at his place, and he is not.

tablished, whereas the family of the wicked, being corrupted, will not endure, in spite of their present wealth and power. Yet although the answer is less satisfying in these individualistic days it is nonetheless sound from the broader view of history.

1. FRET NOT THYSELF. Do not be discontented or indignant at the prosperity of the wicked. It will not endure.

2. THEY SHALL WITHER LIKE THE GRASS. As the green herbiage of the field dries up in the summer heat. This simile is used with great effect in Isaiah 40:8, where mortal plans are contrasted with the eternal purpose of God, "The grass withereth, the flower fadeth; but the word of our God shall stand for ever."

5. HE WILL BRING IT TO PASS. Refers back to verse 4, He shall give thee the petitions of thy heart.

6. THY RIGHTEOUSNESS TO GO FORTH AS THE LIGHT. As the sun grows brighter with the advancing day so will thy righteousness be vindicated as time goes on. The thought is expressed clearly in Proverbs 4:18, "The path of the righteous is as the light of dawn, that shineth more and more unto the perfect day."

10. THOU SHALT LOOK AT HIS PLACE, AND HE IS NOT. For the present the wicked seem powerful. They dominate the scene, but the time will come when they will disappear. You will look for them and not even find them. The same thought is expressed later on in the psalm in verse 36, "I sought him, but he could not be found."

95

11. But the humble shall inherit the land,
    And delight themselves in the abundance of peace.
12. The wicked plotteth against the righteous,
    And gnasheth at him with his teeth.
13. The Lord doth laugh at him;
    For He seeth that his day is coming.
14. The wicked have drawn out the sword, and have bent their bow;
    To cast down the poor and needy,
    To slay such as are upright in the way;
15. Their sword shall enter into their own heart,
    And their bows shall be broken.
16. Better is a little that the righteous hath
    Than the abundance of many wicked.
17. For the arms of the wicked shall be broken;
    But the Lord upholdeth the righteous.
18. The Lord knoweth the days of them that are whole-hearted;
    And their inheritance shall be for ever.
19. They shall not be ashamed in the time of evil;
    And in the days of famine they shall be satisfied.
20. For the wicked shall perish,
    And the enemies of the Lord shall be as the fat of lambs—
    They shall pass away in smoke, they shall pass away.

11. THE HUMBLE SHALL INHERIT THE LAND. This verse is quoted in the Beatitudes of the Gospel (Matthew 5:5).

12-17. The thought changes somewhat. Up to verse 11 the thought was that the wicked themselves would not endure. Now the psalmist says that all their plots would be frustrated and their violences overcome.

13. THE LORD DOTH LAUGH AT HIM. The same thought is expressed in Psalm 2:4, when God beholds the violence of the wicked and "He that sitteth in heaven laugheth."

16. BETTER IS A LITTLE. This verse lends itself to two interpretations. One is the interpretation of the commentator, Rashi: More effective is a handful of men on the side of the righteous than the great host of the wicked. The other explanation, following the commentator, Ibn Ezra, is given here in the text, namely, that the righteous find a greater satisfaction from the little than the wicked can possibly find in abundance.

20. THE FAT OF LAMBS SHALL PASS AWAY IN SMOKE. As the

21. The wicked borroweth, and payeth not;
   But the righteous dealeth graciously, and giveth.
22. For such as are blessed of Him shall inherit the land;
   And they that are cursed of Him shall be cut off.
23. It is of the Lord that a man's goings are established:
   And He delighteth in his way.
24. Though he fall, he shall not be utterly cast down;
   For the Lord upholdeth his hand.
25. I have been young, and now am old;
   Yet have I not seen the righteous forsaken,
   Nor his seed begging bread.
26. All the day long he dealeth graciously, and lendeth;
   And his seed is blessed.
27. Depart from evil, and do good;
   And dwell for evermore.
28. For the Lord loveth justice, and forsaketh not His saints;
   They are preserved for ever;
   But the seed of the wicked shall be cut off.
29. The righteous shall inherit the land,
   And dwell therein for ever.
30. The mouth of the righteous uttereth wisdom,
   And his tongue speaketh justice.

fat of lambs burns upon the altar, dissolves, and disappears.

21. THE WICKED BORROWETH . . . THE RIGHTEOUS . . . GIVETH. In the future the wicked will be impoverished and will need to borrow (and being wicked will not repay), but the righteous will be prosperous (and being righteous will share his wealth).

23-24. God marks out our path, and though we may fall we will not be destroyed.

25. I HAVE BEEN YOUNG. This sentence appropriately closes the traditional grace after meals.

26. The sequence of thought would be clearer if verses 22 and 26 were read as if they were interchanged.

30. THE MOUTH OF THE RIGHTEOUS UTTERETH WISDOM. The righteous will endure because he learns wisdom.

THE LAW OF HIS GOD IS IN HIS HEART. Since his righteousness is not superficial or conventional but is deeply rooted in his heart, his character is consistent and strong. Hence, "none of his steps slide," i. e., he stands firm in the storms of adversity.

97

31. The law of his God is in his heart;
     None of his steps slide.
32. The wicked watcheth the righteous,
     And seeketh to slay him.
33. The LORD will not leave him in his hand,
     Nor suffer him to be condemned when he is judged.
34. Wait for the LORD, and keep His way,
     And He will exalt thee to inherit the land;
     When the wicked are cut off, thou shalt see it.
35. I have seen the wicked in great power,
     And spreading himself like a leafy tree in its native soil.
36. But one passed by, and, lo, he was not;
     Yea, I sought him, but he could not be found.
37. Mark the man of integrity, and behold the upright;
     For there is a future for the man of peace.
38. But transgressors shall be destroyed together;

32-33. Are related in thought to verses 12-15. The plotting of the wicked against the righteous.

35-36. Are related to verses 10-11. The wicked now flourishing "like a leafy tree in its native soil" will soon disappear.

36. BUT ONE PASSED BY, AND, LO, HE WAS NOT. Kimchi understands this verse to mean: But the wicked passed away and no longer existed. As translated here the verse means, that a passer-by would soon fail to see the wicked for he (the wicked) would have passed away.

37-38. THERE IS A FUTURE FOR THE MAN OF PEACE. BUT TRANS-GRESSORS SHALL BE DESTROYED TOGETHER. These verses epitomize the thought of the psalm.

O N most of the earlier psalms the psalmist prays for deliverance from his sinful and hypocritical enemies. In Psalm 32, however, he turns inward and becomes aware of his own sin. This self-judgment grows sterner in Psalm 38. There is only a passing reference to his adversaries. The psalm describes the agonies of body and soul which have come to him because of his own sinfulness. He asks that God have mercy upon him. "Rebuke me not in thine anger."

The future of the wicked shall be cut off.
39. But the salvation of the righteous is of the Lord;
He is their stronghold in the time of trouble.
40. And the Lord helpeth them, and delivereth them;
He delivereth them from the wicked, and saveth them,
Because they have taken refuge in Him.

3 A PSALM OF DAVID, TO MAKE MEMORIAL.

2. O Lord, rebuke me not in Thine anger;
Neither chasten me in Thy wrath.
3. For Thine arrows are gone deep into me,
And Thy hand is come down upon me.
4. There is no soundness in my flesh because of Thine indignation;
Neither is there any health in my bones because of my sin.
5. For mine iniquities are gone over my head;
As a heavy burden they are too heavy for me.

The spirit of this psalm is beautifully expressed in the poem written by Israel Abrahams as a paraphrase of the thought of Section 38 in Gabirol's poem "The Royal Crown":

> When all within is dark
> And Thy just angers rise
> From Thee I turn to Thee
> And find love in Thine eyes.

1. TO MAKE MEMORIAL. This heading is used also for Psalm 70. It may mean that the psalm is to be used for the purpose of reminding us in happier times of our days of sorrow.

2. REBUKE ME NOT IN THINE ANGER. Though God is justly angered at him, the psalmist pleads for pity. Almost the identical phrase is used in Psalm 6:2, "O Lord, rebuke me not in Thine anger," etc.

3-9. A description of his physical agonies which are the result of his sins. This description is not metaphorical, describing the ills of the soul as if they were the ills of the body. He actually means that all his bodily pain is the outcome of his spiritual unsoundness. He says (verse 4), "Neither is there any health in my bones because of my sin."

5. GONE OVER MY HEAD. My sins have become like a vast flood which overwhelms me.

99

6. My wounds are noisome, they fester,
    Because of my foolishness.
7. I am bent and bowed down greatly;
    I go mourning all the day.
8. For my loins are filled with burning;
    And there is no soundness in my flesh.
9. I am benumbed and sore crushed;
    I groan by reason of the moaning of my heart.
10. Lord, all my desire is before Thee;
    And my sighing is not hid from Thee.
11. My heart fluttereth, my strength faileth me;
    As for the light of mine eyes, it also is gone from me.
12. My friends and my companions stand aloof from my plague;
    And my kinsmen stand afar off.
13. They also that seek after my life lay snares for me;
    And they that seek my hurt speak crafty devices,
    And utter deceits all the day.
14. But I am as a deaf man, I hear not;
    And I am as a dumb man that openeth not his mouth.

6. BECAUSE OF MY FOOLISHNESS. The psalmist frequently relates righteousness to wisdom, and sin to folly. It is the fool who says in his heart that there is no God and therefore grows corrupt (Psalm 14:1). So, too, Psalm 36:4, says that the wicked abandon wisdom and thus abandon goodness: "He hath left off to be wise, to do good."

10-15, describes the psalmist as deserted by all his friends. It is only to God to Whom he can turn for help.

10. MY DESIRE IS BEFORE THEE. Though no one else listens to me now, Thou, O God, knowest the desires of my heart and hearest every sigh.

11. THE LIGHT OF MINE EYES. The dimming of the eyes in sickness or sorrow is frequently described in the Psalms. See comment to Psalm 6:8.

14. DEAF . . . DUMB. I am cut off from the world. There are none who will listen to me, and I have no one to whom to speak.

16-23. The third part of the psalm, in which the poet turns to God to help and to heal him.

15. Yea, I am become as a man that heareth not,
    And in whose mouth are no arguments.
16. For in Thee, O Lord, do I hope;
    Thou wilt answer, O Lord my God.
17. For I said: 'Lest they rejoice over me;
    When my foot slippeth, they magnify themselves against me.'
18. For I am ready to halt,
    And my pain is continually before me.
19. For I do declare mine iniquity;
    I am full of care because of my sin.
20. But mine enemies are strong in health;
    And they that hate me wrongfully are multiplied.
21. They also that repay evil for good
    Are adversaries unto me, because I follow the thing
        that is good.
22. Forsake me not, O Lord;
    O my God, be not far from me.
23. Make haste to help me,
    O Lord, my salvation.

17. LEST THEY REJOICE. The psalmist frequently asks that God deprive his enemies of the satisfaction of gloating over him. Thus Psalm 35:19, "Let not them that are wrongfully mine enemies rejoice over me."

18. READY TO HALT. About to stumble and fall.

20. MINE ENEMIES ARE STRONG IN HEALTH. I do not fret or complain of the health and power of mine enemies. I confess that my weakness is due to my sins. "For I do declare mine iniquity" (verse 19).

23. MAKE HASTE TO HELP ME. This urgent plea is repeated in Psalm 40:14, "O Lord, make haste to help me."

THIS psalm is closely connected with the preceding one. The psalmist, in pain and sorrow thought at first that he would not speak but would brood in silence. Yet his very brooding increases his pain. He, therefore, cries out, asking how long he would live and pleading for a little respite before he finally leaves his earthly home.

Psalm 39

39. FOR THE LEADER, FOR JEDUTHUN. A PSALM OF DAVID.

2. I said: 'I will take heed to my ways,
   That I sin not with my tongue;
   I will keep a curb upon my mouth,
   While the wicked is before me.'
3. I was dumb with silence, I held my peace, had no comfort;
   And my pain was held in check.
4. My heart waxed hot within me;
   While I was musing, the fire kindled;
   Then spoke I with my tongue:
5. 'LORD, make me to know mine end,
   And the measure of my days, what it is;
   Let me know how short-lived I am.
6. Behold, Thou hast made my days as hand-breadths;
   And mine age is as nothing before Thee;
   Surely every man at his best estate is altogether vanity.   Selah
7. Surely man walketh as a mere semblance;
   Surely for vanity they are in turmoil;
   He heapeth up riches, and knoweth not who shall gather them.

1. FOR JEDUTHUN. Jeduthun is mentioned with Heman in I Chronicles 16:41 and 42, as the musicians appointed by David to accompany the sacrifices with their music. Two other psalms (62 and 77) are headed "for Jeduthun."

2. THAT I SIN NOT WITH MY TONGUE. I thought I would keep silent lest in my resentment I sin by complaining against God's just punishment.

WHILE THE WICKED IS BEFORE ME. The commentator, Kimchi, interprets this as follows: I hope to keep silent especially in the presence of the wicked who would rejoice at my sorrow.

4. MY HEART WAXETH HOT. My pains increase. Therefore, "then spoke I with my tongue."

5-7, speaks of the transiency of human life. The psalmist wants to know how brief his life will be. In verse 7, he describes the vanity of piling up wealth. It is not in order to grow rich that he asks to be healed.

9. MAKE ME NOT THE REPROACH OF THE BASE. See comment on Psalm 38:17.

102

8. And now, Lord, what wait I for?
   My hope, it is in Thee.
9. Deliver me from all my transgressions;
   Make me not the reproach of the base.
10. I am dumb, I open not my mouth;
    Because Thou hast done it.
11. Remove Thy stroke from off me;
    I am consumed by the blow of Thy hand.
12. With rebukes dost Thou chasten man for iniquity,
    And like a moth Thou makest his beauty to
        consume away;
    Surely every man is vanity.   Selah
13. Hear my prayer, O Lord, and give ear unto my cry;
    Keep not silence at my tears;
    For I am a stranger with Thee,
    A sojourner, as all my fathers were.
14. Look away from me, that I may take comfort,
    Before I go hence, and be no more.'

40. FOR THE LEADER. A PSALM OF DAVID.

13. I AM A STRANGER WITH THEE, A SOJOURNER. Thus, David
in his prayer at the induction of Solomon said (I Chronicles
29:15): "For we are strangers before Thee, and sojourners, as
all our fathers were: our days on the earth are as a shadow."
The psalmist means that we are strangers and sojourners, guests
in God's house. Therefore we ask Him to be gracious unto us.

14. LOOK AWAY FROM ME. Turn Thine anger from me that
I may recover strength.

BEFORE I GO HENCE, AND BE NO MORE. The author of the
Psalms had no definite idea of a life after death where the sorrows of the righteous might be redressed. He says that soon he
will cease to exist. For the little time that he has left, he pleads,
"that I may take comfort."

THE two preceding psalms describe the physical misery
and the spiritual unhappiness of the psalmist. This psalm must
have been written after his recovery from sickness. It sounds a

103

2. I waited patiently for the LORD;
   And He inclined unto me, and heard my cry.
3. He brought me up also out of the tumultuous pit, out of
      the miry clay;
   And he set my feet upon a rock, He established my goings.
4. And He hath put a new song in my mouth, even praise
      unto our God;
   Many shall see, and fear,
   And shall trust in the LORD.
5. Happy is the man that hath made the LORD his trust,
   And hath not turned unto the arrogant, nor unto such as
      fall away treacherously.
6. Many things hast Thou done, O LORD my God,
   Even Thy wondrous works, and Thy thoughts toward us;
   There is none to be compared unto Thee!
   If I would declare and speak of them,
   They are more than can be told.
7. Sacrifice and meal-offering Thou hast no delight in;
   Mine ears hast Thou opened;
   Burnt-offering and sin-offering hast Thou not required.

jubilant note, thanking God for His mercy, and declaring that God is to be worshipped, not by the offering of sacrifice but by delighting to do His will in righteousness.

2. I WAITED PATIENTLY . . . HE HEARD MY CRY. The piteous prayer of the preceding psalm has at last been answered.

TUMULTUOUS PIT. The commentator, Kimchi, explains this to mean a pit tumultuous with water which would drown him who fell into it.

4. A NEW SONG. Since God's mercies are always renewed, man's song of gratitude to God must always spring anew from the heart.

SHALL SEE, AND FEAR, AND TRUST. They shall be awe-struck at God's wondrous help to me and, therefore, shall themselves trust in God in the time of their trouble.

5. HAPPY IS THE MAN. The same thought is expressed by the prophet Jeremiah (17:7), "Blessed is the man that trusteth in the Lord, and whose trust the Lord is."

UNTO THE ARROGANT. He does not put his trust in the power-

8. Then said I: 'Lo, I am come
With the roll of a book which is prescribed for me;
9. I delight to do Thy will, O my God;
Yea, Thy law is in my inmost parts.'
10. I have preached righteousness in the great congregation,
Lo, I did not refrain my lips;
O Lord, Thou knowest.
11. I have not hid Thy righteousness within my heart;
I have declared Thy faithfulness and Thy salvation;
I have not concealed Thy mercy and Thy truth from the great
congregation.
12. Thou, O Lord, wilt not withold Thy compassions from me;
Let Thy mercy and Thy truth continually preserve me.
13. For innumerable evils have compassed me about,
Mine iniquities have overtaken me, so that I am not able to
look up;
They are more than the hairs of my head, and my heart hath
failed me.
14. Be pleased, O Lord, to deliver me;
O Lord, make haste to help me.

ful, arrogant mortals. Thus, Psalm 146:3, "Put not your trust
in princes."

SUCH AS FALL AWAY TREACHEROUSLY. Those who treacherously turn away from God's law.

7. SACRIFICE . . . THOU HAST NO DELIGHT IN. Expresses the
though of Micah 6:6-8, "Shall I come before Him with burnt
offerings? . . . It hath been told thee . . . what the Lord doth
require of thee: only to do justly . . ."

8. I AM COME WITH THE ROLL OF A BOOK. I have come before
God with the book of His law. Thus, verse 9, "Thy law is in
my inmost parts."

12. THOU WILT NOT WITHHOLD THY COMPASSIONS. As I have
not refrained from proclaiming Thy righteousness "in the great
congregation" (verse 10).

13-18. Reverts from the exultant spirit of the first part of
the psalm to the recollections of sorrow described in the two
preceding psalms. Many of the phrases of this section of the
psalm are found in other psalms. Thus, verse 15: "Let them be

15. Let them be ashamed and abashed together
   That seek after my soul to sweep it away;
   Let them be turned backward and brought to confusion
   That delight in my hurt.
16. Let them be appalled by reason of their shame
   That say unto me: 'Aha, aha.'
17. Let all those that seek Thee rejoice and be glad in Thee;
   Let such as love Thy salvation say continually:
   'The LORD be magnified.'
18. But, as for me, that am poor and needy,
   The Lord will account it unto me;
   Thou art my help and my deliverer; O my God, tarry not.

41. FOR THE LEADER. A PSALM OF DAVID.

2. Happy is he that considereth the poor;
   The LORD will deliver him in the day of evil.
3. The LORD preserve him, and keep him alive, let him be
   called happy in the land;

ashamed," etc., is found in Psalm 70:3. "That say unto me 'aha, aha' " is found (though phrased differently) in Psalm 35:21, 25.

18. THE LORD WILL ACCOUNT IT UNTO ME. The commentator, Kimchi, takes this to mean that since I am poor and needy God will take my suffering to be an atonement for my sins. Since I have endured sorrow I have learned God's will.

O MY GOD, TARRY NOT. The psalm ends with the same urgent plea for help as Psalm 38:23, "Make haste to help me, O Lord, my salvation."

THE psalmist, hurt at the hypocrisy of his enemies and their gloating over his misfortunes, realizes how meritorious "is he who is considerate to the poor." It is upon the basis of his own sympathy for human suffering that he turns to God, asking for help in his own sorrow.

2-4. HAPPY IS HE . . . THE LORD WILL DELIVER HIM . . . THE LORD SUPPORT HIM UPON THE BED OF ILLNESS. He who is willing to help others in their suffering will himself receive God's help.

5. HEAL MY SOUL, FOR I HAVE SINNED AGAINST THEE. The com-

And deliver not Thou him unto the greed of his
  enemies.
4. The LORD support him upon the bed of illness;
  Mayest Thou turn all his lying down in his sickness.
5. As for me, I said: 'O LORD, be gracious unto me;
  Heal my soul; for I have sinned against Thee.'
6. Mine enemies speak evil of me:
  'When shall he die, and his name perish?'
7. And if one come to see me, he speaketh falsehood;
  His heart gathereth iniquity to itself;
  When he goeth abroad, he speaketh of it.
8. All that hate me whisper together against me,
  Against me do they devise my hurt:
9. 'An evil thing cleaveth fast unto him;
  And now that he lieth, he shall rise up no more.'
10. Yea, mine own familiar friend, in whom I trusted,
    who did eat of my bread,
  Hath lifted up his heel against me.

mentator, Ibn Ezra, takes this to mean, heal me in spite of the fact that I have sinned against Thee. But other commentators understand the verse as follows: my physical ailments are due to my inner unworthiness. Therefore, heal my soul which is sinful and I may find health and atonement.

6-9. The enemies gloat at his misfortunes.

9. AN EVIL THING CLEAVETH FAST UNTO HIM. His enemies say that evil (misfortune) has overtaken him and he "shall rise up no more." The Hebrew word here used for "evil thing" is *beliyaal*. The word occurs frequently in the Bible. In Deuteronomy 15:9, it is used in the sense of an evil thought. The Talmud (b. Sanhedrin 111 b) derives it from the two words which mean "without yoke," as referring to those who have thrown off the "yoke of the kingdom of God" and are, therefore, unrestrained and evil. Here it means, a horrible sickness adheres to him.

10. Not only my enemies but even my friends have turned against me.

HATH LIFTED UP HIS HEEL. Either as a gesture of contempt or to kick me or trip me.

107

11. But Thou, O Lord, be gracious unto me, and raise me up,
   That I may requite them.
12. By this I know that Thou delightest in me,
   That mine enemy doth not triumph over me.
13. And as for me, Thou upholdest me because of mine integrity,
   And settest me before Thy face for ever.
14. Blessed be the Lord, the God of Israel,
   From everlasting and to everlasting.
   Amen, and Amen.

11. RAISE ME UP. From the bed of sickness.

14. BLESSED BE THE LORD. This verse is not part of the psalm but is the closing sentence of praise (a doxology) ending the first of the five Books of Psalms. Similarly, Psalm 72:18-19, constitute a doxology ending the second Book.

FROM EVERLASTING TO EVERLASTING. From the long past to the endless future. The same phrase is used in Psalm 90:2, describing God's eternity, "From everlasting to everlasting, Thou art God."

AMEN, AND AMEN. The response of the congregation to the blessing just recited. Thus, in Nehemiah 8:6, after "Ezra blessed the Lord," the people recited, "Amen, Amen."

For further discussion of the word "amen" see article "Amen" in the *Jewish Encyclopedia*, Vol. I.

Book Two

~~~

$\mathcal{I}$T is the consensus of modern scholarly opinion that the Book of Psalms as we now have it is the combination of many previous smaller collections. (See Introduction, page 6 ff.) It is not necessary to go into a detailed argument in support of this opinion, but a few of the more obvious arguments may be mentioned. Book Two ends with the statement, "The prayers of David the son of Jesse are ended." (Psalm 70:20.) Yet, in spite of that statement, there is a psalm ascribed to David in Book Three, two psalms in Book Four, and fifteen psalms in Book Five. Evidently the sentence: "The prayers of David are ended," was appended to the end of Book Two at a time when that was a separate and complete collection. It also is to be noted that whereas Book One uses, almost exclusively, the name *JHWH* for God, Books Two and Three use (with few exceptions) the name *Elohim*. This clearly points to the fact that Books Two and Three were part of one collection whose editor preferred to use *Elohim* as the name of God.

Book Two itself must have been composed of two earlier collections. Psalms 42 to 49 have the heading, "of the sons of Korah" (a Levitical family), and Psalms 51 to 70 (with the exception of 66 and 67) have the heading, "Of David." It is interesting to note that in this collection of "David" psalms found in Book Two, there are two psalms which are duplicates of the David psalms found in the collection which constitute Book One. Thus, Psalm 53 is virtually the exact duplicate of Psalm 14 in the earlier collection, and Psalm 70 is identical with Psalm 40:14-18.

Psalm 42

42. FOR THE LEADER; MASCHIL OF THE SONS OF KORAH.

2. As the hart panteth after the water brooks,
   So panteth my soul after Thee, O God.
3. My soul thirsteth for God, for the living God:
   'When shall I come and appear before God?'
4. My tears have been my food day and night,
   While they say unto me all the day: 'Where is thy God?'

In Book Two, besides the "Sons of Korah" collection and the "David" collection, there is one (Psalm 50) described as "A Psalm of Asaph" (another Levitical family), one anonymous (Psalm 71), and one described as "A Psalm of Solomon," (Psalm 72).

A PSALM of longing for God. The author seems to be a Levite for he speaks of leading the multitude to the Temple of God, and in Psalm 43, which evidently is a sequel to Psalm 42, he speaks of praising God upon the harp (verse 4). This Levite, in the mountains where the Jordan rises (Hermon), longs for the day when he can come to the Temple of God. He speaks as if he were a captive prevented by his adversaries from participating in a joyous pilgrimage to the sanctuary.

1. MASCHIL. A technical term. See note to Psalm 32:1.

SONS OF KORAH. Korah was the great-grandson of Levi. In Numbers 26:11, we are told that although Korah was destroyed for his rebellion against Moses and Aaron, his sons did not die. The descendants of Korah are described in the Book of Chronicles as a Levitical guild. In I Chronicles 26:19, they are spoken of as doorkeepers of the Temple. And in II Chronicles 20:19, they are described as singers: "The Levites . . . of the children of the Korahites, stood up to praise the Lord, the God of Israel, with an exceeding loud voice."

2. AS THE HART PANTETH. As a stag in a parched land yearns for water brooks "so panteth my soul after Thee." The metaphor of God as a refreshing stream or fountain of water is ex-

5. These things I remember, and pour out my soul within me,
   How I passed on with the throng, and led them to the house
      of God,
   With the voice of joy and praise, a multitude keeping holyday.
6. Why art thou cast down, O my soul?
   And why moanest thou within me?
   Hope thou in God; for I shall yet praise Him
   For the salvation of His countenance.

pressed clearly by the Prophet Jeremiah 2:13, "They have forsaken Me, the fountain of living waters."

4. MY TEARS HAVE BEEN MY FOOD. In my sorrow I have neg-
lected physical nourishment. I seem to feed on my tears alone.
That description of sorrow, in which tears are the only food, is
also given in Psalm 80:6, "Thou hast fed them with the bread
of tears."

WHERE IS THY GOD? A thought frequently expressed in the
Psalms. The enemies say that the psalmist's sorrows proved
either that there is no God to defend the unfortunate or that
God has forsaken him. So, too, in Psalm 115:2, the psalmist
pleads for help so that the nations may not say: "Where now is
their God?"

5. THESE THINGS I REMEMBER. This refers to what follows: I
remember how I joyfully marched with the throng in the procession to the House of God. A vivid picture of the joyous pilgrimage to the Temple in Jerusalem is given in the Mishnah.
The pilgrims are described as gathering in the chief city of the
district and spending the night there. At dawn they are awak-
ened by the words: "Come, let us go up to Zion, the city of our
God." They form a procession with each pilgrim carrying his
gaily decorated basket of first-fruits. A flute player leads the
march to Jerusalem up to the gates of the Temple. (Mishnah
Bikkurim, 3.)

6. WHY ART THOU CAST DOWN? This appeal of the psalmist to
his own soul that it be not cast down but that it continue to
hope in God, occurs as a refrain here in verse 6 and recurs also
in verse 12.

III

7. O my God, my soul is cast down within me;
   Therefore do I remember Thee from the land of Jordan,
   And the Hermons, from the hill Mizar.
8. Deep calleth unto deep at the voice of Thy cataracts;
   All Thy waves and Thy billows are gone over me.
9. By day the LORD will command His lovingkindness,
   And in the night His song shall be with me,
   Even a prayer unto the God of my life.
10. I will say unto God my Rock: 'Why hast Thou forgotten me?
    Why go I mourning under the oppression of the enemy?'
11. As with a crushing in my bones, mine adversaries taunt me;
    While they say unto me all the day: 'Where is thy God?'
12. Why art thou cast down, O my soul?
    And why moanest thou within me?
    Hope thou in God; for I shall yet praise Him,
    The salvation of my countenance, and my God,

7. MY SOUL IS CAST DOWN. As if in reference to the preceding verses where he rallies his soul to overcome despair. Since, however, his soul is still "cast down," he strengthens himself by thinking of God's house in Zion, although he is in "the land of the Jordan, the Hermons," i. e., the land to the north where the Jordan rises in the mountains.

8. DEEP CALLETH UNTO DEEP. At the rainy season the Jordan leaps in roaring cataracts. The waterfalls seem to call to each other. This description of the tumultuous waters recalls a favorite metaphor of the Psalms which speaks of the waters of sorrow threatening to sweep away the soul. Thus, for example, Psalm 69:2, "Save me, O God; for the waters are come in even unto the soul."

9. In the midst of his sorrow the psalmist reassures himself that God will comfort him by day with his loving kindness and by night with the joy of song and "prayer unto the God of my life."

11. CRUSHING IN MY BONES. The bones, the framework of the body, are frequently spoken of in the Psalms in connection with penetrating sorrow or pain. Psalm 6:3, says: "My bones are affrighted."

43. Be Thou my judge, O God, and plead my cause against an
      ungodly nation;
  O deliver me from the deceitful and unjust man.
2. For Thou art the God of my strength; why hast Thou cast
    me off?
  Why go I mourning under the oppression of the enemy?
3. O send out Thy light and Thy truth; let them lead me;
  Let them bring me unto Thy holy mountain, and to Thy
    dwelling-places;
4. Then will I go unto the altar of God, unto God, my exceeding
    joy;
  And praise Thee upon the harp, O God, my God.
5. Why art thou cast down, O my soul?
  And why moanest thou within me?
  Hope thou in God; for I shall yet praise Him,
  The salvation of my countenance, and my God.

THIS psalm is clearly a continuation of Psalm 42. It has no separate heading although it is in the group of the psalms "of the sons of Korah." Also, it continues the thought of the psalmist who longs to come to God's Holy Temple, and it ends with the refrain used twice in Psalm 42: "Why art thou cast down, O my soul . . ."

1. BE THOU MY JUDGE, O GOD. The psalmist frequently describes his struggle with his enemies as if he and they were in a court of law and they are accusing him unjustly. Hence, he asks God, Who knows the truth, to be his Judge and "deliver me from the deceitful." Thus, God the Judge becomes the Defender of the innocent. The metaphor of the law court is also found in Psalm 35:11.

3. SEND OUT THY LIGHT. Psalm 42 speaks of God as a fountain of living water. Psalm 43 speaks of God as a guiding light. Both of these vivid metaphors are combined in Psalm 36:10, "For with Thee is the fountain of life; in Thy light do we see light."

4. UNTO THE ALTAR OF GOD. The Levites sang their songs during the offering of the sacrifices. Therefore, the author of the psalm, probably a Levite, visualizes himself as standing by the side of the altar and praising God with songs upon a harp.

Psalm 44

₁

44.FOR THE LEADER; [A PSALM] OF THE SONS OF KORAH.   MASCHIL.

2. O God, we have heard with our ears, our fathers have told us;
   A work Thou didst in their days, in the days of old.
3. Thou with Thy hand didst drive out the nations, and didst
      plant them in;
   Thou didst break the peoples, and didst spread them abroad.
4. For not by their own sword did they get the land in
      possession,
   Neither did their own arm save them;
   But Thy right hand, and Thine arm, and the light of Thy
      countenance,
   Because Thou wast favourable unto them.
5. Thou art my King, O God;

*T*HIS is the first psalm written in the plural. The psalmist
does not refer to his own sorrows but to the misfortunes of the
people of Israel. In this prayer the people of Israel acknowl-
edges that all its victories in the past were won by God's might
not by Israel's own strength; but now Israel has been defeated
by its enemies and has been scattered among the nations and
God no longer goes forth with its armies. Yet Israel asserts that,
in spite of its suffering, its trust is still in God. The psalm ends
with a plea to God to awake to Israel's rescue.

It is difficult to assign a date for this psalm. Since the psalmist says of God, "Thou hast scattered us among the nations,"
this psalm apparently must have been written after the Exile,
and since the psalmist also says to God, "Thou goest not forth
with our hosts, Thou makest us to turn back from the adversary," it is evident the psalm was written at a time when the
nation still had its armies which could march forth to war.
Clearly, then, the psalm was written after the Exile, when the
Jewish state was re-established. Just when in this period cannot
be exactly determined. The commentator, Kimchi, speaks of
the hostile hosts as the armies of Persians and Medes.

2-4. OUR FATHERS HAVE TOLD US . . . THOU WITH THY HAND.
We have the tradition from the days of our fathers that it was
not their own sword (verse 4) which conquered for them the

114

Command the salvation of Jacob.
6. Through Thee do we push down our adversaries;
   Through Thy name do we tread them under that rise up
   against us.
7. For I trust not in my bow,
   Neither can my sword save me.
8. But Thou hast saved us from our adversaries,
   And hast put them to shame that hate us.
9. In God have we gloried all the day,
   And we will give thanks unto Thy name for ever.   Selah
10. Yet Thou hast cast off, and brought us to confusion;
    And goest not forth with our hosts.
11. Thou makest us to turn back from the adversary;
    And they that hate us spoil at their will.

land of Canaan but "Thy right hand, and Thine arm."

3. DIDST PLANT THEM. The metaphor of God planting Israel
in the land of Canaan to flourish like a tree is found in Exodus
15:17, "Thou bringest them in, and plantest them in the mountain of Thine inheritance."

5-9. Indicates that this tradition which we have received
from our fathers is also our own conviction. We know that God
is our King Who has "saved us from our adversaries."

7. This verse is exceptionally in the singular. Its thought,
not to trust in the bow and arrow but in God, is expressed in
Psalm 20:8, "Some trust in chariots, and some in horses, but we
will make mention of the name of the Lord our God."

9. SELAH. Indicates the end of the first mood of the psalm.
Here the thought changes. The psalmist turns from the past
with its history of God's help, to the present time with its dis-
appointments.

10-17. God seems to have abandoned the children of Israel.
They are slaughtered, exiled, sold as slaves, and become a byword among the nations for their calamities.

10. GOEST NOT FORTH WITH OUR HOSTS. Refers either to the
older custom of taking the Ark of the Covenant out to battle,
or simply that God is no longer with the armies of Israel and
therefore they are defeated.

115

12. Thou hast given us like sheep to be eaten;
    And hast scattered us among the nations.
13. Thou sellest Thy people for small gain,
    And hast not set their prices high.
14. Thou makest us a taunt to our neighbours,
    A scorn and a derision to them that are round
       about us.
15. Thou makest us a byword among the nations,
    A shaking of the head among the peoples.
16. All the day is my confusion before me,
    And the shame of my face hath covered me,
17. For the voice of him that taunteth and blasphemeth;
    By reason of the enemy and the revengeful.
18. All this is come upon us; yet have we not
       forgotten Thee,
    Neither have we been false to Thy covenant.
19. Our heart is not turned back,

12. SHEEP TO BE EATEN . . . SCATTERED US. As a flock when it is attacked by ravenous beasts, is scattered about in all directions.

13. THOU SELLEST THY PEOPLE FOR SMALL GAIN. After a nation was defeated, the captives were sold as slaves. If the defeat was severe and many slaves were available, the market was glutted with them and their price was low.

15. A BY-WORD . . . SHAKING OF THE HEAD. The miseries of Israel are so manifold as to become proverbial amongst the nations.

18-23. In spite of the calamities which have befallen it, Israel has not forgotten God.

18. THY COVENANT. The covenant made with Abraham and renewed on Mount Sinai that Israel would be God's people dedicated to His commandments. For fuller discussion of the idea of Covenant see comment to Psalm 25:10.

20. A PLACE OF JACKALS. The cities are "crushed" into ruins where jackals lurk.

SHADOW OF DEATH. The same term is used as in Psalm 23:4, "the valley of the shadow of death."

21. SPREAD FORTH OUR HANDS. In prayer.

Neither have our steps declined from Thy path;
20. Though Thou hast crushed us into a place of jackals,
   And covered us with the shadow of death.
21. If we had forgotten the name of our God,
   Or spread forth our hands to a strange god;
22. Would not God search this out?
   For He knoweth the secrets of the heart.
23. Nay, but for Thy sake are we killed all the day;
   We are accounted as sheep for the slaughter.
24. Awake, why sleepest Thou, O Lord?
   Arouse Thyself, cast not off for ever.
25. Wherefore hidest Thou Thy face,
   And forgettest our affliction and our oppression?
26. For our soul is bowed down to the dust;
   Our belly cleaveth unto the earth.
27. Arise for our help,
   And redeem us for Thy mercy's sake.

23. NAY, BUT FOR THY SAKE ARE WE KILLED. We suffer because of our unyielding loyalty to Thy service.

24-27. The psalm ends with a prayer that God no longer hide His face from Israel but that He should "rise . . . and redeem us for Thy mercy's sake."

24. AWAKE, WHY SLEEPEST THOU, O LORD. A bold metaphor used also in Psalm 78:65, "Then the Lord awaked as one asleep."

PSALM 45 is a marriage psalm, written in honor of the nuptials of a king and his royal bride. The first half of the psalm describes the ideal king whose throne is founded upon "truth and meekness and righteousness." The second half of the psalm turns to the royal bride, bidding her forget her parents and promising her children who shall become princes in the land.

The commentator, Rashi, takes this psalm to be metaphorical, a psalm of love between the students of the Torah and the people of Israel. This same type of metaphorical explanation is used in traditional interpretations of the Song of Songs. If the psalm is not to be taken metaphorically it becomes necessary to

117

45. FOR THE LEADER; UPON SHOSHANNIM; [A PSALM] OF THE
SONS OF KORAH. MASCHIL. A SONG OF LOVES.

2. My heart overfloweth with a goodly matter;
   I say: 'My work is concerning a king';
   My tongue is the pen of a ready writer.
3. Thou art fairer than the children of men;
   Grace is poured upon thy lips;
   Therefore God hath blessed thee for ever.
4. Gird thy sword upon thy thigh, O mighty one,
   Thy glory and thy majesty.
5. And in thy majesty prosper, ride on,
   In behalf of truth and meekness and righteousness;

determine which king is it whose marriage is referred to in this psalm. It must be a king who married a foreign princess. The psalmist asks the princess to "forget thine own people and thy father's house" (verse 11). He calls upon her to identify herself with the people and the faith of Israel. It is difficult to be certain which of the royal marriages recorded in Scriptures fit these requirements. It may well refer to the marriage of King Solomon with the Egyptian princess (I Kings 3:1).

1. SHOSHANNIM. Lilies. Probably the name of a melody to which the psalm was to be sung.

2. This verse is the prologue of the author declaring that the theme awakens his imagination ("My heart overfloweth"), and inspires him so that his words come as rapidly as those which flow from the "pen of a ready writer."

3-10. A description of the king, his personal beauty, and the ethical foundation of his throne.

3. THOU ART FAIRER. The king is described as physically beautiful just as Saul is described in I Samuel 9:2, as "there was not among the children of Israel a goodlier person than he."

GRACE . . . UPON THY LIPS. May refer either to his gracious smile, or, as Kimchi takes it, to his gracious speech.

4-5. IN BEHALF OF TRUTH AND MEEKNESS. The king's sword, that is the king's power, is used in behalf of noble causes. A similar description of the ideal king is given in Isaiah, Chapter 11, where the messianic king is depicted as one who will judge

118

And let thy right hand teach thee tremendous things.
6. Thine arrows are sharp—
The peoples fall under thee—
[They sink] into the heart of the king's enemies.
7. Thy throne given of God is for ever and ever;
A sceptre of equity is the sceptre of thy kingdom.
8. Thou hast loved righteousness, and hated wickedness,
Therefore God, thy God, hath anointed thee
With the oil of gladness above thy fellows.
9. Myrrh, and aloes, and cassia are all thy garments;
Out of ivory palaces stringed instruments have made thee **glad.**
10. Kings' daughters are among thy favourites;
At thy right hand doth stand the queen in gold of Ophir.

with righteousness, decide with equity for the meek but will slay the wicked.

7. The Hebrew permits the translation, "Thy Throne, O God," but Kimchi and Saadia (quoted by Ibn Ezra), take it to mean as translated, "Thy throne given by God."

THY THRONE . . . FOR EVER. God promises that the seed of David will be established as a permanent dynasty. See Psalm 18:51, "To David and to his seed for ever more." But the dynasty must be righteous in order to endure.

8. THOU HAST LOVED RIGHTEOUSNESS. Since the king has been righteous God fulfills his promise to David and his throne is established. Note the description of the establishment of the throne of David through righteousness, Isaiah 9:6, "Upon the throne of David . . . to establish it . . . through justice . . . for ever."

OIL OF GLADNESS. This refers either to the oil with which he was anointed as king, and which is described as an oil of gladness because of his auspicious reign, or else to the oil with which guests are anointed at joyous banquets, as in Psalm 23:5, "Thou hast anointed my head with oil."

9. MYRRH, ALOES, CASSIA. The names of these three perfumes are not translated. The three words given are the Hebrew words which have been adopted into the English language.

10-17 or 18. The writer addresses the new queen, describing her happy life and the exalted status of her descendants.

119

11. 'Hearken, O daughter, and consider, and incline thine ear;
    Forget also thine own people, and thy father's house;
12. So shall the king desire thy beauty;
    For he is thy lord; and do homage unto him.
13. And, O daughter of Tyre, the richest of the people
    Shall entreat thy favour with a gift.'
14. All glorious is the king's daughter within the palace;
    Her raiment is of chequer work inwrought with gold.
15. She shall be led unto the king on richly woven stuff;
    The virgins her companions in her train being brought
        unto thee.
16. They shall be led with gladness and rejoicing;
    They shall enter into the king's palace.
17. Instead of thy fathers shall be thy sons,

    11. FORGET THINE OWN PEOPLE. Clearly refers to a princess that comes from another land.

    13. AND, O DAUGHTER OF TYRE. If the text is to be taken as here translated then the princess comes from Tyre and not from Egypt. But many of the commentators take the text to mean: "The daughter of Tyre will come with a gift and the riches of the people will entreat thy favor."

    14-16. The description of the procession of queen and her maidens to the king's palace.

    18. I WILL MAKE THY NAME TO BE REMEMBERED. The commentator, Ibn Ezra, says that this may be taken in two ways, either God's name will be praised, etc., or it refers to the king whose throne will be established.

𝒜 SONG written after a great deliverance. It describes God as Israel's refuge. Trusting in Him the people have no fear even in a time of world calamity. God destroys mighty armies, causing wars to cease and reigning as Lord of all the earth. While this psalm has a general application, it seems to have been inspired by some specific occasion, some deliverance which clearly manifested God's saving power. The commentator, Ibn Ezra, quotes the opinion that the psalm commemorates the de-

Whom thou shalt make princes in all the land.
18. I will make thy name to be remembered in all generations;
Therefore shall the peoples praise thee for ever and ever.

46. FOR THE LEADER; [A PSALM] OF THE SONS OF KORAH; UPON
ALAMOTH. A SONG.

2. God is our refuge and strength,
A very present help in trouble.
3. Therefore will we not fear, though the earth do change,
And though the mountains be moved into the heart of the seas;
4. Though the waters thereof roar and foam,
Though the mountains shake at the swelling thereof.   Selah
5. There is a river, the streams whereof make glad the city of God,
The holiest dwelling-place of the Most High.

feat of the armies of Sennacherib when "the Assyrians came down like a wolf on the fold." (See the description of the defeat of Sennacherib's army, II Kings 19.) This theory of the origin of the psalm seems to be borne out by the similarity of the thought of the psalm and its language with that of Isaiah who describes that great deliverance which took place in his day. This psalm, beginning with the great proclamation, "God is our refuge and our strength," was the basis of Luther's famous hymn "Ein feste Burg ist unser Gott," the classic hymn of the Protestant Reformation.

1. UPON ALAMOTH. The word means "damsels" and may mean that this hymn was to be sung by soprano voices. But the commentator, Rashi, takes *Alamoth* to mean an instrument, an interpretation which is aided by I Chronicles 15:20, where *Alamoth* seems to refer to an instrument.

2. A VERY PRESENT HELP. The Hebrew expresses the thought of a help that is easily found, an ever available help.

3-4. THOUGH THE EARTH DO CHANGE . . . THE MOUNTAINS BE MOVED . . . THE WATERS ROAR. A description of a natural cataclysm—earthquakes and storms. It is, however, metaphorical for historical calamities when armies overrun peaceful lands like a flood, and cities are destroyed as with an earthquake.

5. THERE IS A RIVER. In contrast with the destructive flood of

121

6. God is in the midst of her, she shall not be moved;
   God shall help her, at the approach of morning.
7. Nations were in tumult, kingdoms were moved;
   He uttered His voice, the earth melted.
8. The LORD of hosts is with us;
   The God of Jacob is our high tower.   Selah
9. Come, behold the works of the LORD,
   Who hath made desolations in the earth.
10. He maketh wars to cease unto the end of the earth;
    He breaketh the bow, and cutteth the spear in sunder;
    He burneth the chariots in the fire.
11. 'Let be, and know that I am God;
    I will be exalted among the nations, I will be exalted
    in the earth.'

invading armies God is like a gentle stream which "makes glad the city of God." This same metaphor is found in Isaiah 8:6. God's help is described as "the waters of Shiloah that go softly." While the invading armies of Assyria are described as "the waters of the River (i. e., Euphrates) mighty and many" which "shall sweep through Judah."

6. AT THE APPROACH OF MORNING. After the night of anxious watching, God's help will come at the dawn of the day of deliverance. It was in the morning that the people beheld the army of Sennacherib destroyed. (Isaiah 37:36.)

8. THE LORD OF HOSTS IS WITH US. This confident refrain is repeated at the end of the entire psalm (verse 12). The phrase, "The Lord of hosts," means, the Lord of the hosts of Israel and also the Lord of the hosts of the heavens. See comment to Psalm 24:10.

9-10. WHO HATH MADE DESOLATIONS. The meaning is made clear by the succeeding verse. God destroys invading armies and thus "maketh wars to cease." This description of God establishing universal peace by destroying the weapons of war is strongly reminiscent of the description in Isaiah of the swords which will be beaten into plow-shares. (Isaiah 2:4.)

11. LET BE, AND KNOW. God speaks to the nations: Cease your violence and know that I am God. So, too, in Isaiah, the swords

12. The Lord of hosts is with us;
The God of Jacob is our high tower.   Selah

47. FOR THE LEADER; A PSALM OF THE SONS OF KORAH.

2. O clap your hands, all ye peoples;
Shout unto God with the voice of triumph.
3. For the Lord is most high, awful;
A great King over all the earth.
4. He subdueth peoples under us,
And nations under our feet.
5. He chooseth our inheritance for us,
The pride of Jacob whom He loveth.   Selah
6. God is gone up amidst shouting,
The Lord amidst the sound of the horn.

and spears will be destroyed and the nations will "go up to the mountain of the Lord" acknowledging Him as their Lord.

This psalm is closely connected with the preceding one. It is a development of the theme at the close of Psalm 46, that God is king of all the earth. This psalm is appropriately used as introduction to the service of the sounding of the Shofar on the New Year.

2. CLAP YOUR HANDS. In joy. In a similar manner all of nature expresses its joy at the presence of God. "Let the floods clap their hands . . . the mountains sing for joy" (Psalm 98:8).

3. MOST HIGH, AWFUL. Awe-inspiring.

4. HE SUBDUETH PEOPLES . . . HE CHOOSETH OUR INHERITANCE. The fact that God conquered the people of Canaan and gave the land as an inheritance to Israel is proof that He is Master of history and Lord of all the earth. Thus, Deuteronomy 32:8-9, expresses the general principle that God's conquest of Canaan is part of His general Lordship: "When He gave to the nations their inheritance."

5. THE PRIDE OF JACOB. The Targum, the Aramaic translation, takes this as referring to the Temple.

6. GOD IS GONE UP AMIDST SHOUTING. This need not be taken

7. Sing praises to God, sing praises;
   Sing praises unto our King, sing praises.
8. For God is the King of all the earth;
   Sing ye praises in a skilful song.
9. God reigneth over the nations;
   God sitteth upon His holy throne.
10. The princes of the peoples are gathered together,
    The people of the God of Abraham;
    For unto God belong the shields of the earth;
    He is greatly exalted.

48. A SONG; A PSALM OF THE SONS OF KORAH.

2. Great is the LORD, and highly to be praised,
   In the city of our God, His holy mountain,

literally as an actual ascension to the skies, but means, as the commentator, Kimchi, understands it, that God is exalted amidst the shouts and songs and praises of men.

8. A SKILFUL SONG. The Hebrew word is *Maschil*, the same word as is used as the heading of a number of psalms.

10. THE PRINCES OF THE PEOPLES. The rulers of all nations; when they acknowledge God's sovereignty, they are "the people of the God of Abraham." Thus, Rashi and Ibn Ezra say that Abraham's name is mentioned because it was he who brought many people to the worship of God.

THE SHIELDS OF THE EARTH. This may mean that God is the protection of the earth (as Rashi takes it). He is described in Psalm 89:19, "For the Lord is our shield." Or it may mean that to God belong the *princes* of the earth who protect their people. This is the interpretation of Ibn Ezra and of most commentators.

THIS psalm is closely connected in thought with the two preceding ones. It speaks of Zion as a strong fortress. Its strength comes from God who dwells within it. It refers back to the invasion spoken of in Psalm 46, and how the invading armies were suddenly scattered. Thus, this psalm, too, may well re-

3. Fair in situation, the joy of the whole earth;
   Even mount Zion, the uttermost parts of
      the north,
   The city of the Great King.
4. God in her palaces
   Hath made Himself known for a stronghold.
5. For, lo, the kings assembled themselves,
   They came onward together.
6. They saw, straightway they were amazed;
   They were affrighted, they hasted away.
7. Trembling took hold of them there,
   Pangs, as of a woman in travail.
8. With the east wind
   Thou breakest the ships of Tarshish.

fer to the dramatic destruction of the armies of Sennacherib which were encamped around Jerusalem.

The psalm is recited in the synagogue on Mondays.

2. HIGHLY TO BE PRAISED. God merits the highest praise of man. The same sentence is used in Psalm 145:3.

3. THE JOY OF THE WHOLE EARTH. Jerusalem is so beautiful and imposing a city that the earth rejoices at the sight of it. This phrase, used of Jerusalem, is likewise found in Lamentations 2:15, "Is this the city that men called . . . the joy of the whole earth?"

ZION, THE UTTERMOST PARTS OF THE NORTH. Mount Zion is in the northern part of the city of Jerusalem.

4. HATH MADE HIMSELF KNOWN. God, through His deliverance, has made Himself known as the stronghold (i. e., defender) of Jerusalem.

5-9. Reverts to the theme expressed in Psalm 46, the invasion of the enemy and God's destruction of the invading armies.

5. THE KINGS ASSEMBLED. Most of the great invading armies of the ancient empires were composed of the armies of various confederate kings.

6. THEY SAW. They saw the impregnable might of Zion and "were affrighted."

8. EAST WIND. The east wind in Palestine is particularly de-

125

9. As we have heard, so have we seen
   In the city of the LORD of hosts, in the city of our God—
   God establish it for ever.   Selah
10. We have thought on Thy lovingkindness, O God,
    In the midst of Thy Temple.
11. As is Thy name, O God,
    So is Thy praise unto the ends of the earth;
    Thy right hand is full of righteousness.
12. Let mount Zion be glad,
    Let the daughters of Judah rejoice,
    Because of Thy judgments.
13. Walk about Zion, and go round about her;
    Count the towers thereof.

structive. Thus, in Jeremiah 18:17, "I will scatter them as with an east wind."

THE SHIPS OF TARSHISH. Tarshish is a seacoast city, either Tartessus in Spain or Carthage. The ships of Tarshish are the great seagoing vessels. The phrase is therefore used as a symbol of power. In Isaiah 2:11-17, the prophet speaks of the mighty objects which God will bring low; and he enumerates the "cedars of Lebanon," the "oaks of Bashan," the "high mountains," and the "ships of Tarshish."

The verse is metaphorical. God has destroyed the powerful armies of the invader as an east-wind breaks the great ships of Tarshish.

9. AS WE HAVE HEARD, SO HAVE WE SEEN. What we learned by tradition, namely, that God was the help of our fathers, that we have now seen in our own experience.

10. WE HAVE THOUGHT. In our worship in the Temple, in our prayers, we have meditated on Thy lovingkindness.

11. AS IS THY NAME SO IS THY PRAISE UNTO THE ENDS OF THE EARTH. As Thy name is known all over the earth so art Thou praised everywhere.

13-15. WALK ABOUT ZION. Observe the towers, the ramparts, and the palaces of Zion. All these outward manifestations of strength depend upon God "for such is our God, God is our high tower and our fortress."

14. Mark ye well her ramparts,
Traverse her palaces;
That ye may tell it to the generation following.
15. For such is God, our God, for ever and ever;
He will guide us eternally.

14. Mark ye well her ramparts,
Traverse her palaces;
That ye may tell it to the generation following.
15. For such is God, our God, for ever and ever;
He will guide us eternally.

49. FOR THE LEADER; A PSALM OF THE SONS OF KORAH.
2. Hear this, all ye peoples;
Give ear, all ye inhabitants of the world,
3. Both low and high,
Rich and poor together.
4. My mouth shall speak wisdom,
And the meditation of my heart shall be understanding.

THIS psalm is related in thought to Psalm 37. The theme of Psalm 37 is that the wicked and the powerful will perish. Therefore, the psalmist appeals to the righteous not to "fret thyself because of evil-doers." In this psalm the transiency of wealth is likewise stressed but the emphasis is not placed upon the sinful but upon the materialistic. No wealth is permanent, nor can it redeem its possessor from the grave.

The mood of this psalm is closely related to that of the Wisdom Literature (Proverbs and Job). Many of its phrases are found repeatedly in these books, particularly in the Book of Proverbs. Thus, "wisdom and understanding" is found in Proverbs 4:5, 8:1, etc.; the phrase, "parable and dark saying" (verse 5) is found in Proverbs 1:6; the contrast between the wise and the fool (verse 11) is made frequently in the Book of Proverbs.

This psalm is the last one of the group of eight headed "Of the sons of Korah."

2. ALL YE PEOPLES. The theme of the psalm is a universal one dealing with the question of life and death, therefore, the psalmist addresses not only the people of Israel but *all* peoples.

3. LOW AND HIGH . . . RICH AND POOR. The theme is of interest to all classes and all conditions of men.

4. MY MOUTH . . . THE MEDITATION OF MY HEART. My spoken words and my unspoken thoughts. The same phrase is found in

Psalm 49

5

5. I will incline mine ear to a parable;
   I will open my dark saying upon the harp.
6. Wherefore should I fear in the days of evil,
   When the iniquity of my supplanters compasseth me about,
7. Of them that trust in their wealth,
   And boast themselves in the multitude of their riches?
8. No man can by any means redeem his brother,
   Nor give to God a ransom for him—
9. For too costly is the redemption of their soul,
   And must be let alone for ever—
10. That he should still live alway,
    That he should not see the pit.
11. For he seeth that wise men die,
    The fool and the brutish together perish,

Psalm 19:15, "Let the words of my mouth and the meditation of my heart."

5. I WILL INCLINE MINE EAR. The thoughts which I will express come to me from God and I incline my ear to listen to them.

PARABLE AND DARK SAYING. Riddle. Both words are found in the Book of Proverbs and refer to the puzzling problems of life.

6. WHEREFORE SHOULD I FEAR. Equivalent to the thought in Psalm 37, namely, why fret about the wicked who will "soon wither like grass"?

THE INIQUITY OF MY SUPPLANTERS. The Hebrew text is difficult and various interpretations are offered. The text as translated here means, why should I be afraid when surrounded by the iniquity of those who would push me aside or dispossess me?

8. NO MAN CAN . . . REDEEM HIS BROTHER NOR GIVE . . . A RANSOM. According to the ancient Hebrew law a man could pay a ransom to be redeemed from the penalty of death in the case of certain crimes. Thus, Exodus 21:29-30, the law discussing the owner of an ox which has killed a man or a woman, says: "Its owner also shall be put to death. If there be laid on him a ransom, then he shall give for the redemption of his life whatsoever is laid upon him." The psalmist here means that no one can

128

And leave their wealth to others.
12. Their inward thought is, that their houses shall continue for
ever,
And their dwelling-places to all generations;
They call their lands after their own names.
13. But man abideth not in honour;
He is like the beasts that perish.
14. This is the way of them that are foolish,
And of those who after them approve their sayings.   Selah
15. Like sheep they are appointed for the nether-world;
Death shall be their shepherd;
And the upright shall have dominion over them in the morning;
And their form shall be for the nether-world to wear away,
That there be no habitation for it.

give God such a ransom to redeem the soul of a brother from
death.

9. Continues the thought of the preceding sentence. Such a
ransom could be "too costly," beyond all price.

MUST BE LET ALONE FOR EVER. The attempt to ransom a life
from death is futile and might as well be abandoned.

10. NOT SEE THE PIT. The grave, the nether-world, death.

12. THEIR HOUSES FOR EVER . . . THEY CALL THEIR LANDS AFTER
THEIR OWN NAMES. No matter how great is the estate which a
man accumulates he will not abide in its possession. Thus,
"man abideth not in honour" (verse 13), i. e., in the glory of
his possessions.

14-15. THIS IS THE WAY. Those who follow the foolish belief
that man can enjoy his material possessions forever will discover
that they will be led like sheep to the nether-world and death
will be their shepherd.

THE UPRIGHT SHALL HAVE DOMINION IN THE MORNING. The
commentator, Kimchi, takes the phrase "in the morning" to
mean on the day of judgment when the upright shall triumph
over the wicked. Rashi takes it to mean on the day of deliverance, namely, on earth. But perhaps the simplest meaning and
the one which comports best with the general spirit of the
Psalms is that the wicked die and the righteous awaken to an-

16. But God will redeem my soul from the power of
     the nether-world;
    For He shall receive me.   Selah
17. Be not thou afraid when one waxeth rich,
    When the wealth of his house is increased;
18. For when he dieth he shall carry nothing away;
    His wealth shall not descend after him.
19. Though while he lived he blessed his soul:
    'Men will praise thee, when thou shalt do well
      to thyself';

other day. Surviving the wicked, the righteous triumph over them in life. In Psalm 30:6, the phrase "in the morning" is used in this simple, earthly sense. "Weeping may tarry for the night, but joy cometh in the morning."

THAT THERE BE NO HABITATION FOR IT. The Hebrew phrase is a difficult one. As translated here it means the wicked shall disappear in death and thus have no habitation either on earth or in the nether-world.

16. WILL REDEEM MY SOUL FROM . . . THE NETHER-WORLD. That does not mean that the righteous will not die, but that he will be saved from an untimely death. This thought is clear in the parallelism in Psalm 30:4, "Thou broughtest up my soul from the nether-world; Thou didst keep me alive, that I should not go down to the pit."

HE SHALL RECEIVE ME. The commentator, Kimchi, takes this to refer to immortality, but Rashi explains it to mean simply that God will receive me or take me to walk upon the road of righteousness.

See, however, the comment to Psalm 6:6. Kimchi, taking this verse to refer to immortality, must have sensed the strong feeling of unity with God expressed by the psalmist. This mood of the kinship of the finite with the Infinite is at least "introductory" to the development of the idea of immortality.

17. BE NOT THOU AFRAID. This repeats the general thought of the psalm and of Psalm 38, namely, that one should not fear or fret at the dominating power of wealth since it is ephemeral.

19. WHEN THOU SHALT DO WELL TO THYSELF. As translated

20. It shall go to the generation of his fathers;
They shall never see the light.
21. Man that is in honour understandeth not;
He is like the beasts that perish.

50. A PSALM OF ASAPH.

God, God, the Lord, hath spoken, and called
the earth
From the rising of the sun unto the going down
thereof.

here, the verse seems to mean that the powerful boast that during their lifetime of self-indulgence they win the admiration of
all. However, the medieval commentaries understand the verse
to mean: The righteous will praise you if you take proper care
of your soul rather than of your body.

20. IT SHALL GO. According to the commentator, Ibn Ezra,
"it" refers to the soul of the wicked mentioned in verse 19,
meaning their soul shall join their fathers (i. e., in death).

NEVER SEE THE LIGHT. The light of day.

21. IN HONOUR UNDERSTANDETH NOT. This refrain is used in
slightly different form in verse 13. Verse 13 means that man
will not permanently enjoy the glory and honor of his possessions, while this closing thought is that man, in the midst
of the glory of wealth, does not understand how ephemeral it is.

A PSALM in the prophetic spirit. The preceding psalm was
in the mood of the Wisdom Literature, speaking of the wise
and the fool, of wisdom and understanding, and the problems
of life which concern all men. This psalm addresses itself to
Israel especially. It calls Israel to judgment in the presence of
God. The subject of discussion between Israel and God is the
familiar prophetic theme as to the meaning of the sacrificial
rite and its relationship to the ethical life. First, God summons
those who believe that the sacrifices in themselves are pleasing
to God. To them He says, thanksgiving and prayer are of
greater importance. From the ritualistic he turns to the wicked

2. Out of Zion, the perfection of beauty,
   God hath shined forth.
3. Our God cometh, and doth not keep silence;
   A fire devoureth before Him,
   And round about Him it stormeth mightily.
4. He calleth to the heavens above,
   And to the earth, that He may judge His people:
5. 'Gather My saints together unto Me;
   Those that have made a covenant with Me by sacrifice.'
6. And the heavens declare His righteousness;
   For God, He is judge.   Selah
7. 'Hear, O My people, and I will speak;
   O Israel, and I will testify against thee:
   God, thy God, am I.
8. I will not reprove thee for thy sacrifices;

and reproves them for their hypocrisy. The psalm expresses almost the identical thought found in Isaiah 1:10-17.

The psalm is headed, "A Psalm of Asaph," one of the Levitical guild of singers. This is the only Psalm of Asaph in Book Two. In Book Three there is a group of ten psalms (73-83) with that heading.

1. ASAPH. Asaph is mentioned in I Chronicles 16:4-5, as the chief of the Levitical musicians whose task it was "to celebrate and to thank and praise the Lord, the God of Israel." And in I Chronicles 25:1, the *sons* of Asaph were to accompany the services of the Temple "with psalteries and harps and cymbals."

1-6. The prologue of the psalm. It is marked off from the body of the psalm by the word *Selah*. In the prologue, God calls His people to judgment.

1. GOD, GOD, THE LORD. These three names of God (*El, Elohim, JHWH*) occur also in Joshua 22:22, when the tribe of Reuben takes its oath, "God, God, the Lord, He knoweth."

2. ZION, THE PERFECTION OF BEAUTY. The beauty of Zion is likewise described in Psalm 48:3, "Fair in situation, the joy of the whole earth."

GOD HATH SHINED FORTH. God's radiance appears.

3. A FIRE . . . IT STORMETH. God appeared on Mount Sinai

132

And thy burnt-offerings are continually before Me.
9. I will take no bullock out of thy house,
   Nor he-goats out of thy folds.
10. For every beast of the forest is Mine,
    And the cattle upon a thousand hills.
11. I know all the fowls of the mountains;
    And the wild beasts of the field are Mine.
12. If I were hungry, I would not tell thee;
    For the world is Mine, and the fulness thereof.
13. Do I eat the flesh of bulls,
    Or drink the blood of goats?
14. Offer unto God the sacrifice of thanksgiving;
    And pay thy vows unto the Most High;
15. And call upon Me in the day of trouble;
    I will deliver thee, and thou shalt honour Me.'

(Exodus 19:16) amidst "thunders and lightnings." In Isaiah 29:6, God's coming is described as accompanied "with thunder, and with earthquake, with whirlwind and tempest, and the flame of a devouring fire." So here, as God comes to judge His people, there is flame and storm.

5. MY SAINTS. My righteous or pious ones.

A COVENANT WITH ME BY SACRIFICE. When Moses read the Book of the Covenant to Israel they offered sacrifices to God.

8-13. God says: I do not need your sacrifices since the world and all its beasts and fowl are Mine.

8. I WILL NOT REPROVE THEE FOR THY SACRIFICES. I do not accuse you of failing to bring sacrifices to Me, for, indeed, you have brought them continually, but I tell you that I do not need them since all the earth is Mine. You are not giving me a gift, of which I may have use, for "do I eat the flesh of bulls?" (verse 13).

14. THE SACRIFICE OF THANKSGIVING. This does not seem to mean the regular "thanksgiving sacrifice" (the *Todah*), but rather that we offer God our thanksgiving as if it were a sacrifice on the altar. Both the commentators, Rashi and Kimchi, take this phrase in this spiritual sense. Furthermore, this interpretation is confirmed by the succeeding lines, "pay thy vows

133

16. But unto the wicked God saith:
    'What hast thou to do to declare My statutes,
    And that thou hast taken My covenant in thy mouth?
17. Seeing thou hatest instruction,
    And castest My words behind thee.
18. When thou sawest a thief, thou hadst company with him,
    And with adulterers was thy portion.
19. Thou hast let loose thy mouth for evil,
    And thy tongue frameth deceit.
20. Thou sittest and speakest against thy brother;
    Thou slanderest thine own mother's son.

unto the Most High and call upon me in the day of trouble."

This thought, that God prefers spirituality to the ritual of sacrifice is expressed vigorously by the Prophet Jeremiah (7:21-23): "Thus saith the Lord of hosts: add your burnt offerings unto your sacrifice, and eat ye flesh (i. e., eat *ye* the flesh) for I spoke not unto your fathers, nor commanded them . . . concerning burnt offerings or sacrifices; but this thing I commanded them, saying: 'hearken unto My voice.' "

16-22. From those well-meaning, pious people who believed that offering of sacrifices constituted the sole worship of God, the psalmist now turns to the hypocritical and denounces them for their sin.

16-17. THOU HAST TAKEN MY COVENANT IN THY MOUTH. Many of those who profess to obey God's law and covenant are hypocritical, hating instruction, and casting His words behind them.

18-20. Enumerates the sins of the wicked and seems to refer particularly to the Ten Commandments. Thus, verse 17 mentions theft and adultery; verse 19, deceit and falsehood; verse 20, speaks of slander even against one's own family.

21. SHOULD I HAVE KEPT SILENCE? The Hebrew permits the translation as a declarative rather than an interrogative sentence: "I have kept silence," meaning "I have not punished you hitherto." The commentator, Ibn Ezra, takes the sentence in this sense.

Because I had kept silence and have not punished you, you thought that "I was such a one as thyself," i. e., that I approved

21. These things hast thou done, and should I have kept silence?
    Thou hadst thought that I was altogether such a one as thyself;
    But I will reprove thee, and set the cause before thine eyes.
22. Now consider this, ye that forget God,
    Lest I tear in pieces, and there be none to deliver.
23. Whoso offereth the sacrifice of thanksgiving honoureth Me;
    And to him that ordereth his way aright
    Will I show the salvation of God.'

51. FOR THE LEADER. A PSALM OF DAVID; 2. WHEN NATHAN THE
PROPHET CAME UNTO HIM, AFTER HE HAD GONE IN TO BATH-SHEBA.

of wickedness, that I was not a God of righteousness. Therefore,
"I will reprove thee."

SET THE CAUSE BEFORE THINE EYES. I will make the case and
My decision clear to you.

22. LEST I TEAR IN PIECES. The metaphor of God as a lion.
The same metaphor is used in Hosea 5:14, "For I will be as a
young lion to the house of Judah; I will tear and go away."

23. Sums up both halves of the psalm. To those who thought
that mere sacrifice was enough he says, offer "the (spiritual)
sacrifice of thanksgiving," and to those who were wicked he
says, that "to him that ordereth his way aright will I show the
salvation of God."

THIS psalm is the first of a group of seventeen psalms with
the heading, "of David." In this collection there are eight
psalms with titles which connect the psalm with specific events
in David's life. This psalm is one of the eight being headed: "A
Psalm of David when Nathan the prophet came unto him, after
he had gone into Bath-sheba." In the narrative of David and
Bath-sheba, the wife of Uriah the Hittite (II Samuel 12), the
prophet Nathan relates the parable of the rich man and the
poor man and the poor man's ewe lamb. The parable ends with
Nathan's statement to David: "Thou art the man." David, con-
science-stricken, declares, "I have sinned against the Lord"
(verse 13). This psalm is a development of the theme of that

135

3. Be gracious unto me, O God, according to Thy mercy;
      According to the multitude of Thy compassions blot
         out my transgressions.
4. Wash me thoroughly from mine iniquity,
      And cleanse me from my sin.
5. For I know my transgressions;
      And my sin is ever before me.
6. Against Thee, Thee only, have I sinned,
      And done that which is evil in Thy sight;

terse confession. David pleads with God to forgive him and "to wash me thoroughly from mine iniquity."

3. BE GRACIOUS . . . THY MERCY. Although God punishes iniquity, His lovingkindness is greater than His sternness. David relies upon God's abundant mercy and asks for an undeserved forgiveness. In Exodus 34:6-7, God is described as visiting the iniquity of fathers unto the fourth generation, but that description is prefaced with: "The Lord, the Lord, God, merciful and gracious . . . keeping mercy unto the thousandth generation, forgiving iniquity, transgression," etc.

3-4. TRANSGRESSIONS . . . INIQUITY . . . SIN. For the definition of these three types of sin see comment on Psalm 32:1-2.

BLOT OUT . . . WASH ME . . . CLEANSE ME. Blotting out sin visualizes a book of record, a frequent figure in biblical literature. "Wash" is the same verb which is used of cleansing garments. "Cleanse me," means "purify me," a term that is used in purifying from leprosy and disease.

6. AGAINST THEE ONLY, HAVE I SINNED. Although I have done evil to Uriah, the husband of Bath-sheba, sending him forth to his death in battle, the greater sin is against Thee, since I have violated Thy laws of justice. This sentence seems to refer directly to the statement which David makes to Nathan in II Samuel 12:13, "I have sinned against the Lord."

THAT THOU MAYEST BE JUSTIFIED. I make this confession, acknowledging my sin, that all may know that Thou wilt be justified if Thou dost punish me, and wilt reveal Thyself to all as a righteous Judge.

7. BROUGHT FORTH IN INIQUITY. This sin is not my only evil

That Thou mayest be justified when Thou speakest,
And be in the right when Thou judgest.
7. Behold, I was brought forth in iniquity,
And in sin did my mother conceive me.
8. Behold, Thou desirest truth in the inward parts;
Make me, therefore, to know wisdom in mine
inmost heart.
9. Purge me with hyssop, and I shall be clean;
Wash me, and I shall be whiter than snow.

deed. I am thoroughly corrupt from my very birth. I begin life
with impulses which tend to drag me into iniquity.

The statement of the psalmist sounds like the doctrine of
Original Sin, a doctrine widely held in the Christian Church,
namely, that because of the sin of Adam all mortals are in-
herently sinful. This doctrine of Original Sin is not prevalent
in Judaism. While the poisoning effect of Adam's sin is referred
to in Rabbinic Literature the general tendency of Jewish
thought is that each one is responsible for his own iniquity. It
is true, the Rabbis say that a man has evil *inclination* (*Yetzer
Ho-ra*), nevertheless, with God's help, man can resist temptation, and, therefore, each is responsible for his sins. The Talmud (b. Maccoth 24 a) says that while Moses said, "God visits
the sins of the fathers upon the children" (which would indicate inherited guilt), Ezekiel came and annulled that statement
by saying (Ezekiel 18:4): "The soul that sinneth, *it* shall die"
(thus proclaiming individual responsibility).

What David, therefore, means here is that from his very
birth he has been prone to sin. See article "Sin," *Jewish Encyclopedia* Vol. XI.

8. THE INWARD PARTS . . . MINE INMOST HEART. God desires
not only righteousness in action but purity of motive. Hence
the psalmist asks God's help to purify his heart.

9. WITH HYSSOP. When the priest purified the leper he
sprinkled him with hyssop. (Leviticus 14:1-7.)

WHITER THAN SNOW. The same simile, comparing spiritual
purity to snow, is expressed in Isaiah 1:18, "Though your sins
be as scarlet, they shall be as white as snow."

137

10. Make me to hear joy and gladness;
   That the bones which Thou hast crushed **may** rejoice.
11. Hide Thy face from my sins,
   And blot out all mine iniquities.
12. Create me a clean heart, O God;
   And renew a stedfast spirit within me.
13. Cast me not away from Thy presence;
   And take not Thy holy spirit from me.
14. Restore unto me the joy of Thy salvation;
   And let a willing spirit uphold me.
15. Then will I teach transgressors Thy ways;
   And sinners shall return unto Thee.
16. Deliver me from bloodguiltiness, O God, **Thou God**
   of my salvation;

10. THAT THE BONES WHICH THOU HAST CRUSHED MAY REJOICE.
That my body as well as my soul may rejoice. "Bones," the
framework of the body, is frequently used in the psalms as a
symbol for the body itself.

12. CREATE ME A CLEAN HEART. He sums up his plea (9-10)
with the vivid prayer that his (David's) heart, in spite of all its
many evil impulses, be made, by God's mercy, clean and noble.

13. CAST ME NOT AWAY. Let me not feel estranged from Thee
and deprived of the sense of communion with "Thy holy spirit."

14. A WILLING SPIRIT. A spirit which will spontaneously
choose righteousness.

16. FROM BLOODGUILTINESS. Either refers specifically to the
sin of having brought about the death of Uriah, the husband
of Bath-sheba, or generally to all sins of violence.

17. OPEN THOU MY LIPS. Inspire Thou me to sing Thy praise.
The same idea is expressed in Psalm 40:4, "And He hath put
a new song in my mouth." This sentence, "O Lord, open Thou
my lips . . ." is used in the service as the introduction to the
Tefillah, the daily petitional prayer.

18-19. THOU DELIGHTEST NOT IN SACRIFICE . . . THE SACRIFICES
OF GOD ARE A BROKEN SPIRIT. These two verses, in the spirit of
the prophets, also voice the mood of Psalm 50 in which God
says: I do not need your sacrifices; it would be better if you

138

So shall my tongue sing aloud of Thy righteousness.
17. O Lord, open Thou my lips;
    And my mouth shall declare Thy praise.
18. For Thou delightest not in sacrifice, else would I
    give it;
    Thou hast no pleasure in burnt-offering.
19. The sacrifices of God are a broken spirit;
    A broken and a contrite heart, O God, Thou wilt
    not despise.
20. Do good in Thy favour unto Zion;
    Build Thou the walls of Jerusalem.
21. Then wilt Thou delight in the sacrifices of righteousness,
    in burnt-offering and whole offering;
    Then will they offer bullocks upon Thine altar.

offer Me your thanksgiving and pray to Me in your trouble.

The thought that the most acceptable sacrifice to God is a humble and contrite spirit is beautifully expressed in the Songs of Unity (For the First Day) composed about the thirteenth century and attributed to Judah, the Pious: "Out of the broken fragments of my heart will I build an altar unto Thee."

20-21. Some modern commentators consider these two final verses to be a later addition to the psalm. This opinion is based upon two grounds, one, that verse 20, asking God to build the walls of Jerusalem, must have been written after Jerusalem was destroyed and therefore during or after the Exile, and, also, that verse 21, which speaks of God's delight in burnt offerings, contradicts the more spiritual mood of the body of the psalm. However, it may well be argued that these two verses *were* part of the original psalm, and that the building of the walls of Jerusalem was a prayer not to rebuild *broken* walls but to complete the building of the walls which David started and which indeed were not completed until the time of Solomon. See I Kings 3:1, "He (Solomon) had made an end of building . . . the house of the Lord, and the wall of Jerusalem round about." As for the ritual spirit of the last verse it may well be that the psalmist means that if we are pure of heart and contrite in spirit then the offerings upon the altar will be acceptable.

52. FOR THE LEADER. MASCHIL OF DAVID; 2. WHEN DOEG THE
EDOMITE CAME AND TOLD SAUL, AND SAID UNTO HIM:
'DAVID IS COME TO THE HOUSE OF AHIMELECH.'

3. Why boastest thou thyself of evil, O mighty man?
The mercy of God endureth continually.
4. Thy tongue deviseth destruction;
Like a sharp razor, working deceitfully.
5. Thou lovest evil more than good;
Falsehood rather than speaking righteousness.   Selah

THIS psalm is the second in this group of seventeen entitled "of David." It is also the second of the eight psalms within the group which have in their title a reference to a specific incident in David's career. The incident to which the heading of this psalm refers is: "When Doeg the Edomite came and told Saul, and said unto him: 'David is come to the house of Ahimelech'" (verse 2). This incident is described at length in I Samuel 22. David took refuge in the house of Ahimelech, the priest, and Doeg, an officer of Saul, informed Saul of this fact. Saul, in vengeance, put Ahimelech and his fellow-priests to death.

The psalm is similar in thought to that of Psalm 37. It speaks to the evil man and tells him that his might will not protect him against Divine punishment. It assures the righteous that he will endure.

1. MASCHIL. For the explanation of this technical term see the comment to Psalm 32:1.

3. WHY BOASTEST THOU . . . THE MERCY OF GOD ENDURETH. Thy might, oh evil man, will pass away but the mercy of God being eternal will preserve the righteous.

4. THY TONGUE . . . LIKE A SHARP RAZOR. This seems to refer to Doeg's informing Saul that Ahimelech had sheltered David.

The tongue of the slanderer and informer is here compared to a razor which cuts deep wounds. Elsewhere in the Psalms the slanderous tongue is compared to other cutting instruments such as the sword or the arrow. Thus, "The workers of iniquity

6. Thou lovest all devouring words,
   The deceitful tongue.
7. God will likewise break thee for ever,
   He will take thee up, and pluck thee out of thy tent,
   And root thee out of the land of the living.   Selah
8. The righteous also shall see, and fear,
   And shall laugh at him:
9. 'Lo, this is the man that made not God his stronghold;
   But trusted in the abundance of his riches,
   And strengthened himself in his wickedness.'

who have whet their tongue like a sword, and have aimed their arrow, a poisoned word," Psalm 64:3-4.

WORKING DECEITFULLY. The razor cuts suddenly, before the victim is aware that he is wounded. Hence "deceitfully."

6. DEVOURING WORDS. Words which work destruction.

7. BREAK THEE . . . PLUCK THEE . . . ROOT THEE OUT. Various metaphors for God's destruction of the wicked. The last metaphor, "root thee out," is a familiar one in the Psalms. Those who prosper are described as flourishing like a tree and therefore those who will be destroyed are to be uprooted. In Psalm 37:35, the wicked is described as "spreading himself like a leafy tree in its native soil."

SELAH marks a division between the first thought of the psalm and the second. Up to this point the fall of the wicked was predicted. From here to the end, the psalm speaks of God's defense of the righteous.

8. SHALL SEE, AND FEAR. The righteous will see the destruction of the wicked and will be awe-struck at the manifestation of God's might.

9. LO, THIS IS THE MAN THAT MADE NOT GOD HIS STRONGHOLD. The wicked relied upon his own strength and it has failed him. The converse of the idea is expressed in Jeremiah 17:7-8, "Blessed is the man that trusteth in the Lord, and whose trust the Lord is. For he shall be as a tree . . ." Here, too, as in the passage from Jeremiah, the righteous man who *does* make God his stronghold is described in verse 10 as a flourishing tree.

141

10. But as for me, I am like a leafy olive-tree in the house of God;
I trust in the mercy of God for ever and ever.
11. I will give Thee thanks for ever, because Thou hast done it;
And I will wait for Thy name, for it is good, in the presence of
Thy saints.

53. FOR THE LEADER; UPON MAHALATH. MASCHIL OF DAVID.
2. The fool hath said in his heart: 'There is no God';
They have dealt corruptly, and have done abominable iniquity;
There is none that doeth good.
3. God looked forth from heaven upon the children of men,
To see if there were any man of understanding, that did seek
after God.
4. Every one of them is unclean, they are together become impure;
There is none that doeth good, no, not one.

10. OLIVE TREE IN THE HOUSE OF GOD. The psalmist uses two
metaphors which describe the blessings which come to him who
receives God's help. One metaphor is that he who trusts in God
flourishes like a tree; and the other, that he shall have the joy
of dwelling in God's house. In this verse, both these metaphors
are combined. The righteous will flourish like a tree planted in
God's house. The same combination of the two metaphors is
found in Psalm 92:13-14, "The righteous shall flourish like the
palm-tree . . . planted in the House of the Lord."

11. AND I WILL WAIT FOR THY NAME. I will wait for Thee and
for the manifestation of Thy help. Thus, similarly, Psalm 27
ends with the words: "Yea, wait thou for the Lord."

THY SAINTS. Thy righteous ones.

*T*HIS psalm is another version of Psalm 14 which is found
in the earlier collection of the "Psalms of David" (Book I). See
comment to Psalm 14 and the comment on the few variants
from Psalm 14 given herewith.

1. MAHALATH. The word may mean sickness, and thus may
refer to the title of some melody to which this psalm was sung.
Or, as the commentator, Rashi, takes it, it may be the name of
a musical instrument.

5. 'Shall not the workers of iniquity know it,
Who eat up My people as they eat bread,
And call not upon God?'
6. There are they in great fear, where no fear was;
For God hath scattered the bones of him that encampeth
against thee;
Thou hast put them to shame, because God hath
rejected them.
7. Oh that the salvation of Israel were come out of Zion!
When God turneth the captivity of His people,
Let Jacob rejoice, let Israel be glad.

54.FOR THE LEADER; WITH STRING-MUSIC. MASCHIL OF DAVID; 2. WHEN
THE ZIPHITES CAME AND SAID TO SAUL: 'DOTH NOT DAVID HIDE HIM-
SELF WITH US?'

MASCHIL. For this technical term see comment to Psalm 32.

3. GOD LOOKED FORTH. In Psalm 14, *JHWH* is used as the name of God, and here *Elohim* is used. The editor of Books Two and Three of the Psalms uses the word *Elohim* instead of *JHWH* whenever possible. See introduction to Book Two.

6. WHERE NO FEAR WAS. This is not found in Psalm 14. It means they are afraid when there is nothing to fear. They are the victims of an unreasoning panic.

The rest of this verse differs from Psalm 14 which speaks of God helping the righteous generation. Here the psalm speaks of God scattering those who encamp against the righteous.

THIS psalm is the third one of the eight in whose title there is a definite reference to an incident in the life of David. The incident is described in the heading: "When the Ziphites came and said to Saul: 'Doth not David hide himself with us?'" This incident is given in I Samuel 23:19 ff. It happens that in this instance the heading of the psalm uses the exact words which are given in the Book of Samuel.

The psalmist expresses the familiar prayer for help against violent enemies and anticipates his thanks to God when he will have been delivered.

143

3. O God, save me by Thy name,
   And right me by Thy might.
4. O God, hear my prayer;
   Give ear to the words of my mouth.
5. For strangers are risen up against me,
   And violent men have sought after my soul;
   They have not set God before them.   Selah
6. Behold, God is my helper;
   The Lord is for me as the upholder of my soul.
7. He will requite the evil unto them that lie in
      wait for me;

3. SAVE ME BY THY NAME. The meaning is clear from the second line of the couplet.

BY THY MIGHT. When we call upon God's Name we invoke His help. Thus, Psalm 20:2, "The name of the God of Jacob set thee up on high."

RIGHT ME. Vindicate me. Declare that I am in the right.

5. THEY HAVE NOT SET GOD BEFORE THEM. Those who do evil forget God. Similarly Psalm 36:2, "There is no fear of God before his eyes."

8-9. He visualizes his grateful thanks to God after he will have been delivered. He will come with a free-will offering and with prayers of thanksgiving.

9. MINE EYE HATH GAZED UPON MINE ENEMIES. Mine eyes will see mine enemies destroyed, or, mine eyes will see what they desire to see done to mine enemies. The phrase is a frequent one in the Psalms. Thus, Psalm 118:7, "The Lord is for me as my helper; and I shall gaze upon them that hate me."

THE psalmist complains, not of his enemies, but of his former friends who have become treacherous and deceitful. The city in which he dwells has suddenly become unsafe. Treachery and violence fill its streets. He wishes that he could fly away to safety. "Oh that I had wings like a dove!" (verse 7). He asks God to destroy the hypocritical and he expresses his confidence that his trust in God will sustain him.

Destroy Thou them in Thy truth.

8. With a freewill-offering will I sacrifice unto Thee;
   I will give thanks unto Thy name, O LORD, for it is good.
9. For He hath delivered me out of all trouble;
   And mine eye hath gazed upon mine enemies.

Psalm 55
3

55. FOR THE LEADER; WITH STRING-MUSIC. MASCHIL OF DAVID.

2. Give ear, O God, to my prayer;
   And hide not Thyself from my supplication.
3. Attend unto me, and answer me;
   I am distraught in my complaint, and will moan;

The Targum and many of the older commentators connect this psalm with the treachery of David's friend and counsellor, Ahithophel, who deserted David to join in the rebellion of Absalom. (See II Samuel 15.) However, it is not possible to assign the psalm definitely to David's time. David would hardly speak of "oppression" in the city of Jerusalem (verse 12), nor would he speak of walking with his friends to "the house of God" (verse 15) which seems to refer to the Temple which was not built until after David's day.

The heading "of David" must be understood as a reminiscence of the treachery of Absalom and Ahithophel.

1. MASCHIL. For the explanation of this technical term see comment on Psalm 32.

2. GIVE EAR. The same prayer that God listen to the plea of the psalmist as is found, for example, in Psalm 54:4, "O God . . . give ear to the words of my mouth."

HIDE NOT THYSELF. As a man might hide himself. Thus, in Isaiah 58:7, the prophet pleads with the people: "Is it not to deal thy bread to the hungry . . . that thou hide not thyself from thine own flesh?" (i. e., from thine own kin). The psalmist seems also to have in mind the idea that God will "hide himself" from the wicked. Thus (Isaiah 1:15), "When ye spread forth your hands I will hide Mine eyes from you . . . your hands are full of blood." He, therefore, pleads that he is not wicked but the victim of wickedness, therefore, "hide not Thyself from my supplication."

145

4. Because of the voice of the enemy,
   Because of the oppression of the wicked;
   For they cast mischief upon me,
   And in anger they persecute me.
5. My heart doth writhe within me;
   And the terrors of death are fallen upon me.
6. Fear and trembling come upon me,
   And horror hath overwhelmed me.
7. And I said: 'Oh that I had wings like a dove!
   Then would I fly away, and be at rest.
8. Lo, then would I wander far off,
   I would lodge in the wilderness. Selah
9. I would haste me to a shelter
   From the stormy wind and tempest.'
10. Destroy, O Lord, and divide their tongue;
    For I have seen violence and strife in the city.
11. Day and night they go about it upon the walls thereof;
    Iniquity also and mischief are in the midst of it.
12. Wickedness is in the midst thereof;
    Oppression and guile depart not from her broad place.
13. For it was not an enemy that taunted me,
    Then I could have borne it;

7-9. The psalmist wishes he could flee like a dove from the scene of treachery and violence. The dove could always fly away from the city to his lonely and secure dwelling place in the clefts of the rock. Thus, Song of Songs 2:14, "O my dove, that art in the clefts of the rock, in the covert of the cliff."

10. DIVIDE THEIR TONGUE. The commentator, Rashi, takes this to mean: Divide their councils so that like the men of the Tower of Babel they may not understand each other and thus their plans become confused.

12. BROAD PLACE. The open square of the city around the gates where people gathered and justice was dealt out. There, in the broad place, the place of justice, the psalmist finds "oppression and guile."

13-16. The psalmist says that it is not his known enemies who oppress him now but an intimate friend whose treachery suddenly makes life unsafe.

14-15. He addresses his former friend directly. He describes

Neither was it mine adversary that did magnify
  himself against me,
Then I would have hid myself from him.
14. But it was thou, a man mine equal,
  My companion, and my familiar friend;
15. We took sweet counsel together,
  In the house of God we walked with the throng.
16. May He incite death against them,
  Let them go down alive into the nether-world;
  For evil is in their dwelling, and within them.
17. As for me, I will call upon God;
  And the LORD will save me.
18. Evening, and morning, and at noonday, will I
    complain, and moan;
  And He hath heard my voice.
19. He hath redeemed my soul in peace so that none
    came nigh me;
  For they were many that strove with me.
20. God shall hear, and humble them,
  Even He that is enthroned of old,   Selah
  Such as have no changes,
  And fear not God.

how, in the past, they would take counsel together and walk
with the festive throng to the Temple of God.

16. GO DOWN ALIVE INTO THE NETHER-WORLD. This may be a
reminiscence of the story of Korah, the rebel of whom the Bible
says that the earth opened and swallowed him alive (Numbers
16:32-33). The commentator, Rashi, takes this to mean simply
that they would die suddenly; in the prime of their life they
would go down quickly to death.

18. EVENING, MORNING, NOON-DAY. The usual and natural
times for prayer. Thus, Daniel 6:11, speaks of praying three
times a day. And Jewish tradition provides three fixed periods
for daily prayer: Evening (Maariv), noon or afternoon (Min-
chah), and morning (Shacharis).

20. SUCH AS HAVE NO CHANGES, AND FEAR NOT GOD. The Aramaic translation (the Targum), and the commentator, Ibn
Ezra, take this to mean, those who do not change their evil
ways. It may also mean, those whose life has not changed from

147

21. He hath put forth his hands against them that were at
     peace with him;
     He hath profaned his covenant.
22. Smoother than cream were the speeches of his mouth,
     But his heart was war;
     His words were softer than oil,
     Yet were they keen-edged swords.
23. Cast thy burden upon the Lord, and He will sustain
     thee;
     He will never suffer the righteous to be moved.
24. But Thou, O God, wilt bring them down into the
     nethermost pit;
     Men of blood and deceit shall not live out half their days;
     But as for me, I will trust in Thee.

health to sickness or from wealth to poverty, i. e., those who
have had no vicissitudes and therefore do not fear God.

22. The psalmist elaborates the theme of his former friend's
hypocrisy and deceitfulness. The hypocritical words are
"smoother than cream" but their evil intention makes them
"keen-edged swords." Evil words are frequently described as
destructive weapons. (See comment on Psalm 52:4.)

23. CAST THY BURDEN UPON THE LORD. Just as the wicked cannot rely upon their strength because God will destroy it, so the
righteous need not depend upon their own strength alone. God
will help them carry their burdens.

24. SHALL NOT LIVE OUT HALF THEIR DAYS. This may be taken
in connection with verse 16, "Let them go down alive into the
nether-world." They will die prematurely.

THIS is the fourth psalm of the group of eight which contain a specific reference in the title to some incident in the life
of David. The incident which is referred to here is "when the
Philistines took him in Gath." The full account of this event is
found in I Samuel 21:11 ff. David fled to Gath, and when he
was recognized by the Philistines as the one who had slain
Goliath, his life was endangered and he had to feign madness
in order to escape.

56. FOR THE LEADER; UPON JONATH-ELEM-REHOKIM. [A PSALM] OF DAVID; MICHTAM; WHEN THE PHILISTINES TOOK HIM IN GATH.

2. Be gracious unto me, O God, for man would swallow me up;
   All the day he fighting oppresseth me.
3. They that lie in wait for me would swallow me up all the day;
   For they are many that fight against me, O Most High,
4. In the day that I am afraid,
   I will put my trust in Thee.
5. In God—I will praise His word—
   In God do I trust, I will not be afraid;
   What can flesh do unto me?
6. All the day they trouble mine affairs;
   All their thoughts are against me for evil.

In this psalm the poet speaks of the enemies which lie in ambush for him; but he trusts in God for has He not in the past "delivered my soul from death . . . my feet from stumbling?"

1. JONATH-ELEM-REHOKIM. The phrase is of dubious meaning. It seems to mean "the silent dove of those at a distance." The Aramaic translation (the Targum) understands this phrase to refer to Israel, "the silent dove"; but in all likelihood it is the name of a well-known melody to which this psalm was sung. See Introduction and also the comment to Psalm 9:1.

2. FOR MAN WOULD SWALLOW ME UP. The enemy is described as a ravenous beast, generally as a lion, ready to swallow up his victims.

5. This refrain, marking the close of a stanza, is used again in verses 11 and 12.

I WILL PRAISE HIS WORD. God's word of deliverance, God's assurance of help. Thus in Psalm 130:5, "I wait for the Lord . . . and in His word do I hope."

WHAT CAN FLESH DO UNTO ME? When God is on my side what harm can mortal man do to me? Almost the identical phrase is found in Psalm 118:6, "The Lord is for me; I will not fear; what can man do unto me?"

6. ALL THE DAY THEY TROUBLE MINE AFFAIRS. The Hebrew permits the following translation also; all the day they pervert my words.

149

Psalm 56

7

7. They gather themselves together, they hide themselves,
 They mark my steps;
 According as they have waited for my soul.
8. Because of iniquity cast them out;
 In anger bring down the peoples, O God.
9. Thou hast counted my wanderings;
 Put Thou my tears into Thy bottle;
 Are they not in Thy book?
10. Then shall mine enemies turn back in the day that I call;
 This I know, that God is for me.
11. In God—I will praise His word—
 In the Lord—I will praise His word—
12. In God do I trust, I will not be afraid;

7. THEY HIDE THEMSELVES . . . THEY MARK MY STEPS. Describing his enemies in ambush.

8. IN ANGER. May God in His indignation at their evil intention cast them down.

9. MY TEARS INTO THY BOTTLE. A bold but tender metaphor. God remembers all our sorrows. He counts our tears.

IN THY BOOK. A more familiar metaphor in the Bible. God keeps a record of all the deeds and experiences of man. Thus Malachi 3:16, "The Lord . . . heard and a book of remembrance was written before Him."

10. GOD IS FOR ME. With God on my side I fear no enemy. The same phrase is found in Psalm 118:6, "The Lord is for me; I will not fear."

13-14. The psalmist will pay to God the vows which he had promised in times of danger. The same thought is found in Psalm 54:8-9, "With a freewill-offering will I sacrifice unto Thee . . . for He hath delivered me."

14. MY SOUL FROM DEATH . . . MY FEET FROM STUMBLING. This verse and the preceding one closely resemble the verses in Psalm 116:8, 9, "Thou hast delivered my feet from stumbling, I shall walk before the Lord in the land of the living."

IN THE LIGHT OF THE LIVING. For the psalmist, the greatest boon is to be given long life in which to serve God on earth. This thought is repeated all through the Psalms. Thus, Psalm

150

What can man do unto me?
13. Thy vows are upon me, O God;
I will render thank-offerings unto Thee.
14. For Thou hast delivered my soul from death;
Hast Thou not delivered my feet from stumbling?
That I may walk before God in the light of the living.

57. FOR THE LEADER; AL-TASHHETH. [A PSALM] OF DAVID;
MICHTAM; WHEN HE FLED FROM SAUL, IN THE CAVE.

2. Be gracious unto me, O God, be gracious unto me,
For in Thee hath my soul taken refuge;
Yea, in the shadow of Thy wings will I take refuge,
Until calamities be overpast.

27:13, " (I would have despaired) if I had not believed to look
upon the goodness of the Lord in the land of the living."

*T*HIS psalm is the fifth of the group whose heading contains a specific reference to an event in the life of David, "when
he fled from Saul, in the cave." The incident referred to, is, in
all likelihood, the one described in I Samuel 24.

The mood of the psalm is one of confidence in God in a
time of calamity. The psalmist is sure that "in the shadow of
Thy wings will I take refuge, until the calamities be overpast"
(verse 2). Strengthened by his trust in God, the psalmist anticipates the day when "I will sing praises unto Thee among the
nations" (verse 10).

1. AL-TASHHETH. Means, "do not destroy." This phrase evidently refers to a melody to which this psalm is to be sung. It
is used as a heading also for the next two psalms.

MICHTAM. For the explanation of this technical term see
comment on Psalm 16:1.

2. BE GRACIOUS UNTO ME. The plea for God's grace is similar
to the one which opens Psalm 56.

THE SHADOW OF THY WINGS. This beautiful metaphor of
God's sheltering love is used frequently in the Psalms. See
Psalm 17:8, "Hide me in the shadow of Thy wings."

151

3. I will cry unto God Most High;
   Unto God that accomplisheth it for me.
4. He will send from heaven, and save me,
   When he that would swallow me up taunteth;   Selah
   God shall send forth His mercy and His truth.
5. My soul is among lions, I do lie down among them
      that are aflame;
   Even the sons of men, whose teeth are spears and
      arrows,
   And their tongue a sharp sword.
6. Be Thou exalted, O God, above the heavens;
   Thy glory be above all the earth.
7. They have prepared a net for my steps,
   My soul is bowed down;
   They have digged a pit before me,
   They are fallen into the midst thereof themselves.   Selah

4. HE THAT WOULD SWALLOW ME UP. The psalmist compares his enemy to a lion who swallows up his prey. The same verb is used in Psalm 56:2.

5. THEM THAT ARE AFLAME. Aflame with murderous rage.

THEIR TONGUE A SHARP SWORD. The familiar metaphor for the destructive tongue. See Psalm 55:22, "His words . . . were keen-edged swords."

6. BE THOU EXALTED. This sentence is a refrain which closes the first part of the psalm and is repeated at the close of the psalm (verse 12). When God defeats the wicked He rises from above the puny strength of man. Thus, Isaiah sees the Lord "sitting upon a throne high and lifted up" (Isaiah 6:1); and in Psalm 21 the psalmist calls upon God to defeat the wicked and thus "be Thou exalted, O Lord" (verse 14).

The second half of the verse carries out the same idea: God's glory rises above all the earth. This description of God's glory dominating both earth and heaven is found also in Psalm 148:13, "His Name alone is exalted; His glory is above the earth and heaven."

7. NET . . . PIT. Describes the "net" and the "pit" which his enemies make ready for him. The thought that they themselves have fallen into the pit which they have dug is expressed

8. My heart is stedfast, O God, my heart is stedfast;
I will sing, yea, I will sing praises.
9. Awake, my glory; awake, psaltery and harp;
I will awake the dawn.
10. I will give thanks unto Thee, O Lord, among the peoples;
I will sing praises unto Thee among the nations.
11. For Thy mercy is great unto the heavens,
And Thy truth unto the skies.
12. Be Thou exalted, O God, above the heavens;
Thy glory be above all the earth.

58. FOR THE LEADER; AL-TASHHETH. [A PSALM] OF DAVID; MICHTAM.

2. Do ye indeed speak as a righteous company?
Do ye judge with equity the sons of men?
3. Yea, in heart ye work wickedness;
Ye weigh out in the earth the violence of your hands.

in Ecclesiastes 10:8, "He that diggeth a pit shall fall into it."

11. THY MERCY IS GREAT UNTO THE HEAVENS. God's mercy and truth fill the universe.

Verses 8 to 12 of this psalm are repeated in Psalm 108:2-6.

THE psalmist denounces the unrighteous judges who do not judge "with equity the sons of men." He compares them to venomous serpents and calls upon God to destroy them and thus demonstrate that "there is a God that judgeth in the earth."

1. For the terms *al-tashheth* and *michtam* see comment to Psalm 57:1.

2. A RIGHTEOUS COMPANY. The Hebrew word for "company" can also be translated, "silence." The commentator, Rashi, therefore takes this phrase to mean: Are ye not silent when ye should speak justice? But Kimchi, and one opinion quoted by Ibn Ezra, understood the text as here translated.

3. IN HEART YE WORK WICKEDNESS. Instead of judging "with equity" ye plan evil in the heart. The opposite thought is expressed in Psalm 15:2, "He that . . . worketh righteousness, and speaketh truth in his heart."

153

Psalm 58

4

4. The wicked are estranged from the womb;
   The speakers of lies go astray as soon as they are born.
5. Their venom is like the venom of a serpent;
   They are like the deaf asp that stoppeth her ear;
6. Which hearkeneth not to the voice of charmers,
   Or of the most cunning binder of spells.
7. Break their teeth, O God, in their mouth;
   Break out the cheek-teeth of the young lions, O LORD.
8. Let them melt away as water that runneth apace;
   When he aimeth his arrows, let them be as though they were
   cut off.
9. Let them be as a snail which melteth and passeth away;

YE WEIGH OUT. In the scales of justice these evil judges
weigh out violence. The scales of justice are also referred to in
Job 31:6, "Let me be weighed in a just balance."

4. ESTRANGED FROM THE WOMB. The wicked are described as
being prone to sin from their very birth. The psalmist uses the
same phrase of himself when he confesses his sin, Psalm 51:7,
"Behold, I was brought forth in iniquity."

5-6. He compares the evil done by the unrighteous judges to
the venom of serpents and malignant asps who cannot be
charmed by the snake charmer.

7. The metaphor changes from a snake to a lion.

8-10. The various metaphors in these verses refer to the
rapid destruction of the wicked, for which he prays.

8. MELT AWAY AS WATER. As a mountain cataract, after a rain
storm is over, empties out quickly and becomes a dry river bed.

9. AS A SNAIL WHICH MELTETH. The commentators, Rashi and
Kimchi, both translate this unusual word by the French word
"limace," which means, "snail." The figure evidently refers to
the fact that the snail leaves a slimy track and seems to use up
its body as it crawls along.

10. BEFORE YOUR POTS, etc. The metaphor here also means to
give the idea of rapid destruction. The explanation offered by
the commentator, Kimchi, is as follows: Thorns make a rapid
flame, yet even before the pots can feel the heat of this quick
flame the whirlwind sweeps away the raw meat and the flame.

154

Like the untimely births of a woman, that have not seen
the sun.

10. Before your pots can feel the thorns,
He will sweep it away with a whirlwind, the raw and
the burning alike.

11. The righteous shall rejoice when he seeth the vengeance;
He shall wash his feet in the blood of the wicked.

12. And men shall say: 'Verily there is a reward for the righteous;
Verily there is a God that judgeth in the earth.'

59. FOR THE LEADER; AL-TASHHETH. [A PSALM] OF DAVID; MICHTAM;
WHEN SAUL SENT, AND THEY WATCHED THE HOUSE TO KILL HIM.

11-12. The psalm concludes with a picture of God's vengeance against the wicked and the universal recognition that
God is the righteous Judge.

11. WASH HIS FEET IN BLOOD. A warrior's figure of speech.
So great will be the defeat of the armies of the wicked that their
blood will flow like a stream. The same expression is used in
Psalm 68:24, "That thy foot may wade through blood."

12. A GOD THAT JUDGETH IN THE EARTH. When God destroys
the wicked all men will recognize that there is a stern and
righteous Judge. The same thought is expressed in Psalm 9:6, 9,
after God has "destroyed the wicked" the Lord will have "established His throne for judgment."

THIS is one of the group of psalms whose headings refer
to some specific event in the life of David. The event spoken
of here is "when Saul sent, and they watched the house to kill
him." The full account of the incident is given in I Samuel
19:11 ff. Some commentators discount the possibility that this
psalm was written at that time, since the enemies of which
David speaks in this psalm are referred to as non-Israelites
(verse 6): "God of Israel . . . punish all the nations." Be that
as it may, the description of the enemies running around at
night "like barking dogs" seems to indicate that the author had
in mind the episode in David's life referred to in the title.

155

2. Deliver me from mine enemies, O my God;
   Set me on high from them that rise up against me.
3. Deliver me from the workers of iniquity,
   And save me from the men of blood.
4. For, lo, they lie in wait for my soul;
   The impudent gather themselves together against me;
   Not for my transgression, nor for my sin, O LORD.
5. Without my fault, they run and prepare themselves;
   Awake Thou to help me, and behold.
6. Thou therefore, O LORD God of hosts, the God of
      Israel,
   Arouse Thyself to punish all the nations;

1. AL-TASHHETH. Means, "do not destroy." This phrase, used in the heading of the two previous psalms evidently refers to a well-known melody to which this Psalm was sung. See comment to Psalm 57:7.

MICHTAM. For a discussion of this technical term see comment to Psalm 16:1.

2. SET ME ON HIGH. In a high fortress, secure from attack.

3. THE MEN OF BLOOD. A vigorous epithet describing men of violence. The same phrase is used in Psalm 55:24, "men of blood and deceit."

4-5. NOT FOR MY TRANSGRESSION . . . WITHOUT MY FAULT. I do not merit their hostility.

5. AWAKE THOU. This appeal to God to arouse Himself as if from sleep is expressed in even bolder words in Psalm 44:24, "Awake, why sleepest Thou, O Lord."

SELAH. As usual, *selah* marks the end of a thought, but in this case does not mark the end of a main division of the psalm. In this psalm, as in a number of other psalms, the main divisions are indicated by a refrain. Verse 10 is the refrain which is repeated also in verse 18.

7. AT EVENING, THEY HOWL LIKE A DOG. In the oriental cities dogs range the streets at night, howling, looking for food. Another instance of this comparison of violent men with dogs is to be found in Psalm 22:17, "For dogs have encompassed me."

8. BELCH OUT their barking and howling.

Show no mercy to any iniquitous traitors.   Selah
7. They return at evening, they howl like a dog,
And go round about the city.
8. Behold, they belch out with their mouth;
Swords are in their lips:
'For who doth hear?'
9. But Thou, O Lord, shalt laugh at them;
Thou shalt have all the nations in derision.
10. Because of his strength, I will wait for Thee;
For God is my high tower.
11. The God of my mercy will come to meet me;
God will let me gaze upon mine adversaries.

SWORDS. The familiar comparison of the words of the violent
with destructive swords. See Psalm 55:22, "His words . . . keen-
edged swords."

FOR WHO DOTH HEAR? The enemies are quoted as expressing
the thought which the psalmist frequently ascribes to them,
namely, where is God, or, who will save our victims from us?
Here the enemies say, "who is there (i. e., there is no God) to
hear our barking against the victim."

9. THOU SHALT LAUGH. In response to the pretentious self-
confidence of the violent, God will laugh in derision. The same
thought is found in Psalm 2:4, "He that sitteth in heaven
laugheth, the Lord hath them in derision."

10. The refrain; repeated also at the close of the Psalm
(verse 18).

HIS STRENGTH. The commentators are in disagreement as to
whose strength is here referred to. Is it the strength of the
enemy or the strength of God? Judging by the second version of
the refrain where the psalmist addresses God, "O my Strength,"
it is likely that in verse 10 "His strength" means God's strength.
The commentator, Ibn Ezra, takes the sentence in this way. It
must therefore be understood as follows: Because of *Thy*
strength I will wait for Thee. It is not infrequent that the
psalmist uses the second and third person in the same sentence
even though it refers to the same person.

11. GAZE UPON MINE ADVERSARIES. He will let me see the

157

12. Slay them not, lest my people forget,
   Make them wander to and fro by Thy power, and
      bring them down,
   O Lord our shield.
13. For the sin of their mouth, and the words of their lips,
   Let them even be taken in their pride,
   And for cursing and lying which they speak.
14. Consume them in wrath, consume them, that they be
      no more;
   And let them know that God ruleth in Jacob,
   Unto the ends of the earth.   Selah
15. And they return at evening, they howl like a dog,
   And go round about the city;
16. They wander up and down to devour,

destruction of mine enemies. The same phrase is used in Psalm 54:9, "Mine eye hath gazed upon mine enemies."

12. SLAY THEM NOT . . . MAKE THEM WANDER . . . BRING THEM DOWN. If they were suddenly killed, people would soon forget the lesson implied in their destruction; for the dead are soon forgotten from the heart (Psalm 31:13). Let them therefore be brought to a state of weakness so the righteous may see them constantly and know that the "Lord is our Shield."

13. LET THEM BE TAKEN. Let them be ensnared by the net which they weave.

14. SELAH. As in verse 6, marks a subdivision.

15. LIKE A DOG. The second half of this division begins with the description of the enemies as dogs, just as the second half of the first division began.

16. AND TARRY ALL NIGHT. The dogs, howling and hunting, will continue to do so all night unless they find their prey.

THIS psalm is another of the group whose heading refers to a specific event in the life of David. The heading speaks of the time when "he strove with Aram-naharaim . . . and smote Edom . . . twelve thousand." The events referred to are given in detail in II Samuel 8. There we have a description of David's war with Aram and also his war with Edom. Since both wars

And tarry all night if they have not their fill.

17. But as for me, I will sing of Thy strength;
    Yea, I will sing aloud of Thy mercy in the morning;
    For Thou hast been my high tower,
    And a refuge in the day of my distress.

18. O my strength, unto Thee will I sing praises;
    For God is my high tower, the God of my mercy.

60. FOR THE LEADER; UPON SHUSHAN EDUTH; MICHTAM OF DAVID, TO
    TEACH; 2. WHEN HE STROVE WITH ARAM-NAHARAIM AND WITH
    ARAM-ZOBAH, AND JOAB RETURNED, AND SMOTE OF EDOM IN THE
    VALLEY OF SALT TWELVE THOUSAND.

3. O God, Thou hast cast us off, Thou hast broken us down;
   Thou hast been angry; O restore us.

ended in victory it is a little difficult to understand the dejected
mood of this psalm. The psalmist speaks as if the armies of
Israel had been defeated, and yet the heading as well as the
original narrative in II Samuel 8, both describe decisive victories. Perhaps the explanation is that this psalm was written
between the two campaigns. It is evident from verse 11, "Who
will lead me unto Edom," that the psalm was written *before*
the conquest of Edom referred to in the heading. Since Aram is
in the north (Syria) and Edom to the south, it seems easy to
see what must have occurred. When David attacked the Syrians
the people of Edom must have invaded Judea and it was then
that the psalm was written. This invasion by Edom was, however, repelled and Edom was conquered as the heading indicates.

1. SHUSHAN EDUTH. Literally, the "lily of testimony." In all
likelihood this is the title of a melody to which the psalm was
sung. Ibn Ezra gives this as one of his explanations of the
phrase. His second explanation is that it may be the name of an
instrument. See the same heading (in the plural) in Psalm 80.

MICHTAM. For the explanation of this technical term see
comment to Psalm 16:1.

3. THOU HAST CAST US OFF. This plaint, that God has abandoned Israel, and also the expression in verse 12, "Thou goest not forth with our hosts" are both found in Psalm 44:10,

4. Thou hast made the land to shake, Thou hast cleft it;
   Heal the breaches thereof; for it tottereth.
5. Thou hast made Thy people to see hard things;
   Thou hast made us to drink the wine of staggering.
6. Thou hast given a banner to them that fear Thee,
   That it may be displayed because of the truth.   Selah
7. That Thy beloved may be delivered,
   Save with Thy right hand, and answer me.
8. God spoke in His holiness, that I would exult;
   That I would divide Shechem, and mete out the valley
      of Succoth.
9. Gilead is mine, and Manasseh is mine;

"Yet Thou hast cast off, and goest not forth with our hosts."

4. THE LAND TO SHAKE. The psalmist often speaks of the destruction caused by invading armies as if it were the result of a great natural calamity. Here the invasion (presumably of the armies of Edom) is described as if it were an earthquake. God, by permitting the invasion to take place, has "made the land to shake." A similar expression is found in Psalm 46:3, "though the mountains be moved into the heart of the seas," etc.

5. HARD THINGS. Calamities difficult to endure.

WINE OF STAGGERING. The cup of heavy wine which makes the drinker helpless and ridiculous. The same expression is used a number of times in the Bible. Thus, e. g., Isaiah 51:17, "Thou hast drunken . . . the cup of staggering."

6. THOU HAST GIVEN A BANNER. Though God has punished us, He has also set up a banner around which we can rally.

BECAUSE OF THE TRUTH. The commentator, Ibn Ezra, takes this word "truth" to mean "faith." God has given us a banner because of our faith in Him; but the phrase can mean simply that God has set up a banner in order to vindicate His truth.

7. THY BELOVED. Israel.

8-10. The psalmist recalls the promise of God that David will rule all of Palestine and even surrounding countries.

SHECHEM. Is in the northern part of Palestine.

SUCCOTH. The commentator, Rashi, says that he does not know where this place is. It probably is east of the Jordan.

Ephraim also is the defence of my head;
Judah is my sceptre.

10. Moab is my washpot; upon Edom do I cast my shoe;
Philistia, cry aloud because of me!
11. Who will bring me into the fortified city?
Who will lead me unto Edom?
12. Hast not Thou, O God, cast us off?
And Thou goest not forth, O God, with our hosts.
13. Give us help against the adversary;
For vain is the help of man.
14. Through God we shall do valiantly;
For He it is that will tread down our adversaries.

9. GILEAD. In the northeast.

MANASSEH IS MINE. Half of the tribe of Manasseh settled in Gilead.

EPHRAIM . . . THE DEFENCE OF MY HEAD; JUDAH MY SCEPTRE. The strong tribe of Ephraim will be my defense while the dominion will center in my tribe of Judah.

10. The verse deals with the surrounding lands.

MOAB MY WASHPOT; UPON EDOM DO I CAST MY SHOE. Both expressions describe the complete conquest of these two countries. The commentator, Ibn Ezra, says it means that Moab will be washed clean, i. e., of its possessions; and Kimchi says that "cast my shoe" means, "I shall tread Edom under foot." It may be that both expressions refer to the menial service which the captives will perform. One will bring my washing pot and to the other I will fling my shoes as I take them off.

CRY ALOUD. In terror.

11. Here the psalmist turns from a vision of his future conquest to the actual task in hand. Edom must be conquered and he asks, who will show me how to enter the fortified cities of Edom?

14. WE SHALL DO VALIANTLY. We shall do battle like heroes. The same phrase is used of God Himself in Psalm 118:15, "the right hand of the Lord doeth valiantly."

FOR HE IT IS. Our victories are not due to our own strength. It is God Who is the Master of history.

61. FOR THE LEADER; WITH STRING-MUSIC. [A PSALM] OF DAVID.
2. Hear my cry, O God;
    Attend unto my prayer.
3. From the end of the earth will I call unto Thee, when
    my heart fainteth;
    Lead me to a rock that is too high for me.
4. For Thou hast been a refuge for me,
    A tower of strength in the face of the enemy.
5. I will dwell in Thy Tent for ever;

*T*HE psalmist, far away from the sanctuary, longs for the Divine habitation. He anticipates the day when he will again be in the sanctuary and "sing praise" and "daily perform my vows." The yearning for the sanctuary expressed in this psalm is also the theme of Psalm 42, "When shall I come and appear before God?" (verse 3). This psalm also contains a prayer for the welfare of the king. Such a prayer constitutes the chief theme of Psalm 21.

It is difficult to think of this psalm as being written by David. He would hardly speak of himself in the third person thus: "Mayest Thou add days unto the king's days." It is for this reason, and also because of the fact that sentence 8 contains a prayer that the king be enthroned *forever* that the Aramaic translation (the Targum) offers the explanation that the king referred to is the messianic king.

3. FROM THE END OF THE EARTH WILL I CALL. Because of this phrase the commentator, Kimchi, offers the explanation that the psalm may refer to Israel in exile. However, the psalmist may have visualized David in the land of the Philistines, far from Jerusalem.

A ROCK . . . TOO HIGH FOR ME. Too high for me to climb without Thine aid.

5. I WILL DWELL IN THY TENT FOR EVER . . . THE COVERT OF THY WINGS. This verse combines two of the psalmist's most beautiful descriptions of God's protection. The phrase, "I will dwell in Thy tent for ever," recalls the closing verse of Psalm

I will take refuge in the covert of Thy wings.   Selah
6. For Thou, O God, hast heard my vows;
   Thou hast granted the heritage of those that fear
      Thy name.
7. Mayest Thou add days unto the king's days!
   May his years be as many generations!
8. May he be enthroned before God for ever!
   Appoint mercy and truth, that they may preserve him.
9. So will I sing praise unto Thy name for ever,
   That I may daily perform my vows.

23: "And I shall dwell in the house of the Lord for ever."

6. THE HERITAGE OF THOSE THAT FEAR THY NAME. The wicked will not long possess their wealth and power. The righteous will ultimately inherit the earth. Here, the psalmist anticipates as if it were an accomplished fact that God has already bestowed the heritage due to those who revere His name. We find the same thought expressed in Psalm 37:9, "For evil-doers shall be cut off; but those that wait for the Lord, they shall inherit the land."

7-8. A prayer asking long life for the king. The phrase, "May he be enthroned before God for ever," led the Aramaic translation (the Targum) to assume that this must refer to the messianic king whose reign will be eternal. However, to ask eternal life for a king was a prevailing and almost a formal custom. Thus, the Chaldeans, speaking to King Nebuchadnezzar, said: "O king, live for ever" (Daniel 2:4). This phrase, "enthroned forever," may also refer to the promise which God made to David that his dynasty will endure forever. This explanation is supported by the following sentence: "Appoint mercy and truth that they may preserve him." In II Samuel 7, when God, through the prophet Nathan makes the promise of a perpetual dynasty to David, He says: "My mercy shall not depart from him" (verse 15).

9. The closing sentence reverts to the psalmist's hope to return to the sanctuary where he will praise God's name in prayer and fulfill the vows which he had made.

62. FOR THE LEADER; FOR JEDUTHUN. A PSALM OF DAVID.

2. Only for God doth my soul wait in stillness;
   From Him cometh my salvation.
3. He only is my rock and my salvation,
   My high tower, I shall not be greatly moved.
4. How long will ye set upon a man,
   That ye may slay him, all of you,
   As a leaning wall, a tottering fence?
5. They only devise to thrust him down from his height, delighting
   in lies;
   They bless with their mouth, but they curse inwardly.   Selah

A DECLARATION of confidence in God. Though his enemies conspire against him he waits patiently for God's help. Only God's help can be relied upon. Human power and material wealth are but as "vanity."

The psalm is closely related in thought to Psalm 49. There, too, the transiency of wealth is pointed out and God is described as our only Redemption. The phrase in Psalm 49:3, "both low" (in Hebrew, *b'nai adam*) "and high" (in Hebrew, *b'nai ish*), is used also in this psalm, verse 10.

1. FOR JEDUTHUN. Jeduthun is mentioned in I Chronicles 16:42, as one of David's Levitical musicians.

2. WAIT IN STILLNESS. This thought, that man should wait patiently and quietly for God's help, is frequently expressed in the more personal psalms. It is also found in the Book of Lamentations 3:26, "It is good that a man should quietly wait for the salvation of the Lord."

3. I SHALL NOT BE GREATLY MOVED. I may find sorrow but I shall not be completely overthrown. The same thought is expressed in Psalm 37:24, "Though he fall, he shall not be utterly cast down."

4. This verse is addressed to his enemies.

WILL YE SET UPON A MAN? The Hebrew verb for "set" is a difficult one. The commentator, Rashi, takes it to mean, how long will ye conspire? As translated here it means, how long will ye maliciously attack?

164

6. Only for God wait thou in stillness, my soul;
   For from Him cometh my hope.
7. He only is my rock and my salvation,
   My high tower, I shall not be moved.
8. Upon God resteth my salvation and my glory;
   The rock of my strength, and my refuge, is in God.
9. Trust in Him at all times, ye people;
   Pour out your heart before Him;
   God is a refuge for us.   Selah
10. Men of low degree are vanity, and men of high degree are a lie;
    If they be laid in the balances, they are together lighter than
    vanity.

AS A LEANING WALL, A TOTTERING FENCE. As if your victim
were a wall about to fall down.

5. BLESS . . . CURSE. The familiar description of his enemies
as hypocrites. See Psalm 28:3, "who speak peace with their
neighbors, but evil is in their hearts."

SELAH. Marks the end of the first of the three stanzas. The
second stanza begins with the same sentence as the first and
speaks of God as "rock," "salvation," "high tower," "glory,"
"refuge."

9. POUR OUT YOUR HEART. The rich imaginativeness of biblical literature frequently translates a common physical action
into a high spiritual expression. Thus, the lifting of the hands,
a gesture in the sacrificial ritual, becomes the gesture of prayer.
The tearing of the garments as a physical sign of mourning becomes the spiritual exercise of sincere contrition. Thus, Joel
2:13, "rend your heart, and not your garments, and turn unto
the Lord." Here, too, the ritual of pouring out the libations at
the altar becomes a symbol for the uninhibited utterance of the
soul, "Pour out your heart before Him."

10. The third stanza declares that there is no sure reliance
except in God.

LOW DEGREE, HIGH DEGREE . . . LIGHTER THAN VANITY. You
cannot trust in the help of human beings whether they be humble or great. They cannot be of permanent help. If they were
put into one pan of a balance and nothing in the other (the

165

11. Trust not in oppression,
     And put not vain hope in robbery;
     If riches increase, set not your heart thereon.
12. God hath spoken once,
     Twice have I heard this:
     That strength belongeth unto God;
13. Also unto Thee, O Lord, belongeth mercy;
     For Thou renderest to every man according
        to his work.

text says: "vanity" or a "breath") the vanity or the nothingness would outweigh them all.

11. TRUST NOT in violence or in wealth. In what then can we trust? The answer is given in the last two sentences.

12. ONCE ... TWICE. It is a Hebrew idiom characteristic particularly of proverbial language to mention a number and then increase it by one. Thus, in Proverbs 6:16, "There are six things which the Lord hateth, yea, seven which are an abomination unto Him." Also Proverbs 30:15, "There are three things that are never satisfied, yea, four that say not: 'enough.'" So here in the psalm: "God hath spoken once, twice have I heard this." The two things which the psalmist has heard are, first, "strength belongeth unto God," and, "unto Thee belongeth mercy."

13. TO EVERY MAN ACCORDING TO HIS WORK. This connects with the opening sentence. I wait for the Lord in patient silence because I know that God will defeat the wicked and give every man the due reward for his work.

The American naturalist, John Burroughs, expresses the same thought in his poem, "Waiting":

> Serene I fold my hands and wait
> For lo mine own shall come to me.

ANOTHER psalm whose heading refers to a specific event in the life of David. The heading reads: "When he was in the wilderness of Judah." The commentators are in doubt as to exactly which event this statement refers. If it refers to the

63. A PSALM OF DAVID, WHEN HE WAS IN THE WILDERNESS OF JUDAH.

2. O God, Thou art my God, earnestly will I seek Thee;
   My soul thirsteth for Thee, my flesh longeth for Thee,
   In a dry and weary land, where no water is.
3. So have I looked for Thee in the sanctuary,
   To see Thy power and Thy glory.
4. For Thy lovingkindness is better than life;
   My lips shall praise Thee.

period of his flight from Saul, as Kimchi takes it, then the sentence in verse 12, "The king shall rejoice in God" presents a difficulty since David was not yet king at the time and it is hardly likely that the psalmist would be praising King Saul from whose presence David was fleeing for his life. Therefore, Kimchi takes verse 12 to mean: he who *deserves* to be king (i. e. David) will rejoice in God. Rashi, however, takes the blessing in verse 12 to refer to David *after* he became king. In that case, the heading, "when he was in the wilderness of Judah," must refer to an event during David's own reign. This could only have been when he fled from Jerusalem during Absalom's revolt.

The psalm is closely connected in mood and thought with Psalm 61 and expresses the longing to be in God's house. Like Psalm 61, it also includes a blessing for the welfare of the king. The psalm is likewise akin in thought and language to Psalm 42. The opening metaphor of this psalm, comparing the longing for God to thirst in a dry and parched land, is precisely the metaphor used in the opening of Psalm 42. In fact, some of the phrases are almost identical. Thus, "My soul thirsteth for Thee," is used in Psalm 63:2, and "My soul thirsteth for God," in Psalm 42:3.

2. IN A DRY AND WEARY LAND. A vivid expression. A land parched by the sun and listless in the heat.

3. SO HAVE I LOOKED. As one longs for the water brooks in a parched land so have I looked for Thee.

3-4. THY POWER AND THY GLORY . . . THY LOVINGKINDNESS. The Bible frequently combines the description of God's might with that of His gentleness, His power with His lovingkindness.

167

5. So will I bless Thee as long as I live;
   In Thy name will I lift up my hands.
6. My soul is satisfied as with marrow and fatness;
   And my mouth doth praise Thee with joyful lips;
7. When I remember Thee upon my couch,
   And meditate on Thee in the night-watches.
8. For Thou hast been my help,
   And in the shadow of Thy wings do I rejoice.
9. My soul cleaveth unto Thee;

Thus, here, both the stern and the kindly virtues are mentioned together. So, too, in the preceding psalm (verses 12 and 13), "strength belongeth unto God, also unto Thee belongeth mercy." The Talmud calls attention to this blending of Divine attributes in biblical literature and says (b. Megillah 31 a), "Wherever you find God's greatness mentioned there also you find His gentleness."

4. THY LOVINGKINDNESS IS BETTER THAN LIFE. It is interesting to observe the variety of interpretations given to this passage. The Aramaic translation (the Targum) says: "Better is the life in the world to come which in Thy lovingkindness Thou givest to the righteous than the life (of material pleasure) which Thou givest to the wicked in this world." The commentator, Kimchi, gives a philosophic interpretation: Better is the intelligence which in Thy lovingkindness Thou bestowest upon man than the physical life which Thou givest to all animal creation. Ibn Ezra says: Better even than life is Thy lovingkindness in dwelling in the midst of Israel. If Ibn Ezra's comment be taken in an individual rather than a communal sense the verse would mean: Thy lovingkindness in giving us communion with Thee is more precious than life itself.

5. IN THY NAME WILL I LIFT UP MY HANDS. In prayer. To call upon God's name, to pray in God's name, or to call upon or to pray to God. However, when the passage in Deuteronomy 10:20, speaks of swearing in God's name, it means literally, to use His name alone in oaths and not the name of any other god. "Him thou shalt serve; and by His name shalt thou swear."

6. MY SOUL IS SATISFIED AS WITH MARROW AND FATNESS. In

Thy right hand holdeth me fast.
10. But those that seek my soul, to destroy it,
   Shall go into the nethermost parts of the earth.
11. They shall be hurled to the power of the sword;
   They shall be a portion for foxes.
12. But the king shall rejoice in God;
   Every one that sweareth by Him shall glory;
   For the mouth of them that speak lies shall
      be stopped.

this verse the marrow and fatness of the sacrificial animal is used to indicate a spiritual satisfaction of the soul. In Psalm 36:9, the flesh of the sacrifice is similarly used as a metaphor for spiritual satisfaction, "They are abundantly satisfied with the fatness of Thy house."

7. WHEN I REMEMBER THEE UPON MY COUCH . . . IN THE NIGHT-WATCHES. The psalmist frequently speaks of his prayerful meditations in the watches of the night.

IN THE NIGHT-WATCHES. In biblical times the night was divided into three watches (not four as in Roman times). See Judges 7:19, which speaks of the "middle watch."

8. MY SOUL . . . THY RIGHT HAND. The commentator, Ibn Ezra, connects both halves of this verse as follows: My soul can maintain its loyalty to Thee because Thy right hand helps me. God aids us in our faith.

10. THE NETHERMOST PARTS OF THE EARTH. To the underworld, the abode of death.

11. A PORTION FOR FOXES. Or jackals, which prey upon the battlefield.

12. The king and all who invoke God's name shall "rejoice" and "glory," but falsehood shall be permanently defeated.

THE psalmist asks God in Psalm 64 to preserve him from the conspiracy of evil-doers. He is confident that God will requite the wicked and that the righteous, seeing the downfall of the wicked, will perceive God's moral government of the world. The thought of this psalm is found in many previous psalms.

64. FOR THE LEADER. A PSALM OF DAVID.

2. Hear my voice, O God, in my complaint;
Preserve my life from the terror of the enemy.
3. Hide me from the council of evil-doers;
From the tumult of the workers of iniquity;
4. Who have whet their tongue like a sword,
And have aimed their arrow, a poisoned word;
5. That they may shoot in secret places at the blameless;
Suddenly do they shoot at him, and fear not.
6. They encourage one another in an evil matter;
They converse of laying snares secretly;
They ask, who would see them.

3. THE TUMULT OF THE WORKERS OF INIQUITY. The Hebrew word for "tumult" used here implies a crowd, a mob.

4. A SWORD . . . THEIR ARROW. A frequent metaphor, comparing the slanderous words to a murderous weapon. See Psalm 55:22, "His words . . . were keen-edged swords."

5. AND FEAR NOT. The wicked seem to have no fear of Divine punishment.

6. THEY ASK, WHO WOULD SEE THEM. The psalmist frequently ascribes this thought to the wicked. The wicked believes that there is no God to see, to hear or to punish. The same thought is used in Psalm 59:8, "Behold, they belch out with their mouth 'for who doth hear?' "

7. THEY SEARCH OUT INIQUITIES . . . IN THE INWARD THOUGHT. They seek to invent new ways of harming the innocent.

8. God's punishment fits their crime. Since they "aim their arrow" (verse 4) "suddenly" (verse 5) "God doth shoot at them with an arrow suddenly" (verse 8). Some of the commentators take the word, "suddenly," as applying to the next phrase. Thus, sudden are their wounds, but as translated it means: "Thence (i. e., from God) are their wounds."

9. THEIR OWN TONGUES A STUMBLING. They are trapped by their own conspiracy.

SHAKE THE HEAD. In derision. The same thought is found in Psalm 22:8, "They that see me laugh me to scorn . . . they shake the head."

7. They search out iniquities, they have accomplished a diligent search;
   Even in the inward thought of every one, and the deep heart.
8. But God doth shoot at them with an arrow suddenly;
   Thence are their wounds.
9. So they make their own tongue a stumbling unto themselves;
   All that see them shake the head.
10. And all men fear;
   And they declare the work of God,
   And understand His doing.
11. The righteous shall be glad in the Lord, and shall take refuge in Him;
   And all the upright in heart shall glory.

Psalm 64

11

10. AND ALL MEN FEAR. All will be awe-struck at God's punishment of the wicked. They will "understand His doing"; they will be convinced that God's justice rules the world.

11. THE UPRIGHT IN HEART SHALL GLORY. The same thought is found at the end of the preceding psalm. "Everyone that sweareth by Him shall glory" (Psalm 63:12).

A PSALM of thanksgiving. God has abundantly blessed the earth. The harvest is plentiful. The people have gathered in the sanctuary, waiting to begin their praise to God. The vision of the psalmist extends beyond the prosperity of his own people: he speaks of "God as the confidence of all the ends of the earth," and visualizes "all flesh" coming to worship God. This vision has found noble expression in the medieval poem recited in the Additional Services of the New Year.

> All the world shall come to serve Thee
> And bless Thy glorious Name
> And Thy righteousness triumphant
> The islands shall acclaim.
> . . . .
> With the coming of Thy Kingdom
> The hills shall break into song.
> And the islands laugh exultant
> That they to God belong.
> *Translated by* ZANGWILL.

171

65. FOR THE LEADER. A PSALM. A SONG OF DAVID.

2. Praise waiteth for Thee, O God, in Zion;
   And unto Thee the vow is performed.
3. O Thou that hearest prayer,
   Unto Thee doth all flesh come.
4. The tale of iniquities is too heavy for me;
   As for our transgressions, Thou wilt pardon them.
5. Happy is the man whom Thou choosest, and
      bringest near,
   That he may dwell in Thy courts;
   May we be satisfied with the goodness of Thy house,
   The holy place of Thy temple!

1. A PSALM, A SONG. These two words found in the heading
of many psalms are not quite synonymous. The word *mizmor* is
used in the heading of fifty-seven psalms. It literally means an
"instrumental melody" and has come to be applied technically
to the Psalms and rarely occurs elsewhere in the Bible. It is,
therefore, translated simply "a psalm."

The word *shir* generally occurs in connection with the word
mizmor. It simply means, a "song," and is applied frequently in
the Bible to secular songs as well as to sacred ones. While *mizmor*, translated "a psalm," implies instrumental music, *shir*,
translated "a song," implies vocal music.

2. PRAISE WAITETH FOR THEE. The Aramaic translation (the
Targum) and the commentator, Rashi, connect this verse with
Psalm 62:2, "Only for God doth my soul wait in stillness." The
word for "waiteth," in Psalm 65:2, and the word for "stillness,"
in Psalm 62:2, come from the same Hebrew root. Hence, both
the Targum and Rashi take this verse to mean, silence is praise
to Thee O God; which Rashi amplifies by saying that no
amount of words can ever express the full praise of God. Hence,
even silence is worship. But Ibn Ezra takes it as translated here
and understands the phrase to mean that the congregation is
assembled in the Temple (i. e. for the harvest festival) and is
waiting for the service to begin so that they may utter their
praise of God.

6. With wondrous works dost Thou answer us in
     righteousness,
   O God of our salvation;
   Thou the confidence of all the ends of the earth,
   And of the far distant seas;
7. Who by Thy strength settest fast the mountains,
   Who art girded about with might;
8. Who stillest the roaring of the seas, the roaring of their waves,
   And the tumult of the peoples;
9. So that they that dwell in the uttermost parts stand in awe of
     Thy signs;
   Thou makest the outgoings of the morning and evening to
   rejoice.

3. UNTO THEE DOTH ALL FLESH COME. All mankind shall, some day, come to the Sanctuary on Zion to praise the Lord. Thus, Isaiah 2:3, "And many peoples shall go and say: Come ye, let us go . . . to the house of the God of Jacob." Also Isaiah 56:7, "Their sacrifices shall be acceptable upon Mine altar; for My house shall be called a house of prayer for all peoples."

4. THE TALE OF INIQUITIES. The number of my iniquities. Although our iniquities make us unworthy to appear in God's House, God will pardon us, and, therefore: (verse 5) "Happy is the man whom *Thou* . . . bringest near that he may dwell in Thy courts."

6. THE CONFIDENCE OF . . . ALL THE EARTH. All mankind must rely upon God's support. For (verse 7), He is the Master of nature; He establishes the mountains, and (verse 8) controls the sea and the tumultuous violence of the nations. Therefore (verse 9), "they that dwell in the uttermost parts stand in awe of Thy signs" (i. e., of the signs of Thy majesty).

9. THE OUTGOINGS OF THE MORNING AND EVENING. East and west, the whole world. Thus, Psalm 113:3, "From the rising of the sun unto the going down thereof the Lord's name is to be praised." (See also Malachi 1:11): "From the rising of the sun even unto the going down of the same, My name is great among the nations, and in every place offerings are presented unto My name."

173

Psalm 65

10

10. Thou hast remembered the earth, and watered her,
        greatly enriching her,
    With the river of God that is full of water;
    Thou preparest them corn, for so preparest Thou her.
11. Watering her ridges abundantly,
    Settling down the furrows thereof,
    Thou makest her soft with showers;
    Thou blessest the growth thereof.
12. Thou crownest the year with Thy goodness;
    And Thy paths drop fatness.
13. The pastures of the wilderness do drop;
    And the hills are girded with joy.
14. The meadows are clothed with flocks;
    The valleys also are covered over with corn;
    They shout for joy, yea, they sing.

66. FOR THE LEADER. A SONG, A PSALM.

10-14. A vivid description of the bountiful blessings which God bestows upon the earth. He sends plentiful rain; the pastures are crowded with flocks and the valleys covered with corn.

10. THE RIVER OF GOD. Namely, the rain from heaven.

12. THY PATHS DROP FATNESS. A bold metaphor of God walking through the world and wherever He goes the earth is enriched. Kimchi says: "The clouds which are God's pathways drop fatness" (i. e. rain).

13. THE PASTURES OF THE WILDERNESS. The wilderness does not mean the desert but the uncultivated pasture land. Thus, Jeremiah 23:10, "The pastures of the wilderness are dried up."

13-14. THE HILLS ARE GIRDED WITH JOY . . . THEY SHOUT FOR JOY, YEA, THEY SING. Nature, blessed by God, rejoices aloud. The same thought is expressed in Psalm 96:12, "Let the field exult and all that is therein; then shall all the trees of the wood sing for joy."

ANOTHER psalm of thanksgiving for God's bountiful gifts and for His protection to Israel. The psalm ends with the same thought with which the preceding psalm began. Psalm 65 began

174

Shout unto God, all the earth;
2. Sing praises unto the glory of His name;
   Make His praise glorious.
3. Say unto God: 'How tremendous is Thy work!
   Through the greatness of Thy power shall Thine
      enemies dwindle away before Thee.
4. All the earth shall worship Thee,
   And shall sing praises unto Thee;
   They shall sing praises to Thy name.'   Selah
5. Come, and see the works of God;
   He is terrible in His doing toward the children of men.
6. He turned the sea into dry land;
   They went through the river on foot;
   There let us rejoice in Him!
7. Who ruleth by His might for ever;
   His eyes keep watch upon the nations;
   Let not the rebellious exalt themselves.   Selah

with the realization that our sins hinder us from praising God with a whole heart and that, therefore, God forgives us so that He may bring us near to His courts. Psalm 66 ends with the same idea: "If I had regarded iniquity in my heart, the Lord would not hear."

Both psalms are universal in spirit: Psalm 65:3, "Unto Thee doth all flesh come"; Psalm 66:4, "All the earth shall worship Thee."

1. This psalm and the succeeding psalm are not ascribed to David although they have the same heading: "A song, a Psalm" as Psalm 65, to which heading Psalm 65 adds "of David."

1-4. The introductory invocaton of the psalm. It calls upon all the earth to join in praise and worship of God.

3. THINE ENEMIES DWINDLE. The Hebrew word used for "dwindle" also means "to deceive." Therefore, the older commentators, Kimchi, Rashi, and Ibn Ezra, take this phrase to mean: thine enemies will confess their former falsehoods. But the present translation gives this phrase the same meaning which is given to the identical phrase in Psalm 18:45, "the sons of the stranger dwindle away before me."

5-7. Begins the main thought of the psalm. The psalmist

175

8. Bless our God, ye peoples,
   And make the voice of His praise to be heard;
9. Who hath set our soul in life,
   And suffered not our foot to be moved.
10. For Thou, O God, hast tried us;
    Thou hast refined us, as silver is refined.
11. Thou didst bring us into the hold;
    Thou didst lay constraint upon our loins.
12. Thou hast caused men to ride over our heads;
    We went through fire and through water;
    But Thou didst bring us out unto abundance.
13. I will come into Thy house with burnt-offerings,

speaks of God's achievement in the history of Israel.

5. TERRIBLE IN HIS DOING. Awe-inspiring in His works.

6. THE SEA INTO DRY LAND . . . THE RIVER ON FOOT. The Red Sea. The "river" would seem to refer to the Jordan which the children of Israel crossed on foot in the time of Joshua. However, the "river" need not necessarily refer to the Jordan since the balanced style of the Psalms frequently requires a verbal variation from one line of the couplet to the other. Hence, in spite of the use of the word "river," both lines of the couplet may well refer to the Red Sea which the people of Israel crossed on foot.

7. That event in Jewish history is generalized into a declaration of God's rulership over all nations.

HIS EYES KEEP WATCH. God knows all the events in the lives of the nations. Therefore, "Let not the rebellious exalt themselves." The same thought is expressed in Psalm 33:13, "The Lord looketh from heaven; He beholdeth all the sons of men."

8-12. Is a generalized characterization of Jewish history. Through our sufferings, though we went through fire and water (verse 12), God has "set our soul in life" (verse 9), and "refined us" (verse 10) by the flames of suffering.

9. OUR FOOT TO BE MOVED. He has kept us from stumbling and falling. The same phrase is found in Psalm 121:3, "He will not suffer thy foot to be moved."

10. REFINED US, AS SILVER IS REFINED. This metaphor is fre-

176

I will perform unto Thee my vows,
14. Which my lips have uttered,
And my mouth hath spoken, when I was in distress.
15. I will offer unto Thee burnt-offerings of fatlings,
With the sweet smoke of rams;
I will offer bullocks with goats.   Selah
16. Come, and hearken, all ye that fear God,
And I will declare what He hath done for my soul.
17. I cried unto Him with my mouth,
And He was extolled with my tongue.
18. If I had regarded iniquity in my heart,
The Lord would not hear;

quently found in the Bible. God purifies Israel in the furnace of suffering. Thus, Zechariah 13:9, "I will bring the third part (of Israel) through the fire, and will refine them as silver is refined."

11. INTO THE HOLD. Into the net or dungeon.

CONSTRAINT. A weight or a shackle. The whole sentence describes Israel as captured and imprisoned.

12. MEN TO RIDE OVER OUR HEADS. The Egyptian monuments show pictures of the conqueror riding in his chariot over the bodies of his captives.

THROUGH FIRE AND THROUGH WATER. Fire and flood are symbols of extreme danger. The same expression is found in Isaiah 43:2, "When thou passest through the waters, I will be with thee, when thou walkest through the fire, thou shalt not be burned."

13-15. I will fulfill all my vows unto God and bring to His altar all the offerings which I had promised in the days of my distress.

16-20. Declares that all these sacrificial offerings become meaningful only when accompanied by sincere prayer and purity of heart. Therefore, verse 16 speaks of what God has done "for my soul." I pray to Him and extol Him but if my prayers had not been sincere He would not have listened. "If I had regarded iniquity in my heart, the Lord would not hear" (verse 18).

177

19. But verily God hath heard;
He hath attended to the voice of my prayer.
20. Blessed be God,
Who hath not turned away my prayer, nor His mercy
from me.

67. FOR THE LEADER; WITH STRING-MUSIC. A PSALM, A SONG.

2. God be gracious unto us, and bless us;
May He cause His face to shine toward us;   Selah
3. That Thy way may be known upon earth,
Thy salvation among all nations.

19. BUT GOD HATH HEARD. To be understood in the sense of
Psalm 65:4, that God has forgiven whatever iniquities there
were in my heart and therefore has now heard my prayer. For
this reason the psalmist ends with a blessing to God for having
bestowed "His mercy" and "not turned away my prayer."

THE third of the three thanksgiving hymns. Like the preceding ones it thanks God for the bounties of nature and turns
to all mankind to join in worship of Him. The fact that there
are three thanksgiving psalms, each dealing with the theme of
the harvest, naturally suggests the three harvest festivals, Passover, Shabuoth, and Succoth. It would, however, be difficult
definitely to ascribe each psalm to one particular holiday. It
seems probable, however, that the second of the three, Psalm
66, was intended for Passover inasmuch as it speaks of the Red
Sea (verse 6). In that case, Psalm 67, the third, can well be a
Shabuoth hymn, since it uses the priestly blessing in such a way
as to suggest God's revelation at Mount Sinai. At all events, it
would not be inappropriate for that festival. The first of the
three psalms, 65, would then be for Succoth, which is not unlikely since Succoth came at the end of the year, and the psalm
speaks of "crowning the year with Thy goodness" (verse 12).
Thus, we would have all three of the psalms of thanksgiving
in their calendar order. For Succoth, at the end (and the beginning) of the year, Psalm 65; for Passover, Psalm 66; for

4. Let the peoples give thanks unto Thee, O God;
   Let the peoples give thanks unto Thee, all of them.
5. O let the nations be glad and sing for joy;
   For Thou wilt judge the peoples with equity,
   And lead the nations upon earth.   Selah
6. Let the peoples give thanks unto Thee, O God;
   Let the peoples give thanks unto Thee, all of them.
7. The earth hath yielded her increase;
   May God, our own God, bless us.
8. May God bless us;
   And let all the ends of the earth fear Him.

Shabuoth, Psalm 67. But this, of course, is only conjectural.

2. GOD BE GRACIOUS . . . CAUSE HIS FACE TO SHINE. The psalmist uses the language of the priestly blessing, Numbers 6:25,
"The Lord make His face to shine upon thee, and be gracious
unto thee."

3. THAT THY WAY MAY BE KNOWN UPON EARTH. When God is
gracious unto Israel, and the effect of His blessing becomes
manifest, and all the world can thus learn and know of His
way and His "salvation."

4-5. Calls upon all nations to thank God and to rejoice that
He is the Judge of the world and, therefore, "will judge the
peoples with equity."

5. LEAD THE NATIONS UPON EARTH. As a shepherd leads his
flock. The phrase is frequently used of Israel, namely, that God
leads Israel. But here it is used to express the fact that God is
the universal shepherd and all mankind is His flock.

7. MAY GOD, OUR OWN GOD BLESS US. The translation leaves
an unwarranted impression of an emphasis on "our *own* God."
The phrase is simply "the Lord our God." Usually it is written
"*JHWH* our God" but in Book Two the editor prefers
Elohim.

8. THE ENDS OF THE EARTH FEAR HIM. Those who fear the
Lord, i. e., revere Him, became a technical phrase for all the
non-Jews who accepted the worship of God. The sentence,
therefore, means, let all the peoples of the earth come to worship Him.

179

Psalm 68

68. FOR THE LEADER. A PSALM OF DAVID, A SONG.

2. Let God arise, let His enemies be scattered;
   And let them that hate Him flee before Him.
3. As smoke is driven away, so drive them away;
   As wax melteth before the fire,
   So let the wicked perish at the presence of God.
4. But let the righteous be glad, let them exult
     before God;
   Yea, let them rejoice with gladness.

A MAJESTIC psalm describing God's work in the life of Israel and in the history of all nations. It visualizes God manifesting Himself on earth, leading Israel to Canaan, choosing Mount Zion as His dwelling place, conquering the Canaanitish nations, and finally accepting the homage of all peoples. Although the text of the psalm is in a number of places difficult, the sequence of thought is clear and logical. Verses 1-7 constitute a prologue depicting the manifestation of God's Presence and asking the people to greet Him with songs of praise. Verses 8-18 describe God's conquest of Canaan and His choice of mount Zion. From verse 18 on, the psalm turns from the past to the future. Verses 18-24 describe God as defeating His enemies; verse 25 to the end: Israel and all nations praise Him.

There is a wide difference of opinion among scholars as to the date of this psalm headed, "of David." Some believe that it is really of Davidic origin. Some place it even earlier and point out the resemblance between the latter part of the psalm and the early biblical epics such as the Song of Deborah (Judges 5). Others place it as late as the Maccabean period. In fact, the psalm could well have been written at any time between the days of David and the Maccabean period. Its general mood is somewhat akin to that of Deutero-Isaiah (Isaiah 40-55), namely, that God will manifest His Presence, that He will save His people, and win all nations to His service.

2. LET GOD ARISE . . . ETC. Except for a change from the second to the third person, this verse is identical with the verse in

5. Sing unto God, sing praises to His name;
Extol Him that rideth upon the skies, whose name is the LORD;
And exult ye before Him.
6. A father of the fatherless, and a judge of the widows,
Is God in His holy habitation.
7. God maketh the solitary to dwell in a house;
He bringeth out the prisoners into prosperity;
The rebellious dwell but in a parched land.
8. O God, when Thou wentest forth before Thy people,
When Thou didst march through the wilderness; Selah

Numbers recited when the ark moved forward. The sentence
there is, "Rise up, O Lord, and let Thine enemies be scattered,
and let them that hate Thee flee before Thee." (Numbers
10:35.)

3. SMOKE . . . WAX. Describing the rapid dispersal of the enemies before God. The rapid melting of wax is used even of
mountains "melting away before God." Thus, Psalm 97:5,
"The mountains melted like wax at the presence of the Lord."

5. RIDETH UPON THE SKIES. In poetic imagery God is visualized as riding in His chariot above the skies.

6. A FATHER OF THE FATHERLESS . . . IS GOD IN HIS HOLY
HABITATION. Although God is imaginatively described as riding
in splendor through the heavens, the psalmist never fails to
think of Him as manifested on earth in the Temple, on Mount
Zion (His holy habitation), and as an ethical spirit in the lives
of men, "Father of the fatherless," etc. The fatherless and the
widow were considered to be God's especial care. The biblical
legislation (Exodus 22:21), provides for their protection. God
is frequently described as taking up the cause of these unfortu-
nates. Thus, Psalm 10:14, "Thou hast been the helper of the
fatherless."

7. THE SOLITARY TO DWELL IN A HOUSE . . . BRINGETH OUT THE
PRISONERS. God finds a home for the homeless and brings freedom to the captives, while the rebellious will dwell as in a
"parched land."

8. Here the thought changes and the psalmist sketches the

181

9. The earth trembled, the heavens also dropped at the presence of God;
   Even yon Sinai trembled at the presence of God, the God of Israel.
10. A bounteous rain didst Thou pour down, O God;
   When Thine inheritance was weary, Thou didst confirm it.
11. Thy flock settled therein;
   Thou didst prepare in Thy goodness for the poor, O God.
12. The LORD giveth the word;
   The women that proclaim the tidings are a great host.

beginnings of Israel's history, telling that God brought the people through the desert into the Promised Land.

THOU WENTEST BEFORE THY PEOPLE. God led them with pillars of fire and cloud.

SELAH. Here, *Selah* does not mark the end of a thought but is presumably a musical notation calling for a triumphant flourish of a trumpet.

9. THE EARTH TREMBLED. The earthquakes and the storms which herald God's appearance upon earth.

10. THINE INHERITANCE. The people, Israel, is frequently described as God's inheritance. Thus, Deuteronomy 9:29, "Yet they are Thy people and Thine inheritance."

11. THY FLOCK. Israel.

THE POOR. The psalmist means either the humble who are often referred to in the Psalms as being under God's special protection, or the people of Israel who had lived for forty years in the wilderness.

12. Here follows a description of God's conquest of Canaan.

GIVETH THE WORD. God commands the victory. At God's word the land was won.

THE WOMEN THAT PROCLAIM THE TIDINGS. The women stayed at home, proclaimed the tidings of victory, and sang songs of triumph. Thus, I Samuel 18:6-7, "When David returned from the slaughter of the Philistine, the women came out of all the cities of Israel, singing and dancing, to meet King Saul with timbrels, with joy, and with three-stringed instruments."

13. KINGS OF ARMIES. The Canaanitish kings.

13. Kings of armies flee, they flee;
    And she that tarrieth at home divideth the spoil.
14. When ye lie among the sheepfolds,
    The wings of the dove are covered with silver,
    And her pinions with the shimmer of gold.
15. When the Almighty scattereth kings therein,
    It snoweth in Zalmon.
16. A mountain of God is the mountain of Bashan;
    A mountain of peaks is the mountain of Bashan.
17. Why look ye askance, ye mountains of peaks,

SHE THAT TARRIETH AT HOME. The women divide the spoils.

14. WHEN YE LIE . . . THE WINGS OF THE DOVE . . . HER PINIONS. This verse is difficult to interpret. The first line, "when ye lie among the sheepfolds," is taken from the rebuke which Deborah uttered against the tribe of Reuben for refusing to join in the battle against Sisera. Judges 5:16, "Why sattest thou among the sheepfolds?" The rest of the verse (wings of the dove, etc.) has been given many explanations. The most likely one, is that the silver and the gold are descriptions of the various valuable objects captured as spoil. The whole sentence would, therefore, mean: why do you stay home when there is all this precious booty to be captured? Another explanation is based upon the fact that the dove is often used as a metaphor for Israel. Hence, the wings of the dove, covered with silver, etc., is a description of Israel's glory. The verse would, therefore, mean: even though you stay among the sheepfolds and do not join in battle, God will, without your aid, make Israel glorious.

15. ZALMON. The name of a mountain mentioned in Judges 9:48.

16-19. God speaks of His preference for Mount Zion over the more majestic mountains of Palestine.

16. A MOUNTAIN OF GOD . . . A MOUNTAIN OF PEAKS IS BASHAN. Bashan (very likely Mount Hermon), is an imposing mountain. It has three peaks, yet God did not select it for His Sanctuary.

17. Addresses the mountains and asks them why are they jealous of Mount Zion and tells them that in spite of their

183

At the mountain which God hath desired for His abode?
Yea, the Lord will dwell therein for ever.
18. The chariots of God are myriads, even thousands upon
thousands;
The Lord is among them, as in Sinai, in holiness.
19. Thou hast ascended on high, Thou hast led captivity
captive;
Thou hast received gifts among men,
Yea, among the rebellious also, that the Lord God might
dwell there.
20. Blessed be the Lord, day by day He beareth our burden,
Even the God who is our salvation.   Selah
21. God is unto us a God of deliverances;
And unto God the Lord belong the issues of death.
22. Surely God will smite through the head of His enemies,
The hairy scalp of him that goeth about in his guiltiness.

looking "askance" at it God "will dwell therein" for ever.

18. The psalm imagery frequently moves to and fro between
visions of God in heaven and God in His earthly habitation.
Thus, verse 18, he speaks of the chariots of God. The myriads
possibly refer to the myriads of angels. Thus, "The Lord came
from Sinai . . . He came from the myriads holy." (Deuteronomy
33:2.)

AS IN SINAI. As God appeared on Mount Sinai in holiness.

19. ASCENDED ON HIGH. Having won the victory, God re-
ascends. Even the rebellious bring Him gifts of submission.

THAT GOD MAY DWELL THERE. When they see the manifestation of God's victorious strength even the rebellious submit so
that God may dwell in their midst as Ruler.

20. Turning from the past to the present and future, the
psalmist says that as in the lives of our fathers, so every day God
"bears our burdens."

21. THE ISSUES OF DEATH. Whether any illness will result in
death or not depends upon God. An analogous phrase is used
in Proverbs 4:23, "Keep thy heart; for out of it are the issues of
life."

22. SURELY GOD WILL SMITE. As God defeated the Canaanit-

184

23. The LORD said: 'I will bring back from Bashan,
   I will bring them back from the depths of the sea;
24. That thy foot may wade through blood,
   That the tongue of thy dogs may have its portion
      from thine enemies.'
25. They see Thy goings, O God,
   Even the goings of my God, my King, in holiness.
26. The singers go before, the minstrels follow after,
   In the midst of damsels playing upon timbrels:
27. 'Bless ye God in full assemblies,
   Even the LORD, ye that are from the fountain of Israel.'
28. There is Benjamin, the youngest, ruling them,
   The princes of Judah their council,
   The princes of Zebulun, the princes of Naphtali.
29. Thy God hath commanded thy strength;
   Be strong, O God, Thou that hast wrought for us

ish kings so will He defeat the violent men of the present and of the future.

23. I WILL BRING BACK FROM BASHAN. The Aramaic translation (the Targum) takes this to mean that in messianic times God will bring back Israel to its home, but Ibn Ezra and Kimchi take this sentence as referring to the enemy. The sentence seems to mean: I will bring back the enemy who are hiding in the mountain land of Bashan and they will be defeated so that "thy foot may wade through blood," etc. A sanguinary image, but typical of an ancient warfare. The same expression is used in Psalm 58:11.

25 ff. A vision of a triumphal procession in which the tribes march united, side by side, led by musicians.

25. THY GOINGS. Means either, Thy way in the world, or, perhaps, Thy triumphant procession.

27. FROM THE FOUNTAIN OF ISRAEL. The commentators understand this to mean: all you who are descendants of Israel.

28. BENJAMIN . . . RULING THEM. Benjamin is mentioned first because Saul, the first king, came from the tribe of Benjamin.

JUDAH, ZEBULUN, NAPHTALI, both southern kingdom and northern kingdom will be united.

185

30. Out of Thy temple at Jerusalem,
    Whither kings shall bring presents unto Thee.
31. Rebuke the wild beast of the reeds,
    The multitude of the bulls, with the calves of the peoples,
    Every one submitting himself with pieces of silver;
    He hath scattered the peoples that delight in war!
32. Nobles shall come out of Egypt;
    Ethiopia shall hasten to stretch out her hands unto God.
33. Sing unto God, ye kingdoms of the earth;
    O sing praises unto the Lord;   Selah
34. To Him that rideth upon the heavens of heavens, which
    are of old;
    Lo, He uttereth His voice, a mighty voice.
35. Ascribe ye strength unto God;
    His majesty is over Israel,

30. THY TEMPLE . . . WHITHER KINGS SHALL BRING PRESENTS. The rulers of the earth will come to do homage to Thee.

31. THE WILD BEAST OF THE REEDS. This seems to refer to the crocodiles in the reeds by the Nile and, therefore, is a metaphor for Egypt.

BULLS AND CALVES. A metaphor for the violent nations. All will submit and pay tribute as a mark of their submission. Having submitted, they will acknowledge God's kingship and worship Him in all the future. Therefore, verse 33, "Sing unto God, ye kingdoms of the earth."

33. SELAH. Here, the word *Selah* does not mark a transition of thought but a musical flourish. This is evident from the fact that the sentence after it is a continuation of the thought of the sentence which precedes it, namely, "Sing praises unto the Lord . . . to Him that rideth."

36. AWFUL IS GOD. Awe-inspiring is God.

BLESSED BE GOD. The psalm ends with a benediction as did Psalm 66. If the two benedictions are taken together they will be seen to describe the attributes of God which usually are combined (in Psalm 68): "Blessed be God who gives strength and power," and (in Psalm 66): "Blessed be God who bestoweth mercy."

And His strength is in the skies.
36. Awful is God out of thy holy places;
The God of Israel, He giveth strength and power
    unto the people;
Blessed be God.

69. FOR THE LEADER; UPON SHOSHANNIM. [A PSALM] OF DAVID.
2. Save me, O God;
For the waters are come in even unto the soul.
3. I am sunk in deep mire, where there is no standing;
I am come into deep waters, and the flood overwhelmeth me.
4. I am weary with my crying; my throat is dried;
Mine eyes fail while I wait for my God.
5. They that hate me without a cause are more than the
    hairs of my head;

A PRAYER for deliverance in time of trouble. The psalmist describes himself as sunk in a miry pit whose waters are threatening to overwhelm him. Because of his misfortunes he has become a byword and a mockery. His enemies seek to destroy him. He asks that God punish them. He looks forward to the time when he will praise God for his own deliverance and for the deliverance of Zion and the cities of Judah.

Because of the thought and the phraseology some modern commentators believe that this psalm was written either by the Prophet Jeremiah or by some disciple writing in his spirit. The description of the deep mire is reminiscent of Jeremiah's imprisonment in the pit. (See Jeremiah 38.) Phrases such as "for Thy sake I have borne reproach" (verse 8), and "Zion and the cities of Judah" (verse 36) are characteristic of the Prophet Jeremiah (Jeremiah 15:15 and 33:10). While it is not unlikely that this psalm was written under the influence of the prophet, yet it is difficult to draw definite conclusions from literary resemblances. The psalm also resembles Psalms 22 and 40.

2. WATERS . . . UNTO THE SOUL. The waters have risen high enough to threaten my life; to take my soul.

3. DEEP MIRE. Thus, Psalm 40:3, "He brought me up . . . out of the miry clay."

187

They that would cut me off, being mine enemies wrongfully,
are many;
Should I restore that which I took not away?
6. O God, Thou knowest my folly;
And my trespasses are not hid from Thee.
7. Let not them that wait for Thee be ashamed through me, O
LORD God of hosts;
Let not those that seek Thee be brought to confusion through
me, O God of Israel.
8. Because for Thy sake I have borne reproach;
Confusion hath covered my face.
9. I am become a stranger unto my brethren,
And an alien unto my mother's children.
10. Because zeal for Thy house hath eaten me up,
And the reproaches of them that reproach Thee are fallen upon
me.
11. And I wept with my soul fasting,
And that became unto me a reproach.
12. I made sackcloth also my garment,
And I became a byword unto them.
13. They that sit in the gate talk of me;
And I am the song of the drunkards.
14. But as for me, let my prayer be unto Thee, O LORD, in an
acceptable time;

6. THOU KNOWEST MY FOLLY. The parallel word "trespasses"
in the other half of the couplet indicates that "folly" means
"sin." The Bible frequently describes "sin" as "folly." Thus,
Psalm 38:6, "My wounds . . . fester because of my foolishness."

7. LET NOT THEM . . . BE ASHAMED THROUGH ME. Let not those
who seek Thee be disappointed and discouraged because of my
misfortunes.

8. FOR THY SAKE I HAVE BORNE REPROACH. Because of my
loyalty to Thee have I been mocked by the wicked. The same
phrase is found in Jeremiah 15:15, "For Thy sake I have
suffered taunts."

9. A STRANGER UNTO MY BRETHREN AND AN ALIEN. Even those
who are closest to me are so shocked and terrified at my suffering that they abandon me, fearing to be involved in my fate.
The same thought is expressed in Psalm 38:12, "My friends . . .

O God, in the abundance of Thy mercy,
Answer me with the truth of Thy salvation.

15. Deliver me out of the mire, and let me not sink;
    Let me be delivered from them that hate me, and
    out of the deep waters.
16. Let not the waterflood overwhelm me,
    Neither let the deep swallow me up;
    And let not the pit shut her mouth upon me.
17. Answer me, O LORD, for Thy mercy is good;
    According to the multitude of Thy compassions turn
    Thou unto me.
18. And hide not Thy face from Thy servant;
    For I am in distress; answer me speedily.
19. Draw nigh unto my soul, and redeem it;
    Ransom me because of mine enemies.
20. Thou knowest my reproach, and my shame, and
    my confusion;
    Mine adversaries are all before Thee.
21. Reproach hath broken my heart; and I am sore sick;
    And I looked for some to show compassion, but there
    was none;
    And for comforters, but I found none.
22. Yea, they put poison into my food;
    And in my thirst they gave me vinegar to drink.

stand aloof from my plague; my kinsmen stand afar off."

10. BECAUSE ZEAL . . . HATH EATEN ME UP. The second half
of the couplet explains this line. Because I have been zealous in
coming to Thy house (or defending Thy majesty) Thine enemies hate me and seek to destroy me.

12-13. A BYWORD . . . THE SONG OF THE DRUNKARDS. A familiar
thought in the Psalms. I have become the subject of mockery
and scorn.

14. AS FOR ME. This sentence from the psalmist has appropriately been taken as the closing sentence of the first paragraph
of every Morning Service (mah tovu).

15-16. Reverts to the metaphor of the miry pit and the flood.

21-22. The psalmist hoped for compassion and comfort but
no one would be friendly to him. They even put "poison into
my food" and "gave me vinegar to drink."

189

23. Let their table before them become a snare;
    And when they are in peace, let it become a trap.
24. Let their eyes be darkened, that they see not;
    And make their loins continually to totter.
25. Pour out Thine indignation upon them,
    And let the fierceness of Thine anger overtake them.
26. Let their encampment be desolate;
    Let none dwell in their tents.
27. For they persecute him whom Thou hast smitten;
    And they tell of the pain of those whom Thou hast wounded.
28. Add iniquity unto their iniquity;
    And let them not come into Thy righteousness.
29. Let them be blotted out of the book of the living,
    And not be written with the righteous.
30. But I am afflicted and in pain;

23-29. The psalmist, in his indignation, asks God to punish the wicked.

23. LET THEIR TABLE . . . BECOME A SNARE. This is explained by the second half of the couplet. At the table where they should be at peace among friends, let them be trapped.

24. EYES . . . DARKENED . . . LOINS TOTTER. Evidences of physical weakness. The eye loses its clarity and the legs stagger.

27. WHOM THOU HAST SMITTEN. Thou, O God, hast punished me; but they, although I have not offended them, add to my misfortunes. The same thought is expressed in Job 19:21, "Have pity on me, O ye, my friends, for the Hand of God hath touched me."

28. ADD INIQUITY . . . LET THEM NOT COME INTO THY RIGHTEOUSNESS. The opposite of what the psalmist asks for himself in Psalm 65:4, 5. There he pleaded with God to forgive his sins and bring him near to His courts. Here he asks that God shall not forgive the wicked so that they may not come into His righteous Presence, but that they "be blotted out of the book of the living." The prayer that God forgive not their iniquity is found in Jeremiah 18:23, "Forgive not their iniquity neither blot out their sin."

29. THE BOOK OF THE LIVING. A familiar biblical metaphor. God keeps a record of those who shall live. Thus, Moses (Ex-

Let Thy salvation, O God, set me up on high.
31. I will praise the name of God with a song,
    And will magnify Him with thanksgiving.
32. And it shall please the LORD better than a bullock
    That hath horns and hoofs.
33. The humble shall see it, and be glad;
    Ye that seek after God, let your heart revive.
34. For the LORD hearkeneth unto the needy,
    And despiseth not His prisoners.
35. Let heaven and earth praise Him,
    The seas, and every thing that moveth therein.
36. For God will save Zion, and build the cities of Judah;
    And they shall abide there, and have it in possession.
37. The seed also of His servants shall inherit it;
    And they that love His name shall dwell therein.

odus 32:32) prays in his sorrow, "Blot me, I pray Thee, out of Thy book which Thou hast written."

31-32. When God will have delivered him the psalmist will praise God. These prayers of praise will "please God better than a bullock." The thought that prayers are more acceptable than animal sacrifice is expressed in Psalm 51:18-19. "Thou delightest not in sacrifice, else would I give it . . . the sacrifices of God are a broken spirit."

34. HIS PRISONERS. The commentator, Ibn Ezra, takes this to refer to Israel in exile, but the rest of the psalm would indictate that it refers to those whom God has afflicted and whom He will forgive and heal.

36. GOD WILL SAVE ZION, AND BUILD THE CITIES OF JUDAH. This sentence does not necessarily mean that the psalm was composed after the exile.It merely indicates that it was written when the capital was in danger and many of the cities were ruined. Such ruination occurred often before the final Destruction.

PSALM 70 is taken from the other collection of psalms headed "Of David" (in Book One). It is identical with the text of Psalm 40:14-18, except for the fact that here, in Book Two, the editor has changed *JHWH* to *Elohim*.

191

70. FOR THE LEADER. [A PSALM] OF DAVID; TO MAKE MEMORIAL.

2. O God, to deliver me,
   O LORD, to help me, make haste.
3. Let them be ashamed and abashed
   That seek after my soul;
   Let them be turned backward and brought to confusion
   That delight in my hurt.
4. Let them be turned back by reason of their shame
   That say: 'Aha, aha.'
5. Let all those that seek Thee rejoice and be glad in Thee;
   And let such as love Thy salvation say continually:
   'Let God be magnified.'
6. But I am poor and needy;
   O God, make haste unto me;
   Thou art my help and my deliverer;
   O LORD, tarry not.

71. In Thee, O LORD, have I taken refuge;
   Let me never be ashamed.
2. Deliver me in Thy righteousness, and rescue me;
   Incline Thine ear unto me, and save me.
3. Be Thou to me a sheltering rock, whereunto I may
   continually resort,

1. TO MAKE MEMORIAL. For the explanation of this phrase see comment to Psalm 38:1.

For the rest of the psalm see comment to Psalm 40:14-18.

ALTHOUGH this psalm is strongly reminiscent of many previous psalms (particularly Psalms 22, 31, 35, and 40), and although many of its passages seem actually to have been taken from other psalms, the poem as a whole has strong individuality and deep feeling. It gives earnest expression to the thought frequently found in the Psalms that God is our refuge, that He will deliver us from the hands of the ruthless, and from all our troubles. The psalmist looks forward to the day when "My lips shall greatly rejoice when I sing praises unto Thee."

1-3. Are taken almost without change from Psalm 31:2-4.

192

Which Thou hast appointed to save me;
For Thou art my rock and my fortress.
4. O my God, rescue me out of the hand of the wicked,
Out of the grasp of the unrighteous and ruthless man.
5. For Thou art my hope;
O Lord God, my trust from my youth.
6. Upon Thee have I stayed myself from birth;
Thou art He that took me out of my mother's womb;
My praise is continually of Thee.
7. I am as a wonder unto many;
But Thou art my strong refuge.
8. My mouth shall be filled with Thy praise,
And with Thy glory all the day.
9. Cast me not off in the time of old age;
When my strength faileth, forsake me not.
10. For mine enemies speak concerning me,
And they that watch for my soul take counsel
together,
11. Saying: 'God hath forsaken him;
Pursue and take him; for there is none to deliver.'
12. O God, be not far from me;
O my God, make haste to help me.
13. Let them be ashamed and consumed that are adversaries
to my soul;

3. WHEREUNTO I MAY CONTINUALLY RESORT. To which I can flee for refuge whenever I am in danger.

6. UPON THEE HAVE I STAYED MYSELF. Upon Thee have I relied. This sentence is closely akin to Psalm 22:11, "Thou art my God from my mother's womb."

7. I AM AS A WONDER. They are shocked, they marvel at my miseries.

9. CAST ME NOT OFF IN . . . OLD AGE. The thought is connected with that of verse 6: I have relied on Thee from my birth and now that I am old I plead for Thy assistance.

11. GOD HATH FORSAKEN HIM. The wicked behold my misfortunes and are sure that God will no longer help me. The psalmist himself, when he is in despair, sometimes fears that God has forsaken him. Thus, Psalm 22:2, "My God, why hast Thou forsaken me?"

193

Let them be covered with reproach and confusion that
    seek my hurt.
14. But as for me, I will hope continually,
    And will praise Thee yet more and more.
15. My mouth shall tell of Thy righteousness,
    And of Thy salvation all the day;
    For I know not the numbers thereof.
16. I will come with Thy mighty acts, O Lord God;
    I will make mention of Thy righteousness, even of Thine only.
17. O God, Thou hast taught me from my youth;
    And until now do I declare Thy wondrous works.
18. And even unto old age and hoary hairs, O God, forsake me not;
    Until I have declared Thy strength unto the next generation,
    Thy might to every one that is to come;
19. Thy righteousness also, O God, which reacheth unto high
    heaven;

15. I KNOW NOT THE NUMBERS THEREOF. So numerous are the acts of Thy salvation that I cannot count them.

16. I WILL COME WITH THY MIGHTY ACTS. The second half of the couplet makes this clear. I will come into Thy temple to praise Thy mighty acts.

17-18 are analogous in thought to verses 6 and 9.

17. THOU HAST TAUGHT ME FROM MY YOUTH. To trust in Thee. Therefore, now in my old age "forsake me not."

The thought that God will support us all our life, even in old age, is expressed in Isaiah 46:4, "Even to old age I am the same, even to hoar hairs will I carry you."

19. THY RIGHTEOUSNESS . . . UNTO HIGH HEAVEN. Thy goodness is universal.

20. THOU HAST MADE ME SEE . . . SORE TROUBLES . . . QUICKEN ME AGAIN . . . BRING ME UP. Although Thou hast punished me for my sins, revive me now and save me from the depths of the earth (i. e., from death). The same expression is used in Psalm 30:4, "Thou didst keep me alive, that I should not go down to the pit."

22. THE PSALTERY. A musical instrument. The parallel word later in the couplet is "harp."

Thou who hast done great things,
O God, who is like unto Thee?
20. Thou, who hast made me to see many and sore troubles,
Wilt quicken me again, and bring me up again from the
depths of the earth.
21. Thou wilt increase my greatness,
And turn and comfort me.
22. I also will give thanks unto Thee with the psaltery,
Even unto Thy truth, O my God;
I will sing praises unto Thee with the harp,
O Thou Holy One of Israel.
23. My lips shall greatly rejoice when I sing praises unto Thee;
And my soul, which Thou hast redeemed.
24. My tongue also shall tell of Thy righteousness all the day;
For they are ashamed, for they are abashed, that seek
my hurt.

Psalm 72 is headed, "A Psalm of Solomon." The heading creates a difficulty for the traditional commentators when taken in connection with the closing verse: "The prayers of David the son of Jesse are ended." If the psalms recorded heretofore, and this psalm in particular, are to be described as "the prayers of David" then what explanation can there be given for the heading, "A Psalm of Solomon"? The commentators, Rashi and Ibn Ezra, say that the psalm was written prophetically by David in behalf of Solomon, his son. Kimchi says that David wrote this psalm in honor of his son Solomon when Solomon was crowned king. When David was on his deathbed he appointed Solomon, king.

The Aramaic translation (the Targum), has still another explanation, as is indicated by its translation of the first verse which is as follows: "By Solomon spoken in prophecy: 'O God, give Thy righteous law to the king messiah.'" The interpretation of this psalm as a messianic psalm would seem to be borne out by the fact that its description of the righteousness of the king tallies closely with Isaiah's description of the messianic king, given in Isaiah 11. However, the description of the king's wisdom and his prosperity could harmonize just as well with

72. [A PSALM] OF SOLOMON.

1   Give the king Thy judgments, O God,
And Thy righteousness unto the king's son;

2. That he may judge Thy people with righteousness,
And Thy poor with justice.

3. Let the mountains bear peace to the people,
And the hills, through righteousness.

4. May he judge the poor of the people,
And save the children of the needy,
And crush the oppressor.

5. They shall fear Thee while the sun endureth,
And so long as the moon, throughout all generations.

6. May he come down like rain upon the mown grass,
As showers that water the earth.

7. In his days let the righteous flourish,
And abundance of peace, till the moon be no more.

8. May he have dominion also from sea to sea,
And from the River unto the ends of the earth.

9. Let them that dwell in the wilderness bow before him;

the situation in King Solomon's time, the period of the fullest flowering and widest extent of the Israelitish monarchy. Nor is it an argument against the non-messianic interpretation of the psalm that verse 17 says: "May his name endure forever." The king is often greeted with: "May the king live forever." Furthermore, it may refer to his dynasty, or simply to his fame.

1. THY JUDGMENTS . . . THY RIGHTEOUSNESS. Justice comes from God and mortal rulers merely execute God's laws.

2. JUDGE THY PEOPLE WITH RIGHTEOUSNESS. As the ideal king in Isaiah 11:4, "with righteousness shall he judge the poor."

3. MOUNTAINS BEAR PEACE . . . THE HILLS, THROUGH RIGHTEOUSNESS. The result of righteous government is peace. Thus, Isaiah 32:17, "the work of righteousness shall be peace."

5. THEY SHALL FEAR THEE WHILE THE SUN ENDURETH. God's righteousness practiced by the king will lead men to revere Him forever.

6-7. The king's righteousness is like the blessed rain which enriches the land.

And his enemies lick the dust.
10. The kings of Tarshish and of the isles shall render
      tribute;
   The kings of Sheba and Seba shall offer gifts.
11. Yea, all kings shall prostrate themselves before him;
   All nations shall serve him.
12. For he will deliver the needy when he crieth;
   The poor also, and him that hath no helper.
13. He will have pity on the poor and needy,
   And the souls of the needy he will save.
14. He will redeem their soul from oppression and violence,
   And precious will their blood be in his sight;
15. That they may live, and that he may give them of the
      gold of Sheba,
   That they may pray for him continually,
   Yea, bless him all the day.
16. May he be as a rich cornfield in the land upon the top
      of the mountains;
   May his fruit rustle like Lebanon;
   And may they blossom out of the city like grass of the earth.

8-11. The kingdom shall spread over the earth.

10. TARSHISH. A city or a country far over the sea. See the comment on Psalm 48:8. The promise that various kings would bring gifts to the king of Israel as a mark of friendship and homage, was actually fulfilled in the reign of Solomon. I Kings 5:1, "And Solomon ruled over all the kingdoms from the River (i. e., the Euphrates) unto the border of Egypt; they brought presents, and served Solomon all the days of his life."

SHEBA . . . SEBA. Sheba is the northern coast of Arabia, and Seba is, in all likelihood, Ethiopia.

12-15. His pity for the poor and the needy. Compare the description of the ideal king in Isaiah 11:4.

14. PRECIOUS WILL THEIR BLOOD BE IN HIS SIGHT. He will not be indifferent to violence shown to the humble. The same expression is used of God in Psalm 116:15, "Precious in the sight of the Lord is the death of His saints."

16. Reverts to the figure in verse 6, comparing the benevolence of the king to the bountifulness of the earth.

17. May his name endure for ever;
    May his name be continued as long as the sun;
    May men also bless themselves by him;
    May all nations call him happy.
18. Blessed be the LORD God, the God of Israel,

MAY THEY BLOSSOM OUT OF THE CITY. Kimchi understands
this to mean that the blessing will not only be that of a bounteous earth but there will also be human fruitfulness. The people will increase "like the grass of the earth." This increase of
the population occurred in the reign of King Solomon, I Kings
4:20, "Judah and Israel were many, as the sand which is by the
sea in multitude."

17. MAY HIS NAME BE CONTINUED. The Hebrew word here for
"continued" is *yinnon*. The Talmud interprets this in a messianic sense, saying that *yinnon* is one of the names of the messiah. (b. Pesachim 54 a.)

MAY MEN BLESS THEMSELVES BY HIM. His name will be in-
voked as a blessing. This is precisely the blessing which God
gave to Abraham (Genesis 22:18), "And in thy seed shall all
the nations of the earth be blessed; because thou hast hearkened to My voice."

Who only doeth wondrous things;
19. And blessed be His glorious name for ever;
And let the whole earth be filled with His glory.
Amen, and Amen.
20. The prayers of David the son of Jesse are ended.

18-19. Is not part of the psalm but is the sentence of praise
(the doxology) which closes Book Two. It closely resembles the
doxology which closed Book One, Psalm 41:14.

18. WHO ONLY DOETH WONDROUS THINGS. God alone is the
source of all wondrous works. The same thought is expressed in
Psalm 136:4, "To Him who alone doeth great wonders."

19. LET THE WHOLE EARTH BE FILLED WITH HIS GLORY. This
sentence is reminiscent of Isaiah 6:3, "the whole earth is full
of His glory," and of Numbers 14:21, "and all the earth shall
be filled with the glory of the Lord."

AMEN AND AMEN. The response of the people to the doxology. See comment to Psalm 41:14.

20. THE PRAYERS OF DAVID, THE SON OF JESSE, ARE ENDED. This
sentence must have been added by the collator of this Book.
It marks the end of the group of the psalms ascribed to David
and divides it from the psalms ascribed to Asaph which follow.

Book Three

~

HE first eleven psalms of Book III are headed "of Asaph."
Asaph is mentioned in I Chronicles 16:5, as the chief of the
Levites appointed by David "to minister before the ark of the
Lord, and to celebrate and to thank and to praise the Lord."
The sons of Asaph are mentioned in the reign of Josiah as
Levitical singers, II Chronicles 35:15. They are also mentioned
in Ezra 2:41, among those who returned from the Babylonian
Exile. The Asaph family had functioned as Levitical singers for
centuries. Hence, any psalm headed "A Psalm (or Maschil) of
Asaph" belongs to a family or guild collection whose separate
psalms may have been written at any period from the time of
David until after the Exile. The heading, "of Asaph," therefore,
can give us no indication as to the date of the psalm.

While the Asaph psalms occasionally deal with personal
themes such as the prosperity of the wicked and the misfortunes
of the righteous, the favorite subject of the Asaph psalms is the
history of Israel. The psalms describe either an invasion or the
exile, or present a long historical retrospect in order to prove a
definite theory as to the relationship which existed between
God and Israel.

73. A PSALM OF ASAPH.
   Surely God is good to Israel,
   Even to such as are pure in heart.
2. But as for me, my feet were almost gone;
   My steps had well nigh slipped.
3. For I was envious at the arrogant,
   When I saw the prosperity of the wicked.
4. For there are no pangs at their death,
   And their body is sound.

*C*HIS psalm (73), deals with the theme found in Psalms 38 and 49, namely, the prosperity of the wicked. The two previous psalms describe this prosperity as merely transient, and, because of its transiency, the authors call upon the righteous to be patient and not to fret. This psalm goes more deeply into the subject and deals not only with the prosperity of the wicked but also with the suffering of the righteous.

The theme is expounded in an intensely personal manner. The psalmist confesses that when he contrasted the prosperity of the wicked with his own sufferings he had almost lost his faith in the justice of God. But he came to God's sanctuary and learned to be grateful that even in his suffering he had at least the consciousness of God's sustaining Presence. Because of that consciousness he finds inner strength and grows more certain that the wicked will not continue to triumph.

1. PURE IN HEART. God will show His mercy to those whose motives are pure. Thus, Psalm 24 says, that only those who have "a pure heart" will find the joy of God's Presence: "Who shall stand in His holy place? He that hath . . . a pure heart" (Psalm 24:3, 4).

2-4. The psalmist describes how his faith in God had almost vanished when he contrasted the suffering of the innocent with the prosperity of the wicked.

2. MY STEPS HAD WELL NIGH SLIPPED. Of him who stumbles off the path of God (i. e., who abandons the way of righteousness), the psalmist says, "his foot has slipped." Psalm 17:5, de-

5. In the trouble of man they are not;
   Neither are they plagued like men.
6. Therefore pride is as a chain about their neck;
   Violence covereth them as a garment.
7. Their eyes stand forth from fatness;
   They are gone beyond the imaginations of their heart.
8. They scoff, and in wickedness utter oppression;
   They speak as if there were none on high.
9. They have set their mouth against the heavens,
   And their tongue walketh through the earth.

scribes the converse of such apostasy in these words: "My steps
have held fast to Thy paths, my feet have not slipped."

4. NO PANGS . . . THEIR BODY. They die a painless death, and
until the day of their death their body is sound.

5. NEITHER ARE THEY PLAGUED. Not only do the wicked seem
to be blessed with perfect health but they are not plagued by
any other troubles as most men are.

6. PRIDE IS AS A CHAIN. They carry pride like a beautiful
necklace. In Proverbs 1:9, the disciple is urged to carry the instruction of his father and of his mother as "a chaplet of grace.
. . . (i. e., necklace) about thy neck."

VIOLENCE . . . AS A GARMENT. They strut about proudly in
their violence as in a beautiful garment.

7. THEIR EYES STAND FORTH FROM FATNESS. They have all the
food they can possibly want.

THEY ARE GONE BEYOND. They have succeeded beyond their
wildest dreams.

8. AS IF THERE WERE NONE ON HIGH. As the fool who says:
"There is no God." (Psalm 14:1.)

9. THEIR MOUTH AGAINST THE HEAVENS. The commentator,
Ibn Ezra, takes this to mean that they act as if the words of their
mouth were heavenly decrees. But the Aramaic translation (the
Targum) understands it in a way which harmonizes more
closely with the succeeding couplet:—they speak against God.

THEIR TONGUE WALKETH. Their words are influential everywhere.

10. Therefore His people return hither;
    And waters of fulness are drained out by them.
11. And they say: 'How doth God know?
    And is there knowledge in the Most High?'
12. Behold, such are the wicked;
    And they that are always at ease increase riches.
13. Surely in vain have I cleansed my heart,
    And washed my hands in innocency;
14. For all the day have I been plagued,
    And my chastisement came every morning.
15. If I had said: 'I will speak thus',
    Behold, I had been faithless to the generation of
      Thy children.

10. HIS PEOPLE RETURN HITHER. A difficult verse variously interpreted. Rashi's explanation is that because of the prosperity
of the wicked many of the children of Israel turn back from the
paths of righteousness and join them.

WATERS OF FULLNESS ARE DRAINED. This verse, too, has received various interpretations. Most translators follow Kimchi
who interprets it to mean that they will drink the full draught
of God's cup of punishment. The whole verse, according to
Kimchi, would, therefore, be: God's people are attracted by the
prosperity of the wicked and drain the cup of sinful joy, and,
therefore, will be punished.

11. HOW DOTH GOD KNOW? The psalmist frequently ascribes
this thought to the wicked. They ask: "How doth God know"
(of what we do), or, "God hath forgotten" (Psalm 10:11).

13-14. The psalmist asks, of what good is my righteousness
if the wicked prosper and if in spite of my innocence I am
plagued all the day.

13. WASHED MY HANDS IN INNOCENCY. I kept my hands clean
of crime. This phrase is found also in Psalm 26:6, and is likewise used in connection with the law in Deuteronomy 21:6,
namely, that when a body of a slain man is found between two
cities, the elders of both cities should wash their hands in order
to indicate that "our hands have not shed this blood" (verse 7).

15. The psalmist realizes that if he yields to this despond-

16. And when I pondered how I might know this,
    It was wearisome in mine eyes;
17. Until I entered into the sanctuary of God,
    And considered their end.
18. Surely Thou settest them in slippery places;
    Thou hurlest them down to utter ruin.
19. How are they become a desolation in a moment!
    They are wholly consumed by terrors.
20. As a dream when one awaketh,
    So, O LORD, when Thou arousest Thyself, Thou
        wilt despise their semblance.
21. For my heart was in a ferment,
    And I was pricked in my reins.

ency he will discourage his contemporaries, "the generation of Thy children."

16-17. HOW I MIGHT KNOW THIS. When I wondered how I could understand this paradox, i. e., the prosperity of the wicked, etc. "It was wearisome." The problem worried me until "I entered into the sanctuary." When I came into the Temple and meditated and prayed I found the solution, namely, I "considered their end," I realized that wickedness would end in destruction.

18. THOU SETTEST THEM IN SLIPPERY PLACES. They are bound to stumble and fall. In Psalm 35:6, the psalmist prays that God thus punish the wicked: "Let their way be dark and slippery."

20. AS A DREAM. A dream seems real when one is still asleep, but when one wakes it is recognized as insubstantial.

WHEN THOU AROUSEST THYSELF. The psalmist frequently calls upon God to arouse Himself in order to punish the wicked. "Rouse Thee, and awake to my judgment" (Psalm 35:23). Both halves of this couplet are connected in thought. As the dreamer who awakens brushes aside quickly the visions which seemed so terrible during the dream, so God, when He awakens to judgment, will despise the very "semblance" of the wicked.

21-22. Before I came to realize how insubstantial is the power of the wicked I suffered agonies of soul and body.

21. PRICKED IN MY REINS. The Hebrew (as Rashi understood

205

22. But I was brutish, and ignorant;
     I was as a beast before Thee.
23. Nevertheless I am continually with Thee;
     Thou holdest my right hand.
24. Thou wilt guide me with Thy counsel,
     And afterward receive me with glory.
25. Whom have I in heaven but Thee?
     And beside Thee I desire none upon earth.

it) implies sharp, stabbing pains. The "reins," or kidneys, were considered to be the seat of the emotions.

22. I WAS BRUTISH . . . AS A BEAST. I had no more understanding of the destiny of men than an animal has. The same thought is expressed in Psalm 92:7-8, "A brutish man knoweth not (that) when all the workers of iniquity do flourish, it is that they may be destroyed for ever."

23. The rest of the psalm develops the thought expressed in verse 17, namely, that now that I am conscious of Thy Presence, I have found strength to endure my own sorrows and also have confidence that good will triumph over evil.

24. THOU WILT GUIDE ME . . . AND RECEIVE ME WITH GLORY. Kimchi and Ibn Ezra say that "receive me with glory" means in the life after death. If we consider the phrase "receive me" as a parallel to "guide me" in the first couplet, and if we bear in mind the general psalm emphasis on life in this world, the plain meaning of the phrase is simply that God guides me and will bring me near to Him in honor. My career on earth will be widely respected.

25. IN HEAVEN AND UPON EARTH. I worship Thee alone and need no other help but Thine. It is not only Thy help which is all-sufficient, but Thy loving presence. Conscious of communion with Thee my heart is filled with happiness.

26. THE ROCK OF MY HEART. The fortress of my heart.

28. THE NEARNESS OF GOD IS MY GOOD. This sentence expresses the whole theme of the psalm. I shall not be discouraged by the perplexities and paradoxes of life as long as I feel near to Thee. This awareness is happiness and assurance enough.

26. My flesh and my heart faileth;
      But God is the rock of my heart and my portion
         for ever.
27. For, lo, they that go far from Thee shall perish;
      Thou dost destroy all them that go astray from Thee.
28. But as for me, the nearness of God is my good;
      I have made the Lord God my refuge,
      That I may tell of all Thy works.

THIS psalm is closely connected in thought and in language with Psalm 79. It was written at a time of great national calamity. The invaders have entered the sanctuary and destroyed it. They have burned all the places of assembly throughout the land. The psalmist turns to God Who in the past had manifested His sovereign power and asks Him now to recall His ancient covenant and to deliver His people once more.

The date of this psalm is widely disputed. The alternative dates suggested for this psalm are either the time of the desecration of the Temple by the Syrian Greeks, or the destruction of the Temple by the Babylonians four centuries earlier. It is chiefly on the basis of this psalm that some of the modern scholars say that there are psalms which were written as late as the Maccabean era (from 170 B.C.E.). Most of the modern scholars, however, are not convinced that there are any psalms which were written as late as that period. Most of the arguments as to whether this psalm is Maccabean or not depend upon the interpretation of its content and language. Those who believe that this is a Maccabean psalm base their arguments mainly upon verse 4: "They have set up their own signs for signs," which they interpret to mean that when the soldiers of Antiochus Epiphanes, the Syrian-Greek king, entered the sanctuary they desecrated it and put up their own idolatrous altars and symbols. These scholars also say that verse 8 likewise indicates that this is a Maccabean psalm. Verse 8 reads: "They have burned up all the meeting-places of God in the land." If "meeting-places of God" means "synagogues," and the verse refers to a widespread destruction of synagogues, then the statement would in-

74. MASCHIL OF ASAPH.

Why, O God, hast Thou cast us off for ever?
Why doth Thine anger smoke against the flock of Thy pasture?
2. Remember Thy congregation, which Thou hast gotten
    of old,
Which Thou hast redeemed to be the tribe of Thine inheritance;
And mount Zion, wherein Thou hast dwelt.
3. Lift up Thy steps because of the perpetual ruins,
Even all the evil that the enemy hath done in the sanctuary.

dicate a Maccabean date for the psalm, since there were no synagogues at the time of the earlier desecration of the Temple by
the Babylonians. The scholars who doubt that this psalm is as
late as the Maccabean era point out the complete destruction
and burning of the Temple described in verses 6 and 7. This,
they say, can refer only to the destruction of the Temple by the
Babylonians in 586 b.c.e. (II Kings 25:9 and 10), inasmuch as
we know that the Greeks (in Maccabean times) did not destroy
the Temple. They only burned its gates; while the Babylonians
destroyed it completely.

It is impossible to fix a date for the psalm which will not be
open to question based upon some of the verses in the text.
Perhaps a hint of a most likely date is given by the commentator, Kimchi. In discussing verse 9: "There is no more any prophet," Kimchi says that this refers to the death of the prophets
Haggai, Zechariah, and Malachi. These prophets lived in the
early days of the return from the Exile. A writer, living in those
days, still had in mind the complete destruction of the Temple
by the Babylonians and also saw the rise of the various "meeting-places of God" (verse 8) all through Palestine. This psalm
could therefore have been written during some national misfortune in the earlier days of the return from the Exile. This
misfortune, whatever it was, naturally called to mind the earlier
calamity, namely, the complete destruction of the Temple by
the Babylonians.

1. MASCHIL. For the explanation of this technical term see
note to Psalm 32:1.

4. Thine adversaries have roared in the midst of
   Thy meeting-place;
  They have set up their own signs for signs.
5. It seemed as when men wield upwards
  Axes in a thicket of trees.
6. And now all the carved work thereof together
  They strike down with hatchet and hammers.
7. They have set Thy sanctuary on fire;
  They have profaned the dwelling-place of Thy
   name even to the ground.

WHY DOTH THINE ANGER SMOKE? Why does Thine anger
flame? God's anger is frequently described as a flaming fire.
Thus: "Smoke arose up in His nostrils, and fire out of His
mouth did devour" (Psalm 18:9).

2. WHICH THOU HAST GOTTEN OF OLD. The Bible also speaks
of the congregation of Israel as a community which God has
"gotten" or "acquired," having redeemed them from the possession of the Egyptians. Thus: "Till the people pass over that
Thou hast gotten" (Exodus 15:16).

THINE INHERITANCE. Since God has acquired Israel, Israel is
now God's permanent possession, His inheritance.

3. LIFT UP THY STEPS. The frequently expressed appeal to
God to hasten to deliver.

PERPETUAL RUINS. The psalmist visualizes the *complete* destruction of the Temple, such as occurred after the Babylonians
captured it in 586 B.C.E.

4. THEIR OWN SIGNS FOR SIGNS. This need not necessarily refer to the heathen religious symbols which the Syrian-Greeks
brought into the Temple as the advocates of the Maccabean
date of the psalm would say. It could simply mean the military
ensigns of the invading Babylonians.

5-6. WHEN MEN WIELD UPWARDS . . . THE CARVED WORK . . .
THEY STRIKE DOWN. A difficult passage, variously interpreted. It
seems to mean that the enemy, destroying the Temple, appeared like a group of woodsmen, raising their axes against the
trees and chopping down all the carved doorways of the Temple.

8. THE MEETING-PLACES OF GOD. This verse is referred to in

Psalm 74
8

8. They said in their heart: 'Let us make havoc of them altogether';
   They have burned up all the meeting-places of God
      in the land.
9. We see not our signs;
   There is no more any prophet;
   Neither is there among us any that knoweth how long.
10. How long, O God, shall the adversary reproach?
    Shall the enemy blaspheme Thy name for ever?
11. Why withdrawest Thou Thy hand, even Thy right hand?
    Draw it out of Thy bosom and consume them.
12. Yet God is my King of old,
    Working salvation in the midst of the earth.
13. Thou didst break the sea in pieces by Thy strength;
    Thou didst shatter the heads of the sea-monsters in the waters.
14. Thou didst crush the heads of leviathan,

most investigations of the origin of the synagogues. Certainly, when this verse was written there were assembly places either for worship, or perhaps as yet only for study, scattered over the land. See the article "Synagogue" in *Jewish Encyclopedia*, Vol. XI.

9. WE SEE NOT OUR SIGNS. The Temple is destroyed. None of our religious symbols are to be seen any more. Some, however, interpret the word "signs" as "religious festivals" which were considered to be a sign of the covenant between God and Israel. Thus, in Exodus 31:13, the Sabbath is described as follows: "It is a sign between Me and you throughout your generations."

NO MORE ANY PROPHET . . . THAT KNOWETH HOW LONG. There is no one left who can comfort us by foretelling for us when our misfortunes will end.

11. WHY WITHDRAWEST THOU . . . THY RIGHT HAND? Why dost Thou not manifest Thy power? God's right hand is a symbol of His might. Thus, Psalm 118:16, "The right hand of the Lord doeth valiantly."

12-17. Describes God's mighty help in the days gone by.

13-14. THOU DIDST BREAK THE SEA. i. e., divide the Red Sea.

SEA-MONSTERS—LEVIATHAN. These are evidently symbols for the Egyptians. That Egypt is called the "sea monster" (possibly the crocodile), is evident from Ezekiel 29:3, "the King of

210

Thou gavest him to be food to the folk inhabiting
    the wilderness.
15. Thou didst cleave fountain and brook;
    Thou driedst up ever-flowing rivers.
16. Thine is the day, Thine also the night;
    Thou hast established luminary and sun.
17. Thou hast set all the borders of the earth;
    Thou hast made summer and winter.
18. Remember this, how the enemy hath reproached the LORD,
    And how a base people have blasphemed Thy name.
19. O deliver not the soul of Thy turtle-dove unto the wild beast;
    Forget not the life of Thy poor for ever.
20. Look upon the covenant;
    For the dark places of the land are full of the habitations
    of violence.

Egypt, the great dragon in the midst of his rivers." The word translated as "dragon" is the same word which is translated here as "sea-monster." In Isaiah 27:1, the mythical sea monster, leviathan, is used as parallel to the word *tanin* which is translated here "sea-monster." For the later rabbinic legends about leviathan, see article "Leviathan" in *Jewish Encyclopedia*, Vol. VIII.

THOU GAVEST HIM TO BE FOOD. The bodies of the Egyptians cast up by the Red Sea became food for the jackals inhabiting the desert; or it may mean, retaining the metaphor of the fish or sea-monster, that it became food for those who dwell by the Red Sea.

15. CLEAVE FOUNTAIN. God split the rock so that a fountain of water gushed forth. Exodus 17:6.

DRIEDST UP . . . RIVERS. The dividing of the Jordan in the days of Joshua.

17. ALL THE BORDERS OF THE EARTH. This can mean either that God fixes the outermost points of the world, or that He establishes the borders between nations, as Deuteronomy 32:8, "He set the borders of the peoples."

19. THE SOUL OF THY TURTLE-DOVE. Israel is often spoken of in the metaphor of a dove.

20. LOOK UPON THE COVENANT. Remember the covenant

21. O let not the oppressed turn back in confusion;
    Let the poor and needy praise Thy name.
22. Arise, O God, plead Thine own cause;
    Remember Thy reproach all the day at the hand of
    the base man.
23. Forget not the voice of Thine adversaries,
    The tumult of those that rise up against Thee which
    ascendeth continually.

75. FOR THE LEADER; AL-TASHHETH. A PSALM OF ASAPH, A SONG.

2. We give thanks unto Thee, O God,
   We give thanks, and Thy name is near;
   Men tell of Thy wondrous works.

which You made with our fathers. Thus, in Exodus 6:5, God says to Moses that He is aware of the suffering of the children of Israel in Egypt, "and I have remembered My covenant."

23. THE TUMULT . . . WHICH ASCENDETH. The shouting of the rebellious rises up to God day after day.

*T*HIS psalm bears a close resemblance in language and thought to the prayer of Hannah in I Samuel 2:1-10. Both poems symbolize mortal pride as an animal proudly lifting and tossing its horns; and both speak of God destroying the arrogant.

The psalm is also related in thought and language to the next psalm (76) which refers rather definitely to the sudden destruction of the army of Sennacherib which encamped around Jerusalem in the days of King Hezekiah. Psalm 75 must have been written under the influence of the same dramatic event. The psalmist begins with expressing his gratitude to God, and then introduces God Himself as a speaker Who declares that He will execute judgment against the violent. Therefore, let not the wicked be haughty for they shall soon be destroyed and the righteous shall triumph.

2. THY NAME IS NEAR. Means simply, "Thou art near." We invoke God's name that He might come near to help us. See also, Psalm 52:11, "I will wait for Thy Name."

3. 'When I take the appointed time,
   I Myself will judge with equity.
4. When the earth and all the inhabitants thereof
   are dissolved,
   I Myself establish the pillars of it.'   Selah
5. I say unto the arrogant: 'Deal not arrogantly';
   And to the wicked: 'Lift not up the horn.'
6. Lift not up your horn on high;
   Speak not insolence with a haughty neck.
7. For neither from the east, nor from the west,
   Nor yet from the wilderness, cometh lifting up.
8. For God is judge;
   He putteth down one, and lifteth up another.

3-6. God's words to the wicked.

3. THE APPOINTED TIME. The wicked will, indeed, triumph for awhile but that is only because God is waiting for the appointed time which He has designated for judgment. In Psalm 102:14, the psalmist pleads with God to have mercy upon Zion, "for the appointed time is come."

4. WHEN THE EARTH IS DISSOLVED I ESTABLISH THE PILLARS OF IT. When the violence of the wicked seems to destroy the very foundation of society I will firmly re-establish the security of men and nations. The same expression is used in the Song of Hannah, I Samuel 2:8, "for the pillars of the earth are the Lord's, and He hath set the world upon them."

5. LIFT NOT UP YOUR HORN. The phrase is clear from the parallel expression in the first verse of the couplet: "Deal not arrogantly." The bull or the stag raises and tosses his horns in arrogant pride. A similar thought is expressed in the next verse by the phrase, "haughty neck," which refers to the head held stiffly and arrogantly.

7-8. NEITHER FROM THE EAST . . . COMETH LIFTING UP . . . GOD IS JUDGE . . . AND LIFTETH UP. These verses, addressed to the wicked, mean that not from your wandering or conquests east and west will you find reason for pride (lifting up the head). God is the judge. From Him alone comes human glory. The expression that God "putteth down and lifteth up" is likewise found

213

9. For in the hand of the LORD there is a cup, with foaming
        wine, full of mixture,
    And He poureth out of the same;
    Surely the dregs thereof, all the wicked of the earth shall
        drain them, and drink them.
10. But as for me, I will declare for ever,
    I will sing praises to the God of Jacob.
11. All the horns of the wicked also will I cut off;
    But the horns of the righteous shall be lifted up.

76. FOR THE LEADER; WITH STRING-MUSIC. A PSALM OF ASAPH, A SONG.

2. In Judah is God known;
   His name is great in Israel.
3. In Salem also is set His tabernacle,
   And His dwelling-place in Zion.

---

in the Song of Hannah, I Samuel 2:7, "He bringeth low, He also lifteth up."

9. IN THE HAND OF THE LORD . . . A CUP . . . THE DREGS THEREOF. This metaphor is frequently used in the Psalms and in the Prophets. God will give those whom He desires to punish a cup of confusion or "staggering" which they must drain to the very dregs. See Isaiah 51:17, "Stand up O Jerusalem, Thou hast drunk at the hand of the Lord . . . the cup of staggering, and drained it."

11. THE HORNS OF THE WICKED. The pride of the wicked will be broken and the righteous will triumph.

*T*HIS psalm continues the thought of the preceding psalm and speaks of God's judgment against the invaders of Jerusalem. The reference to the armies of Sennacherib which were completely destroyed near Jerusalem in the reign of Hezekiah, is quite clear in verses 6 and 7 which speak of the dead sleep which fell upon the riders and horses. Moreover, the Greek translation (the Septuagint), in its heading to the psalm, says: "With regard to the Assyrians."

2. IN JUDAH IS GOD KNOWN. He is known as a helper and a

4. There He broke the fiery shafts of the bow;
   The shield, and the sword, and the battle. Selah
5. Glorious art Thou and excellent, coming down from the mountains of prey.
6. The stout-hearted are bereft of sense, they sleep their sleep;
   And none of the men of might have found their hands.
7. At Thy rebuke, O God of Jacob,
   They are cast into a dead sleep, the riders also and the horses.
8. Thou, even Thou, art terrible;
   And who may stand in Thy sight when once Thou art angry?
9. Thou didst cause sentence to be heard from heaven;
   The earth feared, and was still,
10. When God arose to judgment,
    To save all the humble of the earth. Selah
11. Surely the wrath of man shall praise Thee;
    The residue of wrath shalt Thou gird upon Thee.

defense. The same phrase is used in Psalm 48:4, "God in her palaces hath made Himself known for a stronghold."

3. IN SALEM. The name means "peace" and is an abbreviation of the name "Jerusalem."

5. THE MOUNTAINS OF PREY. The commentator, Rashi, takes this to mean, the mountains where the beasts of prey lurk. The metaphor seems to be that God descends upon the enemy like a lion from the mountain ravine.

6-7. Describes the sudden sleep, the sleep of death, which overtook the army of the Assyrians.

9. SENTENCE TO BE HEARD. Thy sentence of judgment.

11. THE WRATH OF MAN SHALL PRAISE THEE. The very wrath of the violent will lead to the manifestation of Thy just rebukes, and those will redound to Thy praise.

THE RESIDUE OF WRATH SHALT THOU GIRD. This second line of the couplet must have substantially the same meaning as the first line, namely, that God's glory will become manifest when He punishes the wrath of the violent. Specifically, the sentence means that whatever violence remains after Thou hast punished most of the wicked, "the residue" will also redound to Thy majesty. Thou wilt gird it on Thee as a glorious garment. An analogous use of the idea of girding oneself with a mood or

12. Vow, and pay unto the LORD your God;
    Let all that are round about Him bring presents unto Him
        that is to be feared;
13. He minisheth the spirit of princes;
    He is terrible to the kings of the earth.

77. FOR THE LEADER; FOR JEDUTHUN. A PSALM OF ASAPH.

2. I will lift up my voice unto God, and cry;
    I will lift up my voice unto God, that He may give ear unto me.
3. In the day of my trouble I seek the Lord;
    With my hand uplifted, [mine eye] streameth in the night
        without ceasing;
    My soul refuseth to be comforted.
4. When I think thereon, O God, I must moan;

with an achievement as if with a garment is found in Psalm
73:6, where it is said of the wicked that "violence covereth
them as a garment."

12. BRING PRESENTS UNTO HIM. As a mark of submission.

13. HE MINISHETH. Diminisheth. He will cut down or destroy. He will break the spirit of violent kings.

A SONG of anguish. The psalmist, in his grief, "refuseth to
be comforted." He has arrived at the state of mind where he
asks himself the question (verse 10): "Hath God forgotten to
be gracious?" Yet he soon realizes that such a conclusion would
be a mark of spiritual weakness. He, therefore, recalls God's
deliverance of Israel in the past when, accompanied by dramatic manifestations of natural forces, God led His "people like a
flock by the hand of Moses and Aaron." The commentator,
Kimchi, interprets this psalm as referring to the Exile. Indeed,
the tragic mood of the psalm is such that it could well have
been written during the first bitter days of Israel in Babylon.

1. JEDUTHUN. Jeduthun is mentioned in I Chronicles 16:42,
as one of David's Levitical musicians. See also Psalm 62:1.

2-10. The psalmist describes his anguish of soul and tells
how neither prayer nor meditation seems to comfort him.

When I muse thereon, my spirit fainteth.   Selah
5. Thou holdest fast the lids of mine eyes;
   I am troubled, and cannot speak.
6. I have pondered the days of old,
   The years of ancient times.
7. In the night I will call to remembrance my song;
   I will commune with mine own heart;
   And my spirit maketh diligent search:
8. 'Will the Lord cast off for ever?
   And will He be favourable no more?
9. Is His mercy clean gone for ever?
   Is His promise come to an end for evermore?
10. Hath God forgotten to be gracious?
   Hath He in anger shut up His compassions?'   Selah

3. MY HAND UPLIFTETH. In prayer.

REFUSETH TO BE COMFORTED. This is almost the exact phrase
which Jeremiah uses when he describes mother Rachel weeping
for her exiled children: "Rachel weeping for her children; she
refuseth to be comforted," Jeremiah 31:15. It is not far-fetched
to assume that the psalmist remembered that vision of Jeremiah
in which the prophet referred to the exile of the northern kingdom. Now that the people of the southern kingdom are also in
exile the psalmist uses the same expression.

5. THOU HOLDEST FAST THE LIDS. The commentator, Kimchi,
explains this to mean that God has punished him by troubling
his heart with such bitter thoughts that he cannot sleep during
the night. Thus, God holds open the lids of his eyes.

6. I HAVE PONDERED. I have meditated about the events of
the past but could find no comfort from them.

7. I WILL CALL TO REMEMBRANCE. I will recall my own joyous prayers in the past.

MY SPIRIT MAKETH DILIGENT SEARCH. I search for thoughts
that will strengthen me, yet, in spite of my prayers and recollections these unhappy questions return: "Will the Lord cast off
forever?" (verse 8); "Is His mercy clean gone forever?" (verse
9); "Hath God forgotten to be gracious?" (verse 10).

10. HATH HE IN ANGER SHUT UP HIS COMPASSION? Has His

217

11. And I say: 'This is my weakness,
    That the right hand of the Most High could change.
12. I will make mention of the deeds of the LORD;
    Yea, I will remember Thy wonders of old.
13. I will meditate also upon all Thy work,
    And muse on Thy doings.'
14. O God, Thy way is in holiness;
    Who is a great god like unto God?
15. Thou art the God that doest wonders;
    Thou hast made known Thy strength among the
        peoples.

anger imprisoned His mercy so that it cannot come forth?

11-13. The psalmist resolves to conquer his weakness and to find strength in his present grief from recollections of God's help in ages past.

11. MY WEAKNESS. It is a proof of weakness in me that I allow myself to believe that God's right hand which delivered us in the past would now change from strength to weakness. Therefore, "I will make mention of the deeds of the Lord" (verse 12), and will find strength again from those recollections.

RIGHT HAND . . . COULD CHANGE. Isaiah 50:2 uses the same idea, denying that God's hand could change from strength to weakness: "Is my hand shortened that it cannot redeem?"

14-15. THY WAY IS IN HOLINESS; WHO IS . . . LIKE UNTO GOD . . . THAT DOEST WONDERS. The whole passage is based upon the description of God's holiness and incomparable power given in the Song by the Red Sea, (Exodus 15:11), "Who is like unto Thee, O Lord, among the mighty . . . glorious in holiness . . . doing wonders?"

16. THINE ARM REDEEMED THY PEOPLE. Thy might delivered Israel. This phrase is based upon the phraseology of the Song by the Red Sea: "Thou stretchest out Thy right hand . . . hast led the people that Thou hast redeemed," (Exodus 15:12, 13).

THE SONS OF JACOB AND JOSEPH. The prophets and the psalmist frequently mention these names together in order to describe all of Israel. It is not quite clear however, why Joseph should be mentioned, since the "sons of Jacob" would include all of the

16. Thou hast with Thine arm redeemed Thy people,
    The sons of Jacob and Joseph.   Selah
17. The waters saw Thee, O God;
    The waters saw Thee, they were in pain;
    The depths also trembled.
18. The clouds flooded forth waters;
    The skies sent out a sound;
    Thine arrows also went abroad.
19. The voice of Thy thunder was in the whirlwind;
    The lightnings lighted up the world;
    The earth trembled and shook.

tribes. The Aramaic translation (the Targum), says: "The sons whom Jacob begot and Joseph sustained," referring to the fact that Joseph, as viceroy in Egypt, saved the lives of all the children of Israel. Another possible explanation is that Joseph (meaning the tribes of Ephraim and Manasseh, his two sons), represented the most powerful element of the northern kingdom. However, this explanation is not quite satisfactory. Had the psalmist said "Judah and Joseph," the phrase would be logical, but the name "Jacob" includes all of the tribes, both northern and southern. Perhaps the explanation is that just as Jacob was the ancestor of tribes so was Joseph the ancestor of two great tribes (namely, Ephraim and Manasseh). Thus, although Jacob and Joseph were father and son, they were both progenitors of tribes.

17-21. All of nature, sea and sky, were startled at the coming of God to redeem His people. The panic of the waters is described also in Psalm 114:3, "The sea saw it and fled."

17. THEY WERE IN PAIN. In an agony of fear.

18. THINE ARROWS. The lightning.

19. THE WHIRLWIND. The Hebrew word here used literally means a "wheel," and in medieval astronomy had come to mean the revolving spheres of the heavens. The commentator, Kimchi, therefore, takes this verse as meaning: Thy thunder was in the heavens. However, the translation "whirlwind," given here, corresponds to the use of the same word in Psalm 83:14, where it is translated "whirling dust."

219

20. Thy way was in the sea,
      And Thy path in the great waters,
      And Thy footsteps were not known.
21. Thou didst lead Thy people like a flock,
      By the hand of Moses and Aaron.

78. MASCHIL OF ASAPH.

Give ear, O my people, to my teaching.
Incline your ears to the words of my mouth.
2. I will open my mouth with a parable;
      I will utter dark sayings concerning days of old.
3. That which we have heard and known,
      And our fathers have told us,
4. We will not hide from their children,
      Telling to the generation to come the praises of the LORD,

20. THY WAY WAS IN THE SEA . . . THY FOOTSTEPS WERE NOT KNOWN. The psalmist seems to mean that God, unseen, led the people afoot through the divided waters of the Red Sea.

21. BY THE HAND OF MOSES AND AARON. i. e. under the leadership of Moses and Aaron. The same phrase is used in the Book of Numbers 33:1, "Israel . . . went forth out of the land of Egypt . . . under the hand of Moses and Aaron."

THIS Asaph psalm presents a detailed retrospect of the history of Israel in order to prove that in spite of God's constant deliverance, the people repeatedly rebelled against Him. God has been merciful, but Israel has been ungrateful. This theory of Israel's past is frequently developed in the Bible, particularly in Judges 2:11-23, where the author describes how God would send judge after judge to deliver Israel and how, nevertheless, time and time again the people would go astray. It is noteworthy that the Bible, unlike every other history of the past, not only does not undertake to glorify Israel but frankly points out its weaknesses. The hero of the Bible is not Israel, but God alone.

The thought of this psalm is repeated in Psalms 105 and

And His strength, and His wondrous works that He hath done. Psalm 78

5. For He established a testimony in Jacob,
   And appointed a law in Israel,
   Which He commanded our fathers,
   That they should make them known to their children;
6. That the generation to come might know them, even the chil-
   dren that should be born;
   Who should arise and tell them to their children,
7. That they might put their confidence in God,
   And not forget the works of God,
   But keep His commandments;
8. And might not be as their fathers,
   A stubborn and rebellious generation;
   A generation that set not their heart aright,
   And whose spirit was not stedfast with God.

106. Its language is akin to that of the song in Deuteronomy
32. It is difficult, however, to fix an exact date for the psalm.
Some modern scholars have analyzed the list of plagues given
in verses 43-51, and have tried to correlate the list with the list
of plagues in what they consider to be the basic documents into
which these scholars analyze the Pentateuch (the Jahwist, the
Elohist, the Priestly Codes). However, it is difficult to arrive at
a precise date by this method. It is not unlikely, however, that
this psalm is later than the prophet Isaiah, since it makes use
of the expression "the Holy One of Israel" (verse 41), a phrase
which is used almost exclusively in Isaiah. Also, it would seem
to have been written after the northern kingdom was destroyed.
(See verses 60 and 61.)

1. MASCHIL. See note to Psalm 32:1.

1-4. An introductory statement calling upon the people to
listen to his words.

2. DARK SAYINGS. The phrase is a parallel to the word "parable." The same parallel is found in the introductory phrase of
Psalm 49, "I will incline mine ear to a parable; I will open my
dark saying upon the harp."

5-8. These verses refer to the God-given duty to hand down
the traditions of the past from father to son in order that chil-

9. The children of Ephraim were as archers handling the bow,
   That turned back in the day of battle.
10. They kept not the covenant of God,
    And refused to walk in His law;
11. And they forgot His doings,
    And His wondrous works that He had shown them.
12. Marvellous things did He in the sight of their fathers,
    In the land of Egypt, in the field of Zoan.
13. He cleaved the sea, and caused them to pass through;
    And He made the waters to stand as a heap.
14. By day also He led them with a cloud,
    And all the night with a light of fire.
15. He cleaved rocks in the wilderness,
    And gave them drink abundantly as out of the great deep.

dren may avoid the sins of their fathers. This duty to preserve the memory of the past is given as a definite command in Deuteronomy 4:9, "Take heed . . . lest thou forget the things which thine eyes saw . . . make them known unto thy children and thy children's children."

7-8. The purpose of teaching Israel's history was that the coming generations "forget not the works of God" (verse 7), and that they may be careful not "to be as their fathers, a stubborn and rebellious generation" (verse 8). The phrase, "stubborn and rebellious," is identical with that used of an incorrigible son (Deuteronomy 21:18).

9. CHILDREN OF EPHRAIM . . . ARCHERS . . . THAT TURNED BACK. The commentators, Ibn Ezra and Rashi, say that this refers to a premature expedition of the children of Ephraim in the early days of Israel's stay in Egypt. They marched against the Philistines and were defeated. This explanation is based upon a tradition found in the Midrash (Exodus Rabba 22:11). The Midrashic story is, in turn, based upon a rather obscure verse in I Chronicles 7:21, which speaks of the sons of Ephraim "whom the men of Gath . . . slew because they came down to take away their cattle." However, we need not take this verse literally (as Ibn Ezra and Rashi do) as referring to a specific event, but may understand it symbolically, namely, that

222

16. He brought streams also out of the rock,
    And caused waters to run down like rivers.
17. Yet went they on still to sin against Him,
    To rebel against the Most High in the desert.
18. And they tried God in their heart
    By asking food for their craving.
19. Yea, they spoke against God;
    They said: 'Can God prepare a table in the wilderness?
20. Behold, He smote the rock, that waters gushed out,
    And streams overflowed;
    Can He give bread also?
    Or will He provide flesh for His people?'
21. Therefore the LORD heard, and was wroth;
    And a fire was kindled against Jacob,

Ephraim (the northern kingdom) failed in their duty to God as unreliable archers might fail their commander on the day of battle. So interpreted, the verse becomes still clearer when taken with verse 57 where Ephraim is rejected "like a deceitful bow." The psalmist there explains why God rejected Ephraim, i. e., the northern tribes, and forsook the tabernacle of Shiloh which was in their territory. At all events, verse 10 ff. ("They kept not the covenant of God") does not refer back to Ephraim but to the entire people of Israel, describing how quickly they forgot the miracles that God performed in their behalf in Egypt and in the desert.

12. ZOAN. A district in Egypt.

13. WATERS . . . AS A HEAP. The same phrase used in the Song by the Red Sea, "The floods stood upright as a heap" (Exodus 15:8).

15. CLEAVED ROCKS. When Moses divided the rock to give Israel water. (Exodus 17:6.)

18. THEY TRIED GOD IN THEIR HEART BY ASKING FOOD. Their murmurings in the wilderness before the giving of the manna. (Exodus 16:8.)

21. A FIRE WAS KINDLED. The event referred to in Numbers 11:1, "When the Lord heard it, His anger was kindled; and the fire of the Lord burnt among them."

223

And anger also went up against Israel;
22. Because they believed not in God,
And trusted not in His salvation.
23. And He commanded the skies above,
And opened the doors of heaven;
24. And He caused manna to rain upon them for food,
And gave them of the corn of heaven.
25. Man did eat the bread of the mighty;
He sent them provisions to the full.
26. He caused the east wind to set forth in heaven;
And by His power He brought on the south wind.
27. He caused flesh also to rain upon them as the dust,
And winged fowl as the sand of the seas;
28. And He let it fall in the midst of their camp,
Round about their dwellings.
29. So they did eat, and were well filled;
And He gave them that which they craved.
30. They were not estranged from their craving,
Their food was yet in their mouths,
31. When the anger of God went up against them,

24. THE CORN OF HEAVEN. The phrase is made clear by the parallel in the first half of the couplet. It means the manna.

25. THE BREAD OF THE MIGHTY. Most of the commentators take this to mean the bread of the angels, i. e., the manna. In Psalm 29:1, "O ye sons of might," refers to the angels.

26-27. EAST WIND . . . CAUSED FLESH TO RAIN. Refers to the fall of quail in the desert as related in Numbers 11:31, "And there went forth a wind from the Lord, and brought across quails from the sea, and let them fall by the camp."

30. THEY WERE NOT ESTRANGED FROM THEIR CRAVING. They had not yet stilled their appetite for flesh when punishment came upon them "when the anger of God went up against them" (verse 31). In Numbers 11:33, the event is described as follows: "While the flesh was yet between their teeth . . . the anger of the Lord was kindled."

32-39. The psalmist arrives at a general conclusion from the above events, namely, that they frequently sinned and would frequently repent: "turn back and seek God earnestly" (verse

And slew of the lustiest among them,
And smote down the young men of Israel.
32. For all this they sinned still,
And believed not in His wondrous works.
33. Therefore He ended their days as a breath,
And their years in terror.
34. When He slew them, then they would inquire after **Him,**
And turn back and seek God earnestly.
35. And they remembered that God was their Rock,
And the Most High God their Redeemer.
36. But they beguiled Him with their mouth,
And lied unto Him with their tongue.
37. For their heart was not stedfast with Him,
Neither were they faithful in His covenant.
38. But He, being full of compassion, forgiveth **iniquity,**
and destroyeth not;
Yea, many a time doth He turn His anger away,
And doth not stir up all His wrath.
39. So He remembered that they were but flesh;
A wind that passeth away, and cometh not **again.**

34), but their repentance was never permanent; "they beguiled Him . . . and lied unto Him" (verse 36) but God, "full of compassion" (verse 38), knowing "that they were but flesh," forgave them again and again.

38. BUT HE, BEING FULL OF COMPASSION. According to the Talmud (b. Kiddushin 30 a), this verse is the middle verse of the Psalter, and the Hebrew word for "wood", in Psalm 80:14, is the middle *word* of the entire Book of Psalms.

Every word in Scriptures was counted and the separate totals of the various books recorded. By noting which was the middle sentence and the middle word of each biblical book, they could be certain that, as the books were recopied, no sentence or word would ever drop out undetected. See the article *Masorah, Jewish Encyclopedia*, Vol. VIII, particularly page 366, column 1.

Verse 38 has been embodied in the Prayerbook as the introduction to the Evening Services and to the penitential prayers (*Tachanun*) at the close of the daily Morning Service.

225

40. How oft did they rebel against Him in the wilderness,
    And grieve Him in the desert!
41. And still again they tried God,
    And set bounds to the Holy One of Israel.
42. They remembered not His hand,
    Nor the day when He redeemed them from the adversary.
43. How He set His signs in Egypt,
    And His wonders in the field of Zoan;
44. And turned their rivers into blood,
    So that they could not drink their streams.
45. He sent among them swarms of flies, which devoured them;
    And frogs, which destroyed them.
46. He gave also their increase unto the caterpillar,
    And their labour unto the locust.
47. He destroyed their vines with hail,
    And their sycomore-trees with frost.
48. He gave over their cattle also to the hail,
    And their flocks to fiery bolts.
49. He sent forth upon them the fierceness of His anger,
    Wrath, and indignation, and trouble,
    A sending of messengers of evil.
50. He levelled a path for His anger;
    He spared not their soul from death,
    But gave their life over to the pestilence;

40-55. A more detailed recapitulation of the deliverance from Egypt and the march through the desert to the promised land.

43. ZOAN. A district in Egypt.

49. A SENDING OF MESSENGERS. Some of the commentators say that "messengers" here means "destroying angels," while others say it simply refers to the plagues as instruments of God's will.

51. THE FIRST-FRUITS OF THEIR STRENGTH. This phrase is frequently used in the Bible to mean the first born child. Thus, Genesis 49:3, "Reuben, thou art my first-born ... the first-fruits of my strength."

52. TO GO FORTH LIKE SHEEP. The same phrase is used in the preceding psalm, "Thou didst lead Thy people like a flock" (Psalm 77:21).

54. TO THE MOUNTAIN. May refer to Mount Sinai, but the

51. And smote all the first-born in Egypt,
    The first-fruits of their strength in the tents of Ham;
52. But He made His own people to go forth like sheep,
    And guided them in the wilderness like a flock.
53. And He led them safely, and they feared not;
    But the sea overwhelmed their enemies.
54. And He brought them to His holy border,
    To the mountain, which His right hand had gotten.
55. He drove out the nations also before them,
    And allotted them for an inheritance by line,
    And made the tribes of Israel to dwell in their tents.
56. Yet they tried and provoked God, the Most High,
    And kept not His testimonies;
57. But turned back, and dealt treacherously like their fathers;
    They were turned aside like a deceitful bow.
58. For they provoked Him with their high places,
    And moved Him to jealousy with their graven images.
59. God heard, and was wroth,
    And He greatly abhorred Israel;
60. And He forsook the tabernacle of Shiloh,
    The tent which He had made to dwell among men;
61. And delivered His strength into captivity,
    And His glory into the adversary's hand.
62. He gave His people over also unto the sword;

context seems to indicate that it refers to Canaan, the mountainous land.

55. INHERITANCE BY LINE. They measured out the land with a measuring line and divided it up by lot.

THEIR TENTS. The tents of the Canaanites whom they conquered.

57. DECEITFUL BOW. An unreliable bow on which the archer cannot depend. The same phrase is found in Hosea 7:16, "They are become like a deceitful bow." This verse is connected with the thought of verse 9, "The children of Ephraim . . . handling the bow."

From here on to the end, the psalmist tells why God abandoned the northern kingdom and the sanctuary of Shiloh situated within its territory and preferred Zion and Judah.

58 ff. Because "they provoked Him . . . with graven images

And was wroth with His inheritance.
63. Fire devoured their young men;
And their virgins had no marriage-song.
64. Their priests fell by the sword;
And their widows made no lamentation.
65. Then the Lord awaked as one asleep,
Like a mighty man recovering from wine.
66. And He smote His adversaries backward;
He put upon them a perpetual reproach.
67. Moreover He abhorred the tent of Joseph,
And chose not the tribe of Ephraim;
68. But chose the tribe of Judah,
The mount Zion which He loved.
69. And He built His sanctuary like the heights,
Like the earth which He hath founded for ever.
70. He chose David also His servant,
And took him from the sheepfolds;
71. From following the ewes that give suck He brought him,

... He abhorred Israel ... forsook the tabernacle of Shiloh,"
God permitted the invaders to destroy the northern kingdom
(verses 61-64).

64. THEIR WIDOWS MADE NO LAMENTATION. So great was the
devastation that even the customary funeral rites were abandoned.

65 to the end. God now selects Zion and Judah and the
house of David.

65. THE LORD AWAKED. This bold metaphor occurs frequently in the Psalms. Thus, "Awake, why sleepest Thou, O Lord?"
(Psalm 44:24).

67. CHOSE NOT THE TRIBE OF EPHRAIM. God's rejection of the
northern kingdom.

69. LIKE THE HEIGHTS. Either like a high palace or a lofty
mountain.

70 to the end. He chooses David, the shepherd, to be the
shepherd of Israel.

72. THE INTEGRITY OF HIS HEART. Thus, in I Kings 9:4, God
says to Solomon referring to David, his father, "as David thy
father walked, in integrity of heart."

To be shepherd over Jacob His people, and Israel His inheritance.

72. So he shepherded them according to the integrity of his heart;
And led them by the skillfulness of his hands.

79. A PSALM OF ASAPH.

O God, the heathen are come into Thine inheritance;
They have defiled Thy holy temple;
They have made Jerusalem into heaps.

2. They have given the dead bodies of Thy servants to be food
unto the fowls of the heaven,
The flesh of Thy saints unto the beasts of the earth.

3. They have shed their blood like water
Round about Jerusalem, with none to bury them.

4. We are become a taunt to our neighbours,
A scorn and derision to them that are round about us.

5. How long, O LORD, wilt Thou be angry for ever?
How long will Thy jealousy burn like fire?

THIS psalm is related in subject matter to Psalm 74. Both speak of the enemies who had invaded Jerusalem and destroyed the Temple. For the discussion of the date of the psalm see introduction to Psalm 74.

1. THE HEATHEN . . . INTO THINE INHERITANCE. This phrase is used by Jeremiah speaking of the destruction of Jerusalem, "strangers are come into the sanctuaries of the Lord's house" (Jeremiah 51:51).

MADE JERUSALEM INTO HEAPS. This phrase is likewise used by Jeremiah, "Jerusalem shall become heaps," i. e., of ruins (Jeremiah 26:18).

4. A TAUNT TO OUR NEIGHBOURS. A familiar thought in the Psalms. When our enemies see us suffer they mock us. See Psalm 44:14, "Thou makest us a taunt to our neighbours."

5. HOW LONG, O LORD . . . FOR EVER. A puzzling expression. "How long" and "for ever" seem to contradict each other. Possibly it means, how long, O Lord, will Your anger seem perpetual, or, how long wilt Thou rage against us ceaselessly. A similar phrase is used in Psalm 74:10, "How long . . . shall the enemy blaspheme . . . for ever?"

229

6. Pour out Thy wrath upon the nations that know Thee not,
And upon the kingdoms that call not upon Thy name.
7. For they have devoured Jacob,
And laid waste his habitation.
8. Remember not against us the iniquities of our forefathers;
Let Thy compassions speedily come to meet us;
For we are brought very low.
9. Help us, O God of our salvation, for the sake of the
glory of Thy name;
And deliver us, and forgive our sins, for Thy name's sake.
10. Wherefore should the nations say: 'Where is their God?'
Let the avenging of Thy servants' blood that is shed
Be made known among the nations in our sight.
11. Let the groaning of the prisoner come before Thee;
According to the greatness of Thy power set free

THY JEALOUSY BURN LIKE FIRE. The Bible frequently speaks
of God as a jealous God. He will brook no rival worship. Man
must make an absolute choice between the One God and idolatry. God's jealousy, like God's anger, is often described by the
metaphor of a raging fire. Thus, "For the Lord thy God is a
devouring fire, a jealous God" (Deuteronomy 4:24).

8. THE INIQUITIES OF OUR FOREFATHERS. The thought that
our forefathers have repeatedly sinned against God was developed in Psalm 78, and is a familiar theme in the Asaph psalms.

10. WHERE IS THEIR GOD? The psalmist frequently describes
the enemy as mocking Israel and saying, where is their God on
whom they rely for help? (Cf. Psalm 42:4.)

AVENGING OF THY SERVANTS' BLOOD. In ancient times if a man
were murdered a relative would have the responsibility of ex-
acting punishment. This relative was called "the avenger of the
blood." The humble and the fatherless who had no relatives to
protect them relied upon the king to exact punishment for violence done them. Ultimately it was God who held "precious the
blood" of his righteous ones. God would not permit violence to
go unpunished. Thus, "He doth avenge the blood of His servants (Deuteronomy 32:43).

12. SEVENFOLD. A round number, meaning many times.

230

those that are appointed to death;

12. And render unto our neighbours sevenfold into their bosom
    Their reproach, wherewith they have reproached Thee, O Lord.
13. So we that are Thy people and the flock of Thy pasture
    Will give Thee thanks for ever;
    We will tell of Thy praise to all generations.

80. FOR THE LEADER; UPON SHOSHANNIM. A TESTIMONY. A PSALM
    OF ASAPH.

2. Give ear, O Shepherd of Israel,
   Thou that leadest Joseph like a flock;
   Thou that art enthroned upon the cherubim, shine forth.
3. Before Ephraim and Benjamin and Manasseh, stir up
     Thy might,
   And come to save us.

THIS psalm prays that God restore the northern kingdom,
and, therefore, must have been written after the destruction of
the northern kingdom and, in all likelihood, a considerable
time after that destruction, since the spirit of rivalry between
north and south had been forgotten and the psalmist, living in
Judah, pleads to God to restore the northern tribes.

1. SHOSHANNIM. Lilies. Probably the name of a melody to
which this psalm was sung.

A TESTIMONY. This word may be part of the title of the
melody. See comment to Psalm 60:1.

2. THAT LEADEST JOSEPH LIKE A FLOCK. In Psalm 77:21, the
psalmist says, "Thou didst lead Thy *people* like a flock," but
here the prayer is a special prayer for the descendants of Joseph,
that is, for Ephraim and Manasseh, the northern kingdom.

ENTHRONED UPON THE CHERUBIM. This phrase, frequently
used, has two meanings. It refers to God in the heavens surrounded by the cherubim (the angels), and has also come to
refer to God as hovering over the ark which was adorned with
two golden cherubim. Thus, I Samuel 4:4, "The ark of the
covenant of the Lord of hosts, who sitteth upon the cherubim."

3. EPHRAIM, BENJAMIN AND MANASSEH. Ephraim and Manasseh were the children of Joseph, the brother of Benjamin.

231

4. O God, restore us;
   And cause Thy face to shine, and we shall be saved.
5. O Lord God of hosts,
   How long wilt Thou be angry against the prayer of Thy people?
6. Thou hast fed them with the bread of tears,
   And given them tears to drink in large measure.
7. Thou makest us a strife unto our neighbours;
   And our enemies mock as they please.
8. O God of hosts, restore us;
   And cause Thy face to shine, and we shall be saved.
9. Thou didst pluck up a vine out of Egypt;
   Thou didst drive out the nations, and didst plant it.
10. Thou didst clear a place before it,
    And it took deep root, and filled the land.
11. The mountains were covered with the shadow of it,
    And the mighty cedars with the boughs thereof.
12. She sent out her branches unto the sea,

Hence, these three tribes were the children of Rachel whom Jeremiah describes as weeping for her children when the northern kingdom was destroyed. (Jeremiah 31:15.)

4. O GOD RESTORE US; CAUSE THY FACE TO SHINE. This sentence is a refrain which is repeated in verses 8 and 20 to mark the close of each division of the thought.

5-8. The psalmist asks God to have pity on His people.

6. THE BREAD OF TEARS . . . TEARS TO DRINK. The same phrase is used in Psalm 42:4, "My tears have been my food day and night."

7. A STRIFE UNTO OUR NEIGHBOURS. They fight over the division of the spoil.

9 to the end. Describes Israel as a vine which God has transplanted from Egypt to the Holy Land. This metaphor is used a number of times in the Bible, but its finest expression is found in Isaiah 5:1-7. The Rabbis are likewise fond of comparing Israel to a vine. The Midrash (Exodus Rabba XLIV, 1) develops the metaphor of the vine in great detail. The description given in this psalm of all that God did for his vine (Israel) parallels Isaiah's famous sermon, Isaiah 5.

12. SHE SENT OUT. i. e. The vine sends out her branches.

232

And her shoots unto the River.
13. Why hast Thou broken down her fences,
    So that all they that pass by the way do pluck her?
14. The boar out of the wood doth ravage it,
    That which moveth in the field feedeth on it.
15. O God of hosts, return, we beseech Thee;
    Look from heaven, and behold, and be mindful of this **vine,**
16. And of the stock which Thy right hand hath planted,
    And the branch that Thou madest strong for Thyself.
17. It is burned with fire, it is cut down;
    They perish at the rebuke of Thy countenance.
18. Let Thy hand be upon the man of Thy right hand,
    Upon the son of man whom Thou madest strong for **Thyself.**
19. So shall we not turn back from Thee;
    Quicken Thou us, and we will call upon Thy name.
20. O LORD God of hosts, restore us;
    Cause Thy face to shine, and we shall be saved.

The Hebrew word for "vine" used here is a feminine noun.

THE RIVER. The Euphrates.

14. THE WOOD. According to the Talmud this is the middle word of the Book of Psalms. See note to Psalm 78:38.

18. THE MAN OF THY RIGHT HAND. The commentator, Kimchi, explains this to mean, "Israel whom Thou hast delivered by Thy right hand."

19. QUICKEN THOU US. Revive us.

SALM 81 is a call to worship God with music and song on a festival day. As is usually the case in the Asaph psalms, this psalm goes on from the call to worship to a discussion of Jewish history. It speaks of the sinfulness of our ancestors and bids the people obey God's Law that He might protect them.

This psalm is recited in the synagogue on Thursday at the close of the morning service. It was one of the regular Levitical Psalms recited at the daily sacrifice on Thursday (m. Tamid VII, 4). The Talmud also prescribes this psalm for *Mussaf* (the additional service) for the New Year (b. Rosh Hashonah 4a and b).

233

81. FOR THE LEADER; UPON THE GITTITH. [A PSALM]
OF ASAPH.

2. Sing aloud unto God our strength;
   Shout unto the God of Jacob.
3. Take up the melody, and sound the timbrel,
   The sweet harp with the psaltery.
4. Blow the horn at the new moon,
   At the full moon for our feast-day.
5. For it is a statute for Israel,
   An ordinance of the God of Jacob.
6. He appointed it in Joseph for a testimony,
   When He went forth against the land of Egypt.

1. GITTITH. A melody from Gath, or the song of David's Gittite guard, or the name of an instrument. See Psalm 8:1.

4. THE HORN AT THE NEW MOON. The word for "horn" here is *shofar*, meaning a wind instrument made from the horn of an animal. But the Law in Numbers 10:10, seems to prescribe *metal* trumpets to be used at the new moon. For that reason the Aramaic translation (the Targum) translates the verse as follows: "And blow the horn at the new moon of Tishri," i. e., at the New Year, thus accounting for the psalmist's use of *shofar* instead of trumpet.

THE FULL MOON FOR OUR FEAST-DAY. The two great holidays, Passover and Succoth, occurred in the middle of the month at the time of the *full* moon.

5-6. ORDINANCE OF THE GOD OF JACOB . . . IN JOSEPH FOR A TESTIMONY. Just as in Psalm 77:16, Jacob and Joseph are used to include the entire people of Israel (both kingdoms). But the commentator, Rashi, basing his comment upon the talmudic legend (in b. Rosh Hashonah 10 b and b. Sota 36 b), takes the name "Joseph" to refer not to the tribe but to Joseph the individual, and interprets verse 6 as follows: when Joseph went forth in Egypt, i. e., when he came out of prison on the New Year, he said: "The speech of one that I knew not did I hear." Joseph referred to the angel Gabriel who had taught him the seventy languages of the world while he was in prison.

The speech of one that I knew not did I hear:
7. 'I removed his shoulder from the burden;
His hands were freed from the basket.
8. Thou didst call in trouble, and I rescued thee;
I answered thee in the secret place of thunder;
I proved thee at the waters of Meribah.   Selah
9. Hear, O My people, and I will admonish thee:
O Israel, if thou wouldest hearken unto Me!
10. There shall no strange god be in thee;
Neither shalt thou worship any foreign god.
11. I am the LORD thy God,
Who brought thee up out of the land of Egypt;
Open thy mouth wide, and I will fill it.

However, as translated here the thought is closer to the plain meaning of the text: When "He (God) marched forth to punish the Egyptians."

6. THE SPEECH OF ONE THAT I KNEW NOT. Both the commentators, Ibn Ezra and Kimchi, take the subject to be the people Israel, not Joseph (as Rashi takes it). Israel heard in Egypt a language that he knew not, a language that he did not understand. This idea is expressed in Psalm 114:1, "When Israel came forth out of Egypt, the house of Jacob from a people of strange language."

7-11. God speaks to Israel, reminding him how He had delivered him and how Israel nevertheless rebelled.

8. SECRET PLACE OF THUNDER. The dark, impenetrable clouds.

PROVED THEE AT MERIBAH. In Exodus 17:7, "And the name of the place was called Massah, and Meribah, because of the striving of the children of Israel, and because they tried the Lord."

10-11. WORSHIP ANY FOREIGN GOD. I AM THE LORD THY GOD. This parallels closely the opening verse of the Ten Commandments. (Exodus 20:2-3.)

11. I AM THE LORD . . . OPEN THY MOUTH WIDE, AND I WILL FILL IT. If you will worship Me alone I will shower My bounties upon you.

235

Psalm 81

12. But My people hearkened not to My voice;
    And Israel would none of Me.
13. So I let them go after the stubbornness of their heart,
    That they might walk in their own counsels.
14. Oh that My people would hearken unto Me,
    That Israel would walk in My ways!
15. I would soon subdue their enemies,
    And turn My hand against their adversaries.
16. The haters of the LORD should dwindle away before Him;
    And their punishment should endure for ever.
17. They should also be fed with the fat of wheat;
    And with honey out of the rock would I satisfy thee.'

82. A PSALM OF ASAPH.

God standeth in the congregation of God;

12-17. God continues to speak but not to Israel of old. He now addresses the Israelites who are contemporary with the psalmist, and tells them how their forefathers repeatedly rebelled against Him.

16. THE HATERS . . . SHOULD DWINDLE. The same phrase is found in Psalm 66:3, "Thine enemies dwindle away before Thee."

17. THE FAT OF WHEAT. The richness of wheat.

HONEY OUT OF THE ROCK. This refers to the wild honey that is found in the crevices of the rocks. Thus, Deuteronomy 32:13, "He made him to suck honey out of the crag."

THIS psalm, chanted by the Levites in the Temple on Tuesdays (m. Tamid 7:4), is recited daily in the synagogue on that day at the close of the morning service.

The psalm is closely akin in thought to Psalm 58. Both psalms rebuke unjust judges and remind them that God is the true Judge.

1. GOD STANDETH IN THE CONGREGATION OF GOD. The commentator, Ibn Ezra, takes the words "congregation of God" to mean the Godly congregation, namely, Israel (as in Numbers

236

In the midst of the judges He judgeth:
2. 'How long will ye judge unjustly,
   And respect the persons of the wicked?   Selah
3. Judge the poor and fatherless;
   Do justice to the afflicted and destitute.
4. Rescue the poor and needy;
   Deliver them out of the hand of the wicked.
5. They know not, neither do they understand;
   They go about in darkness;
   All the foundations of the earth are moved.
6. I said: Ye are godlike beings,
   And all of you sons of the Most High.
7. Nevertheless ye shall die like men,
   And fall like one of the princes.'
8. Arise, O God, judge the earth;

27:17, "that the congregation of the Lord be not as sheep which have no shepherd"). The verse then means that God is in the midst of Israel and He speaks to the judges, rebuking them for their injustices.

2. RESPECT THE PERSONS OF THE WICKED. The law denounces the "respecting" of any persons, low or great. The judge must be just and must never give an unjust decision out of respect for any person, rich or poor. Thus, "Ye shall do no unrighteousness in judgment; thou shalt not respect the person of the poor, nor favour the person of the mighty." (Leviticus 19:15.)

3. THE POOR AND FATHERLESS. These are God's especial wards. "He doth execute justice for the fatherless and widow." (Deuteronomy 10:18.)

5. THEY KNOW NOT . . . THE FOUNDATIONS OF THE EARTH ARE MOVED. The judges, being ignorant, destroy the ethical foundations of human life on earth.

6. I SAID: YE ARE GOD-LIKE BEINGS. God speaks: I appointed you as judges and thus made you God-like by allowing you to be the vehicles of My justice.

7. NEVERTHELESS YE SHALL DIE . . . FALL LIKE ONE OF THE PRINCES. In your pride you imagine you are immortal. Remember that you will die like ordinary men. And since you are un-

237

For Thou shalt possess all the nations.

83. A SONG, A PSALM OF ASAPH.

2. O God, keep not Thou silence;
   Hold not Thy peace, and be not still, O God.
3. For, lo, Thine enemies are in an uproar;
   And they that hate Thee have lifted up the head.
4. They hold crafty converse against Thy people,
   And take counsel against Thy treasured ones.
5. They have said: 'Come, and let us cut them off from
      being a nation;
   That the name of Israel may be no more in remembrance.'
6. For they have consulted together with one consent;
   Against Thee do they make a covenant;

just judges you will fall suddenly like the wicked princes. The heathen princes are the judges in their respective lands. When they practice violence instead of justice, they perish. So shall you fall, if you are unjust.

8. JUDGE THE EARTH. A fitting close to the psalm. Be Thou, O God, the Judge. Since there is no unrighteousness in Thee, Thou wilt possess and govern all the world as Judge and King.

THIS psalm is the last one of the twelve Asaph psalms (eleven psalms here, 73 to 83, and Psalm 50 in the preceding Book).

The psalmist turns to God for help in behalf of Israel against the confederation of enemies. He asks God to defeat this hostile confederation as He had defeated Israel's enemies in the early days. When God will achieve His victory all the nations of the earth will know that He is the Master of mankind.

To which confederation of enemies does the psalmist refer? Inasmuch as Assyria is included among the nations mentioned, the psalm must have been written some time before Assyria became the great world-power of the east and was just one nation in a larger confederation. Thus, the psalm may refer to the con-

7. The tents of Edom and the Ishmaelites;
   Moab, and the Hagrites;
8. Gebal, and Ammon, and Amalek;
   Philistia with the inhabitants of Tyre;
9. Assyria also is joined with them;
   They have been an arm to the children of Lot.   **Selah**
10. Do Thou unto them as unto Midian;
    As to Sisera, as to Jabin, at the brook Kishon;
11. Who were destroyed at En-dor;
    They became as dung for the earth.
12. Make their nobles like Oreb and Zeeb,
    And like Zebah and Zalmunna all their princes;
13. Who said: 'Let us take to ourselves in possession
    The habitations of God,'

federation of enemies against Israel in the days of Jehoshaphat (II Chronicles 20).

2. KEEP NOT THOU SILENCE. DO NOT IGNORE OUR PLIGHT. A frequent plea in the Psalms. Thus, "Thou hast seen, O Lord; keep not silence" (Psalm 35:22).

4. THY TREASURED ONES. Israel is described as God's treasured possession. "Ye shall be Mine own treasure from among all peoples" (Exodus 19:5).

7. THE TENTS OF EDOM. The men of Edom and the Ishmaelites were Bedouins who dwelled in tents. The various nations mentioned in verses 7, 8, 9, constitute a virtual encirclement of Palestine.

9. AN ARM TO THE CHILDREN OF LOT. Lot, the nephew of Abraham, was the father of Moab and Ammon (Genesis 19:37, 38). The verse therefore means, Assyria was an ally ("an arm") to Moab and Ammon.

10-18. DO THOU UNTO THEM . . . The psalmist calls upon God to defeat this confederation as He defeated Israel's enemies in the past.

10. MIDIAN defeated by Gideon (Judges 8).

SISERA . . . JABIN. Defeated by Deborah (Judges 4:2).

12. OREB . . . ZEEB. Midianite generals (Judges 7:25).

ZEBAH AND ZALMUNNA. Midianite princes (Judges 8:6).

239

14. O my God, make them like the whirling dust;
      As stubble before the wind.
15. As the fire that burneth the forest,
      And as the flame that setteth the mountains ablaze;
16. So pursue them with Thy tempest,
      And affright them with Thy storm.
17. Fill their faces with shame;
      That they may seek Thy name, O Lord.
18. Let them be ashamed and affrighted for ever;
      Yea, let them be abashed and perish;
19. That they may know that it is Thou alone whose
         name is the Lord,
      The Most High over all the earth.

14. WHIRLING DUST. The same Hebrew word is used here as the word in Psalm 77:19 which was translated as "whirlwind."

STUBBLE BEFORE THE WIND. The stubble or the chaff is blown away by the slightest wind. Thus, Psalm 1:4, "They are like the chaff which the wind driveth away."

19. The verse concludes the psalm with the thought that when God conquers the wicked, the world learns that the "Most High" is monarch "over all the earth."

THE first of four Korah psalms. Most of the Korah psalms are at the beginning of Book Two, Psalms 42 to 49. While the Korah psalms deal with a number of subjects, as do the Asaph psalms, they, too, have a favorite theme. The favorite theme of the Asaph psalms is the lessons of Jewish history. The favorite mood of the Korah psalms is a longing for the sanctuary.

This psalm is a typical Korah psalm, expressing an earnest wish to come to the sanctuary on Mount Zion. Thus it is closely akin to Psalms 42 and 43, both Korah psalms. One difference, however, between the Korah psalms here in Book Three and those in Book Two is that those in Book Two prefer to use *Elohim* as the name of God, and here *JHWH* is used.

It is difficult to date this psalm, except to say that it is pre-exilic. It must have been written at the time of the monarchy,

84. FOR THE LEADER; UPON THE GITTITH. A PSALM OF THE SONS OF KORAH.

2. How lovely are Thy tabernacles, O LORD of hosts!
3. My soul yearneth, yea, even pineth for the courts of the LORD;
   My heart and my flesh sing for joy unto the living God.
4. Yea, the sparrow hath found a house, and the swallow a nest for herself,
   Where she may lay her young;
   Thine altars, O LORD of hosts,
   My King, and my God—.
5. Happy are they that dwell in Thy house,
   They are ever praising Thee.   Selah

inasmuch as it includes a blessing for God's anointed (verse 10).

3. MY SOUL YEARNETH. The typical Korahite mood. Thus, "My soul thirsteth for God, for the living God" (Psalm 42:3).

MY SOUL . . . MY HEART . . . MY FLESH. Soul, heart, and flesh are mentioned together in Psalm 16:9, "My heart is glad, and my glory (i. e., "my soul") rejoiceth; my flesh also . . ."

4. THE SPARROW . . . A NEST . . . THINE ALTARS. The medieval commentators find this verse difficult inasmuch as it was contrary to the Jewish Law to allow birds to nest in the Temple. The commentator, Kimchi, therefore, says that this is a psalm of David and refers to the days before the Temple was built, when God's altars were erected in various "high places," as Shiloh and Nob. In these "high places" there was no prohibition against the nesting of the birds. The commentator, Rashi, says that this refers to the period when the Temple had been destroyed, and it means that the sparrows are nesting among the ruins of the altars. However, the meaning of the text becomes simple if the sentence, "thine altars," be not taken together with the previous sentence, "the sparrow her nest." The meaning would be, even the birds have a home. So is Thy sanctuary a dwelling place for me. Or, as the birds yearn to return to their nests, so do I yearn for Thine altars, O God. In other words: "so to me are Thine altars."

5. HAPPY ARE THEY THAT DWELL. This sentence is used as

241

Psalm 84
6

6. Happy is the man whose strength is in Thee;
   In whose heart are the highways.
7. Passing through the valley of Baca they make it
     a place of springs;
   Yea, the early rain clotheth it with blessings.
8. They go from strength to strength,
   Every one of them appeareth before God in Zion.
9. O LORD God of hosts, hear my prayer;
   Give ear, O God of Jacob.   Selah
10. Behold, O God our shield,
    And look upon the face of Thine anointed.
11. For a day in Thy courts is better than a thousand;

an introduction for Psalm 145 in the Prayerbook and is recited daily in the synagogue.

6. IN WHOSE HEART ARE THE HIGHWAYS. This verse is sometimes translated: "Happy the man . . . in whose heart are Thy ways." However, the Hebrew does not warrant this translation. It means, happy the man who thinks constantly of the road to the sanctuary. Read it as if it were, in whose heart are the highways to the Temple.

7. MAKE IT A PLACE OF SPRINGS. Such devoted pilgrims passing through the valley of Baca make it a place of springs. The verse may mean that the pilgrims journey fearlessly through arid valleys as if the valleys were lined with wells and springs.

8. FROM STRENGTH TO STRENGTH. They do not weary on the journey. Their eagerness to come to the sanctuary buoys them up. A similar expression is found in Isaiah 40:31, "they that wait for the Lord shall renew their strength."

10. LOOK UPON THE FACE OF THINE ANOINTED. Look with favor on the king.

11. A DAY IN THY COURTS IS BETTER THAN A THOUSAND. All the commentators understand this to mean, "is better than a thousand elsewhere."

I HAD RATHER STAND AT THE THRESHOLD . . . OF MY GOD, THAN TO DWELL IN THE TENTS OF WICKEDNESS. It is a greater joy to stand even at the outer door of God's house than to be an honored guest within the dwelling places of the wicked. Perhaps

242

I had rather stand at the threshold of the house of my God,
Than to dwell in the tents of wickedness.
12. For the LORD God is a sun and a shield;
The LORD giveth grace and glory;
No good thing will He withhold from them that
walk uprightly.
13. O LORD of hosts,
Happy is the man that trusteth in Thee.

85. FOR THE LEADER. A PSALM OF THE SONS OF KORAH.

2. LORD, Thou hast been favourable unto Thy land,
Thou hast turned the captivity of Jacob.

this Korahite singer thought of this comparison because one of
the functions of the Korahite Levites was to stand guard at the
threshold of the Temple. "The Korahites . . . keepers of the
gates of the Tent" (I Chronicles 9:19).

12. GOD IS A SUN AND A SHIELD. God is our light and our protector.

THEM THAT WALK UPRIGHTLY. Thus, similarly, Psalm 15:1
asks, "who shall sojourn in Thy tabernacle," and answers
(verse 2): "he that walketh uprightly."

THE psalmist praises God for having restored Israel to his
land. After the psalmist praises God for that act of mercy, he
again asks, in verse 5, "Restore us, O God" and asks further,
"Wilt Thou be angry with us for ever?" These two parts of the
psalm seem to contradict each other. If God has already restored Israel why does the psalmist still pray for restoration? The
commentator, Ibn Ezra, says that the psalmist thanks God for
having restored us from the Babylonian exile, and that now
he asks that God bring us back from the present exile. It is,
however, not necessary to make that assumption. After the return from Babylon the tiny community was in a desperate
situation for many years. The Temple was in ruins; Jerusalem
was uninhabitable; the nations roundabout were hostile. The
psalm, therefore, could well have been written in the early days

243

Psalm 85

3

3. Thou hast forgiven the iniquity of Thy people,
   Thou hast pardoned all their sin. Selah
4. Thou hast withdrawn all Thy wrath;
   Thou hast turned from the fierceness of Thine anger.
5. Restore us, O God of our salvation,
   And cause Thine indignation toward us to cease.
6. Wilt Thou be angry with us for ever?
   Wilt Thou draw out Thine anger to all generations?
7. Wilt Thou not quicken us again,
   That Thy people may rejoice in Thee?
8. Show us Thy mercy, O Lord,
   And grant us Thy salvation.
9. I will hear what God the Lord will speak;
   For He will speak peace unto His people, and to
       His saints;

of the return. The psalmist thanks God for having brought them back to their land. He now asks God to show further mercy by establishing the community.

3. THOU HAST FORGIVEN THE INIQUITY. Israel had been exiled for its sin. Now the fact that God has restored them is proof that God has forgiven.

5-8. The thought changes. The miseries of the small community living amid the ruins of the Judean cities indicate that they must have sinned further and incurred God's anger. Therefore he asks God to "cause Thine indignation toward us to cease" (verse 5).

7. QUICKEN US AGAIN. Revive us once more as Thou didst revive us when Thou didst bring us back from Babylon. Thus, "Thou . . . wilt quicken me again," (Psalm 71:20).

9-14. The psalmist states the circumstances under which God will forgive Israel and "speak peace unto His people" (verse 9), namely, if they will "not turn back to folly" (verse 9). God's deliverance "is nigh them that fear Him" (verse 10). If we revere God then we may hope "that glory may dwell in our land" (verse 10).

11. Describes the virtues that men must practice: mercy and truth, righteousness and peace. These virtues must unite into character; they must "kiss each other."

But let them not turn back to folly.
10. Surely His salvation is nigh them that fear Him;
That glory may dwell in our land.
11. Mercy and truth are met together;
Righteousness and peace have kissed each other.
12. Truth springeth out of the earth;
And righteousness hath looked down from heaven.
13. Yea, the LORD will give that which is good;
And our land shall yield her produce.
14. Righteousness shall go before Him,
And shall make His footsteps a way.

86. A PRAYER OF DAVID.

Incline Thine ear, O LORD, and answer me;
For I am poor and needy.

12. TRUTH . . . OUT OF THE EARTH AND RIGHTEOUSNESS . . . FROM HEAVEN. If men will cause truth to grow on earth God will send down righteous government from heaven and will also cause the land to produce its bounty, "our land shall yield her produce" (verse 13).

The psalm closes with the general statement that man's righteousness must build a highway for God's footsteps on earth. The same thought is expressed in II Isaiah, who lived at the time which we have assigned for this psalm, Isaiah 40:3, "Clear ye in the wilderness . . . a highway for our God."

PRAYER of David. This is the only psalm in Book Three with a heading referring to David. It is virtually a mosaic of phrases from earlier psalms. David asks God to help him "in the day of trouble" (verse 7). He knows that God will answer him and that all nations seeing God's help to him (and to Israel) will come and worship God and "they shall glorify Thy name" (verse 9).

At the end of the psalm, David repeats the statement, "violent men have sought after my soul" (verse 14). He asks God to give "strength unto Thy servant" (verse 16).

1. INCLINE THINE EAR. A phrase similar to this is found in

Psalm 86

2

2. Keep my soul, for I am godly;
   O Thou my God, save Thy servant that trusteth in Thee.
3. Be gracious unto me, O Lord;
   For unto Thee do I cry all the day.
4. Rejoice the soul of Thy servant;
   For unto Thee, O Lord, do I lift up my soul.
5. For Thou, Lord, art good, and ready to pardon,
   And plenteous in mercy unto all them that call upon Thee.
6. Give ear, O Lord, unto my prayer;
   And attend unto the voice of my supplications.
7. In the day of my trouble I call upon Thee;
   For Thou wilt answer me.
8. There is none like unto Thee among the gods, O Lord;
   And there are no works like Thine.
9. All nations whom Thou hast made shall come and prostrate
   themselves before Thee, O Lord;
   And they shall glorify Thy name.
10. For Thou art great, and doest wondrous things;
    Thou art God alone.

Psalm 17:6, "Incline Thine ear unto me, hear my speech."

2. I AM GODLY. The Hebrew word is *hasid*, meaning kindly or pious. The word may also be taken as a passive and, therefore, may mean: "I am the recipient of Thy loving-kindness." Thus, the verse would mean: "Preserve my life, O God, for Thou art ever kind to me."

5. THOU ART GOOD . . . PLENTEOUS IN MERCY. This description, together with that in verse 15, "full of compassion . . . slow to anger," follows the description of God's attributes spoken to Moses in Exodus 34:6, "The Lord, God, merciful and gracious, forgiving iniquity . . .," etc.

9. ALL NATIONS SHALL COME. The same universalistic hope which is found frequently in the Psalms and in the Prophets. See Psalm 22:28, "all the kindreds of the nations shall worship before Thee."

11. MAKE ONE MY HEART. The "double heart" is hypocritical. The "single heart" is sincere.

13. MY SOUL FROM THE NETHER-WORLD. Thou hast saved me from death.

246

11. Teach me, O LORD, Thy way, that I may walk in Thy truth;
    Make one my heart to fear Thy name.
12. I will thank Thee, O Lord my God, with my whole heart;
    And I will glorify Thy name for evermore.
13. For great is Thy mercy toward me;
    And Thou hast delivered my soul from the lowest nether-world.
14. O God, the proud are risen up against me,
    And the company of violent men have sought after my soul,
    And have not set Thee before them.
15. But Thou, O Lord, art a God full of compassion and gracious,
    Slow to anger, and plenteous in mercy and truth.
16. O turn unto me, and be gracious unto me;
    Give Thy strength unto Thy servant,
    And save the son of Thy handmaid.
17. Work in my behalf a sign for good;
    That they that hate me may see it, and be put to shame,
    Because Thou, LORD, hast helped me, and comforted me.

87. A PSALM OF THE SONS OF KORAH; A SONG.

14. HAVE NOT SET THEE BEFORE THEM. They do not think of Thee; therefore, they are wicked and violent.

16. THE SON OF THY HANDMAID. David describes himself in humble terms as the child of a servant in God's house. Thus, "I am Thy servant, the son of Thy handmaid" (Psalm 116:16).

17. WORK IN MY BEHALF A SIGN FOR GOOD. Show me a token of your love. The commentator, Kimchi, says that David meant, let me be king of Israel and that will be a sign to all the wicked that Thou art protecting me against them. The commentator, Rashi, says that David asks that God give him a proof that He has forgiven his iniquity.

A KORAHITE psalm, depicting the beauty of Zion and describing the reverence which God's sanctuary will receive all over the world. Zion is to become the center of God's world-wide kingdom. The psalm is written in the universalistic spirit of the prophet Isaiah and that of Psalm 66.

1. HIS FOUNDATIONS. The psalm begins without introduction

247

Psalm 87
1

His foundation is in the holy mountains.
2. The LORD loveth the gates of Zion
  More than all the dwellings of Jacob.
3. Glorious things are spoken of Thee,
  O city of God.   Selah
4. 'I will make mention of Rahab and Babylon as among them
    that know Me;
  Behold Philistia, and Tyre, with Ethiopia;
  This one was born there.'

and speaks of the Temple as God's foundation upon the holy mountains (of Jerusalem).

2. Zion is God's most beloved place in all of Israel.

3. GLORIOUS THINGS ARE SPOKEN. The glorious things spoken of Zion constitute the theme of the rest of the psalm.

4. RAHAB. Isaiah's term for Egypt "for Egypt helpeth in vain . . . therefore have I called her arrogancy" (Isaiah 30:7). The Hebrew word for arrogancy is *rahab*. These nations, Egypt, Babylonia, Philistia are "among them that know Me." These nations have come to know God.

THIS ONE WAS BORN THERE. A number of interpretations have been offered for this verse together with the following verse: "Of Zion it shall be said: This man and that was born in her." The Aramaic translation (the Targum) takes it to mean that these various lands can be praised for only one famous king, born there, but Zion is praised for David and for Solomon.

But verse 6 permits a more universalistic interpretation of the entire psalm. The verse reads, "The Lord shall count in the register of the peoples: this one was born there." That seems to imply that God, in His book of registry of all nations, will say of everyone, of whatever birth he may be, that he was born in Zion, that he is a citizen of God's commonwealth. Certainly, this interpretation is in harmony with Isaiah 2:2-3, "The mountain of the Lord's house shall be established as the top of the mountains, and all nations shall flow into it. And many peoples shall go and say: let us go up to the mountain of the Lord." It also seems to express the mood of Isaiah 19:24-25, "In that day shall Israel be the third with Egypt and with Assyria, a blessing

248

5. But of Zion it shall be said: 'This man and that was born in her;
And the Most High Himself doth establish her.'
6. The LORD shall count in the register of the peoples:
'This one was born there.'   Selah
7. And whether they sing or dance,
All my thoughts are in thee.

88. A SONG, A PSALM OF THE SONS OF KORAH; FOR THE LEADER; UPON
MAHALATH LEANNOTH. MASCHIL OF HEMAN THE EZRAHITE.

in the midst of the earth; for that the Lord of hosts hath blessed
him, saying: 'Blessed be Egypt My people, and Assyria the work
of My hands, and Israel Mine inheritance.' "

7. WHETHER THEY SING OR DANCE. This closing sentence is
difficult to interpret though it clearly portrays the mood of
messianic happiness. They shall all sing and dance and all my
thoughts are in the Zion of the future.

THIS psalm is ascribed to Heman, the Ezrahite, and the
next psalm, 89, is ascribed to Ethan, the Ezrahite. Both these
men are named as Levitical singers in I Chronicles 15:17.
Heman and Ethan are also mentioned in I Kings 5:11, among
the four great sages in the time of Solomon. Whether or not the
Levites and the Sages were the same persons cannot be determined. For fuller discussion of the subject, see the article
"Heman," *Jewish Encyclopedia,* Vol. VI, page 343.

The psalm is a cry of anguish. The poet is in utter despair.
He is broken in body and crushed in soul. This psalm is unusual in that it does not even end with a note of anticipated deliverance. Although this psalm uses many of the phrases found
in previous psalms, it gives a profoundly moving impression of
the outpourings of an anguished soul.

1. MAHALATH LEANNOTH. The heading "Mahalath" has been
used before as the heading for Psalm 53. It may mean "sickness." And "Leannoth" may mean "to respond" or, perhaps
with different punctuation, "to be afflicted." Both words may
be the name of some plaintive melody.

249

2. O LORD, God of my salvation,
   What time I cry in the night before Thee,
3. Let my prayer come before Thee,
   Incline Thine ear unto my cry.
4. For my soul is sated with troubles,
   And my life draweth nigh unto the grave.
5. I am counted with them that go down into the pit;
   I am become as a man that hath no help;
6. Set apart among the dead,
   Like the slain that lie in the grave,
   Whom Thou rememberest no more;
   And they are cut off from Thy hand.
7. Thou hast laid me in the nethermost pit,
   In dark places, in the deeps.
8. Thy wrath lieth hard upon me,
   And all Thy waves Thou pressest down.   Selah
9. Thou hast put mine acquaintance far from me;
   Thou hast made me an abomination unto them;
   I am shut up, and I cannot come forth.

MASCHIL. For explanation of this technical term see comment to Psalm 32:1.

2. WHAT TIME I CRY. The Hebrew word for the phrase translated here "what time" is *yom* which means "day." Therefore, the commentator, Rashi, says that the verse means: by day and by night I call upon Thee. But the commentators, Ibn Ezra and Kimchi, take the word to mean "time" and connect it with the following verse ("let my prayer come"). Thus, it means, whenever I cry "let my prayer come before Thee" (verse 3).

6. SET APART AMONG THE DEAD. I am put aside as if I were dead.

WHOM THOU REMEMBEREST NO MORE. The dead have a shadowy existence, forgetting and forgotten. Psalm 6:6, "In death there is no remembrance of Thee."

8. THY WRATH LIETH HARD UPON ME. The phrase is explained by the second half of the couplet: "Thine anger like a flood presses me down."

9. MINE ACQUAINTANCE FAR FROM ME . . . AN ABOMINATION TO THEM; I AM SHUT UP. The psalmist means that he is com-

10. Mine eye languisheth by reason of affliction;
    I have called upon Thee, O Lord, every day,
    I have spread forth my hands unto Thee.
11. Wilt Thou work wonders for the dead?
    Or shall the shades arise and give Thee thanks?   Selah
12. Shall Thy mercy be declared in the grave?
    Or Thy faithfulness in destruction?
13. Shall Thy wonders be known in the dark?
    And Thy righteousness in the land of forgetfulness?
14. But as for me, unto Thee, O Lord, do I cry,
    And in the morning doth my prayer come to meet Thee.
15. Lord, why castest Thou off my soul?
    Why hidest Thou Thy face from me?
16. I am afflicted and at the point of death from my youth up;
    I have borne Thy terrors, I am distracted.
17. Thy fierce wrath is gone over me;
    Thy terrors have cut me off.
18. They came round about me like water all the day;
    They compassed me about together.

pletely isolated from his friends; that sickness keeps him confined to the house; he meets no one. He may even mean that he is a leper, forbidden to meet other people.

10. MINE EYE LANGUISHETH. A familiar expression in the Psalms. One of the marks of sickness and grief is that the eye loses its brightness and grows dim. Thus, "I am in distress; mine eye wasteth away" (Psalm 31:10).

11. SHALL THE SHADES . . . GIVE THEE THANKS? The psalmist often says that the dead can no longer praise God. Thus, "The dead praise not the Lord" (Psalm 115:17).

12-13. The dead cannot know anything of God's marvelous works.

13. THE LAND OF FORGETFULNESS. Another reference to death. See comment to verse 6.

14-19. Although the psalmist is in despair he still prays to God, asking, "Why hidest Thou Thy face from me?" (verse 15).

18. LIKE WATER. The frequent metaphor in the Psalms: trouble engulfs us like a flood.

251

19. Friend and companion hast Thou put far from me,
    And mine acquaintance into darkness.

89. MASCHIL OF ETHAN THE EZRAHITE.

2. I will sing of the mercies of the LORD for ever;
   To all generations will I make known
   Thy faithfulness with my mouth.
3. For I have said: 'For ever is mercy built;
   In the very heavens Thou dost establish Thy faithfulness.
4. I have made a covenant with My chosen,
   I have sworn unto David My servant:
5. For ever will I establish thy seed,
   And build up thy throne to all generations.' Selah
6. So shall the heavens praise Thy wonders, O LORD,
   Thy faithfulness also in the assembly of the holy ones.
7. For who in the skies can be compared unto the LORD,
   Who among the sons of might can be likened unto the LORD,
8. A God dreaded in the great council of the holy ones,

19. MINE ACQUAINTANCE INTO DARKNESS. The phrase, "Thou hast put" from the first half of the verse must be understood also with the latter half. Thus: "Thou hast put mine acquaintance into darkness; I can no longer see any friends; I live in gloomy solitude."

*F*OR explanation of the name "Ethan the Ezrahite" see introduction to the previous psalm.

The theme of the psalm is the promise which God gave to David that his dynasty would be eternal. This promise seems now to have been set aside, "Thou hast abhorred the covenant of Thy servant" (verse 40). The king, the descendant of David, is dethroned. This psalm could well have been written at the very beginning of the exile when Jehoiachin, the young king of Judah, was taken captive to Babylon.

2-5. The psalmist begins with a general statement of God's eternal mercy and faithfulness, evidenced by the covenant which He made with David to establish his seed upon the throne forever.

And feared of all them that are round about Him?
9. O Lord God of hosts,
Who is a mighty one, like unto Thee, O Lord?
And Thy faithfulness is round about Thee.
10. Thou rulest the proud swelling of the sea;
When the waves thereof arise, Thou stillest them.
11. Thou didst crush Rahab, as one that is slain;
Thou didst scatter Thine enemies with the arm of
Thy strength.
12. Thine are the heavens, Thine also the earth;
The world and the fulness thereof, Thou hast founded them.
13. The north and the south, Thou hast created them;
Tabor and Hermon rejoice in Thy name.
14. Thine is an arm with might;
Strong is Thy hand, and exalted is Thy right hand.
15. Righteousness and justice are the foundation of Thy throne;
Mercy and truth go before Thee.
16. Happy is the people that know the joyful shout;

3. FOR EVER IS MERCY BUILT. God's mercy is built to last for ever.

6-19. God is praised by heavenly hosts. He controls the forces of nature. Happy is the people which relies upon His help.

6. IN THE ASSEMBLY OF THE HOLY ONES. The heavenly hosts. This cannot mean the holy ones on earth but must refer to the angels, since the first couplet speaks of the heavens praising God's wonders.

7. SONS OF MIGHT. The angels. Thus, "Ascribe unto the Lord, ye sons of might" (Psalm 29:1). So, too, in verse 8, "the council of the holy ones" refers to the heavenly hosts.

10-14. The scene of God's workings changes from the heavens to the forces of nature on earth.

11. RAHAB. Egypt, as in Psalm 87:4, and refers to God's power manifested at the Red Sea. He crushed Egypt (or Egypt's sea).

13. TABOR AND HERMON. The highest mountains in Palestine.

15-19. God's power as a moral force in the world.

16. HAPPY IS THE PEOPLE THAT KNOW THE JOYFUL SHOUT.

253

They walk, O LORD, in the light of Thy countenance.
17. In Thy name do they rejoice all the day;
   And through Thy righteousness are they exalted.
18. For Thou art the glory of their strength;
   And in Thy favour our horn is exalted.
19. For of the LORD is our shield;
   And of the Holy One of Israel is our king.
20. Then Thou spokest in vision to Thy godly ones,
   And saidst: 'I have laid help upon one that is mighty;
   I have exalted one chosen out of the people.
21. I have found David My servant;
   With My holy oil have I anointed him;
22. With whom My hand shall be established;
   Mine arm also shall strengthen him.
23. The enemy shall not exact from him;
   Nor the son of wickedness afflict him.
24. And I will beat to pieces his adversaries before him,
   And smite them that hate him.
25. But My faithfulness and My mercy shall be with him;
   And through My name shall his horn be exalted.
26. I will set his hand also on the sea,

The commentator, Rashi, basing his comment on the fact that the word for "joyful shout" means also the "blast of the shofar" says, happy is the people that knows how to appease God's indignation on the New Year's day when the shofar is sounded. But perhaps it simply means: the people that know the shout of triumph which rises when the king is crowned and mounts his throne. Thus, "God is gone up amid shouting, the Lord amidst the sound of the horn" (Psalm 47:6).

18. OUR HORN IS EXALTED. We are triumphant (as a stag raises its horns in pride).

This general introduction describing God's might in the heavens, over nature, and in the moral sphere is now followed by a detailed statement (verses 20-38) of His promise to David that his dynasty will remain forever upon the throne. This promise is given in II Samuel 7:11-17. The psalmist follows closely the language of that passage.

20. THOU SPOKEST . . . TO THY GODLY ONES. The commenta-

And his right hand on the rivers.
27. He shall call unto Me: Thou art my Father,
My God, and the rock of my salvation.
28. I also will appoint him first-born,
The highest of the kings of the earth.
29. For ever will I keep for him My mercy,
And My covenant shall stand fast with him.
30. His seed also will I make to endure for ever,
And his throne as the days of heaven.
31. If his children forsake My law,
And walk not in Mine ordinances;
32. If they profane My statutes,
And keep not My commandments;
33. Then will I visit their transgression with the rod,
And their iniquity with strokes.
34. But My mercy will I not break off from him,
Nor will I be false to My faithfulness.
35. My covenant will I not profane,
Nor alter that which is gone out of My lips.
36. Once have I sworn by My holiness:
Surely I will not be false unto David;

tor, Rashi says, to the prophets, Nathan and Gad. (See II Samuel 24:11.) But the commentator, Ibn Ezra, says, to seers like Heman and Ethan and the prophets.

HELP UPON ONE THAT IS MIGHTY. I add my strength to his (i. e., to David's), as verse 22, "Mine arm also shall strengthen him."

22. WITH WHOM MY HAND SHALL BE ESTABLISHED. My hand will be firm to help him.

23. SHALL NOT EXACT. Tribute.

26. THE SEA . . . THE RIVERS. His kingdom will extend from the Mediterranean to Mesopotamia.

27. THOU ART MY FATHER. See II Samuel 7:14, "I will be to him for a father."

31-33. If his sons violate My law I will punish them "with the rod . . . with strokes" (verse 33). Cf. II Samuel 7:14, "I will chasten him with the rod of men."

34. BUT MY MERCY WILL I NOT BREAK. Although I will pun-

255

37. His seed shall endure for ever,
    And his throne as the sun before Me.
38. It shall be established for ever as the moon;
    And be stedfast as the witness in the sky.' Selah
39. But Thou hast cast off and rejected,
    Thou hast been wroth with Thine anointed.
40. Thou hast abhorred the covenant of Thy servant;
    Thou hast profaned his crown even to the ground.
41. Thou hast broken down all his fences;
    Thou hast brought his strongholds to ruin.
42. All that pass by the way spoil him;
    He is become a taunt to his neighbours.
43. Thou hast exalted the right hand of his adversaries;
    Thou hast made all his enemies to rejoice.
44. Yea, Thou turnest back the edge of his sword,
    And hast not made him to stand in the battle.
45. Thou hast made his brightness to cease,

ish him I will not break My promise that his dynasty will be
eternal. See II Samuel 7:15, "but my mercy shall not depart
from him."

37. HIS SEED SHALL ENDURE . . . AS THE SUN. The same expression is used in Psalm 72:17, "May his name be continued as
long as the sun."

38. STEDFAST AS THE WITNESS IN THE SKY. Who is the witness in the sky? The commentator, Kimchi, says, the moon; and
the commentator, Rashi, speaks of the sun and the moon as
witnesses in the sky. But the witness may simply mean God
Himself as in Jeremiah 42:5, "The Lord be a true and faithful
witness."

39-52. The psalmist now contrasts these great promises with
the bitter actuality of contemporary facts. He says: "Thou hast
cast off and rejected . . . Thine anointed" (verse 39); "profaned
his crown . . . brought his strongholds to ruin" (verses 40-41);
"turnest back the edge of his sword" (verse 44), (i. e., makest
him retreat).

46. THE DAYS OF HIS YOUTH HAST THOU SHORTENED . . . COV-
ERED HIM WITH SHAME. This seems clearly to refer to the young
king Jehoiachin, who came to the throne at the age of eighteen

And cast his throne down to the ground.
46. The days of his youth hast Thou shortened;
    Thou hast covered him with shame.   Selah
47. How long, O Lord, wilt Thou hide Thyself for ever?
    How long shall Thy wrath burn like fire?
48. O remember how short my time is;
    For what vanity hast Thou created all the children of men!
49. What man is he that liveth and shall not see death,
    That shall deliver his soul from the power of the grave?   Selah
50. Where are Thy former mercies, O Lord,
    Which Thou didst swear unto David in Thy faithfulness?
51. Remember, Lord, the taunt of Thy servants;
    How I do bear in my bosom [the taunt of] so many peoples;
52. Wherewith Thine enemies have taunted, O Lord,
    Wherewith they have taunted the footsteps of Thine anointed.
53. Blessed be the Lord for evermore.
    Amen, and Amen.

and reigned for only three months (II Kings 24:8) and then
was captured by the Babylonians who destroyed Jerusalem and
kept the king in prison for thirty-seven years (II Kings 25:27 ff.).

The psalmist now appeals to God and asks that God cease
His wrath for human life is short (verse 48).

48. FOR WHAT VANITY HAST THOU CREATED . . . MEN. For what
vain hopes does our life persist?

49. WHAT MAN IS HE THAT . . . SHALL NOT SEE DEATH? All of
us will soon die, therefore, O God, send us Thy deliverance
that I may behold it in my lifetime.

51. THE TAUNT OF THY SERVANTS. The taunts hurled at Thy
servants.

52. They have taunted me and taunted "Thine anointed,"
the unhappy king.

The phrase "the footsteps of Thine anointed" can well be
a reference to the picture of Jehoiachin being led through the
streets of Babylon and taunted by the mob.

53. BLESSED BE THE LORD. This verse is not part of the psalm
but is the prayer of praise, the doxology, which ends the Book.
Cf. the doxology which ends Book Two, Psalm 72:18-19, and
that which ended Book One, Psalm 41:14.

257

Book Four

&

BOOK Four (Psalms 90 to 106) forms a unit with Book Five (Psalms 107 to 150) just as Books Two and Three were closely connected. A striking literary evidence of this grouping is the choice of name for God used in these books. Books Two and Three prefer *Elohim* as the name of God and tend to avoid the name *JHWH*. Books Four and Five prefer the name *JHWH* and avoid the name *Elohim*. In fact, the word *Elohim* is used only seven times in Books Four and Five. Of these seven uses of *Elohim*, six are in Psalm 108 and one in Psalm 144. Both these psalms are mosaics of material from previous psalms.

Another characteristic common to Books Four and Five is that the most of the psalms here do not have a heading ascribing them to any author.

Psalm 90

1

90. A PRAYER OF MOSES THE MAN OF GOD.
Lord, Thou hast been our dwelling-place in all
generations.
2. Before the mountains were brought forth,
Or ever Thou hadst formed the earth and the world,

*T*HIS psalm vividly contrasts God's eternity and the transiency of human life. From this contrast the psalmist draws the
conclusion that we must "number our days that we may get us
a heart of wisdom" (verse 12). He prays also that God give us
joy in our brief life (that we may "be glad all our days," verse
14), and that God give permanence to our work: "establish
Thou . . . the work of our hands" (verse 17).

The heading ascribes this psalm to Moses. The commentator, Ibn Ezra, offers two reasons why this psalm must be the
work of Moses, our teacher; first, the psalm is in the plural,
thus differing from most of the Psalms of David; and, secondly,
Moses describes God as "our dwellingplace" (verse 1) which
is the same expression which he used in the hymn which he
sang before his death. "The eternal God is a dwellingplace"
(Deuteronomy 33:27). The commentator, Rashi, says that all
the psalms from 90 to 100 are by Moses; that is to say, the
heading, "A prayer of Moses," is the common title for all of
these psalms. Rashi bases this opinion upon a statement in the
Midrash Tehillim (see also the Yalkut to this psalm).

This psalm is recited in a group of psalms in the Saturday
morning service.

1. THE MAN OF GOD. The same title is used as the heading to
the Song of Moses in Deuteronomy 33:1, "Moses, the man of
God." The commentator, Ibn Ezra, in his commentary to Deuteronomy, says that the phrase indicates that Moses spoke under
the inspiration of prophecy. The phrase "man of God" would
therefore mean "the God-inspired man."

OUR DWELLINGPLACE. The psalmist frequently speaks of
God as our Host in whose habitation we are sheltered (e. g.,
Psalm 23), but here God Himself is our eternal dwellingplace.

Even from everlasting to everlasting, Thou art God.
3. Thou turnest man to contrition;
   And sayest: 'Return, ye children of men.'
4. For a thousand years in Thy sight
   Are but as yesterday when it is past,
   And as a watch in the night.

See also in the next psalm, "Thou hast made the Lord ... the
Most High, thy habitation" (Psalm 91:9). The commentator,
Ibn Ezra, says that this means that although generations may
come and go the house in which they lived remains permanent.
So, although man is transient, God, our dwelling-place, is
eternal.

2. BEFORE THE MOUNTAINS. The mountains are here mentioned first as being the most ancient and permanent part of
the earth. Thus, Genesis 49:26, "the utmost bound of the everlasting hills."

FROM EVERLASTING TO EVERLASTING. Some of the commentators (and the Targum, the Aramaic translation) say that this
means, in this world and in the world to come. But the commentator, Kimchi, says it means, from the eternity before creation and to all the eternity in the future. See Psalm 41:14.

3. MAN TO CONTRITION. The Hebrew word for "contrition"
means "crushing." Hence, the phrase is frequently translated,
"Thou turnest man to dust." This translation would be consistent with the following sentence: "Return, ye children of
men." The whole verse would then have the meaning expressed in Genesis 3:19, that men will "return unto the ground for
out of it wast thou taken; for dust thou art, and unto dust shalt
thou return." But in the metaphorical sense as translated here
(and as the comentator Rashi takes it), the sentence is quite
logical. God turns man to humility or contrition saying, return,
i. e., repent, ye children of men.

4. A WATCH IN THE NIGHT. In Roman times the night was
divided into four watches, but in biblical times into three
watches. This is evident from Judges 7:19, where the writer
speaks of "the middle watch."

5. Thou carriest them away as with a flood; they are as a sleep;
   In the morning they are like grass which groweth up.
6. In the morning it flourisheth, and groweth up;
   In the evening it is cut down, and withereth.
7. For we are consumed in Thine anger,
   And by Thy wrath are we hurried away.
8. Thou hast set our iniquities before Thee,
   Our secret sins in the light of Thy countenance.
9. For all our days are passed away in Thy wrath;
   We bring our years to an end as a tale that is told.
10. The days of our years are threescore years and ten,
    Or even by reason of strength fourscore years;
    Yet is their pride but travail and vanity;
    For it is speedily gone, and we fly away.
11. Who knoweth the power of Thine anger,

5. LIKE GRASS WHICH GROWETH UP. The metaphor, comparing the transiency of man's life to the rapid withering of the grass under the burning sun, is used frequently in the Bible. Thus, "For they shall soon wither like the grass" (Psalm 37:2). See also the use of this metaphor in Isaiah 40:6-9, "All flesh is grass; the grass withereth, the flower fadeth; but the word of our God shall stand for ever."

9. AS A TALE THAT IS TOLD. The Hebrew word used here for "tale" can mean "a breath." The commentators, Kimchi and Ibn Ezra, both say that it means, our days are as transient as a single word that is uttered.

11. THY WRATH ACCORDING TO THE FEAR . . . DUE UNTO THEE. The commentators, Ibn Ezra and Kimchi, explain this verse to mean that God is angry at us in proportion to the fear or reverence which we owe Him. He who, because of his status and knowledge, owes God a larger measure of reverence, will receive a greater punishment for his violation of God's law. The commentators connect this with the incident described in Leviticus 10:3, when the sons of Aaron were put to death for bringing strange fire, and Scripture implies it was precisely because they were in such an exalted position that their punishment was so great. "Through them that are nigh unto Me I will be sanctified" (Leviticus 10:3).

And Thy wrath according to the fear that is due unto Thee?

12. So teach us to number our days,
    That we may get us a heart of wisdom.
13. Return, O LORD; how long?
    And let it repent Thee concerning Thy servants.
14. O satisfy us in the morning with Thy mercy;
    That we may rejoice and be glad all our days.
15. Make us glad according to the days wherein Thou hast afflicted
    us,
    According to the years wherein we have seen evil.
16. Let Thy work appear unto Thy servants,
    And Thy glory upon their children.
17. And let the graciousness of the Lord our God be upon us;
    Establish Thou also upon us the work of our hands;
    Yea, the work of our hands establish Thou it.

12. TO NUMBER OUR DAYS. That is to say: teach us the number of our days; teach us to realize how brief our life is so that we will not be wasteful of our time. Thus, "Lord, make me to know . . . the measure of my days" (Psalm 39:5).

13. RETURN O LORD. Return from Thine anger. Be not withdrawn from us. Thus, "Return, O Lord, deliver my soul" (Psalm 6:5).

14. IN THE MORNING. The psalmist frequently asks for God's help in the morning. It means that after the long night of weeping and prayer he hopes to see God's deliverance when the morning dawns. "Weeping may tarry for the night, but joy cometh in the morning." (Psalm 30:6.)

17. LET THE GRACIOUSNESS OF THE LORD. The same phrase is used in Psalm 27:4: "To behold the graciousness of the Lord." See the comment to that verse.

THIS psalm is described in the Talmud as The Song of Accidents or Misfortunes, or The Song of Plagues (b. Shebuoth 15 b). Both descriptions are based upon the fact that the psalmist speaks of God's protection against pestilence and other dangers in life. The psalm is closely akin in language to Psalm 90 and to the poem in Deuteronomy 32.

91. O thou that dwellest in the covert of the
   Most High,
 And abidest in the shadow of the Almighty;
2. I will say of the LORD, who is my refuge and my fortress,
 My God, in whom I trust,
3. That He will deliver thee from the snare of the fowler,
 And from the noisome pestilence.
4. He will cover thee with His pinions,
 And under His wings shalt thou take refuge;
 His truth is a shield and a buckler.
5. Thou shalt not be afraid of the terror by night,
 Nor of the arrow that flieth by day;
6. Of the pestilence that walketh in darkness,
 Nor of the destruction that wasteth at noonday.
7. A thousand may fall at thy side,
 And ten thousand at thy right hand;
 It shall not come nigh thee.
8. Only with thine eyes shalt thou behold,
 And see the recompense of the wicked.

This psalm is recited in a group of psalms on Saturday morning and is also used in the evening prayer on Saturday night at the close of the services. Perhaps its use on Saturday night comes from the thought that now that we are entering a week of work we pray that God may protect us from danger. The mood of the psalm explains also its traditional use as part of the funeral service.

1. THE COVERT OF THE MOST HIGH. The hiding place which God provides against pursuing enemies. Thus, "Thou hidest them in the covert of Thy presence from the plottings of man" (Psalm 31:21).

THE SHADOW OF THE ALMIGHTY. This may mean the shade of His roof or the shadow of the rock protecting us from the sun as in Isaiah 32:2. "A covert from the tempest . . . the shadow of a great rock in a weary land."

3. THE SNARE OF THE FOWLER. A favorite metaphor in the Psalms describing danger as a net spread by the fowler to entrap birds. Thus, "They that seek after my life lay snares for me" (Psalm 38:13).

9. For thou hast made the LORD who is my refuge,
 Even the Most High, thy habitation.
10. There shall no evil befall thee,
 Neither shall any plague come nigh thy tent.
11. For He will give His angels charge over thee,
 To keep thee in all thy ways.
12. They shall bear thee upon their hands,
 Lest thou dash thy foot against a stone.
13. Thou shalt tread upon the lion and asp;
 The young lion and the serpent shalt thou trample
 under feet.
14. 'Because he hath set his love upon Me, therefore will
 I deliver him;
 I will set him on high, because he hath known My name.
15. He shall call upon Me, and I will answer him;
 I will be with him in trouble;
 I will rescue him, and bring him to honour.
16. With long life will I satisfy him,
 And make him to behold My salvation.'

THE NOISOME PESTILENCE. The destructive pestilence. The commentator, Ibn Ezra, takes the phrase to mean the sudden and unexpected pestilence.

5-10. Describes how confident the man will be who trusts in God. Neither the terror by night nor destruction at noonday, nor the sight of thousands falling about him will terrify him, since God is his refuge.

11. HE WILL GIVE HIS ANGELS CHARGE. The angels, God's messengers, whom He sends as protection to man. The same expression is used in Exodus 23:20, "Behold, I send an angel before thee, to keep thee by the way." For fuller discussion of the subject of angels in Jewish literature see article "Angelology" in the *Jewish Encyclopedia*, Vol. I.

14. HE HATH KNOWN MY NAME. This is to say, he hath known Me and relies upon Me. Thus Psalm 9:11, "They that know Thy name will put their trust in Thee."

16. WITH LONG LIFE. The Hebrew means literally, "with length of days." The same phrase is used in Proverbs 3:2, "For length of days, and years of life, . . . will they add to thee."

265

92. A PSALM, A SONG. FOR THE SABBATH DAY.
2. It is a good thing to give thanks unto the LORD,
   And to sing praises unto Thy name, O Most High;
3. To declare Thy lovingkindness in the morning,
   And Thy faithfulness in the night seasons,
4. With an instrument of ten strings, and with the psaltery;
   With a solemn sound upon the harp.
5. For Thou, LORD, hast made me glad through Thy work;
   I will exult in the works of Thy hands.
6. How great are Thy works, O LORD!
   Thy thoughts are very deep.
7. A brutish man knoweth not,
   Neither doth a fool understand this.
8. When the wicked spring up as the grass,
   And when all the workers of iniquity do flourish;
   It is that they may be destroyed for ever.

THIS psalm is headed "for the Sabbath day," and is listed among the psalms recited by the Levites in the Temple (m. Tamid 7:4). It is still used as a Sabbath psalm in the synagogues.

2-4. An introductory invocation calling upon the worshippers to praise God with prayer and instrumental music. Note the similar invocation in Psalm 81:2-5.

6. THY THOUGHTS ARE VERY DEEP. God's wondrous works are beyond our power to describe. Thus, "If I would declare and speak of them, they are more than can be told" (Psalm 40:6).

7. A BRUTISH MAN. The man who lacks understanding is bewildered and terrified at the power of the wicked but the man who is not brutish, but has spiritual perception, knows that "when the workers of iniquity do flourish" they will be "destroyed for ever." The same thought is expressed in Psalm 73:22. There, the psalmist says that at first he could not understand why the wicked were so powerful, and he explains his obtuseness in these words: "I was brutish and ignorant." A similar idea is expressed in the Ethics of the Fathers. Hillel says: "A man void of intelligence cannot be sensitive to sin nor can an ignorant person be pious." (Ethics of the Fathers 2:6.)

266

9. But Thou, O LORD, art on high for evermore.
10. For, lo, Thine enemies, O LORD,
    For, lo, Thine enemies shall perish;
    All the workers of iniquity shall be scattered.
11. But my horn hast Thou exalted like the horn of the wild-ox;
    I am anointed with rich oil.
12. Mine eye also hath gazed on them that lie in wait for me,
    Mine ears have heard my desire of the evil-doers that rise
        up against me.
13. The righteous shall flourish like the palm-tree;
    He shall grow like a cedar in Lebanon.
14. Planted in the house of the LORD,
    They shall flourish in the courts of our God.
15. They shall still bring forth fruit in old age;
    They shall be full of sap and richness;
16. To declare that the LORD is upright,
    My Rock, in whom there is no unrighteousness.

13-16. The righteous are compared to palm trees and cedars
planted in the court of God. This is the combination of two
favorite metaphors of the Psalms, that the righteous shall flourish like a tree and that it is a blessing to dwell in God's house.
See comment to Psalm 52:10. A palm tree (verse 13) is vigorous even when old; hence "full of sap and richness" (verse 15).

16. THE LORD IS UPRIGHT. The phrase is explained by the
second half of the couplet: "There is no unrighteousness in
Him." His actions are always just. The same expression is used
in Deuteronomy 32:4, "A God of faithfulness and without
iniquity, just and right is He."

Psalm 93 is listed in the Mishnah (Tamid 7:4), as the
psalm which the Levites sang on Friday. It is still recited
on Friday in the synagogue service.

The psalm is a declaration that God is king of the universe.
It is, in a sense, an introduction to the group of psalms from
95 to 100. All these psalms emphasize the thought that God is
king. Hence, modern commentators refer to these psalms (93,
95 to 100) as the "Theocratic" psalms. The thought of God as

93. The LORD reigneth; He is clothed in majesty;
The LORD is clothed, He hath girded Himself with
strength;
Yea, the world is established, that it cannot be moved.
2. Thy throne is established of old;
Thou art from everlasting.
3. The floods have lifted up, O LORD,
The floods have lifted up their voice;
The floods lift up their roaring.

king dominates the entire Bible and later Jewish literature.
The idea begins with God as the King of Israel, the mortal
kings of Israel being merely His earthly representatives. Thus
(in Samuel), when the people of Israel ask for a king, Samuel
reminds them that God is their King. "Ye said unto me: nay,
but a king shall reign over us; when the Lord your God was
your king" (I Samuel 12:12). The idea of God as King over
Israel is extended to the Kingship of God over all the world.
Thus, "The Lord shall reign for ever and ever" (Exodus
15:18). Both thoughts, namely, that God is God of Israel and
also the King of all the world, are embodied in the formula of
every blessing. Thus: "Praised be Thou O Lord, *our* God, King
of the *Universe*."

The commentators, Rashi and Kimchi, say that this psalm,
as well as the other King psalms up to Psalm 100, refer to the
messianic days, i. e., when men will obey the Divine law and
will practice justice and mercy, then will God's majesty be
manifest to all and He will be acknowledged as King of all the
world.

1. CLOTHED IN MAJESTY . . . GIRDED WITH STRENGTH. The
psalmist frequently speaks of God's attributes as a glorious garment wrapped about Him.

2. THY THRONE IS ESTABLISHED OF OLD. All other earthly
thrones are temporary. God's Kingship is the only permanent
dominion in the world. Thus, "from everlasting to everlasting,
Thou art God" (Psalm 90:2).

5. THY TESTIMONIES ARE VERY SURE. Thy law, Thy moral
commandments to man. The commentator, Ibn Ezra, connects

4. Above the voices of many waters,
   The mighty breakers of the sea,
   The LORD on high is mighty.
5. Thy testimonies are very sure,
   Holiness becometh Thy house,
   O LORD, for evermore.

94. O LORD, Thou God to whom vengeance belongeth,
   Thou God to whom vengeance belongeth, shine forth.

this statement with the close of Psalm 19, where, just as in this psalm, the psalmist begins with a description of God in nature, "the heavens declare the glory of God" and ends with the idea that God is the guide to the ethical life: "the law of the Lord is perfect . . ." Upon the basis of the comparison, Ibn Ezra says that great as is the evidence which nature presents of God's infinite might, the evidence of His greatness found in His moral law is still more telling.

HOLINESS BECOMETH THY HOUSE. The mood of holiness is appropriate to Thine earthly dwelling-place, O Master of the world and Guide of human life.

THIS psalm is listed in the Mishnah (Tamid 7:4), as the psalm which the Levites sang on Wednesday. It is still the special psalm for Wednesday in the synagogue service.

The psalm speaks of God Who will execute vengeance against the unjust. God is the true Judge and all those who judge unjustly will be punished by Him. Thus, the psalm is closely connected with Psalm 82 which likewise speaks of God as the Supreme Judge.

1. GOD TO WHOM VENGEANCE BELONGETH. The violence done to the weak and the humble will not go unavenged. Even though the humble may have no mortal "redeemer of the blood" to avenge them, nevertheless, God Who protects the fatherless, will punish those who would do them harm. This is the meaning of the phrase in Deuteronomy 32:35, "vengeance is Mine." See also Psalm 79:10, "Let the avenging of Thy ser-

269

2

2. Lift up Thyself, Thou Judge of the earth;
   Render to the proud their recompense.
3. Lord, how long shall the wicked,
   How long shall the wicked exult?
4. They gush out, they speak arrogancy;
   All the workers of iniquity bear themselves loftily.
5. They crush Thy people, O Lord,
   And afflict Thy heritage.
6. They slay the widow and the stranger,
   And murder the fatherless.
7. And they say: 'The Lord will not see,
   Neither will the God of Jacob give heed.'
8. Consider, ye brutish among the people;
   And ye fools, when will ye understand?
9. He that planted the ear, shall He not hear?
   He that formed the eye, shall He not see?
10. He that instructeth nations, shall not He correct,
    Even He that teacheth man knowledge?

vants' blood that is shed be made known among the nations."

2. THE PROUD. The haughty and the violent.

6. THE WIDOW . . . THE STRANGER . . . THE FATHERLESS. Those who have no one else to protect them can rely upon God.

7. THE LORD WILL NOT SEE. The wicked believe that God does not see their cruel deeds. The same thought is expressed in Psalm 10:11: "He hath said in his heart; God hath forgotten, He will never see." But, the psalmist continues, "Thou hast seen . . . Thou hast been the helper of the fatherless" (Psalm 10:14).

8. YE BRUTISH. Ye ignorant who do not understand that God knows the thoughts of the wicked and understands their evil intentions. See Psalm 92:7 ff., "A brutish man knoweth not, when the workers of iniquity do flourish; it is that they may be destroyed for ever."

10. SHALL NOT HE CORRECT? God will instruct and correct the action of human judges as a teacher or a father corrects a child. In Proverbs 3:12, the same function is ascribed to God, "whom the Lord loveth He correcteth, even as a father the son in whom he delighteth."

11. The LORD knoweth the thoughts of man,
    That they are vanity.
12. Happy is the man whom Thou instructest, O LORD,
    And teachest out of Thy law:
13. That Thou mayest give him rest from the days of evil,
    Until the pit be digged for the wicked.
14. For the LORD will not cast off His people,
    Neither will He forsake His inheritance.
15. For right shall return unto justice,
    And all the upright in heart shall follow it.
16. Who will rise up for me against the evil-doers?
    Who will stand up for me against the workers of iniquity?
17. Unless the LORD had been my help,
    My soul had soon dwelt in silence.
18. If I say: 'My foot slippeth',
    Thy mercy, O LORD, holdeth me up.
19. When my cares are many within me,
    Thy comforts delight my soul.

11. THE THOUGHTS . . . THAT THEY ARE VANITY. God knows well how transient are the schemes and the conspiracies of mortals. Thus, Psalm 39:7, "Surely for vanity they are in turmoil."

13. THE PIT BE DIGGED FOR THE WICKED. A familiar thought in the Psalms. The wicked dig a pit for others but they will fall into it themselves. Thus, "let his net that he hath hid catch himself; with destruction let him fall therein" (Psalm 35:8).

15. RIGHT SHALL RETURN UNTO JUSTICE. The commentator, Kimchi, explains that justice and right belong together but the wicked have separated them. According to this interpretation the verse means that the wicked administer the law without righteousness, but when God has corrected the unrighteous judges then righteousness shall return to human justice.

17. UNLESS THE LORD HAD BEEN MY HELP, MY SOUL . . . IN SILENCE. If God had not assisted me I would not have had the courage to resist the violence of the wicked. The same thought is expressed in Psalm 124:1, 4, "If it had not been the Lord who was for us . . .then the proud waters had gone over our soul."

18. MY FOOT SLIPPETH. A thought frequently found in the

20. Shall the seat of wickedness have fellowship with Thee,
    Which frameth mischief by statute?
21. They gather themselves together against the soul
      of the righteous,
    And condemn innocent blood.
22. But the LORD hath been my high tower,
    And my God the rock of my refuge.
23. And He hath brought upon them their own iniquity,
    And will cut them off in their own evil;
    The LORD our God will cut them off.

95. O come, let us sing unto the LORD;
    Let us shout for joy to the Rock of our salvation.
2. Let us come before His presence with thanksgiving,
    Let us shout for joy unto Him with psalms.

Psalms. It means, "I stumble on the path of life." See Psalm
18:37, "Thou hast enlarged my steps under me, and my feet
have not slipped."

A PSALM praising God as King over all of nature, and
pleading with Israel not to rebel against Him as our forefathers
did in the wilderness. Thus, the psalm deals with the same
theme as the Asaph Psalm 78. This psalm and the four following psalms have been recited on Friday night in Ashkenazic
(i. e. in German and East European) synagogues since the six-
teenth century.

1-2. The first two verses are the introductory invocation
calling upon the worshipper to praise God.

3-6. Speaks of God as the Master of nature.

5. THE SEA IS HIS. A similar expression is used, but in the
second person instead of the third, in Psalm 89:12, "Thine are
the heavens, Thine also the earth."

6. BOW DOWN AND BEND THE KNEE, LET US KNEEL. In ancient
times kneeling was one of the usual postures in prayer. Thus,
in Daniel 6:11, we learn that Daniel knelt three times a day,
"and he kneeled upon his knees three times a day, and prayed."

3. For the LORD is a great God,
   And a great King above all gods;
4. In whose hand are the depths of the earth;
   The heights of the mountains are His also.
5. The sea is His, and He made it;
   And His hands formed the dry land.
6. O come, let us bow down and bend the knee;
   Let us kneel before the LORD our Maker;
7. For He is our God,
   And we are the people of His pasture, and the flock of His hand.
   To-day, if ye would but hearken to His voice!
8. 'Harden not your heart, as at Meribah,
   As in the day of Massah in the wilderness;
9. When your fathers tried Me,
   Proved Me, even though they saw My work.

The Mishnah (Yoma VI, 2), tells us that the people in the Temple knelt and prostrated themselves when the priest pronounced the name of God during his confessions. The Talmud (b. Berachoth 34 b) tells us of certain rabbis who knelt at prayer.

To this day it is the custom for the people to prostrate themselves in the synagogue on the Day of Atonement at the same point in the service where the people knelt in the Temple, namely, when the confession of the high priest is read. (See Dembitz, *Services in the Synagogue and Home*, page 300 ff.)

7. TODAY, IF YE WOULD BUT HEARKEN. The commentator, Ibn Ezra, takes this verse in connection with verse 6: let us kneel before God today. However, it can just as well be taken with the following verses as follows: if you would hearken to God today then harden not your heart (verse 8).

8 to the end. Refers to the rebelliousness of our forefathers in the wilderness.

MERIBAH ... MASSAH. The place where the children of Israel murmured against God. See Exodus 17:1-7.

9. YOUR FATHERS TRIED ME. Tested me. Endeavored to discover whether I had strength to help them.

EVEN THOUGH THEY SAW MY WORK. Even though they had

273

10. For forty years was I wearied with that generation,
    And said: It is a people that do err in their heart,
    And they have not known My ways;
11. Wherefore I swore in My wrath,
    That they should not enter into My rest.'*

96. O sing unto the LORD a new song;
   Sing unto the LORD, all the earth.
2. Sing unto the LORD, bless His name;
   Proclaim His salvation from day to day.
3. Declare His glory among the nations,
   His marvellous works among all the peoples.
4. For great is the LORD, and highly to be praised;
   He is to be feared above all gods.

seen what I had done to the Egyptians they nevertheless wanted
to prove and test Me further.

10. THEY HAVE NOT KNOWN MY WAYS. They have indeed seen
My actions but they still did not understand My ways.

11. THEY SHOULD NOT ENTER INTO MY REST. God swore that
the generation that left Egypt should die in the wilderness and
not enter the Promised Land. Palestine is called "the resting
place" or "rest" in Deuteronomy 12:9, "For ye are not as yet
come to the rest and to the inheritance, which the Lord your
God giveth thee."

THIS psalm is a paean of praise of God as King. As in the
preceding psalm, the psalmist calls upon the people to praise
God, the just Judge and the Master of nature. The psalm is
quoted in I Chronicles 16:23-33, as the one which Asaph and
his brethren sang before the ark of God at the command of
King David.

The psalm resembles Psalm 29 in thought and in language.

1. SING UNTO THE LORD A NEW SONG. Since God's mercies are
constantly renewed for us, our worship of Him must never be
permitted to grow hackneyed but must always be creative and

* See Deut. xii. 9.

5. For all the gods of the peoples are things of nought;
   But the Lord made the heavens.
6. Honour and majesty are before Him;
   Strength and beauty are in His sanctuary.
7. Ascribe unto the Lord, ye kindreds of the peoples,
   Ascribe unto the Lord glory and strength.
8. Ascribe unto the Lord the glory due unto His name;
   Bring an offering, and come into His courts.
9. O worship the Lord in the beauty of holiness;
   Tremble before Him, all the earth.
10. Say among the nations: 'The Lord reigneth.'
    The world also is established that it cannot
       be moved;
    He will judge the peoples with equity.

new. Compare also Psalm 33:3, "Sing unto Him a new song."

3. HIS GLORY AMONG THE NATIONS. Israel's experience with God is a lesson to the world. Israel must proclaim to the world God's glorious deeds.

7, 8, 9. This passage is almost identical with the first two verses in Psalm 29 except that in Psalm 29 the invocation is addressed to the "sons of might" and here it is addressed to the kindreds of the peoples. There the angels are called upon to praise God and here all the nations are summoned.

7. KINDREDS means "families."

9. THE BEAUTY OF HOLINESS. The commentators take this to mean, worship the Lord in the Temple which is both beautiful and holy. Beyond its literal meaning, the connotation of this magnificent sentence expresses one of the noblest attitudes of the Bible. To the Hebraic spirit the greatest beauty is to be found not primarily in works of art but in works of righteousness. The highest art is expressed in the perfection of the moral life, in the grandeur of character. The noblest beauty is the beauty of holiness.

10. THE WORLD ALSO IS ESTABLISHED. A similar phrase is found in Psalm 93:2, "Thy throne is established." But here the emphasis is that the world is established because God "will judge the peoples with equity." Therefore all nature will re-

275

11. Let the heavens be glad, and let the earth rejoice;
    Let the sea roar, and the fulness thereof;
12. Let the field exult, and all that is therein;
    Then shall all the trees of the wood sing for joy;
13. Before the LORD, for He is come;
    For He is come to judge the earth;
    He will judge the world with righteousness,
    And the peoples in His faithfulness.

97. The LORD reigneth; let the earth rejoice;
    Let the multitude of isles be glad.
2. Clouds and darkness are round about Him;
    Righteousness and justice are the foundation of His throne.
3. A fire goeth before Him,
    And burneth up His adversaries round about.
4. His lightnings lighted up the world;
    The earth saw, and trembled.

joice, "all the trees of the woods sing for joy." When justice and faithfulness rule the world, even nature seems to smile.

ANOTHER one of the theocratic psalms praising God as Master of the world. At the manifestations of His might nature trembles and all the idolators are ashamed.

Many of the sentences of this psalm are found in other psalms, but due to its fine spirit of jubilant praise the psalm gives the effect of originality.

1. THE LORD REIGNETH . . . ISLES BE GLAD. Since God is King the world is secure. Therefore let all the nations rejoice.

MULTITUDE OF ISLES BE GLAD. This means all the coastlands, which to the psalmist meant all the borders of the inhabited earth.

2. RIGHTEOUSNESS AND JUSTICE. A similar phrase is found in Psalm 89:15.

4. HIS LIGHTNINGS LIGHTED UP THE WORLD. This verse is found in Psalm 77:19.

5. MOUNTAINS MELTED LIKE WAX. A vivid metaphor to describe the weakness of physical nature in the flaming presence

5. The mountains melted like wax at the presence of the LORD,
   At the presence of the Lord of the whole earth.
6. The heavens declared His righteousness,
   And all the peoples saw His glory.
7. Ashamed be all they that serve graven images,
   That boast themselves of things of nought;
   Bow down to Him, all ye gods.
8. Zion heard and was glad,
   And the daughters of Judah rejoiced;
   Because of Thy judgments, O LORD.
9. For Thou, LORD, art most high above all the earth;
   Thou art exalted far above all gods.
10. O ye that love the LORD, hate evil;
    He preserveth the souls of His saints;
    He delivereth them out of the hand of the wicked.
11. Light is sown for the righteous,
    And gladness for the upright in heart.

of God. The prophet Micah uses the same metaphor: "The mountains shall be molten under Him . . . as wax before the fire" (Micah 1:4).

8. ZION HEARD AND WAS GLAD . . . BECAUSE OF THY JUDGMENTS. This verse is found with a slight grammatical change in Psalm 48:12.

10. YE THAT LOVE THE LORD, HATE EVIL. Since God is the God of righteousness only those who hate evil and love righteousness can sincerely worship Him.

11. LIGHT IS SOWN FOR THE RIGHTEOUS. A beautiful metaphor, but rather difficult to explain. The commentator, Ibn Ezra, says that though one may sow little he will reap much. Whatever light the righteous will sow, will grow into a great harvest. The thought of this verse may be taken in connection with the thought of Proverbs 4:18, "The path of the righteous is as the light of dawn, that shineth more and more unto the perfect day." Thus understood, the verse means that there is a radiance which accompanies righteousness, a "beauty of holiness." The path of the righteous, his road through life, glows with light and gladness. Thus, "Light is sown for the righteous, and gladness for the upright in heart."

277

12. Be glad in the LORD, ye righteous;
    And give thanks to His holy name.

98. A PSALM.

O sing unto the LORD a new song;
For He hath done marvellous things;
His right hand, and His holy arm, hath wrought salvation for
    Him.
2. The LORD hath made known His salvation;
    His righteousness hath He revealed in the sight of the nations.
3. He hath remembered His mercy and His faithfulness toward the
    house of Israel;
    All the ends of the earth have seen the salvation of our God.
4. Shout unto the LORD, all the earth;
    Break forth and sing for joy, yea, sing praises.
5. Sing praises unto the LORD with the harp;
    With the harp and the voice of melody.
6. With trumpets and sound of the horn

12. BE GLAD . . . GIVE THANKS. This verse is taken from
Psalm 32:11 and Psalm 30:5.

ANOTHER theocratic psalm. The ideas of the Psalm are
hardly original and, indeed, some of its phrases come from other
sources, yet the psalm is a stirring song of joyous praise.

1. HIS RIGHT HAND . . . HATH WROUGHT SALVATION. God's hand
(a symbol for God's might) has brought deliverance at His
command. This thought is found in Isaiah 59:16, "therefore
His own arm brought salvation unto Him."

3. THE ENDS OF THE EARTH. The world from limit to limit.
This sentence is taken from Isaiah 52:10.

7. LET THE SEA ROAR. This whole description of jubilant nature rejoicing at God's coming to judge the world with equity
is found in Psalm 96:11-13.

ANOTHER theocratic psalm. The specific attribute of
God's kingship described in the preceding psalms was His

Shout ye before the King, the LORD.
7. Let the sea roar, and the fulness thereof;
   The world, and they that dwell therein;
8. Let the floods clap their hands;
   Let the mountains sing for joy together;
9. Before the LORD, for He is come to judge the earth;
   He will judge the world with righteousness,
   And the peoples with equity.

99. The LORD reigneth; let the peoples tremble;
   He is enthroned upon the cherubim; let the earth quake.
2. The LORD is great in Zion;
   And He is high above all the peoples.
3. Let them praise Thy name as great and awful;
   Holy is He.
4. The strength also of the king who loveth justice—
   Thou hast established equity,
   Thou hast executed justice and righteousness in Jacob.

righteous judgment. Here the psalmist speaks of God's holiness.

1. ENTHRONED UPON THE CHERUBIM. This phrase is used in Psalm 80:2. See comment to that phrase.

2. GREAT IN ZION . . . HIGH ABOVE ALL THE PEOPLES. God is revered not only by Israel but is to be revered by all mankind.

3. GREAT AND AWFUL. Great and awe-inspiring.

HOLY IS HE. This phrase is the refrain which is repeated in verse 5 and, with some variation, at the close of the psalm. God's attribute of holiness finds sublime expression in the vision of Isaiah (Isaiah 6) where the angels chant, "Holy, holy, holy, is the Lord of hosts." The holiness of God as an ethical influence in human life is also expressed in Leviticus 19:2, "Ye shall be holy; for I the Lord your God am holy." The rabbis commenting on this verse say that it means that as God is merciful be ye merciful, as God is just be ye just.

4. THE STRENGTH OF THE KING. The commentator, Kimchi, says that the king referred to here is God; but the commentator, Ibn Ezra, gives the meaning as here translated that God is the strength of every mortal king who loves justice.

THOU HAST ESTABLISHED EQUITY. The ultimate source of all

279

5. Exalt ye the LORD our God,
   And prostrate yourselves at His footstool; Holy is He.
6. Moses and Aaron among His priests,
   And Samuel among them that call upon His name,
   Did call upon the LORD, and He answered them.
7. He spoke unto them in the pillar of cloud;
   They kept His testimonies, and the statute that He
   gave them.
8. O LORD our God, Thou didst answer them;
   A forgiving God wast Thou unto them,
   Though Thou tookest vengeance of their misdeeds.
9. Exalt ye the LORD our God,
   And worship at His holy hill;
   For the LORD our God is holy.

justice is God, the pure and the holy. It is He who has established justice through His mortal messengers.

5. PROSTRATE YOURSELVES AT HIS FOOTSTOOL. This means the Temple or perhaps the ark itself. Thus, I Chronicles 28:2, "Then David . . . said . . . it was in my heart to build a house of rest for the ark . . . and for the footstool of our God." The Aramaic translation (the Targum) translates the word "footstool" as "temple." The author of Isaiah 66 had this meaning in mind when God says: How can you build me an earthly temple when "the heaven is my throne and the whole earth is my footstool" (i. e., my Temple). The verse in this psalm means: "prostrate yourselves in the Temple."

6-8. A brief historical retrospect. Unlike the retrospective history in the Asaph Psalm 78, the psalmist here does not speak of the sinfulness of the people but of the nobility of the leaders, Moses, Aaron and Samuel, whom God answered when they prayed to Him. Although they, too, were not without sin, God was "a forgiving God unto them" (verse 8).

7. HE SPOKE UNTO THEM IN THE PILLAR OF CLOUD. A pillar of cloud descended upon the tabernacle whenever the people encamped and then God spoke through the cloud. "When Moses entered the Tent, the pillar of cloud descended, and the Lord spoke with Moses" (Exodus 33:9).

100. A PSALM OF THANKSGIVING.

Shout unto the Lord, all the earth.
2. Serve the Lord with gladness;
Come before His presence with singing.
3. Know ye that the Lord He is God;
It is He that hath made us, and we are His,
His people, and the flock of His pasture.
4. Enter into His gates with thanksgiving,
And into His courts with praise;
Give thanks unto Him, and bless His name.
5. For the Lord is good;
His mercy endureth for ever;
And His faithfulness unto all generations.

*T*HIS psalm concludes the theocratic psalms, and calls upon all the nations to worship God, the King, "Shout unto the Lord, all the earth." The famous Christian hymn beginning:

"All people that on earth do dwell,
Sing to the Lord with cheerful voice,
Him serve with fear; His praise forth tell,
Come ye before Him and rejoice."

is a paraphrase of this psalm and because this is Psalm 100, the hymn is known as "Old Hundred."

This psalm is read in the daily morning service.

3. AND WE ARE HIS. The Hebrew word, translated "his," can also be read to mean "no" or "not." Therefore, some give this translation: it is He that hath made us and *not* we ourselves. However, tradition has adopted the reading upon which the present translation is based. The translation here given fits the context better. The thought sequence is: we are His . . . the flock of His pasture.

5. HIS MERCY ENDURETH FOR EVER. This phrase is the basis of a refrain, " for His mercy endureth for ever," which is used in a number of psalms, e. g., Psalm 106:1, "O give thanks unto the Lord for He is good; for His mercy endureth for ever."

281

101. A PSALM OF DAVID.

> I will sing of mercy and justice;
> Unto Thee, O LORD, will I sing praises.
> 2. I will give heed unto the way of integrity;
> Oh when wilt Thou come unto me?
> I will walk within my house in the integrity of my heart.
> 3. I will set no base thing before mine eyes;
> I hate the doing of things crooked;
> It shall not cleave unto me.
> 4. A perverse heart shall depart from me;
> I will know no evil thing.
> 5. Whoso slandereth his neighbour in secret, him will I destroy;
> Whoso is haughty of eye and proud of heart, him will I
> not suffer.
> 6. Mine eyes are upon the faithful of the land, that they may
> dwell with me;

THE psalm is headed "A Psalm of David." There is one more psalm "of David" in this Book (Psalm 103). This psalm is closely related in thought to Psalm 15, also a psalm "of David." In Psalm 15, David asks: which are the ethical qualities that give man the right to dwell in God's house? Here he tells which ethical qualities must be found in those men whom he will permit to dwell about him in his palace.

1. I WILL SING OF MERCY AND JUSTICE. The commentator, Ibn Ezra, makes the following comment on this verse: whether God be merciful to me or whether He execute stern justice against me, in either case I will sing His praises.

2. WHEN WILT THOU COME UNTO ME? When will I be worthy of Thy presence; or perhaps he means, more specifically, when will God forgive my sins and permit His holy ark to come to the place which I have prepared for it? Thus, "And David was afraid of the Lord that day; and he said, 'how shall the ark of the Lord come unto me?'" (II Samuel 6:9).

3-8. He says that he will keep all evil people away from him.

4. I WILL KNOW NO EVIL THING. The commentator, Kimchi, takes this to mean, I will not become acquainted with any evil man.

He that walketh in a way of integrity, he shall minister unto me.

7. He that worketh deceit shall not dwell within my house;
   He that speaketh falsehood shall not be established before
   mine eyes.
8. Morning by morning will I destroy all the wicked of the land;
   To cut off all the workers of iniquity from the city of the LORD.

102. A PRAYER OF THE AFFLICTED, WHEN HE FAINTETH, AND POURETH
OUT HIS COMPLAINT BEFORE THE LORD.

2. O LORD, hear my prayer,
   And let my cry come unto Thee.
3. Hide not Thy face from me
      in the day of my distress;
   Incline Thine ear unto me;
   In the day when I call answer me speedily.
4. For my days are consumed like smoke,
   And my bones are burned as a hearth.

6. MINE EYES ARE UPON THE FAITHFUL. When I shall select my councillors I will look for those who are faithful to Thee. The second half of the couplet makes this meaning clear: "He that walketh in integrity shall minister to me."

8. MORNING BY MORNING WILL I DESTROY THE WICKED. The morning was the time of day when the king passed judgment upon cases that were brought before him. In the morning, therefore, when I sit as judge I will destroy wickedness. See II Samuel 15:2, "And Absalom used to rise up early, and stand beside the gate, and it was so, that when any man had a suit which should come to the king for judgment . . ." etc.

THIS psalm was probably written during the exile. The psalmist speaks of the love which the exiles have for the very stones and dust of Jerusalem in ruins. He says that the exile has lasted long enough, that the time has come for God to be gracious.

The psalm is appropriately headed, "A prayer of the afflicted when he fainteth, and poureth out his complaint before the Lord."

283

5. My heart is smitten like grass, and withered;
   For I forget to eat my bread.
6. By reason of the voice of my sighing
   My bones cleave to my flesh.
7. I am like a pelican of the wilderness;
   I am become as an owl of the waste places.
8. I watch, and am become
   Like a sparrow that is alone upon the housetop.
9. Mine enemies taunt me all the day;
   They that are mad against me do curse by me.
10. For I have eaten ashes like bread,
    And mingled my drink with weeping.
11. Because of Thine indignation and Thy wrath;
    For Thou hast taken me up, and cast me away.
12. My days are like a lengthening shadow;
    And I am withered like grass.
13. But Thou, O LORD, sittest enthroned for ever;
    And Thy name is unto all generations.
14. Thou wilt arise, and have compassion upon Zion;
    For it is time to be gracious unto her, for the
    appointed time is come.
15. For Thy servants take pleasure in her stones,

5. MY HEART IS SMITTEN LIKE GRASS. As grass is dried up by the blazing sun.

I FORGET TO EAT MY BREAD. My sorrows destroy my desire for food.

6. MY BONES CLEAVE TO MY FLESH. My body is shrivelled up.

7. A PELICAN . . . AN OWL. The commentator, Kimchi, says the call of these birds is a plaintive moan. But in all likelihood these birds are selected as lonely birds, birds of the "wilderness, of the waste places." The psalmist feels alone in a land of exile. This interpretation is supported by the next verse: "A sparrow alone upon the housetop."

9. MINE ENEMIES . . . CURSE BY ME. They use me as an example of misfortune. His enemies would curse as follows: May I become as miserable as he is if I do thus and thus.

10. ASHES LIKE BREAD . . . DRINK WITH WEEPING. The same expression is used in Psalm 80:6, "Thou hast fed them with bread of tears, and given them tears to drink."

And love her dust.

16. So the nations will fear the name of the Lord,
    And all the kings of the earth Thy glory;
17. When the Lord hath built up Zion,
    When He hath appeared in His glory;
18. When He hath regarded the prayer of the destitute,
    And hath not despised their prayer.
19. This shall be written for the generation to come;
    And a people which shall be created shall praise the Lord.
20. For He hath looked down from the height of
    His sanctuary;
    From heaven did the Lord behold the earth;
21. To hear the groaning of the prisoner;
    To loose those that are appointed to death;
22. That men may tell of the name of the Lord in Zion,
    And His praise in Jerusalem;
23. When the peoples are gathered together,
    And the kingdoms, to serve the Lord.
24. He weakened my strength in the way;
    He shortened my days.
25. I say: 'O my God, take me not away in the midst of my days,
    Thou whose years endure throughout all generations.

14. TIME TO BE GRACIOUS . . . THE APPOINTED TIME. The prophet Isaiah, heralding Israel's redemption from exile, uses the same expression: "Bid Jerusalem take heart, proclaim unto her, that her time of service is accomplished" (Isaiah 40:2).

15. TAKE PLEASURE IN HER STONES, AND LOVE HER DUST. Jerusalem is in ruins, but the exiled children of Israel think lovingly of her very dust.

21. THE GROANING OF THE PRISONER. See Psalm 79:11, "Let the groaning of the prisoner come before Thee."

23. THE PEOPLES ARE GATHERED . . . TO SERVE THE LORD. This universalistic thought, that all the world will come to worship God and Zion will be God's metropolis, is frequently expressed in the Psalms. Thus, "All the ends of the earth shall turn unto the Lord; and all the kindreds of the nations shall worship before Thee" (Psalm 22:28).

25. IN THE MIDST OF MY DAYS. While I am yet in the prime of life.

26. Of old Thou didst lay the foundation of the earth;
    And the heavens are the work of Thy hands.
27. They shall perish, but Thou shalt endure;
    Yea, all of them shall wax old like a garment;
    As a vesture shalt Thou change them, and they shall pass away;
28. But Thou art the selfsame,
    And Thy years shall have no end.
29. The children of Thy servants shall dwell securely,
    And their seed shall be established before Thee.'

103. [A PSALM] OF DAVID.
    Bless the LORD, O my soul;
    And all that is within me, bless His holy name.
2. Bless the LORD, O my soul,
    And forget not all His benefits;

26, 27, 28. THE HEAVENS . . . SHALL PERISH . . . WAX OLD LIKE A GARMENT . . . THY YEARS SHALL HAVE NO END. All of nature will vanish but God alone is eternal. This same thought and the same phrases have been embodied in a poem used in the synagogue on the Day of Atonement:

"Before the lights in heaven shone, the Lord did reign.
Though like a garment earth decay,
And heaven all as smoke dissolve,
The Lord will reign for ever."

(See *Union Prayerbook*, Vol. II, page 352.)

29. THEIR SEED SHALL BE ESTABLISHED. God's promise that the children of Israel shall dwell under His protection for ever. Thus, "The seed also of His servants shall inherit it; and they that love His name shall dwell therein" (Psalm 69:37).

THE preceding psalm was written during the exile and the psalmist pleaded that God be gracious unto His people and restore them. This psalm may well have been written after the return. The psalmist is grateful for the mercies of God. But whatever were the circumstances of the community when the psalm was written, the psalm is intensely personal in tone. The

3. Who forgiveth all thine iniquity;
Who healeth all thy diseases;
4. Who redeemeth thy life from the pit;
Who encompasseth thee with lovingkindness
and tender mercies;
5. Who satisfieth thine old age with good things;
So that thy youth is renewed like the eagle.
6. The LORD executeth righteousness,
And acts of justice for all that are oppressed.
7. He made known His ways unto Moses,
His doings unto the children of Israel.
8. The LORD is full of compassion and gracious,
Slow to anger, and plenteous in mercy.
9. He will not always contend;
Neither will He keep His anger for ever.

psalmist invokes his soul to sing praise to God "who healeth all thy diseases" (verse 3), "who satisfieth thine old age with good things" (verse 5), and whose tenderness is that of a compassionate father (verse 13).

3. WHO HEALETH ALL THY DISEASES. God is our healer. The same Divine attribute is mentioned in Exodus 15:26, "I will put none of the diseases upon thee, which I have put upon the Egyptians; for I am the Lord that healeth thee."

5. THY YOUTH IS RENEWED LIKE THE EAGLE. The commentator, Kimchi, cites here the legend of the eagle who soars towards the sun and then plunges suddenly into the sea to emerge young again. However, the psalmist may simply mean that as the eagles seem to be tireless, so will you have the tireless strength of youth. It is in this sense that the prophet Isaiah used this phrase: "They that wait for the Lord shall renew their strength; they shall mount up with wings as eagles; they shall run, and not be weary" (Isaiah 40:31).

7-8. MADE KNOWN HIS WAYS UNTO MOSES. THE LORD IS FULL OF COMPASSION . . . PLENTEOUS IN MERCY. These verses are based upon the famous passage in Exodus 33:13, where Moses pleads with God and asks: "Show me Thy ways," and in Exodus 34:6, the "way" of God is described as "merciful, gracious, abundant in goodness."

10. He hath not dealt with us after our sins,
     Nor requited us according to our iniquities.
11. For as the heaven is high above the earth,
     So great is His mercy toward them that fear Him.
12. As far as the east is from the west,
     So far hath He removed our transgressions from us.
13. Like as a father hath compassion upon his children,
     So hath the LORD compassion upon them that
        fear Him.
14. For He knoweth our frame;
     He remembereth that we are dust.
15. As for man, his days are as grass;
     As a flower of the field, so he flourisheth.
16. For the wind passeth over it, and it is gone;
     And the place thereof knoweth it no more.

10-18. This passage elaborates upon God's mercifulness. It is as great as the distance from heaven to earth. He removes our sin from us as far as the east is from the west (verse 12). He is as compassionate as a father is to his children. The compassion of the parent is ascribed to God also in Isaiah 49:15, but there it speaks of mother-love. Thus, "Zion said, the Lord hath forsaken me. Can a woman forget her sucking child?"

14-16. God is merciful to us because He knows our life is brief and we have not many days on earth in which to see happiness.

16. THE PLACE THEREOF KNOWETH IT NO MORE. This expression means that man vanishes so completely that the places in which he lived do not even remember him. The same expression is used in Job 7:10, "He shall return no more to his house, neither shall his place know him any more."

17. THE MERCY OF THE LORD. Continues the development of the passage in Exodus describing God's forgiveness.

18. Is influenced by the phrase in the Ten Commandments, "showing mercy unto the thousandth generation of them that love Me and keep My commandments," (Exodus 20:6).

20. YE ANGELS OF HIS. As in Psalm 29, the psalmist calls upon the angels to utter their hymns of praise to God. In Isaiah's vi-

17. But the mercy of the LORD is from everlasting to
       everlasting upon them that fear Him,
    And His righteousness unto children's children;
18. To such as keep His covenant,
    And to those that remember His precepts to do them.
19. The LORD hath established His throne in the heavens;
    And His kingdom ruleth over all.
20. Bless the LORD, ye angels of His,
    Ye mighty in strength, that fulfil His word,
    Hearkening unto the voice of His word.
21. Bless the LORD, all ye His hosts;
    Ye ministers of His, that do His pleasure.
22. Bless the LORD, all ye His works,
    In all places of His dominion;
    Bless the LORD, O my soul.

sion (Isaiah 6), it is the angels who proclaim: "Holy, holy, holy,
is the Lord of hosts."

21. YE MINISTERS OF HIS. Ye servants.

22. BLESS THE LORD, ALL YE, HIS WORKS. This psalm begins
with a song within the human soul: "Bless the Lord, O my
soul," and ends with all of the universe praising God.

*T*HIS psalm is closely related to the preceding one. It begins with the same invocation: "Bless the Lord, O my soul."
Psalm 103 spoke of God's greatness and mercy in the history of
Israel. Psalm 104 speaks of God's grandeur in nature. The
psalm describes the creation of the world and follows the account of creation given in Genesis 1. It begins, as does the account in Genesis, with the establishment of the heavens; then
continues with the separation of the sea from the land; then
the springing up of grass and food for cattle and man; then the
creation of the sun and moon; and then the living creatures of
the sea.

Psalm 104 is recited in the synagogue on Sabbath afternoons
during the winter months and is part of the morning services
for the New Moon.

289

104. Bless the LORD, O my soul.

1   O LORD my God, Thou art very great;
    Thou art clothed with glory and majesty.

2. Who coverest Thyself with light as with a garment,
    Who stretchest out the heavens like a curtain;

3. Who layest the beams of Thine upper chambers in the waters,
    Who makest the clouds Thy chariot,
    Who walkest upon the wings of the wind;

4. Who makest winds Thy messengers,
    The flaming fire Thy ministers.

5. Who didst establish the earth upon its foundations,
    That it should not be moved for ever and ever;

6. Thou didst cover it with the deep as with a vesture;
    The waters stood above the mountains.

7. At Thy rebuke they fled,
    At the voice of Thy thunder they hasted away—

8. The mountains rose, the valleys sank down—
    Unto the place which Thou hadst founded for them;

9. Thou didst set a bound which they should not pass over,

1-2. THOU ART CLOTHED WITH GLORY AND MAJESTY . . . LIGHT AS WITH A GARMENT. The divine attributes of glory, majesty, and radiance are metaphorically described in the Psalms as garments of God. Thus, "The Lord reigneth; He is clothed in majesty" (Psalm 93:1).

2. THE HEAVENS LIKE A CURTAIN. Like the curtain or roof of a tent.

3. THE BEAMS OF THINE UPPER CHAMBERS IN THE WATERS. Psalm 24:2 describes the earth as being founded on the waters. Here, the psalmist speaks of heaven as founded above the seas. Or the verse may well refer to the belief that the heavens were composed of water. In the description of the creation (Genesis 1:7), God divides the lower waters (the sea) from the upper waters. The psalm verse would then mean that God builds His "upper chambers" in the midst of the heavenly waters.

4. THY MINISTERS. Thy messengers, Thy servants.

6. THE WATER STOOD ABOVE THE MOUNTAINS. This does not refer to the deluge but to the primeval waters which, according to the account in Genesis, originally covered all the earth.

That they might not return to cover the earth.

10. Who sendest forth springs into the valleys;
They run between the mountains;
11. They give drink to every beast of the field,
The wild asses quench their thirst.
12. Beside them dwell the fowl of the heaven,
From among the branches they sing.
13. Who waterest the mountains from Thine upper chambers;
The earth is full of the fruit of Thy works.
14. Who causest the grass to spring up for the cattle,
And herb for the service of man;
To bring forth bread out of the earth,
15. And wine that maketh glad the heart of man,
Making the face brighter than oil,
And bread that stayeth man's heart.
16. The trees of the LORD have their fill,
The cedars of Lebanon, which He hath planted;
17. Wherein the birds make their nests;
As for the stork, the fir-trees are her house.

7. AT THY REBUKE THEY FLED. At Thy command the waters receded and let the dry land appear.

9. THOU DIDST SET A BOUND. God fixed the limits of the seas for they should not return to cover the earth. Thus, "And said (to the sea): 'thus far shalt thou come, but no further; and here shalt thy proud waves be stayed'" (Job 38:11).

11. THE WILD ASSES QUENCH THEIR THIRST. The wild asses of the desert are described also in Jeremiah 14:6.

14. TO BRING FORTH BREAD OUT OF THE EARTH. This sentence is used in the blessing over bread. "Praised be Thou ... Who bringest forth bread from the earth."

15. MAKING THE FACE BRIGHTER THAN OIL. As translated here the verse refers to the wine spoken of in the preceding sentence, namely, that wine makes the heart glad and, like oil, makes the face bright. But the commentator, Rashi, translates the verse as follows: wine that maketh glad ... and oil which maketh the face bright.

WINE, OIL, BREAD (OR CORN), are often mentioned as the greatest gifts of God. Thus, "The tithe of thy corn (i. e.,

291

18. The high mountains are for the wild goats;
    The rocks are a refuge for the conies.
19. Who appointedst the moon for seasons;
    The sun knoweth his going down.
20. Thou makest darkness, and it is night,
    Wherein all the beasts of the forest do creep forth.
21. The young lions roar after their prey,
    And seek their food from God.
22. The sun ariseth, they slink away,
    And couch in their dens.
23. Man goeth forth unto his work
    And to his labour until the evening.
24. How manifold are Thy works, O LORD!
    In wisdom hast Thou made them all;
    The earth is full of Thy creatures.
25. Yonder sea, great and wide,
    Therein are creeping things innumerable,
    Living creatures, both small and great.
26. There go the ships;

thy bread), thy wine or thine oil" (Deuteronomy 12:17).

18. A REFUGE FOR THE CONIES. For rabbits.

19. THE MOON FOR SEASONS. The ancient calendars were based upon the phases of the moon.

THE SUN KNOWETH HIS GOING DOWN. The psalmist refers here to the sunset, and in verse 22 to the sunrise, and describes the varied life on earth by night and day.

21. THE YOUNG LIONS . . . SEEK THEIR FOOD FROM GOD. Even the beasts of prey are sustained by Divine bounty.

26. THERE IS LEVIATHAN. Leviathan (the great sea monster referred to in Job 40) generally means the crocodile. See note to Psalm 74:15. Here it probably refers to any of the great sea monsters, such as the whales which were plentiful in the Mediterranean in the ancient days.

27-28. ALL OF THEM WAIT FOR THEE . . . THOU MAYEST GIVE THEM THEIR FOOD . . . THOU OPENEST THY HAND. The same thought, the same language is expressed in Psalm 145:15-16, "The eyes of all wait for Thee, Thou givest them their food . . . Thou openest Thy hand."

292

There is leviathan, whom Thou hast formed to sport
therein.
27. All of them wait for Thee,
That Thou mayest give them their food in due season.
28. Thou givest it unto them, they gather it;
Thou openest Thy hand, they are satisfied with good.
29. Thou hidest Thy face, they vanish;
Thou withdrawest their breath, they perish,
And return to their dust.
30. Thou sendest forth Thy spirit, they are created;
And Thou renewest the face of the earth.
31. May the glory of the LORD endure for ever;
Let the LORD rejoice in His works!
32. Who looketh on the earth, and it trembleth;
He toucheth the mountains, and they smoke.
33. I will sing unto the LORD as long as I live;
I will sing praise to my God while I have any being.
34. Let my musing be sweet unto Him;
As for me, I will rejoice in the LORD.

29. THOU HIDEST THY FACE, THEY VANISH. Every living thing
depends upon God's favor. When God withdraws His help
(Thou hidest Thy face) they perish.

30. THOU RENEWEST THE FACE OF THE EARTH. As one generation goes and another generation comes, God renews life
upon the surface of the earth. A similar expression is used in
the daily service, "and in His goodness He reneweth every day
the works of creation."

31. MAY THE GLORY OF THE LORD. This phrase is taken into
the daily morning service as the opening sentence of the paragraph, (Yehi ch'vode), which introduces the group of psalms of
praise.

32. HE TOUCHETH THE MOUNTAINS, AND THEY SMOKE. As in
Exodus 19:18, "Now Mount Sinai was altogether on smoke,
because the Lord descended upon it in fire."

34. LET MY MUSING BE SWEET. Not only my uttered songs but
the musing of my heart. Thus, in Psalm 19:15, "Let the words
of my mouth and the meditation of my heart be acceptable before Thee."

35. Let sinners cease out of the earth,
    And let the wicked be no more.
    Bless the LORD, O my soul.
    Hallelujah.*

105. O give thanks unto the LORD, call upon His name;
     Make known His doings among the peoples.
  2. Sing unto Him, sing praises unto Him;
     Speak ye of all His marvellous works.
  3. Glory ye in His holy name;
     Let the heart of them rejoice that seek the LORD.
  4. Seek ye the LORD and His strength;
     Seek His face continually.
  5. Remember His marvellous works that He hath done,

35. BLESS THE LORD, O MY SOUL. The psalm ends with the phrase with which it began.

HALLELUJAH. Literally, praise ye the Lord. This word is found only in the Psalms and this is the first use of it in the Psalm Book. It is generally used either at the beginning or at the close of a psalm as a call to praise. Only once (in Psalm 135:3) is it used in the middle of a psalm. It is not unlikely that the word "Hallelujah" is misplaced here and should be the opening word for the following psalm, Psalm 105, as the Greek translation, the Septuagint, has it. If "Hallelujah" is taken as the opening word of Psalm 105, then Psalm 104 will properly end with the sentence with which it began: "Bless the Lord, O my soul," and Psalm 105 will properly begin and end with the word "Hallelujah."

𝔓SALMS 105 and 106 are closely related. They both begin and end with "Hallelujah." (See note to the close of the preceding psalm.) Both, together, express a complete idea, namely, the theme developed in Psalm 78, a psalm of Asaph, which describes the history of Israel and speaks of the constant rebellion of our fathers against God. These two ideas, united in

* That is, *Praise ye the LORD.*

294

His wonders, and the judgments of His mouth;
6. O ye seed of Abraham His servant,
Ye children of Jacob, His chosen ones.
7. He is the LORD our God;
His judgments are in all the earth.
8. He hath remembered His covenant for ever,
The word which He commanded to a thousand
generations;
9. [The covenant] which He made with Abraham,
And His oath unto Isaac;
10. And He established it unto Jacob for a statute,
To Israel for an everlasting covenant;
11. Saying: 'Unto thee will I give the land of Canaan,
The lot of your inheritance.'

Psalm 78, are here separated. Psalm 105 speaks of Israel's history, and Psalm 106 describes the rebellious murmurings of our fathers.

Verses 1 to 15 of this psalm are quoted in I Chronicles 16:8-22, as the opening part of the hymn which Asaph and his brethren sang before the ark at the command of David. See note to Psalm 96, which is quoted in the hymn in Chronicles following this psalm.

The two psalms, 105 and 106, must have been written during the exile inasmuch as Psalm 106:46 speaks of the captivity.

1. MAKE KNOWN HIS DOINGS AMONG THE PEOPLES. Israel is commanded to declare to all the world God's wondrous works. The same sentence is used in Psalm 9:12, "declare among the peoples His doings."

6. CHILDREN OF JACOB, HIS CHOSEN ONES. Israel whom God has chosen to make a covenant with him to obey His law and to speak of His work to all nations. This idea is found frequently in the Bible. Thus, "But thou, Israel, My servant, Jacob whom I have chosen, the seed of Abraham, My friend; Thou whom I have taken hold of from the ends of the earth . . . and said unto thee: 'Thou art My servant' " (Isaiah 41:8-9).

11. THE LOT OF YOUR INHERITANCE. The allotment of your inheritance. The land of Canaan was allotted to the children of Israel by measurement and by lot.

295

12. When they were but a few men in number,
     Yea, very few, and sojourners in it,
13. And when they went about from nation to nation,
     From one kingdom to another people,
14. He suffered no man to do them wrong,
     Yea, for their sake He reproved kings:
15. 'Touch not Mine anointed ones,
     And do My prophets no harm.'
16. And He called a famine upon the land;
     He broke the whole staff of bread.
17. He sent a man before them;
     Joseph was sold for a servant;
18. His feet they hurt with fetters,
     His person was laid in iron;
19. Until the time that his word came to pass,
     The word of the LORD tested him.
20. The king sent and loosed him;
     Even the ruler of peoples, and set him free.
21. He made him lord of his house,
     And ruler of all his possessions;
22. To bind his princes at his pleasure,
     And teach his elders wisdom.
23. Israel also came into Egypt;

12-22. This section speaks of God's protection of the patriarchs.

12. BUT A FEW MEN IN NUMBER. Namely, the patriarchs.

SOJOURNERS IN IT. Abraham speaks of himself as a mere sojourner in the land of Canaan. Thus, "I am a stranger and a sojourner with you" (Genesis 23:4).

13. FROM NATION TO NATION. The wanderings of the patriarchs.

14. HE REPROVED KINGS. God reproved the king of Egypt, (Genesis 12:10 ff.) and also Abimelech, the king of Gerar (Genesis 20).

15. MY PROPHETS. The commentators, Ibn Ezra and Kimchi, explain that the patriarchs (who are described as having spoken with God) are to be considered as prophets.

16. THE STAFF OF BREAD. The Bible frequently speaks of bread as the staff which supports the body, hence, "the staff of

And Jacob sojourned in the land of Ham.

24. And He increased His people greatly,
And made them too mighty for their adversaries.

25. He turned their heart to hate His people,
To deal craftily with His servants.

26. He sent Moses His servant,
And Aaron whom He had chosen.

27. They wrought among them His manifold signs,
And wonders in the land of Ham.

28. He sent darkness, and it was dark;
And they rebelled not against His word.

29. He turned their waters into blood,
And slew their fish.

30. Their land swarmed with frogs,
In the chambers of their kings.

31. He spoke, and there came swarms of flies,
And gnats in all their borders.

32. He gave them hail for rain,
And flaming fire in their land.

33. He smote their vines also and their fig-trees;
And broke the trees of their borders.

34. He spoke, and the locust came,
And the canker-worm without number,

life." Thus, "Behold, the Lord doth take away . . . the stay and staff, the stay of bread" (Isaiah 3:1) .

19. UNTIL HIS WORD COME TO PASS. Until Joseph's predictions to the butler and the baker were fulfilled. Joseph remained in prison till "his (Joseph's) word came to pass."

22. TO BIND HIS PRINCES. When Joseph was made viceroy of Egypt he received permission to imprison even the princes of Egypt whenever necessary.

23-38. Israel's stay in Egypt.

23. THE LAND OF HAM. Ham, the son of Noah, was the father of Mizraim, the ancestor of Egypt. (Genesis 10:6.)

25. TO DEAL CRAFTILY. When Israel increased in number, Pharaoh said to his servants: "Come, let us deal wisely (or craftily) with them" (Exodus 1:10).

Here follows a description of the plagues. The plague of darkness which was the ninth plague is mentioned here first.

297

35. And did eat up every herb in their land,
    And did eat up the fruit of their ground.
36. He smote also all the first-born in their land,
    The first-fruits of all their strength.
37. And He brought them forth with silver and gold;
    And there was none that stumbled among His tribes.
38. Egypt was glad when they departed;
    For the fear of them had fallen upon them.
39. He spread a cloud for a screen;
    And fire to give light in the night.
40. They asked, and He brought quails,
    And gave them in plenty the bread of heaven.
41. He opened the rock, and waters gushed out;
    They ran, a river in the dry places.
42. For He remembered His holy word
    Unto Abraham His servant;
43. And He brought forth His people with joy,
    His chosen ones with singing.
44. And He gave them the lands of the nations,

36. THE FIRST-BORN . . . THE FIRST-FRUITS OF ALL THEIR STRENGTH. Psalm 78:51, likewise describes the first-born as "the first-fruits of their strength."

37. NONE THAT STUMBLED. When Israel marched out of Egypt.

39-41. The miracles in the desert: the pillars of cloud, the pillars of fire, the quail, the manna, the water from the rock. The psalm does not mention their rebellions in connection with these miracles as does Psalm 78. It relegates the discussion of these rebellious murmurings to the next psalm.

44. THE LANDS OF THE NATIONS. Of Canaan.

45. THAT THEY MIGHT KEEP HIS STATUTES. God protected Israel only in order that Israel obey His laws.

SEE the introduction to Psalm 105.

1-5. An introductory invocation, calling upon the worshippers to praise God and asking that God grant him (the psalmist) the privilege of beholding the restoration.

And they took the labour of the peoples in
  possession;
45. That they might keep His statutes,
And observe His laws. Hallelujah.

106. HALLELUJAH.

O give thanks unto the LORD; for He is good;
For His mercy endureth for ever.
2. Who can express the mighty acts of the LORD,
Or make all His praise to be heard?
3. Happy are they that keep justice,
That do righteousness at all times.
4. Remember me, O LORD, when Thou favourest Thy people;
O think of me at Thy salvation;
5. That I may behold the prosperity of Thy chosen,
That I may rejoice in the gladness of Thy nation,
That I may glory with Thine inheritance.
6. We have sinned with our fathers,
We have done iniquitously, we have dealt wickedly.

1. GIVE THANKS UNTO THE LORD . . . FOR HIS MERCY ENDURETH
FOR EVER. This formula is frequently used further on in the
Psalms, in Psalm 118 and in Psalm 136, etc.

2. WHO CAN EXPRESS THE MIGHTY ACTS OF THE LORD. The
thought is often expressed in the Psalms that God's greatness is
Infinite and no mortal can describe it all. The Talmud (b.
Berachoth 33 b) tells of a reader in the service who added a
number of laudatory adjectives to the words of praise in the
prayers. Rabbi Haninah rebuked him and said: "Dost thou imagine that thereby thou hast expressed *all* the praises of God?"

3. HAPPY ARE THEY THAT KEEP JUSTICE. We cannot do justice
to all of God's greatness but we can keep justice in our relation-
ships with our fellow-men.

4. REMEMBER ME WHEN THOU FAVOUREST THY PEOPLE. The
psalmist is speaking during the exile and therefore asks that
God give him the joy of living to behold His deliverance of
Israel.

6. WE HAVE SINNED WITH OUR FATHERS. The sins which we
have committed and in punishment for which we have been

7. Our fathers in Egypt gave no heed unto Thy wonders;
    They remembered not the multitude of Thy mercies;
    But were rebellious at the sea, even at the Red Sea.
8. Nevertheless He saved them for His name's sake,
    That He might make His mighty power to be known.
9. And He rebuked the Red Sea, and it was dried up;
    And He led them through the depths, as through a wilderness.
10. And He saved them from the hand of him that hated them,
     And redeemed them from the hand of the enemy.
11. And the waters covered their adversaries;
     There was not one of them left.
12. Then believed they His words;
     They sang His praise.
13. They soon forgot His works;
     They waited not for His counsel;
14. But lusted exceedingly in the wilderness,
     And tried God in the desert.
15. And He gave them their request;
     But sent leanness into their soul.
16. They were jealous also of Moses in the camp,
     And of Aaron the holy one of the LORD.
17. The earth opened and swallowed up Dathan,
     And covered the company of Abiram.

exiled, are similar to the sins which our fathers committed before us. Here follows a long description of the sins of Israel in the desert. In Egypt they did not appreciate God's wonders (verse 7); they rebelled (verse 7) at the Red Sea. After that miracle they did, for the time at least, appreciate God's greatness. They believed His works and sang His praises (verse 12).

But they soon forgot His works (verse 13); they "lusted exceedingly" (verse 14); they cried for food (verse 15); God sent them the quail but "sent leanness into their soul," i. e., He punished them for their presumption. (See Numbers 11:6.)

16-18. The rebellion of Dathan and Abiram against Moses and Aaron. See Numbers 16:3-7.

19. HOREB. Another name for Mount Sinai. Exodus 19:18, refers to the mountain of revelation as "Sinai" while Deuteronomy 4:10, calls the mountain "Horeb."

20. THEY EXCHANGED THEIR GLORY FOR THE LIKENESS OF AN

18. And a fire was kindled in their company;
      The flame burned up the wicked.
19. They made a calf in Horeb,
      And worshipped a molten image.
20. Thus they exchanged their glory
      For the likeness of an ox that eateth grass.
21. They forgot God their saviour,
      Who had done great things in Egypt;
22. Wondrous works in the land of Ham,
      Terrible things by the Red Sea.
23. Therefore He said that He would destroy them,
      Had not Moses His chosen stood before Him in the breach,
      To turn back His wrath, lest He should destroy them.
24. Moreover, they scorned the desirable land,
      They believed not His word;
25. And they murmured in their tents,
      They hearkened not unto the voice of the Lord.
26. Therefore He swore concerning them,
      That He would overthrow them in the wilderness;
27. And that He would cast out their seed among the nations,
      And scatter them in the lands.
28. They joined themselves also unto Baal of Peor,
      And ate the sacrifices of the dead.

ox. The commentator, Ibn Ezra, takes the word "glory" to mean "God," i. e., they exchanged God for a calf.

24. THEY SCORNED THE DESIRABLE LAND. When the spies returned with a fearful report Israel scorned the Promised Land.

27. HE WOULD CAST OUT THEIR SEED AMONG THE NATIONS. The commentator, Kimchi, calls attention to the fact that God had said that the generations of the wilderness would not come into Canaan but that the Pentateuch nowhere says that God, in punishment for their rebellion in the desert, would scatter their children among the nations as the psalmist here says. The psalmist evidently bases his statement upon Ezekiel 20:23, "I lifted up My hand unto them also in the wilderness, (i. e., I swore) that I would scatter them among the nations."

28. THEY JOINED THEMSELVES UNTO BAAL OF PEOR. Here follows a description of Israel's worship of Baal Peor and the sins connected therewith and the punishment which Phinehas

301

29. Thus they provoked Him with their doings,
    And the plague broke in upon them.
30. Then stood up Phinehas, and wrought judgment,
    And so the plague was stayed.
31. And that was counted unto him for righteousness,
    Unto all generations for ever.
32. They angered Him also at the waters of Meribah,
    And it went ill with Moses because of them;
33. For they embittered his spirit,
    And he spoke rashly with his lips.
34. They did not destroy the peoples,
    As the LORD commanded them;
35. But mingled themselves with the nations,
    And learned their works;
36. And they served their idols,
    Which became a snare unto them;
37. Yea, they sacrificed their sons and their daughters unto demons,
38. And shed innocent blood, even the blood of their sons and of
    their daughters,
    Whom they sacrificed unto the idols of Canaan;
    And the land was polluted with blood.
39. Thus were they defiled with their works,
    And went astray in their doings.

executed upon the sinners are all described in Numbers 25.

28. SACRIFICES OF THE DEAD. Kimchi explains this to mean sacrifices offered to the idols who are lifeless. God, by contrast, is referred to as "the living God" (Psalm 42:3) .

32. The rebellion at Meribah (Numbers 20:13), and the sin of Moses who, when he rebuked them, "spoke rashly with his lips" (verse 33). Cf. Deuteronomy 1:37, "the Lord was angry with me for your sakes."

34-36. The early history of Israel in Canaan. They failed to destroy the idolators; they learned idol worship from them (verse 36); they even sacrificed their sons and their daughters unto demons. This refers to human sacrifices used in the worship of the god Moloch. (See Deuteronomy 18:10.)

The psalmist speaks of their repeated sinfulness and God's repeated forgiveness, "many times did He deliver them" (verse 43). This idea of God's repeated deliverance of the Israelites,

302

40. Therefore was the wrath of the Lord kindled against His people,
     And He abhorred His inheritance.
41. And He gave them into the hand of the nations;
     And they that hated them ruled over them.
42. Their enemies also oppressed them,
     And they were subdued under their hand.
43. Many times did He deliver them;
     But they were rebellious in their counsel,
     And sank low through their iniquity.
44. Nevertheless He looked upon their distress,
     When He heard their cry;
45. And He remembered for them His covenant,
     And repented according to the multitude of His mercies.
46. He made them also to be pitied
     Of all those that carried them captive.
47. Save us, O Lord our God,
     And gather us from among the nations,
     That we may give thanks unto Thy holy name,
     That we may triumph in Thy praise.
48. Blessed be the Lord, the God of Israel,
     From everlasting even to everlasting.
     And let all the people say: 'Amen.'
     Hallelujah.

in spite of their repeated sins, is described in Judges 2:16-19.

46. HE MADE THEM ALSO TO BE PITIED OF ALL THOSE THAT CARRIED THEM CAPTIVE. This sentence seems to bring the history down to the exile since it speaks of Israel as captive. In the prayer of Solomon, I Kings 8:50, the same expression is used, "give them compassion before those who carry them captive, that they may have compassion on them."

47. SAVE US, O LORD, GATHER US FROM AMONG THE NATIONS. The closing prayer of the psalm, a prayer for the restoration of Israel.

48. BLESSED BE THE LORD, FROM EVERLASTING EVEN TO EVERLASTING . . . AMEN. This is the doxology or liturgical appendage which closes Book Four. Some commentators believe that this is not a doxology marking the end of the Book but is an integral part of Psalm 106, inasmuch as it is followed by the word "Hallelujah," and "Hallelujah" marks the beginning and close

of this psalm. However, this doxology is so similar to the doxologies which close Books One, Two, and Three that it can hardly be anything else. As for "Hallelujah," it may easily have been misplaced as was the "Hallelujah" at the beginning of Psalm 105. If the "Hallelujah" is placed at the end of verse 47, it would close the psalm properly as follows: "That we may triumph in Thy praise. Hallelujah," (i. e., praise ye the Lord). Then follows the doxology which is almost identical with the previous doxologies.

Book Five

Book Five must have been united with Book Four as a separate collection. This is evident from the fact first, that the psalm which begins Book Five (Psalm 107) closely resembles in style and thought the two psalms which close Book Four. The three psalms, 105, 106, 107, clearly belong together. Furthermore, Books Four and Five, both use the name *JHWH* for God instead of *Elohim* which is the preferred name for God in Books Two and Three. (See introduction to Book Four.)

Book Five contains three special groups of psalms which must have been collected separately: a) the Hallel psalms, 113-118; b) the Songs of Ascent, 120-134; c) the Hallelujah psalms, 135-150.

𝒫salm 107
1

107. 'O give thanks unto the Lord, for He is good,
For His mercy endureth for ever.'
2. So let the redeemed of the Lord say,
Whom He hath redeemed from the hand of the
adversary;
3. And gathered them out of the lands,
From the east and from the west,
From the north and from the sea.
4. They wandered in the wilderness in a desert way;
They found no city of habitation.
5. Hungry and thirsty,

𝒯HIS psalm, a call to the worshippers to sing praise to God, begins with the same invocation as the closing psalm in Book Four: "Oh give thanks unto the Lord, for He is good, for His mercy endureth for ever." The psalm enumerates four different types of human experience in which God delivers men from dire peril, and those rescued learn to be grateful for His mercies.

That this psalm was written soon after the return from the exile seems to be indicated in verses 2 and 3: "Let the redeemed of the Lord say, whom He hath redeemed from the hand of the adversary and gathered them out of the lands."

1-3. The introductory call to the praise of God.

1. O GIVE THANKS . . . The formula of invocation used in Psalms 106, 107 and in Psalm 136.

2. THE REDEEMED OF THE LORD. Probably the exiles who have returned from Babylon.

3. GATHERED THEM FROM THE EAST, FROM THE WEST, FROM THE NORTH AND FROM THE SEA. The Hebrew word for "sea" is also translated "south." It may be that the word "sea" used in this connection refers to the southern part of the Mediterranean (i. e., at the coasts of Egypt).

It seems strange that the psalmist, speaking of those who have returned to Palestine, describes them as coming from all four points of the compass. Did they not all come from the east, from Babylon? Yet Isaiah, too, in heralding their return from Babylon says: "I will bring thy seed from the east, and gather

306

Their soul fainted in them.

6. Then they cried unto the LORD in their trouble,
   And He delivered them out of their distresses.
7. And He led them by a straight way,
   That they might go to a city of habitation.
8. Let them give thanks unto the LORD for His mercy,
   And for His wonderful works to the children of men!
9. For He hath satisfied the longing soul,
   And the hungry soul He hath filled with good.
10. Such as sat in darkness and in the shadow of death,
    Being bound in affliction and iron—

thee from the west; I will say to the north: 'give up,' and to the south: 'keep not back' " (Isaiah 43:5-6).

It is evident that after (and perhaps even before) the destruction of Jerusalem, Jewish communities were established in many lands. Thus, Jeremiah (24:8) speaks of "Zedekiah the king of Judah, and his princes, and the residue of Jerusalem, that remain in this land, and them that dwell in the land of Egypt."

In verses 4-32 the psalmist describes four different types of dangerous experience in which God alone can bring deliverance. At the climax of each incident, when the peril is greatest, the psalmist says: "Then they cried unto the Lord in their trouble, and He delivered them out of their distresses," (verses 6, 13, 19, 28). Each incident ends with a call to man to express his gratitude to God.

4-9. Those who are lost in the desert and are rescued by God's guidance.

9. THE HUNGRY SOUL . . . WITH GOOD. He has given the hungry that which is good, that is, food and sustenance.

10-16. God rescues the prisoners who had been doomed to die.

10. DARKNESS . . . SHADOW OF DEATH. The darkness of the dungeon in which they are condemned to death. The phrase, "shadow of death," is also used in Psalm 23:4, where, as in this instance, it means darkness where the danger of death is lurking.

307

11. Because they rebelled against the words of God,
      And contemned the counsel of the Most High.
12. Therefore He humbled their heart with travail,
      They stumbled, and there was none to help—
13. They cried unto the LORD in their trouble,
      And He saved them out of their distresses.
14. He brought them out of darkness and the shadow of death,
      And broke their bands in sunder.
15. Let them give thanks unto the LORD for His mercy,
      And for His wonderful works to the children of men!
16. For He hath broken the gates of brass,
      And cut the bars of iron in sunder.
17. Crazed because of the way of their transgression,
      And afflicted because of their iniquities—
18. Their soul abhorred all manner of food,
      And they drew near unto the gates of death—
19. They cried unto the LORD in their trouble,
      And He saved them out of their distresses;
20. He sent His word, and healed them,

11. BECAUSE THEY REBELLED. They are imprisoned because of some crime which they had committed.

CONTEMNED THE COUNSEL. Despised the counsel of God.

12. HE HUMBLED THEIR HEART WITH TRAVAIL. With the hard labor of prison or captivity.

THEY STUMBLED. This is used in the same figurative sense as the frequent phrase, "their footsteps stumbled," i. e., they fell down, they almost died. As Isaiah 3:8, where the same verb is used, it is translated, "for Jerusalem is ruined."

14. BROKE THEIR BANDS IN SUNDER. He broke their shackles asunder.

16. THE GATES OF BRASS. The prison gates.

17-22. Those who are dangerously sick are healed through the kindness of God.

17. CRAZED BECAUSE OF . . . THEIR TRANSGRESSION, AFFLICTED BECAUSE OF THEIR INIQUITIES. The Hebrew word used here for "crazed" can be translated "fools." The commentator, Kimchi, therefore, interprets the verse as follows: when sickness first comes a wise man should recognize it as a possible punishment

308

And delivered them from their graves.
21. Let them give thanks unto the LORD for His mercy,
   And for His wonderful works to the children of men!
22. And let them offer the sacrifices of thanksgiving,
   And declare His works with singing.
23. They that go down to the sea in ships,
   That do business in great waters—
24. These saw the works of the LORD,
   And His wonders in the deep;
25. For He commanded, and raised the stormy wind,
   Which lifted up the waves thereof;
26. They mounted up to the heaven, they went down to the deeps;
   Their soul melted away because of trouble;
27. They reeled to and fro, and staggered like a drunken man,
   And all their wisdom was swallowed up—
28. They cried unto the LORD in their trouble,
   And He brought them out of their distresses.
29. He made the storm a calm,
   So that the waves thereof were still.

for sin; but these fools failed to draw a salutary lesson at the onset of their sickness. But also as translated here, the passage is quite clear: sickness is looked upon as a punishment for the violation of God's law. "Their transgression" has led them into mental as well as physical disease.

18. THE GATES OF DEATH. The phrase "gates of death" evidently means the doors of the nether-world, possibly the grave which is the gateway to the nether-world, the abode of death. The same phrase is used in Psalm 9:14, "Thou that liftest me up from the gates of death."

23-32. The fourth instance of peril is a storm at sea. The psalmist describes the storm:

26. THEY MOUNTED UP . . . THEY WENT DOWN. The sailors are lifted towards the skies and dropped towards the depth as the waves toss the ship.

THEIR SOUL MELTED AWAY BECAUSE OF TROUBLE. Their courage melts away in the time of their calamity.

27. THEIR WISDOM WAS SWALLOWED UP. All their skill in navigation becomes useless. They are helpless in the storm.

309

30. Then were they glad because they were quiet,
   And He led them unto their desired haven.
31. Let them give thanks unto the LORD for His mercy,
   And for His wonderful works to the children of men!
32. Let them exalt Him also in the assembly of the people,
   And praise Him in the seat of the elders.
33. He turneth rivers into a wilderness,
   And watersprings into a thirsty ground;
34. A fruitful land into a salt waste,
   For the wickedness of them that dwell therein.
35. He turneth a wilderness into a pool of water,
   And a dry land into watersprings.
36. And there He maketh the hungry to dwell,
   And they establish a city of habitation;

32. LET THEM EXALT HIM IN THE ASSEMBLY OF THE PEOPLE
. . . IN THE SEAT OF THE ELDERS. When they return safely to their
native city, let them praise God before the assembled citizens
and also in the council chamber of the elders. The phrase used
here for "the seat of the elders" (*moshav zekenim*) is used in
modern times for a Home for the Aged.

33-38. Having mentioned four special types of peril in human experience in which only God can bring deliverance, the
psalmist now speaks in wider terms of God's control of human
life. At His command, fertile lands may become sterile and the
wildernesses may become fruitful fields.

34. A SALT WASTE. The author has in mind the barren salt
lands around the Dead Sea. In Deuteronomy 29:22, where the
author speaks of the complete destruction which God will
bring upon the sinful land he says, "And the whole land thereof
is brimstone, and salt . . . it is not sown . . . nor any grass
groweth therein, like the overthrow of Sodom and Gomorrah."

As God can destroy a fertile land so He can also turn "a
wilderness into a pool of water" (verse 35).

39-42. As God's goodness is needed in time of personal peril
and also in the raising of crops, so is His help needed during
the vicissitudes of human history. Verses 39-42 describe God's
rescue of those who suffer oppression and tyranny.

37. And sow fields, and plant vineyards,
Which yield fruits of increase.
38. He blesseth them also, so that they are multiplied greatly,
And suffereth not their cattle to decrease.
39. Again, they are minished and dwindle away
Through oppression of evil and sorrow.
40. He poureth contempt upon princes,
And causeth them to wander in the waste, where there is no way.
41. Yet setteth He the needy on high from affliction,
And maketh His families like a flock.
42. The upright see it, and are glad;
And all iniquity stoppeth her mouth.
43. Whoso is wise, let him observe these things,
And let them consider the mercies of the LORD.

39. THEY ARE MINISHED. Diminished. The sentence refers to the preceding sentence. Those who live in a land which God has blessed with fertility may suffer political vicissitudes; they may be wasted away ("dwindle away") "through oppression of evil."

AND SORROW. Through the oppression of tyrants and its resultant sorrow.

40. HE POURETH CONTEMPT UPON PRINCES. God comes to the rescue of those who are oppressed by tyrants. He pours His contempt upon tyrannous princes sending them into exile. The phrase, "He poureth contempt upon princes," is found also in Job 12:21.

The second part of the sentence, "He causeth them to wander," etc., is also found in the same chapter of Job, 12:24.

41. SETTETH . . . ON HIGH FROM AFFLICTION. He setteth the needy on a high mountain, safe from affliction.

HIS FAMILIES LIKE A FLOCK. As a flock increases. His family will be large.

42. INIQUITY STOPPETH HER MOUTH. The sinful will no longer be able to taunt the humble. The sinful will be silenced.

43. WHOSO IS WISE. This sentence is taken from the last sentence of the Book of Hosea (Hosea 14:10).

LET THEM CONSIDER THE MERCIES OF THE LORD. The psalm-

311

108. A SONG, A PSALM OF DAVID.

2. My heart is stedfast, O God;
   I will sing, yea, I will sing praises, even with my glory.
3. Awake, psaltery and harp;
   I will awake the dawn.
4. I will give thanks unto Thee, O LORD, among the peoples;
   And I will sing praises unto Thee among the nations.
5. For Thy mercy is great above the heavens,
   And Thy truth reacheth unto the skies.
6. Be Thou exalted, O God, above the heavens;
   And Thy glory be above all the earth.
7. That Thy beloved may be delivered,
   Save with Thy right hand, and answer me.
8. God spoke in His holiness, that I would exult;
   That I would divide Shechem, and mete out the valley
      of Succoth.
9. Gilead is mine, Manasseh is mine;
   Ephraim also is the defence of my head;
   Judah is my sceptre.
10. Moab is my washpot;

ist ends with the thought with which he began. The psalm began: "Give thanks unto the Lord for His mercy . . . ," and it ends: "Let them consider the mercies of the Lord."

THIS psalm is a composite of passages from two psalms which appear earlier in the Psalm Book. Verses 2-6 are taken from Psalm 57:8-12. Verses 7-14 are taken from Psalm 60:7-14. The psalmist who selected these two sections to construct a new psalm out of them must have felt that the beginning of Psalm 60, "O God, Thou hast cast us off," was too sombre for the mood which he wished to express. Hence, instead of the sorrowful passage which opened Psalm 60:3-7, he selected the more jubilant passage in Psalm 57:8-12, as the opening of the hymn which he thus constructed.

For comment on the various verses see the original psalms from which this psalm is constructed.

Upon Edom do I cast my shoe;
Over Philistia do I cry aloud.
11. Who will bring me into the fortified city?
Who will lead me unto Edom?
12. Hast not Thou cast us off, O God?
And Thou goest not forth, O God, with our hosts.
13. Give us help against the adversary;
For vain is the help of man.
14. Through God we shall do valiantly;
For He it is that will tread down our adversaries.

109. FOR THE LEADER. A PSALM OF DAVID.

O God of my praise, keep not silence;
2. For the mouth of the wicked and the mouth of deceit
have they opened against me;
They have spoken unto me with a lying tongue.
3. They compassed me about also with words of hatred,
And fought against me without a cause.
4. In return for my love they are my adversaries;
But I am all prayer.
5. And they have laid upon me evil for good,

A PATHETIC cry for help against implacable enemies. The psalm is kindred in spirit to Psalms 35 and 69.

1. O GOD, KEEP NOT SILENCE. The psalmist frequently calls upon God to break His apparent silence to speak out in his behalf and voice His condemnation of the wicked. Thus, "Thou hast seen, O Lord; keep not silence" (Psalm 35:22).

4. IN RETURN FOR MY LOVE THEY ARE MY ADVERSARIES. In a previous psalm, David complains of those to whom he was friendly and who, without any justification, have turned against him. Thus, "Yea, mine own familiar friend, in whom I trusted . . . hath lifted up his heel against me" (Psalm 41:10).

I AM ALL PRAYER. In time of trouble I find my strength in prayer. However, the commentator, Ibn Ezra, explains this to mean: they are my adversaries yet I always have prayed in their behalf. This is precisely the thought which is expressed in Psalm 35:12-13, "They repay me evil for good; but as for me, when they were sick . . . I afflicted my soul with fasting."

313

Psalm 109

5

And hatred for my love:
6. 'Set Thou a wicked man over him;
   And let an adversary stand at his right hand.
7. When he is judged, let him go forth condemned;
   And let his prayer be turned into sin.
8. Let his days be few;
   Let another take his charge.
9. Let his children be fatherless,
   And his wife a widow.
10. Let his children be vagabonds, and beg;
    And let them seek their bread out of their desolate places.

6-19. A harsh imprecation, calling down all manner of punishment. As the present translation correctly takes it, these verses of imprecation are spoken by the wicked against the psalmist. This interpretation is supported by verse 20 which follows this list of curses. The verse reads: "This would mine adversaries effect from the Lord." That is to say, the above misfortunes would mine enemies call down upon me. While this interpretation of verses 6-19 is somewhat preferable, it is not beyond question, since it is hard to imagine the wicked saying of the psalmist: "He remembered not kindness but persecuted the poor" (verse 16), unless, of course, the accusation is taken to be a slanderous statement of the wicked charging the psalmist with cruelty to the poor. At all events, the present translation takes these verses 6-19 to be the curse uttered by the wicked against the psalmist. Hence, sentence 5 must be understood as follows: "They laid upon me evil for good, and hatred for my love, saying:

6. SET THOU A WICKED MAN. Appoint a cruel officer to rule over him.

AN ADVERSARY AT HIS RIGHT HAND. The author visualizes a trial in a law court. At the right hand of the accused stands an adversary to slander him and to contradict his defense. The Hebrew word here for adversary is "satan." *Satan*, in Hebrew, means an opponent or an adversary. Later it came to mean a semi-divine accuser, an emissary of God ("Satan" in the Book of Job who acts as "prosecuting attorney"); thus also (Zechariah

314

11. Let the creditor distrain all that he hath;
And let strangers make spoil of his labour.
12. Let there be none to extend kindness unto him;
Neither let there be any to be gracious unto his fatherless
children.
13. Let his posterity be cut off;
In the generation following let their name be blotted out.
14. Let the iniquity of his fathers be brought to remembrance
unto the Lord;
And let not the sin of his mother be blotted out.
15. Let them be before the Lord continually,

3:1) "and he showed me Joshua the high priest standing before the angel of the Lord, and Satan standing at his right hand to accuse him."

For further development of the idea of Satan see article "Satan" in the *Jewish Encyclopedia*, Volume XI, page 68.

7. LET HIS PRAYER BE TURNED INTO SIN. The word for "sin" used here means literally "failure." Hence, let his prayer fail to win favor. Or if taken in connection with the first half of the couplet, it can mean: when he is judged let him go forth condemned. The wicked hopes that when the psalmist prays to be released, that this very prayer may be counted against him as if it were a sin.

10. SEEK THEIR BREAD OUT OF THEIR DESOLATE PLACES. Let his children wander out of the ruins of his house begging for bread.

11. LET THE CREDITOR DISTRAIN. Seize possession of.

MAKE SPOIL OF HIS LABOUR. Since the victim is described as already dead, this does not mean "exploit him," to take his labor for naught. It must mean, let strangers despoil that for which he has labored.

13. LET HIS POSTERITY BE CUT OFF. Let his descendants be destroyed, i. e., let his family name "be blotted out" (verse 13).

14-15. The curse now goes back into the past. Let God remember the sin of his ancestors that even their memory be blotted out. Not only will he die young and his property be confiscated and his descendants destroyed but even the memory

315

That He may cut off the memory of them from the earth.
16. Because that he remembered not to do kindness,
But persecuted the poor and needy man,
And the broken in heart he was ready to slay.
17. Yea, he loved cursing, and it came unto him;
And he delighted not in blessing, and it is far from him.
18. He clothed himself also with cursing as with his raiment,
And it is come into his inward parts like water,
And like oil into his bones.
19. Let it be unto him as the garment which he putteth on,
And for the girdle wherewith he is girded continually.'
20. This would mine adversaries effect from the LORD,
And they that speak evil against my soul.
21. But Thou, O God the Lord, deal with me for Thy name's sake;
Because Thy mercy is good, deliver Thou me.
22. For I am poor and needy,
And my heart is wounded within me.
23. I am gone like the shadow when it lengtheneth;

of his ancestors will be erased from all human recollection.

16. HE REMEMBERED NOT TO DO KINDNESS . . . PERSECUTED THE POOR. In the sense in which we have taken this whole passage, namely, this is the curse which the wicked invokes upon the psalmist, this sentence must be taken as a slanderous accusation.

17. HE LOVED CURSING, AND IT CAME UNTO HIM. He cursed and he is now accursed. He has never blessed, hence he remains unblessed. A somewhat similar phrase is used in Genesis 12:3, "him that curseth thee will I curse."

18. CLOTHED HIMSELF WITH CURSING AS WITH HIS RAIMENT. The psalmist often speaks of glory and majesty being worn like a garment, and also of violence used as a garment. Thus, "violence covereth them as a garment" (Psalm 73:6).

IT IS COME INTO HIS INWARD PARTS. Because he voluntarily clothed himself with cursing it has now become part of his personality. It enters into his body, into his very bones "like water and like oil" which, when drunk, is absorbed into the body. Therefore, let it become his permanent garment. "The girdle wherewith he is girded continually" (verse 19).

20. The long passage above (verses 6-19), which the psalm-

I am shaken off as the locust.
24. My knees totter through fasting;
    And my flesh is lean, and hath no fatness.
25. I am become also a taunt unto them;
    When they see me, they shake their head.
26. Help me, O Lord my God;
    O save me according to Thy mercy;
27. That they may know that this is Thy hand;
    That Thou, Lord, hast done it.
28. Let them curse, but bless Thou;
    When they arise, they shall be put to shame, but Thy
    servant shall rejoice.
29. Mine adversaries shall be clothed with confusion,
    And shall put on their own shame as a robe.
30. I will give great thanks unto the Lord with my mouth;
    Yea, I will praise Him among the multitude;
31. Because He standeth at the right hand of the needy,
    To save him from them that judge his soul.

ist has quoted as the curse uttered by his enemies against him, is now summed up in the words: "This (i. e., the above) would mine adversaries effect from the Lord," i. e., this is what they would hope to persuade God to do unto me.

23. LIKE THE SHADOW WHEN IT LENGTHENETH. As, at the close of the day, the shadows lengthen, so have I come in my sorrows to the end of my day of life.

SHAKEN OFF AS THE LOCUST. People ignore me; they push me aside indifferently as one shakes off a locust.

25. A TAUNT UNTO THEM . . . THEY SHAKE THEIR HEAD. They mock me; they shake their head in contempt.

27. THAT THIS IS THY HAND. This phrase is explained by the next couplet, "that Thou hast done it," that it is Thou who hast delivered me.

28. LET THEM CURSE, BUT BLESS THOU. This refers to the long curse uttered by the enemies (verses 6-19).

29. CLOTHED WITH CONFUSION. Let their shame cover them as a garment.

31. HE STANDETH AT THE RIGHT HAND OF THE NEEDY. In the place of the accuser, Satan, whom the wicked hoped would

317

110. A PSALM OF DAVID.

The LORD saith unto my lord:
'Sit thou at My right hand,
Until I make thine enemies thy footstool.'

stand at the right hand of the psalmist, it is God, the Beneficent,
who will stand at his right hand and "save him from them that
judge his soul," from those who would condemn him.

THIS psalm has received many interpretations. Yet, though
its language is difficult and therefore permits various explanations, the general mood of the psalm is fairly obvious. It is a
royal psalm, calling down God's blessing on the anointed king.
It is, therefore, related to the other royal psalms, 20, 21 and 45.

The psalm quotes God as speaking to the king, promising
that the king will be "a priest after the manner of Melchizedek"
(verse 4). It is this sentence which has been the occasion for
most of the divergent interpretations. Its plain meaning seems
to be that the king will not only be a righteous judge but also,
in a sense, a holy priest. Since the whole people of Israel is described as a priest people, "Ye shall be unto Me a kingdom of
priests, and a holy nation" (Exodus 19:6), it is natural that the
ideal king shall be visualized as holy, and, in a sense, priestly.
Of course, we do not know that the kings of Israel actually performed priestly functions, although David did wear a priestly
robe and danced before the ark (II Samuel 6:14). We know,
however, that in ancient times, among primitive peoples and
also among civilized nations (as the Egyptians), the function of
royalty and priesthood were often combined.

For explanation of the name Melchizedek see the commentary to verse 4. See also the article "Melchidezek" in the
Jewish Encyclopedia, Volume VIII, page 450.

1. THE LORD SAITH UNTO MY LORD. The commentator, Rashi,
following the talmudic tradition (b. Nedarim 32 b), says that
the word "my lord" refers to Abraham, since the children of

2. The rod of thy strength the LORD will send out of Zion:
'Rule thou in the midst of thine enemies.'
3. Thy people offer themselves willingly in the day of thy warfare;
In adornments of holiness, from the womb of the dawn,
Thine is the dew of thy youth.

Heth addressed Abraham in these words: "Hear us, my lord" (Genesis 23:5). In fact, the Talmud (and Rashi also) takes the entire psalm to refer to Abraham who met Melchizedek (Genesis 14:18).

However, the commentators, Ibn Ezra and Kimchi, say that the psalm refers to King David. The psalm must certainly refer to some king, whether it was King David or a successor.

MY LORD is regularly used in addressing a king. Cf. I Samuel 22:12.

SIT AT MY RIGHT HAND. The right hand is the place of honor, as in Psalm 45:10, "at thy right hand doth stand the queen."

UNTIL I MAKE THINE ENEMIES THY FOOTSTOOL. Until thou shalt tread upon thine enemies; until thou shalt conquer them.

2. THE ROD OF THY STRENGTH. The rod, the symbol of power, or of correction. See Psalm 2, another royal psalm, in which God promises the king, "I will give the nations for thine inheritance . . . thou shalt break them with a rod of iron" (Psalm 2:8-9).

IN THE MIDST OF THINE ENEMIES. Even though surrounded by enemies, be not afraid. Rule fearlessly. I will guide you to victory.

3. THY PEOPLE OFFER THEMSELVES WILLINGLY. When you will need an army your people will gladly volunteer. The same idea is expressed by Deborah in reference to the campaign against the Canaanites, "when the people offer themselves willingly," i. e., as volunteers (Judges 5:2).

ADORNMENTS OF HOLINESS. The commentator, Kimchi, translates this, "in the beauty of holiness," which is one of the descriptions of Zion. He, therefore, takes the verse to mean, the people will gladly volunteer in Zion. However, the verse may mean that the people will volunteer dressed in sacred garments.

319

4. The LORD hath sworn, and will not repent:
'Thou art a priest for ever
After the manner of Melchizedek.'
5. The Lord at thy right hand
Doth crush kings in the day of His wrath.

FROM THE WOMB OF THE DAWN, THINE IS THE DEW OF THY
YOUTH. This difficult sentence has been variously interpreted.
The commentator, Ibn Ezra, takes it to mean that the people
will offer themselves willingly for war; you will see them at the
dawn of day come as freely as the morning dew which thou
didst often see in thy youth when thou wast a shepherd. This
is perhaps the most acceptable interpretation. Moreover, if the
word "youth" can be taken as a collective noun, meaning
"young men," Ibn Ezra's interpretation can be still further
simplified and the text made perhaps a little clearer, as follows:
as the dew comes from the womb of the dawn so will the young
men be thine, i. e., they will be thy soldiers. The word "dew"
therefore refers both to the dawn and, as a natural metaphor,
to the youth. The whole sentence, therefore, can be paraphras-
ed as follows: the people willingly volunteer, clad in holy garments; and from the womb of the dawn the "dewy" youths
come to be thy warriors.

4. THE LORD HATH SWORN, AND WILL NOT REPENT. Will not
annul His oath. The Bible frequently describes God as taking
an oath before making a solemn promise. Thus, God says to
Abraham on Mount Moriah: "By Myself have I sworn that . . .
I will bless thee" (Genesis 22:16).

THOU ART A PRIEST AFTER THE MANNER OF MELCHIZEDEK.
Melchizedek is mentioned in Genesis 14:18. When Abraham
returned from his victory over the four kings: "Melchizedek,
king of Salem brought forth bread and wine; and he was priest
of God the Most High. And he blessed him, and said: 'blessed
be Abram of God Most High'." Melchizedek is thus described
as king (Salem is Jerusalem) and as priest. The psalmist, therefore, says to the king: as Melchizedek combined the functions of
priesthood and royalty so wilt thou be king and priest.

6. He will judge among the nations;
   He filleth it with dead bodies,
   He crusheth the head over a wide land.
7. He will drink of the brook in the way;
   Therefore will he lift up the head.

But perhaps the promise is not meant to be quite so specific. It may mean simply that the king will stand in the presence of God in the sanctuary; just as the promise made to Israel, "ye shall be unto Me a kingdom of priests" (Exodus 19:6), did not mean that they would actually have priestly functions but would be holy and near to God, "ye shall be Mine own treasure among all peoples" (Exodus 19:5), so the king would be like a priest, holy and intimate with God.

From 5 to 7 the psalmist reverts to the picture of the king's victory referred to in verse 1.

5. THE LORD AT THY RIGHT HAND. Verse 1, God asks the king to sit at His right hand. Now, in battle, God marches at the right hand of the king.

6. HE WILL JUDGE. He will execute judgment.

HE FILLETH IT. He filleth the battle-field.

HE CRUSHETH THE HEAD. The same vivid description of the complete defeat of the enemy is found in Psalm 68:22, "Surely God will smite through the head of His enemies."

7. HE WILL DRINK OF THE BROOK . . . WILL HE LIFT UP HIS HEAD. This sentence refers not to God but to the king who, in the heat of battle, will pause to drink from the brook and lift up his head proudly and march on to complete the victory.

THE next two psalms are very closely related. They both begin with "Hallelujah." They are both acrostic psalms.

Psalm 112 makes constant reference to Psalm 111. Furthermore, both psalms together express one complete thought. Psalm 111 speaks of God's works in human life and Psalm 112 completes the thought by describing the happiness that comes to those who obey God's laws.

111. HALLELUJAH.

I will give thanks unto the LORD with my whole heart,
In the council of the upright, and in the congregation.
2. The works of the LORD are great,
Sought out of all them that have delight therein.
3. His work is glory and majesty;
And His righteousness endureth for ever.
4. He hath made a memorial for His wonderful works;
The LORD is gracious and full of compassion.
5. He hath given food unto them that fear Him;
He will ever be mindful of His covenant.
6. He hath declared to His people the power of His works,
In giving them the heritage of the nations.
7. The works of His hands are truth and justice;
All His precepts are sure.

3. HIS WORK IS GLORY . . . HIS RIGHTEOUSNESS ENDURETH. God's greatness is manifested both through His glorious works in nature and through the ethical influence which He exerts in human life.

4. HE HATH MADE A MEMORIAL FOR HIS WORKS. God has commanded man to remember and to tell the story of God's marvelous works. By means of human tradition God has built among men the memorial of His great works of old. Thus, "our fathers have told us, we will not hide from their children, telling to the generation to come the praises of the Lord, and His wondrous works" (Psalm 78:3-4).

5. EVER MINDFUL OF HIS COVENANT. God will never forget the covenant which He made with Abraham to bless his children. Thus, when God saw the affliction of Israel in Egypt He said: "And I heard the groaning of the children of Israel . . . and I have remembered My covenant" (Exodus 6:5).

7-8. HIS PRECEPTS ARE SURE . . . ESTABLISHED FOREVER. The language here describing God's precepts is reminiscent of the description in Psalm 19:8 ff., "The law of the Lord is perfect . . . sure . . . precepts are right," etc.

9. HE HATH COMMANDED HIS COVENANT FOR EVER. Whatever misfortunes may overtake us we must never fall into the

8. They are established for ever and ever,
   They are done in truth and uprightness.
9. He hath sent redemption unto His people;
   He hath commanded His covenant for ever;
   Holy and awful is His name.
10. The fear of the LORD is the beginning of wisdom;
    A good understanding have all they that do thereafter;
    His praise endureth for ever.

112. HALLELUJAH.

   Happy is the man that feareth the LORD,
   That delighteth greatly in His commandments.
2. His seed shall be mighty upon earth;
   The generation of the upright shall be blessed.
3. Wealth and riches are in his house;
   And his merit endureth for ever.

despairing belief that God has annulled His covenant with us.

HOLY AND AWFUL. Holy and awe-inspiring.

10. THE FEAR OF THE LORD IS THE BEGINNING OF WISDOM. Reverence for God, or religion, is the first step toward wisdom. This verse is also found in Proverbs 9:10.

A GOOD UNDERSTANDING. Since the fear, or the reverence, for God is the beginning of wisdom those who follow His laws ("they that do thereafter") will attain a good understanding of life.

SEE introduction to Psalm 111.

1. HAPPY THE MAN . . . THAT DELIGHTETH IN HIS COMMANDMENTS. This sentence is reminiscent of Psalm 1:1-2, "Happy the man . . . his delight is in the law of the Lord."

2. HIS SEED SHALL BE MIGHTY UPON EARTH. One of the blessings which the psalmist cherished most was that his family would endure and prosper. Thus, Psalm 25:13, "His soul shall abide in prosperity; and his seed shall inherit the land."

3. WEALTH AND RICHES. That prosperity is the reward of an ethical life is the favorite idea in the Book of Proverbs and in all the Wisdom Literature. Thus, "Length of days is in her

4. Unto the upright He shineth as a light in the darkness,
     Gracious, and full of compassion, and righteous.
5. Well is it with the man that dealeth graciously and lendeth,
     That ordereth his affairs rightfully.
6. For he shall never be moved;
     The righteous shall be had in everlasting remembrance.
7. He shall not be afraid of evil tidings;
     His heart is stedfast, trusting in the LORD.

right hand (in the right hand of wisdom); in her left hand are riches and honour" (Proverbs 3:16).

HIS MERIT ENDURETH. The commentator, Kimchi, offers two interpretations, first, that his merit will stand him in good stead in the world to come, and (this second interpretation comports better with the spirit of the Psalms) his merit will last in the lives of his descendants. The "merit of the fathers" is a favorite idea in Jewish thought. (See Schechter, *Aspects of Rabbinic Theology*, Chapter 12.)

4. HE SHINETH AS A LIGHT IN THE DARKNESS. God's radiance dispels all sorrow and despair.

5. THAT DEALETH GRACIOUSLY AND LENDETH. The same generosity is referred to in Psalm 37:21, "the righteous dealeth graciously, and giveth."

ORDERETH HIS AFFAIRS RIGHTFULLY. He manages his business justly without doing harm to anyone.

6. HE SHALL NEVER BE MOVED. The same description of the stability of the righteous man closes Psalm 15, "he that doeth these things shall never be moved."

8. UNTIL HE GAZE UPON HIS ADVERSARIES. Until he sees his adversaries defeated. Thus, "only with thine eyes shalt thou behold, and see the recompense of the wicked" (Psalm 91:8).

9. HIS RIGHTEOUSNESS ENDURETH. Parallels verse 8 in the preceding psalm, "they (God's works) are established for ever and ever."

HIS HORN SHALL BE EXALTED. He shall not be ashamed but shall lift his head in just pride as a stag proudly raises his antlers.

8. His heart is established, he shall not be afraid,
   Until he gaze upon his adversaries.
9. He hath scattered abroad, he hath given to the needy;
   His righteousness endureth for ever;
   His horn shall be exalted in honour.
10. The wicked shall see, and be vexed;
    He shall gnash with his teeth, and melt away;
    The desire of the wicked shall perish.

10. HE SHALL GNASH WITH HIS TEETH. The wicked will gnash their teeth in futile vexation at the triumph of the righteous.

THE DESIRE OF THE WICKED SHALL PERISH. This verse is likewise reminiscent of Psalm 1, "the way of the wicked shall perish" (Psalm 1:6).

PSALM 113 is the first of the Hallel psalms, 113-118. The word *hallel*, "praise," refers to the prevailing theme of the psalm, the praise of God, and the frequent use of the word "Hallelujah," which means "praise ye the Lord." These psalms have always been considered a unit in Jewish tradition and were, in all likelihood, composed about the same time. They are recited as a unit in the synagogue services.

The complete Hallel is recited on the first two days of Passover, the two days of Shabuoth, the nine days of Succoth and the eight days of Hanukkah. This enumeration of twenty-one recitations of the complete Hallel applies only to Orthodox congregations outside of Palestine. In Palestine and in Reform congregations everywhere the biblical rule is followed, namely, that Passover has seven days, Shabuoth one, and Succoth eight. The half Hallel (that is, the Hallel with the omission of Psalm 115:1-11 and 116:1-11) is recited on the last six days of Passover and on the New Moon. Considering the group as a unit, it seems fairly evident that they were written in the early days after the return from the exile. In the first place, there are some fairly clear references to the situation of the small community of returned exiles which was surrounded by enemies and man-

113. HALLELUJAH.
Praise, O ye servants of the LORD,
Praise the name of the LORD.
2. Blessed be the name of the LORD
From this time forth and for ever.
3. From the rising of the sun unto the
going down thereof
The LORD's name is to be praised.
4. The LORD is high above all nations,
His glory is above the heavens.

aged nevertheless to rebuild the Temple and the walls of Jerusalem. Secondly, there are many evidences of the influence of the Aramaic language which began to affect the Hebrew language at that time.

Psalm 136 is also known as the Hallel. In order to distinguish this group, 113-118 from Psalm 136, the latter psalm is called "the great Hallel" and this group is called "the Hallel of Egypt" since it makes reference to the redemption from Egypt. (b. Berachoth 26 a).

Psalm 113 is an exalted call to all nations to praise God. Its language, particularly in verses 7-9, is based upon the language of the Song of Hannah in I Samuel 2.

1. YE SERVANTS OF THE LORD. Israel is called God's servants, thus, "but thou, Israel, My servant" (Isaiah 41:8). The psalmist begins with calling upon Israel to praise God and then extends the chorus of praise to include all the nations.

3. THE RISING OF THE SUN UNTO THE GOING DOWN THEREOF. Verse 2 spoke of God's name being blessed forever. This verse speaks of His being praised *everywhere*, from the east (the place of the rising of the sun), to the west (the place of the sun's setting). The same phrase is used by the prophet Malachi (1:11), "from the rising of the sun even unto the going down of the same My name is great among the nations."

4. THE LORD IS HIGH ABOVE ALL NATIONS. The same phrase is found in Psalm 99:2.

HIS GLORY IS ABOVE THE HEAVENS. A similar expression is

326

5. Who is like unto the LORD our God,
   That is enthroned on high,
6. That looketh down low
   Upon heaven and upon the earth?
7. Who raiseth up the poor out of the dust,
   And lifteth up the needy out of the dunghill;
8. That He may set him with princes,
   Even with the princes of His people.
9. Who maketh the barren woman to dwell in her house
   As a joyful mother of children.
   Hallelujah.

found in Psalm 8:2, "glorious is Thy name . . . Whose majesty is rehearsed above the heavens."

5-6. God is enthroned on high but His exalted status does not keep Him distant from the earth. "He looketh down low upon heaven and the earth." He is above them both. He guides and guards them both. The same idea is vividly expressed by the prophet Isaiah (57:15), "for thus saith the high and lofty One . . . I dwell in the high and holy place, with him also that is of a contrite and humble spirit."

7-8. Speaks of God's raising the poor and the needy out of the dunghill; the poor and the needy who have no home and must dwell in the dust and on the dunghill. The entire passage is taken from the Song of Hannah (I Samuel 2:8), except for the closing line, "even with the princes of His people." This line is added by the psalmist to the passage in the Song of Hannah.

9. WHO MAKETH THE BARREN WOMAN TO DWELL . . . A JOYFUL MOTHER OF CHILDREN. Since the psalmist is quoting from the Song of Hannah he thinks here of Hannah who was childless and who later had the joy of becoming the mother of the prophet Samuel. Also, the people of Israel in exile was looked upon as a childless woman; when she was restored she became a "joyful mother of children." This idea is developed by the prophet Isaiah (Isaiah 54:1), "Sing, O barren, thou that didst not bear . . . for more are the children of the desolate than the children of the married wife."

327

114. When Israel came forth out of Egypt,
   The house of Jacob from a people of strange language;
2. Judah became His sanctuary,
   Israel His dominion.
3. The sea saw it, and fled;
   The Jordan turned backward.
4. The mountains skipped like rams,
   The hills like young sheep.
5. What aileth thee, O thou sea, that thou fleest?
   Thou Jordan, that thou turnest backward?

AFTER calling upon all nations to praise God, who helps
the humble, the psalmist now turns to the evidences of God's
wondrous deliverance, "when Israel came forth from Egypt."
The psalm is brief and dramatic. The psalmist describes all nature as astounded at the coming of God to deliver His people.
The psalm is written with careful artistry. Verse 3, "the sea saw
it, and fled," recalls the verse in Psalm 77:17, "The waters saw
Thee, O God . . . they were in pain." But here the author con-
sciously omits the name of God and leaves the sentence
vague. "The sea saw it and fled" (literally "the sea saw and
fled") in order that he may be able to ask: "what ailest thee
that thou fleest?" and then he can climax the psalm with his
answer: "tremble, thou earth, at the presence of the Lord."

1. FROM A PEOPLE OF STRANGE LANGUAGE. The parallelism
indicates that it refers to the Egyptians whose language seemed
unintelligible to the Israelites. See also, "when he went forth
against Egypt, the speech of one that I knew not did I hear"
(Psalm 81:6).

2. JUDAH BECAME HIS SANCTUARY, ISRAEL HIS DOMINION. Some
commentators take this verse literally to mean: Judah, the
southern kingdom, contained His temple (i. e., Zion), while
Israel, the powerful northern kingdom, manifested His dominion. However, the phrase is not to be taken literally. Judah
and Israel are simply parallel words meaning the people of
Israel. The commentator, Ibn Ezra, properly connects the verses
with the verse in Exodus 19:6, which God addresses to the

6. Ye mountains, that ye skip like rams;
Ye hills, like young sheep?
7. Tremble, thou earth, at the presence of the Lord,
At the presence of the God of Jacob;
8. Who turned the rock into a pool of water,
The flint into a fountain of waters.

115. Not unto us, O Lord, not unto us,
But unto Thy name give glory,
For Thy mercy, and for Thy truth's sake.

people of Israel, "ye shall be unto me a kingdom of priests, and a holy nation."

3. THE SEA SAW IT, AND FLED. The excitement manifested by the Red Sea and the Jordan and their "flight" at God's command so as not to hinder Israel's departure from Egypt and the entrance into Canaan. All of this is expressed in Psalm 77:17, "The waters saw Thee, O God; the waters saw Thee, they were in pain; the depths also trembled."

4. THE MOUNTAINS SKIPPED LIKE RAMS. The commentator, Kimchi, says this is a reference to Mount Sinai (and possibly the surrounding hills) which shook at the coming of God.

5-6. The psalmist asks: "What aileth thee, O sea?" that is, "what troubleth thee, O sea, that thou fleest" etc.

7-8. Gives the answer to the above question. The earth trembles at the advent of God who converted rocks into pools of water in the desert (cf. Exodus 17:6) and performed other wonders in behalf of Israel.

8. THE FLINT. The flint, a parallel to the word "rock" in the first half of the couplet. It means the hard, flinty rock.

FOR the sake of His great name, not for our sakes, may God deliver us as God has delivered us in the past. May He keep us in the land of the living that we may praise Him forever.

1. NOT UNTO US. Give glory not unto our name, O Lord, but unto Thy name.

2. Wherefore should the nations say:
   'Where is now their God?'
3. But our God is in the heavens;
   Whatsoever pleased Him He hath done.
4. Their idols are silver and gold,
   The work of men's hands.
5. They have mouths, but they speak not;
   Eyes have they, but they see not;
6. They have ears, but they hear not;
   Noses have they, but they smell not;
7. They have hands, but they handle not;
   Feet have they, but they walk not;
   Neither speak they with their throat.
8. They that make them shall be like unto them;

FOR THY MERCY, AND FOR THY TRUTH'S SAKE. In Psalm 77:9, when the psalmist asks for deliverance, he says, "Is His mercy clean gone for ever?" Here, similarly, the psalmist asks God to demonstrate to the nations that His mercy and His truth are still effective in the world lest the nations will say mockingly, "Where is now their God?" (verse 2).

3. OUR GOD IS IN THE HEAVENS; WHATSOEVER PLEASED HIM HE HATH DONE. The psalmist answers the supposed taunt of the nations by saying to them: judge not from our misery, that there is no God. God is eternally enthroned and our misery is not a proof of God's non-existence or forgetfulness. It is His deliberate punishment for our sins. He has done what has "pleased Him."

4-8. Describes the helplessness of idols in order to indicate that only God can direct human history. Passages of this type, scornful of the helplessness of the idols, are found frequently in the writings of the prophets. Thus, Isaiah 44:9 ff., Jeremiah 10.

8. THEY THAT MAKE THEM SHALL BE LIKE UNTO THEM. Worshippers become like their gods. Since God is holy we become holier in our worship of Him, and since their idols are helpless they become dumb and inert like their gods. Human character is influenced by the nature of its ideals.

330

Yea, every one that trusteth in them.
9. O Israel, trust thou in the Lord!
He is their help and their shield!
10. O house of Aaron, trust ye in the Lord!
He is their help and their shield!
11. Ye that fear the Lord, trust in the Lord!
He is their help and their shield.
12. The Lord hath been mindful of us, He will bless—
He will bless the house of Israel;
He will bless the house of Aaron.
13. He will bless them that fear the Lord,
Both small and great.
14. The Lord increase you more and more,
You and your children.

9-11. The psalmist calls upon all classes of Israel to trust in God who alone can be our "help" and our "shield." He speaks first to Israel, meaning all the people, then to the house of Aaron, meaning the priesthood, who are in the sanctuary, and thirdly he speaks of "ye that fear the Lord" (verse 11). Most of the commentators take this third class to mean the various proselytes, the Gentile converts who join Israel and become those who "fear" (i. e., revere and worship) the Lord. The Bible frequently speaks of the great number of people among the nations who will join themselves unto God. Thus, in the prayer of Solomon (I Kings 8:41): "Moreover concerning the stranger that is not of Thy people Israel, when he shall come out of a far country for Thy name's sake," and also Isaiah 56: 6-7, "Also the aliens, that join themselves unto the Lord . . . love the name of the Lord . . . My house shall be called a house of prayer for all peoples." These willing converts were called "those who fear (i. e., revere) the Lord." The same three classes are addressed in Psalm 118:2-4.

13. SMALL AND GREAT. The humble and the mighty, all will receive God's blessing.

14. THE LORD INCREASE YOU. One of the blessings that the Israelites cherished most was the blessing of many children. Deuteronomy 1:11, "The Lord, the God of your fathers, make

15. Blessed be ye of the Lord,
     Who made heaven and earth.
16. The heavens are the heavens of the Lord;
     But the earth hath He given to the children of men.
17. The dead praise not the Lord,
     Neither any that go down into silence;
18. But we will bless the Lord
     From this time forth and for ever.
     Hallelujah.

116. I love that the Lord should hear
     My voice and my supplications.
2. Because He hath inclined His ear unto me,
     Therefore will I call upon Him all my days.
3. The cords of death compassed me,

you a thousand times so many more as ye are, and bless you." This blessing was particularly appreciated in the small community of the returned exiles.

15. WHO MADE HEAVEN AND EARTH. This phrase is used only in the Psalms. This is the first use of the phrase in the Psalter. It is used again in Psalms 121:2; 124:8; 134:3; 146:6.

16. THE HEAVENS OF THE LORD BUT THE EARTH . . . TO THE CHILDREN OF MEN. God ruleth over the entire universe but permits us to govern our life on earth in accordance with His laws. As Ibn Ezra puts it, man is God's deputy on earth.

17. THE DEAD PRAISE NOT THE LORD. A thought familiar in the Psalms that only the living worship God and therefore we pray that God keep us alive. See Psalm 88:11, "Shall the shades arise and give Thee thanks?"

THAT GO DOWN INTO SILENCE. The silence of death. See Psalm 94:17, where the psalmist wishes to say that had not God assisted him, he would have died. The words used are, "unless the Lord had been my help, my soul had soon dwelt in silence."

THE joy of prayer. The consciousness that God had helped me in the past and that His assurance will comfort me now.

And the straits of the nether-world got hold upon me;
I found trouble and sorrow.
4. But I called upon the name of the LORD:
'I beseech Thee, O LORD, deliver my soul.'
5. Gracious is the LORD, and righteous;
Yea, our God is compassionate.
6. The LORD preserveth the simple;
I was brought low, and He saved me.
7. Return, O my soul, unto thy rest;
For the LORD hath dealt bountifully with thee.
8. For Thou hast delivered my soul from death,
Mine eyes from tears,
And my feet from stumbling.
9. I shall walk before the LORD
In the lands of the living.

Although this psalm has many phrases which are taken from other psalms (as e. g., Psalms 18, 27, 31), it is intensely personal and moving.

2. BECAUSE HE HATH INCLINED . . . THEREFORE WILL I CALL. Because He has answered my prayer in the past I pray for Him with all my heart for the rest of my life.

3. THE CORDS OF DEATH. Either ropes or a net.

THE STRAITS OF THE NETHER-WORLD. The word for "straits" comes from the root that means "narrow", a narrow ravine; the opposite idea is expressed in the phrase "a broad place" which indicates deliverance.

4. DELIVER MY SOUL. Deliver my life.

5. GRACIOUS . . . COMPASSIONATE. The attributes of God described in Exodus 34:6, "The Lord, God, merciful and gracious," etc.

6. PRESERVETH THE SIMPLE. The opposite of "cunning." In Psalm 19:8, "The testimony of the Lord is sure, making wise the simple."

8-9. MY SOUL FROM DEATH, MINE EYES FROM TEARS. A passage very similar to this is found in Psalm 56:14, "Thou hast delivered my soul from death . . . my feet from stumbling . . . that I may walk before God in the light of the living."

333

10. I trusted even when I spoke:
    'I am greatly afflicted.'
11. I said in my haste:
    'All men are liars.'
12. How can I repay unto the LORD
    All His bountiful dealings toward me?
13. I will lift up the cup of salvation,
    And call upon the name of the LORD.
14. My vows will I pay unto the LORD,
    Yea, in the presence of all His people.
15. Precious in the sight of the LORD
    Is the death of His saints.
16. I beseech Thee, O LORD, for I am Thy servant;
    I am Thy servant, the son of Thy handmaid;

10-11. Even when I said that I was greatly afflicted, and even when in my haste I distrusted all mankind, saying, "all men are liars," even then I continued to trust in God.

11. ALL MEN ARE LIARS. The commentator, Rashi, ascribes this statement to David during the rebellion of Absalom. At that time David said in his haste there was no one whom he could trust. The phrase, "in my haste," meaning "in my panic," is also used in a similar sense in Psalm 31:23, "I said in my haste: 'I am cut off from before Thine eyes.'"

13. THE CUP OF SALVATION. The commentator, Rashi, explains this to mean the cup for the libation which accompanied the thanksgiving offering which I bring to Thee for having saved me.

15. PRECIOUS . . . IS THE DEATH OF HIS SAINTS. God will not permit His righteous ones to be slain with impunity. He is the "avenger of their blood." The same phrase is used in Psalm 72:14, where the meaning is clearer than in the present psalm: "He will redeem their soul from oppression and violence, and precious will their blood be in his sight."

THIS is the shortest psalm in the Psalter.

All nations can see how great God's mercy is towards Israel.

334

Thou hast loosed my bands.
17. I will offer to Thee the sacrifice of thanksgiving,
    And will call upon the name of the LORD.
18. I will pay my vows unto the LORD,
    Yea, in the presence of all His people;
19. In the courts of the LORD's house,
    In the midst of thee, O Jerusalem.
    Hallelujah.

117. O praise the LORD, all ye nations;
    Laud Him, all ye peoples.
2. For His mercy is great toward us;
    And the truth of the LORD endureth for ever.
    Hallelujah.

With the redemption of Israel as an object lesson let all nations praise the Lord.

2. THE TRUTH OF THE LORD ENDURETH. As in Psalm 115:1, when God redeems Israel He shows the permanence of His truth. Thus, " (Save us) for Thy mercy, and for Thy truth's sake."

THE closing psalm of the Hallel. The evidences of post-exilic authorship are numerous in this psalm. God had punished Israel but not destroyed it (verse 18). The stone which the builders rejected (verse 22) refers to the restoration or the re-building of the Temple after the exile. A number of other verses seem to point to the situation in the restored community as described in the Books of Nehemiah and Ezra.

While we cannot be certain exactly when the psalm was written, the mood of the psalm is such that it reflects perfectly the time when the Temple was rebuilt after the return, and when the people of Israel came to celebrate the Passover and to dedicate the house of God (Ezra 6:15 ff.). This would make the psalm primarily a Passover psalm. The fact that the phrase in verse 24, "We beseech Thee, O Lord, save now" was recited with special ceremony on the seven days of Succoth, does not

118. 'O give thanks unto the Lord, for He is good,
  For His mercy endureth for ever.'
  2. So let Israel now say,
  For His mercy endureth for ever.
  3. So let the house of Aaron now say,
  For His mercy endureth for ever.
  4. So let them now that fear the Lord say,
  For His mercy endureth for ever.
  5. Out of my straits I called upon the Lord;
  He answered me with great enlargement.
  6. The Lord is for me; I will not fear;
  What can man do unto me?
  7. The Lord is for me as my helper;
  And I shall gaze upon them that hate me.
  8. It is better to take refuge in the Lord
  Than to trust in man.
  9. It is better to take refuge in the Lord
  Than to trust in princes.

argue against this psalm having been written for the Passover celebration at the dedication of the Temple in the year 516 before the Christian era. The use of this refrain in the special Succoth celebrations (*Hoshanoth*) may have begun later.

1. O GIVE THANKS . . . FOR HIS MERCY ENDURETH. See comment on Psalm 106:1.

2-4. ISRAEL . . . AARON . . . THEM THAT FEAR THE LORD. See comment on Psalm 115:9-11.

5. OUT OF MY STRAITS . . . ENLARGEMENT. The enemies hemmed me in but God drove them away and I stand in a broad place. Thus, "Thou hast not given me over into the hand of the enemy; Thou hast set my foot in a broad place" (Psalm 31:9).

6. THE LORD IS FOR ME; I WILL NOT FEAR. This passage is found almost exactly in Psalm 56:10, 12.

7. GAZE UPON THEM THAT HATE ME. A phrase frequently used in the Psalms meaning, I shall see the destruction of them that hate me. Thus, "God will let me gaze upon mine adversaries" (Psalm 59:11).

9. THAN TO TRUST IN PRINCES. If this psalm were indeed writ-

10. All nations compass me about;
 Verily, in the name of the LORD I will cut them off.
11. They compass me about, yea, they compass me about;
 Verily, in the name of the LORD I will cut them off.
12. They compass me about like bees;
 They are quenched as the fire of thorns;
 Verily, in the name of the LORD I will cut them off.
13. Thou didst thrust sore at me that I might fall;
 But the LORD helped me.
14. The LORD is my strength and song;
 And He is become my salvation.
15. The voice of rejoicing and salvation is in the tents
 of the righteous;
 The right hand of the LORD doeth valiantly.
16. The right hand of the LORD is exalted;
 The right hand of the LORD doeth valiantly.
17. I shall not die, but live,
 And declare the works of the LORD.

ten at the time when the returned exiles were rebuilding the Temple then this statement can well refer to the fact that Nehemiah, the leader of the community, had letters from the Persian king, but nevertheless, in spite of the royal letters, the community was in danger. (See Nehemiah 2:7-9.) So in verses 10 and 11, "all nations compass me about" likewise describes the situation at the time of the return. Nehemiah (4:1) speaks of the Arabians, the Ammonites, and the Philistines who surrounded the community.

12. LIKE BEES. The metaphor of the enemies stinging like a swarm of bees is found in Deuteronomy 1:44, "And the Amorites came out against you, and chased you, as bees do."

A FIRE OF THORNS. A quick fire which is easily quenched. Psalm 58:10, also speaks of a fire of thorns. (However, another Hebrew word for thorns is used there.)

14-15. THE LORD IS MY STRENGTH AND SONG . . . THE RIGHT HAND OF THE LORD DOETH VALIANTLY. These phrases are found in the Song by the Red Sea, Exodus 15.

17. I SHALL NOT DIE. Cf. with Psalm 115:17, "The dead praise not the Lord," etc.

337

18. The Lord hath chastened me sore;
But He hath not given me over unto death.
19. Open to me the gates of righteousness;
I will enter into them, I will give thanks unto the Lord.
20. This is the gate of the Lord;
The righteous shall enter into it.
21. I will give thanks unto Thee, for Thou hast
answered me,
And art become my salvation.
22. The stone which the builders rejected
Is become the chief corner-stone.
23. This is the Lord's doing;
It is marvellous in our eyes.

18. THE LORD HATH CHASTENED ME SORE. i. e., sorely.

BUT NOT GIVEN ME OVER UNTO DEATH. The psalmist speaks not only of himself as an individual, referring to his own sickness, but evidently thinks of the vicissitudes of the community during the exile from which God delivered it.

19. THE GATES OF RIGHTEOUSNESS. The pilgrim procession asks that the gates of the Temple be opened. Thus, in Psalm 24 the expression is used, "Lift up your heads, O ye gates." The commentator, Rashi, indicates that the "gates of righteousness" means the Temple, which is the abode of righteousness. Thus, "The Lord bless thee, O habitation of righteousness, O mountain of holiness" (Jeremiah 31:23).

20. THE RIGHTEOUS SHALL ENTER INTO IT. This echoes the thought of Psalm 15 and Psalm 24, "Who shall stand in His holy place; he that hath clean hands."

22. THE STONE WHICH THE BUILDERS REJECTED. Kimchi, Rashi, and Ibn Ezra say this refers to Israel whom all the nations scorned but which has become central in God's plan.

23. THIS IS THE LORD'S DOING. The rebuilding of the Temple is really God's achievement. So, in Nehemiah, when the nations roundabout saw the wall built, "they perceived that this work was wrought of our God" (Nehemiah 6:16).

24. THIS IS THE DAY. This day of celebration, of dedication, and of festival.

338

24. This is the day which the LORD hath made;
    We will rejoice and be glad in it.
25. We beseech Thee, O LORD, save now!
    We beseech Thee, O LORD, make us now to prosper!
26. Blessed be he that cometh in the name of the LORD;
    We bless you out of the house of the LORD.
27. The LORD is God, and hath given us light;
    Order the festival procession with boughs, even unto
        the horns of the altar.
28. Thou art my God, and I will give thanks unto Thee;
    Thou art my God, I will exalt Thee.
29. O give thanks unto the LORD, for He is good,
    For His mercy endureth for ever.

26. BLESSED BE HE THAT COMETH . . . WE BLESS YOU. The
priest answers the pilgrims who said (verse 19): "Open to me
the gates of righteousness." He responds: "Blessed be he that
cometh."

27. THE LORD HATH GIVEN US LIGHT. A reminiscence of the
priestly blessing in Numbers 6:25, "The Lord make His face
to shine upon thee."

ORDER THE FESTIVAL PROCESSION WITH BOUGHS, EVEN UNTO
THE HORNS OF THE ALTAR. The commentators, Ibn Ezra and
Kimchi, translate this verse differently and take it to mean: tie
up the festal offering with cords and bring it to the horns of the
altar. But as translated here it means; decorate the procession
with branches of trees and march to the horns of the altar.

HORNS OF THE ALTAR. For further reference see Leviticus
4:7. The altar had horn-like projections on which the blood of
sacrifices was sprinkled.

PSALM 119 is the longest in the Psalter. It is an octuple
acrostic. There are eight consecutive verses beginning with
the first letter of the alphabet, aleph, then eight beginning with
the second letter of the alphabet, beth, etc. The whole psalm is a
paean of praise to God as teacher. It is a psalm dedicated to the
knowledge of God's law. According to the commentator, Ibn

339

Psalm 119

ALEPH

119. Happy are they that are upright in the way,
Who walk in the law of the Lᴏʀᴅ.

2. Happy are they that keep His testimonies,
That seek Him with the whole heart;

3. Yea, they do no unrighteousness;
They walk in His ways.

4. Thou hast ordained Thy precepts,
That we should observe them diligently.

5. Oh that my ways were directed
To observe Thy statutes!

6. Then should I not be ashamed,
When I have regard unto all Thy commandments.

7. I will give thanks unto Thee with uprightness of heart,
When I learn Thy righteous ordinances.

Ezra, every verse in the psalm has some mention of the law, except verse 122. Thus every verse says either *Torah* (law), or *Eduth* (testimony), or *Chok* (statute), or *Mizvoh* (commandment) or some other synonym. The meaning of *Torah*, generally translated "law," is usually misunderstood. While it also means "legislation" it does not mean legal literature alone. It means also "God's moral law"; it may mean "wisdom." Wisdom, which is personified and speaks in Proverb 8, is identified in rabbinic literature with the Torah. Just as wisdom is described (Proverbs 8:22) as one of God's first creations, so the Torah is described in the Talmud as having been created before the rest of the world (b. Pesachim 54 a). (See article "Torah," *Jewish Encyclopedia*, Vol. XII, p. 197.) The best evidence of the rich connotation of *Torah* is found in this psalm which, dedicated to the Torah, expresses an intimate, personal, and spiritual relationship with God. (For full discussion of the concept of law, or Torah, see Schechter, *Aspects of Rabbinic Theology*, Chapter 8.)

1. UPRIGHT IN THE WAY . . . WALK IN THE LAW. This is reminiscent of Psalm 1, "Happy the man who hath not walked in the counsel of the wicked . . . but his delight is in the law of the Lord."

2. SEEK HIM WITH THE WHOLE HEART. With undivided heart,

340

8. I will observe Thy statutes;
   O forsake me not utterly.
      BETH
9. Wherewithal shall a young man keep his way pure?
   By taking heed thereto according to Thy word.
10. With my whole heart have I sought Thee;
    O let me not err from Thy commandments.
11. Thy word have I laid up in my heart,
    That I might not sin against Thee.
12. Blessed art Thou, O LORD;
    Teach me Thy statutes.
13. With my lips have I told
    All the ordinances of Thy mouth.
14. I have rejoiced in the way of Thy testimonies,
    As much as in all riches.

i. e., with sincerity. The same expression is found in Deuteronomy 6:5, "Thou shalt love thy God with all thy heart."

8. FORSAKE ME NOT UTTERLY. This plea could easily have been spoken in exile. Do not entirely abandon me but come to my help.

9. KEEP HIS WAY PURE BY TAKING HEED THERETO. By taking heed to his way; by paying attention to his way of life shall a young man keep himself pure.

11. THY WORD HAVE I LAID UP IN MY HEART. The word for "laid up" means "concealed" as a precious treasure is concealed. The same expression is used of laying up or treasuring wisdom which is also a synonym for God's law: "My son . . . receive my words . . . and lay up my commandments with thee," (Proverbs 2:1), i. e., keep them as a treasure.

12. BLESSED ART THOU, O LORD. This phrase became the opening of every benediction either in the public liturgy or in private prayer.

13. WITH MY LIPS HAVE I TOLD. The word "lips" must be taken with the phrase in verse 11, "Thy word in my heart." The Psalms frequently combine "the meditations of the heart" and "the words of the lips." (Cf. Psalm 19:15.)

14. THY TESTIMONIES AS MUCH AS IN ALL RICHES. I value Thy law more than all material wealth. This thought is frequently

341

15. I will meditate in Thy precepts,
    And have respect unto Thy ways.
16. I will delight myself in Thy statutes;
    I will not forget Thy word.
    GIMEL
17. Deal bountifully with Thy servant, that I may live,
    And I will observe Thy word.
18. Open Thou mine eyes, that I may behold
    Wondrous things out of Thy law.
19. I am a sojourner in the earth;
    Hide not Thy commandments from me.
20. My soul breaketh for the longing
    That it hath unto Thine ordinances at all times.
21. Thou hast rebuked the proud that are cursed,
    That do err from Thy commandments.
22. Take away from me reproach and contempt;
    For I have kept Thy testimonies.
23. Even though princes sit and talk against me,
    Thy servant doth meditate in Thy statutes.
24. Yea, Thy testimonies are my delight,
    They are my counsellors.
    DALETH
25. My soul cleaveth unto the dust;
    Quicken Thou me according to Thy word.

expressed in this psalm and in the Book of Proverbs. Thus, "for the merchandise of it (i. e., for wisdom or the law) is better than . . . silver . . . than fine gold . . . more precious than rubies" (Proverbs 3:14, 15).

17. DEAL BOUNTIFULLY . . . THAT I MAY LIVE. Be generous to me more than my merits. This phrase is often found in the Psalms. Thus, "I will sing unto the Lord, because He hath dealt bountifully with me" (Psalm 13:6).

19. I AM A SOJOURNER. I am just a stranger and a traveller on earth. My life is brief, therefore I need Thine instruction and guidance. The same thought is expressed in Psalm 39:13, "Hear my prayer, O Lord, for I am a stranger with Thee, a sojourner, as all my fathers were," i. e., my life is as transient as was the life of my fathers.

23. EVEN THOUGH PRINCES SIT AND TALK AGAINST ME. The

26. I told of my ways, and Thou didst answer me;
    Teach me Thy statutes.
27. Make me to understand the way of Thy precepts,
    That I may talk of Thy wondrous works.
28. My soul melteth away for heaviness;
    Sustain me according unto Thy word.
29. Remove from me the way of falsehood;
    And grant me Thy law graciously.
30. I have chosen the way of faithfulness;
    Thine ordinances have I set [before me].
31. I cleave unto Thy testimonies;
    O LORD, put me not to shame.
32. I will run the way of Thy commandments,
    For Thou dost enlarge my heart.

                    HE

33. Teach me, O LORD, the way of Thy statutes;
    And I will keep it at every step.
34. Give me understanding, that I keep Thy law
    And observe it with my whole heart.
35. Make me to tread in the path of Thy commandments;
    For therein do I delight.
36. Incline my heart unto Thy testimonies,
    And not to covetousness.
37. Turn away mine eyes from beholding vanity,

psalmist may mean: princes who sit as judges talk against me.

25. MY SOUL CLEAVETH UNTO THE DUST. My soul adheres to the dust. I am brought low.

QUICKEN THOU ME. Revive me.

31. I CLEAVE UNTO THY TESTIMONIES. I hold loyally to Thy law. Thus, in Deuteronomy 10:20, "Him thou shalt serve; and to Him thou shalt cleave," i. e., remain loyal to God.

32. FOR THOU DOST ENLARGE MY HEART. It may mean, Thou dost relieve my heart from the sorrows which cramp it. The word "enlarge" is used here in the same sense as it is used in Psalm 118:5, "out of my straits I called . . . He answered me with great enlargement."

36. NOT TO COVETOUSNESS. Let me follow Thy commandment to be gracious and generous and guard myself from covetousness.

343

And quicken me in Thy ways.

38. Confirm Thy word unto Thy servant,
Which pertaineth unto the fear of Thee.

39. Turn away my reproach which I dread;
For Thine ordinances are good.

40. Behold, I have longed after Thy precepts;
Quicken me in Thy righteousness.

VAU

41. Let Thy mercies also come unto me, O LORD,
Even Thy salvation, according to Thy word;

42. That I may have an answer for him that taunteth me;
For I trust in Thy word.

43. And take not the word of truth utterly out of my mouth;
For I hope in Thine ordinances;

44. So shall I observe Thy law continually
For ever and ever;

45. And I will walk at ease,
For I have sought Thy precepts;

46. I will also speak of Thy testimonies before kings,
And will not be ashamed.

47. And I will delight myself in Thy commandments,
Which I have loved.

48. I will lift up my hands also unto Thy commandments,
which I have loved;
And I will meditate in Thy statutes.

ZAIN

49. Remember the word unto Thy servant,

38. CONFIRM THY WORD UNTO THY SERVANT, WHICH PERTAINETH UNTO THE FEAR OF THEE. The word "pertaineth" is not found in Hebrew. The commentator, Rashi, takes this sentence to mean: confirm Thy promise to Thy servant, that I may be devoted to the fear of Thee. The commentator, Kimchi, makes a similar comment. As translated here the text means: confirm to Thy servant Thy word which pertaineth, i. e., which concerns or teaches the fear of Thee.

45. I WILL WALK AT EASE. The word for "ease" means literally "broadness," in a broad place freed from enemies who would hem me in.

48. I WILL LIFT UP MY HANDS UNTO THY COMMANDMENTS.

344

Because Thou hast made me to hope.
50. This is my comfort in my affliction,
That Thy word hath quickened me.
51. The proud have had me greatly in derision;
Yet have I not turned aside from Thy law.
52. I have remembered Thine ordinances which are of old, O LORD,
And have comforted myself.
53. Burning indignation hath taken hold upon me, because of the
wicked
That forsake Thy law.
54. Thy statutes have been my songs
In the house of my pilgrimage.
55. I have remembered Thy name, O LORD, in the night,
And have observed Thy law.
56. This I have had,
That I have kept Thy precepts.
HETH
57. My portion is the LORD,
I have said that I would observe Thy words.
58. I have entreated Thy favour with my whole heart;
Be gracious unto me according to Thy word.
59. I considered my ways,
And turned my feet unto Thy testimonies.
60. I made haste, and delayed not,
To observe Thy commandments.
61. The bands of the wicked have enclosed me;
But I have not forgotten Thy law.

Lifting up the hands, perhaps originally a gesture in the sacrificial cult, was a gesture of prayer and in general expressed the
mood of reverence. Here it means: I will revere Thy commandments.

54. IN THE HOUSE OF MY PILGRIMAGE. Here on earth, the
abode in which I am a pilgrim and a sojourner. See comment
to verse 19.

57. MY PORTION IS THE LORD. My inheritance. The knowledge of God is my most precious possession. This thought is expressed a number of times in this psalm. See also Psalm 16:5,
"O Lord, the portion of mine inheritance."

61. THE BANDS OF THE WICKED. The ropes with which they

345

62. At midnight I will rise to give thanks unto Thee
    Because of Thy righteous ordinances.
63. I am a companion of all them that fear Thee,
    And of them that observe Thy precepts.
64. The earth, O Lord, is full of Thy mercy;
    Teach me Thy statutes.

      TETH

65. Thou hast dealt well with Thy servant,
    O Lord, according unto Thy word.
66. Teach me good discernment and knowledge;
    For I have believed in Thy commandments.
67. Before I was afflicted, I did err;
    But now I observe Thy word.
68. Thou art good, and doest good;
    Teach me Thy statutes.
69. The proud have forged a lie against me;
    But I with my whole heart will keep Thy precepts.
70. Their heart is gross like fat;
    But I delight in Thy law.
71. It is good for me that I have been afflicted,
    In order that I might learn Thy statutes.
72. The law of Thy mouth is better unto me
    Than thousands of gold and silver.

      IOD

73. Thy hands have made me and fashioned me;

would tie me, or the net in which they would ensnare me. The word for "bands" is translated "cords" in Psalm 116:3, "the cords of death compass me."

67. BEFORE I WAS AFFLICTED, I DID ERR. This verse must be taken in connection with verse 71, "It is good for me that I have been afflicted." The psalmist means: before I was taught by suffering, I did not have the insight to understand Thy law.

69. THE PROUD HAVE FORGED A LIE AGAINST ME. The haughty and the violent slander the followers of God's law.

70. THEIR HEART IS GROSS LIKE FAT. The wicked are too coarse to be sensitive to sin. The same expression is used in Psalm 17:10, "Their gross heart they have shut tight."

72. THE LAW . . . BETTER THAN GOLD AND SILVER. See comment to verse 14.

Give me understanding, that I may learn Thy commandments.

74. They that fear Thee shall see me and be glad,
    Because I have hope in Thy word.
75. I know, O LORD, that Thy judgments are righteous,
    And that in faithfulness Thou hast afflicted me.
76. Let, I pray Thee, Thy lovingkindness be ready to comfort me,
    According to Thy promise unto Thy servant.
77. Let Thy tender mercies come unto me, that I may live;
    For Thy law is my delight.
78. Let the proud be put to shame, for they have distorted my
    cause with falsehood;
    But I will meditate in Thy precepts.
79. Let those that fear Thee return unto me,
    And they that know Thy testimonies.
80. Let my heart be undivided in Thy statutes,
    In order that I may not be put to shame.
                CAPH
81. My soul pineth for Thy salvation;
    In Thy word do I hope.
82. Mine eyes fail for Thy word,
    Saying: 'When wilt Thou comfort me?'
83. For I am become like a wine-skin in the smoke;
    Yet do I not forget Thy statutes.
84. How many are the days of Thy servant?
    When wilt Thou execute judgment on them that persecute me?

73. THY HANDS HAVE MADE ME. God, who has created man's body, is also the source of his intelligence. Therefore, "give me understanding."

76. BE READY TO COMFORT ME. God is described here as a parent, ready to comfort his children in their sorrow. In Isaiah 66:13, the metaphor of mother love is used, "As one whom his mother comforteth, so will I comfort you."

82. MINE EYES FAIL. The psalmist frequently says when describing sickness or longing or faintness that the eyes grow dim and fail. Thus, "I am weary with my crying . . . mine eyes fail while I wait for my God" (Psalm 69:4).

83. LIKE A WINE-SKIN IN THE SMOKE. Kimchi explains this as follows, as a wine-skin hung in smoke shrivels up.

84. HOW MANY ARE THE DAYS OF THY SERVANT? My life is so

347

85. The proud have digged pits for me,
   Which is not according to Thy law.
86. All Thy commandments are faithful;
   They persecute me for nought; help Thou me.
87. They had almost consumed me upon earth;
   But as for me, I forsook not Thy precepts.
88. Quicken me after Thy lovingkindness,
   And I will observe the testimony of Thy mouth.
       LAMED
89. For ever, O LORD,
   Thy word standeth fast in heaven.
90. Thy faithfulness is unto all generations;
   Thou hast established the earth, and it standeth.
91. They stand this day according to Thine ordinances;
   For all things are Thy servants.
92. Unless Thy law had been my delight,
   I should then have perished in mine affliction.
93. I will never forget Thy precepts;
   For with them Thou hast quickened me.
94. I am Thine, save me;
   For I have sought Thy precepts.
95. The wicked have waited for me to destroy me;
   But I will consider Thy testimonies.
96. I have seen an end to every purpose;

brief. How long will You delay in protecting me from those who persecute me? A similar appeal is found in Psalm 89:48, "O remember how short my time is."

85. DIGGED PITS FOR ME, WHICH IS NOT ACCORDING TO THY LAW. The commentator, Ibn Ezra, explains this as follows: in violation of Thy law against the shedding of innocent blood they have dug pits to ensnare me.

91. THEY STAND THIS DAY. "They" refers to heaven and earth, in the preceding verses. The heavens are maintained in accordance with Thy laws. All things in nature obey Thee as Thy servants.

96. I HAVE SEEN AN END TO EVERY PURPOSE; BUT THY COMMANDMENT IS EXCEEDING BROAD. The word for "purpose" may also be translated "excellence." The verse means: I have seen that every human purpose or excellence is limited or comes

But Thy commandment is exceeding broad.

MEM
97. Oh how love I Thy law!
It is my meditation all the day.
98. Thy commandments make me wiser than mine enemies;
For they are ever with me.
99. I have more understanding than all my teachers;
For Thy testimonies are my meditation.
100. I understand more than mine elders,
Because I have kept Thy precepts.
101. I have refrained my feet from every evil way,
In order that I might observe Thy word.
102. I have not turned aside from Thine ordinances;
For Thou hast instructed me.
103. How sweet are Thy words unto my palate!
Yea, sweeter than honey to my mouth!
104. From Thy precepts I get understanding;
Therefore I hate every false way.
NUN
105. Thy word is a lamp unto my feet,
And a light unto my path.
106. I have sworn, and have confirmed it,
To observe Thy righteous ordinances.
107. I am afflicted very much;

quickly to an end but Thy commandments are broad; they are infinite.

99-100. I HAVE MORE UNDERSTANDING THAN MY TEACHERS . . . THAN MINE ELDERS, BECAUSE I HAVE KEPT THY PRECEPTS. God's law is the source of deepest wisdom, more than any other knowledge. The culture of the soul is greater than mere erudition. This is the significance of the verse in Psalm 19:8, "the testimony of the Lord is sure, making wise the simple."

103. THY WORDS . . . SWEETER THAN HONEY. This phrase is also a reminiscence of Psalm 19:11. God's law is described as "sweeter also than honey and the honeycomb."

105. THY WORD IS A LAMP UNTO MY FEET. The same idea is expressed in Proverbs 6:23, "For the commandment is a lamp and the teaching is light." The same metaphor is implied in the sentence in Psalm 19:9, "The commandment of the Lord

Quicken me, O Lord, according unto Thy word.
108. Accept, I beseech Thee, the freewill-offerings of my
mouth, O Lord,
And teach me Thine ordinances.
109. My soul is continually in my hand;
Yet have I not forgotten Thy law.
110. The wicked have laid a snare for me;
Yet went I not astray from Thy precepts.
111. Thy testimonies have I taken as a heritage for ever;
For they are the rejoicing of my heart.
112. I have inclined my heart to perform Thy statutes,
For ever, at every step.

SAMECH

113. I hate them that are of a double mind;
But Thy law do I love.
114. Thou art my covert and my shield;
In Thy word do I hope.
115. Depart from me, ye evil-doers;
That I may keep the commandments of my God.
116. Uphold me according unto Thy word, that I may live;
And put me not to shame in my hope.
117. Support Thou me, and I shall be saved;
And I will occupy myself with Thy statutes continually.
118. Thou hast made light of all them that err from Thy statutes;
For their deceit is vain.
119. Thou puttest away all the wicked of the earth like dross;
Therefore I love Thy testimonies.

is pure, enlightening the eyes." The law is light, therefore enlightenment. The Talmud (b. Megillah 16 b), commenting on
the verse in Esther 8:16, "The Jews had light and gladness,"
says, "light means the law."

113. OF A DOUBLE MIND. Since here the word for "double
mind" may possibly be translated as "thoughts," the commentator, Kimchi, takes this sentence to mean: I dislike all other
thoughts but only "Thy law do I love." As translated here the
verse means either "cunning" or "hypocrisy" (as "double
heart" in Psalm 12:3) or else it may mean "vacillation" as in I
Kings 18:21, "How long halt ye (i. e. vacillate) between two
opinions."

120. My flesh shuddereth for fear of Thee;
And I am afraid of Thy judgments.
>   AIN
121. I have done justice and righteousness;
Leave me not to mine oppressors.
122. Be surety for Thy servant for good;
Let not the proud oppress me.
123. Mine eyes fail for Thy salvation,
And for Thy righteous word.
124. Deal with Thy servant according unto Thy mercy,
And teach me Thy statutes.
125. I am Thy servant, give me understanding;
That I may know Thy testimonies.
126. It is time for the LORD to work;
They have made void Thy law.
127. Therefore I love Thy commandments
Above gold, yea, above fine gold.
128. Therefore I esteem all [Thy] precepts concerning
all things to be right;
Every false way I hate.
>   PE
129. Thy testimonies are wonderful;
Therefore doth my soul keep them.
130. The opening of Thy words giveth light;
It giveth understanding unto the simple.
131. I opened wide my mouth, and panted;
For I longed for Thy commandments.

120. MY FLESH SHUDDERETH. This verse must be taken with the preceding verse which speaks of God disposing of the wicked as the smelter disposes of worthless dross. Therefore, I, knowing my own unworthiness, "shudder" and "am afraid of Thy judgments."

126. IT IS TIME FOR THE LORD TO WORK; THEY HAVE MADE VOID THY LAW. The rabbinic interpretation takes this verse to mean: the time has come for the righteous to work for the Lord since the wicked have made void Thy law. However, as translated here it means: the wicked have made void Thy law, therefore it is time for God to intervene.

131. I OPENED WIDE MY MOUTH, AND PANTED. A rather vivid

132. Turn Thee towards me, and be gracious unto me,
   As is Thy wont to do unto those that love Thy name.
133. Order my footsteps by Thy word;
   And let not any iniquity have dominion over me.
134. Redeem me from the oppression of man,
   And I will observe Thy precepts.
135. Make Thy face to shine upon Thy servant;
   And teach me Thy statutes.
136. Mine eyes run down with rivers of water,
   Because they observe not Thy law.
                  TZADE
137. Righteous art Thou, O LORD,
   And upright are Thy judgments.
138. Thou hast commanded Thy testimonies in righteousness
   And exceeding faithfulness.
139. My zeal hath undone me,
   Because mine adversaries have forgotten Thy words.
140. Thy word is tried to the uttermost,
   And Thy servant loveth it.
141. I am small and despised;
   Yet have I not forgotten Thy precepts.
142. Thy righteousness is an everlasting righteousness,
   And Thy law is truth.
143. Trouble and anguish have overtaken me;
   Yet Thy commandments are my delight.
144. Thy testimonies are righteous for ever;
   Give me understanding, and I shall live.
                  KOPH
145. I have called with my whole heart; answer me, O LORD;
   I will keep Thy statutes.
146. I have called Thee, save me,

metaphor of eagerness and spiritual hunger. Used in a more physical sense, the same expression is found in Psalm 81:11, "open thy mouth wide, and I will fill it."

   139. MY ZEAL HATH UNDONE ME. Because I am zealous in Thy behalf I have used up my strength and even incurred the enmity of the wicked. The same thought is expressed in Psalm 69:10, "Because zeal for Thy house hath eaten me up."

   140. THY WORD IS TRIED TO THE UTTERMOST. Thy word is pure. It is refined to the uttermost, as gold is refined.

And I will observe Thy testimonies.
147. I rose early at dawn, and cried;
I hoped in Thy word.
148. Mine eyes forestalled the night-watches,
That I might meditate in Thy word.
149. Hear my voice according unto Thy lovingkindness;
Quicken me, O LORD, as Thou art wont.
150. They draw nigh that follow after wickedness;
They are far from Thy law.
151. Thou art nigh, O LORD;
And all Thy commandments are truth.
152. Of old have I known from Thy testimonies
That Thou hast founded them for ever.

RESH

153. O see mine affliction, and rescue me;
For I do not forget Thy law.
154. Plead Thou my cause, and redeem me;
Quicken me according to Thy word.
155. Salvation is far from the wicked;
For they seek not Thy statutes.
156. Great are Thy compassions, O LORD;
Quicken me as Thou art wont.
157. Many are my persecutors and mine adversaries;
Yet have I not turned aside from Thy testimonies.
158. I beheld them that were faithless, and strove with them;
Because they observed not Thy word.
159. O see how I love Thy precepts;
Quicken me, O LORD, according to Thy
lovingkindness.
160. The beginning of Thy word is truth;
And all Thy righteous ordinance endureth for ever.

142. THY RIGHTEOUSNESS, ETC. This sentence is used in the Sabbath afternoon service after the *Tefillah* (the penitential prayer).

148. MINE EYES FORESTALLED THE NIGHT-WATCHES. I kept awake to meditate. The psalmist thinks of himself as a watch-man or sentinel and says: I awoke before the time for my watch in order to "meditate in Thy word."

156. AS THOU ART WONT. The Hebrew can be translated "ac-cording to Thine ordinances." As translated here it means: re-

353

161

161. Princes have persecuted me without a cause;
But my heart standeth in awe of Thy words.

162. I rejoice at Thy word,
As one that findeth great spoil.

163. I hate and abhor falsehood;
Thy law do I love.

164. Seven times a day do I praise Thee,
Because of Thy righteous ordinances.

165. Great peace have they that love Thy law;
And there is no stumbling for them.

166. I have hoped for Thy salvation, O LORD,
And have done Thy commandments.

167. My soul hath observed Thy testimonies;
And I love them exceedingly.

168. I have observed Thy precepts and Thy testimonies;
For all my ways are before Thee.

vive me (quicken me) as Thou hast always done in the past.

164. SEVEN TIMES A DAY DO I PRAISE THEE. Kimchi explains that this does not mean precisely seven times. Seven is simply a round number meaning "often." Thus, "For a righteous man falleth seven times, and riseth up again" (Proverbs 24:16).

176. I HAVE GONE ASTRAY LIKE A LOST SHEEP; SEEK THY SERVANT. The Lord is my Shepherd. As a shepherd seeks a sheep that has gone astray from the flock, so seek me and bring me near to Thee. The same expression is found in Isaiah 53:6, "All we like sheep did go astray."

A SONG of Ascents. This is the first of fifteen psalms headed "A Song of Ascents" (Psalms 120-134). There are many explanations of the term "A Song of Ascents" and these explanations involve the question of the occasions for which these psalms were written or when they were used. The Mishnah in Succah V, 4, says, that there were fifteen steps from the Court of the Women in the Temple to the Court of the Men, these fifteen steps corresponding to the fifteen Songs of Ascents, and that on each step the Levites stood with musical instruments.

354

TAU

169. Let my cry come near before Thee, O LORD;
Give me understanding according to Thy word.
170. Let my supplication come before Thee;
Deliver me according to Thy word.
171. Let my lips utter praise:
Because Thou teachest me Thy statutes.
172. Let my tongue sing of Thy word;
For all Thy commandments are righteousness.
173. Let Thy hand be ready to help me;
For I have chosen Thy precepts.
174. I have longed for Thy salvation, O LORD;
And Thy law is my delight.
175. Let my soul live, and it shall praise Thee;
And let Thine ordinances help me.
176. I have gone astray like a lost sheep; seek Thy servant;
For I have not forgotten Thy commandments.

The Mishnah does not specifically say that the Levites sang one
of these songs on each step as they ascended from one court to
another, but the commentator, Rashi, understands the Mishnah
in this sense. Therefore, the Song of Ascents would mean, songs
for the ascent of the steps, or the songs of the steps. The commentator, Ibn Ezra, quotes an opinion of Saadia to the effect
that the word "ascent" meant a high voice, therefore these were
songs of the ascending or high music. The commentator, Kimchi, says that they are songs of ascent from exile.

The most widely accepted opinion is that they are songs
which the pilgrims sang when they came up to Jerusalem for
the festivals. Zion was in the highlands and the pilgrims, coming three times a year on the festivals, as was required by law,
came *up* to Jerusalem. We know that these pilgrims, coming up
for the festivals, sang while they marched. Thus, Psalm 42:5,
"How I passed on with the throng, and led them to the house
of God, with the voice of joy and praise, a multitude keeping
holyday." We also know from the Mishnah (Bikkurim III, 3),
that the pilgrims marched to music. Thus, these psalms were
songs for the ascent of the pilgrims to Jerusalem on the festivals.

It is not quite certain when they were written or if, indeed,

355

120. A SONG OF ASCENTS.

In my distress I called unto the LORD,
And He answered me.
2. O LORD, deliver my soul from lying lips,
From a deceitful tongue.
3. What shall be given unto thee, and what
shall be done more unto thee, thou deceitful tongue?

they all were written at the same time. Though, judging by
their content, it does seem likely that they were part of one
collection and were fairly contemporaneous. From some of the
psalms one gets the impression that they were written in the
early days of the return from Babylon, after Jerusalem and the
Temple were rebuilt but while the small community was still
surrounded by enemies.

These psalms, together with Psalm 104, are recited in the
synagogue on Sabbath afternoons during the winter.

In Psalm 120, the psalmist calls upon God to save him from
the distress caused by the deceitful and warlike enemies.

1. IN MY DISTRESS I CALLED . . . HE ANSWERED ME. This is virtually the same expression as is used in Psalm 118:5, "Out of
my straits I call upon the Lord; He answered me." God had
answered the psalmist in the past and therefore he prays with
confidence that God will help him now.

2. He asks to be delivered from slanderers, "from a deceitful tongue."

3-4. He addresses the deceitful tongue.

3. WHAT SHALL BE GIVEN UNTO THEE, WHAT SHALL BE DONE
MORE UNTO THEE? This expression is an emphatic Hebrew
idiom meaning, what shall be given, yes, what shall be added to
thee. A similar expression is used by Ruth when she assures
Naomi that nothing will ever part them. She says (Ruth 1:17),
"the Lord do so to me, and more also, if aught but death part
thee and me." She means: may God punish me and add to my
punishment, if, etc.

Woe

4. Sharp arrows of the mighty,
   With coals of broom.
5. Woe is me, that I sojourn with Meshech,
   That I dwell beside the tents of Kedar!
6. My soul hath full long had her dwelling
   With him that hateth peace.
7. I am all peace;
   But when I speak, they are for war.

4. SHARP ARROWS OF THE MIGHTY, WITH COALS OF BROOM.
The broom bush, or juniper, is used in the east for the making
of a very hot charcoal. This sentence is the answer to the question which the psalmist asks of the deceitful tongue. Thus,
what shall be done to thee, thou deceitful tongue? Mayest thou
be pierced with the arrows of the mighty (soldier) and be
burned with the hot charcoal of the broom bush.

5. WOE IS ME, THAT I SOJOURN WITH MESHECH . . . KEDAR.
Meshech is mentioned in Genesis 10:2, as one of the sons of
Japheth, and in Ezekiel 27:13, among the nations apparently
living at a distance. Kedar is one of the sons of Ishmael (Genesis 25:13) and refers to the Bedouin tribes. The psalmist does
not necessarily mean that he actually dwells with these distant
peoples. He uses their names merely as a symbol of untamed,
violent nations. In the next verse he says: my soul hath dwelt
too long with him that hateth peace. He lives among the violent. The violence, as well as the slander mentioned above, is
the cause of his distress.

7. I AM ALL PEACE . . . THEY ARE FOR WAR. No matter how
eager I am to live at peace with them, they are violent and
belligerent.

ON the previous psalm the pilgrim had evidently come from
distant and lawless lands. Now, at last, he is within sight of
Jerusalem. He is about to lift up his eyes unto the sacred mountain. The meaning of the psalm is that although I see the tower-
ing fortress of Zion it is God who is my fortress and protection.

357

121. A SONG OF ASCENTS.

I will lift up mine eyes unto the mountains:
From whence shall my help come?
2. My help cometh from the LORD,
Who made heaven and earth.
3. He will not suffer thy foot to be moved;
He that keepeth thee will not slumber.
4. Behold, He that keepeth Israel
Doth neither slumber nor sleep.
5. The LORD is thy keeper;
The LORD is thy shade upon thy right hand.
6. The sun shall not smite thee by day,

1. UNTO THE MOUNTAINS The various mountains which surround Jerusalem.

WHENCE SHALL MY HELP COME? Does my help come from earthly mountains and man-made citadels? The answer is given in the next verse: " (No) my help cometh from the Lord." It is God's presence in Zion which is the source of our help, not the material city in itself. Thus. "He answereth me out of His holy mountain" (Psalm 3:5). The rest of the psalm changes in the person of address. The pilgrim is now addressed presumably by other pilgrims. The first pilgrim sang the first two verses; the next pilgrim answered him. "He will not suffer thy foot to be moved." The verse means. He will not let thee stumble and fall. This expression is found frequently in the Psalms. Thus, "Bless our God, ye peoples . . . Who hath set our soul in life, and suffered not our foot to be moved" (Psalm 66:8-9).

5. THE LORD IS THY KEEPER. Thy protector.

THY SHADE UPON THY RIGHT HAND. God is a shade, a shelter from the heat and, also, God stands as our protector at our right hand. Both these metaphors are combined in this verse.

6. NOR THE MOON BY NIGHT. It is a belief in the Orient that the moon can be as dangerous as the sun. The commentators, Ibn Ezra and Kimchi, speak of the diseases which can be induced by the rays of the moon. It is a belief in the East that exposure to the moonlight is dangerous. It can cause blindness;

Nor the moon by night.
7. The LORD shall keep thee from all evil;
He shall keep thy soul.
8. The LORD shall guard thy going out and thy coming in,
From this time forth and for ever.

122. A SONG OF ASCENTS; OF DAVID.

I rejoiced when they said unto me:
'Let us go unto the house of the LORD.'
2. Our feet are standing
Within thy gates, O Jerusalem;
3. Jerusalem, that art builded
As a city that is compact together;

just as one may be sunstruck so may he be moonstruck.
7. HE SHALL KEEP THY SOUL. He shall guard thy life.

THE pilgrim has reached the gates of Jerusalem. "Our feet are standing within thy gates, O jerusalem" (verse 2). He thinks back to the days (before the exile) when the city was the center of a government which ruled all the tribes of Israel. He prays for the prosperity of Jerusalem.

1. I REJOICED WHEN THEY SAID: LET US GO . . He recalls the summons to join the pilgrimage. Such a summons is referred to in the Mishnah Bikkurim III, 2. The various pilgrims gathered in the city of the district. They spent the night in "the street" of the city. At dawn the leader of the group called to them with these words: "Come, let us go up to Zion, to the house of the Lord, our God."

2. The pilgrim is now in Jerusalem and observes the city.

3. JERUSALEM THAT ART BUILDED . . . COMPACT TOGETHER. The commentator, Ibn Ezra, takes this to mean that the city is packed full of pilgrims who have come up to celebrate the festival. But the verse may simply mean that Jerusalem, which was in ruins when the Jews returned from Babylon, was first rebuilt sparsely, with houses here and there. Now the pilgrim rejoices to see it built up solidly "packed together."

4. Whither the tribes went up, even the tribes of the LORD,
   As a testimony unto Israel,
   To give thanks unto the name of the LORD.
5. For there were set thrones for judgment,
   The thrones of the house of David.
6. Pray for the peace of Jerusalem;
   May they prosper that love thee.
7. Peace be within thy walls,
   And prosperity within thy palaces.
8. For my brethren and companions' sakes,
   I will now say: 'Peace be within thee.'
9. For the sake of the house of the LORD our God I will
   seek thy good.

4-5. The psalmist now thinks of the glorious past when all of Israel was governed from Jerusalem.

4. WHITHER THE TRIBES WENT UP. To Jerusalem all the tribes came on their pilgrimages.

A TESTIMONY UNTO ISRAEL. "Testimony" is a regular biblical synonym for "law" or for "statute." The verse means that the pilgrimage was a "testimony" or a "law" unto Israel. God commanded them to celebrate the festivals by pilgrimage. In Psalm 81:6, the psalmist, speaking of a festival, says: "He appointed it in Joseph for a testimony."

5. THRONES FOR JUDGMENT, THE THRONES OF THE HOUSE OF DAVID. The kings were also the judges.

6-9. The pilgrim reverts to the present and calls upon his fellow-pilgrims to pray for the welfare of Jerusalem.

9. I WILL SEEK THY GOOD. I will pray for thy happiness, or, I will endeavor to promote thy welfare. When Nehemiah came to join the small community which had returned from Babylon he describes himself as coming to seek their good, i. e., to work for their welfare. (Nehemiah 2:10.)

THE beginning of this psalm is similar to that of Psalm 121. The psalmist lifts up his eyes to God. He declares his absolute dependence upon Him and asks that he may be delivered

123. A SONG OF ASCENTS.
Unto Thee I lift up mine eyes,
O Thou that art enthroned in the heavens.
2. Behold, as the eyes of servants unto the hand of their master,
As the eyes of a maiden unto the hand of her mistress;
So our eyes look unto the LORD our God,
Until He be gracious unto us.
3. Be gracious unto us, O LORD, be gracious unto us;
For we are full sated with contempt.
4. Our soul is full sated
With the scorning of those that are at ease,
And with the contempt of the proud oppressors.

from "the contempt of the proud oppressors." (See verse 4).

2. AS THE EYES OF SERVANTS UNTO THE HAND OF THEIR MAS-
TER. As servants are completely dependent for their welfare
upon the will of their master, so are we dependent upon God
and look to Him to be gracious unto us.

3. WE ARE SATED WITH CONTEMPT. We have suffered as much
contempt as we can possibly endure. The contempt and the
scorn spoken of in verses 3 and 4 can very well refer to the contemptuous scorn with which the surrounding people mocked
the efforts of the returned exiles to rebuild Jerusalem. (See
Nehemiah 2:19.) "But when Sanballat the Horonite, and
Tobiah the servant, the Ammonite, and Geshem the Arabian,
heard it (that we were intending to rebuild the walls of Jerusalem), they laughed us to scorn, and despised us."

4. THOSE THAT ARE AT EASE. The sinful and proud are described by the prophet Amos in these same terms: "Woe to
them that are at ease in Zion" (Amos 6:1). The parallel phrase
in the second sentence of the couplet also makes clear that those
who are described as being "at ease" are the same ones who are
referred to as the "proud oppressors."

HAD it not been for God's help we would have been overwhelmed. The psalmist, in describing the dangers which threat-

1

124. A SONG OF ASCENTS; OF DAVID.

'If it had not been the LORD who was for us,'
Let Israel now say;
2. 'If it had not been the LORD who was for us,
When men rose up against us,
3. Then they had swallowed us up alive,
When their wrath was kindled against us;
4. Then the waters had overwhelmed us,
The stream had gone over our soul;
5. Then the proud waters
Had gone over our soul.'
6. Blessed be the LORD,
Who hath not given us as a prey to their teeth.
7. Our soul is escaped as a bird out of the snare of the fowlers;
The snare is broken, and we are escaped.
8. Our help is in the name of the LORD,
Who made heaven and earth.

ened him and the people of Israel, uses a number of metaphors which are found throughout the Psalter: the flood, the beast of prey, the snare of the fowler. Verses 1-5 constitute one sentence, whose meaning is, if God had not helped us we would have been overwhelmed.

1. LET ISRAEL NOW SAY. Let Israel now bear testimony to God's unfailing help.

5. THEN THE PROUD WATERS. The violent waters. This metaphor, transferring the spirit of haughty violence from man to the waters of the flood, is also found in Job 38:11, "Here shall thy proud waves be stayed." However, the passage in Job uses a different Hebrew word for "proud" than is used here.

HAD GONE OVER OUR SOUL. The Hebrew word *Nefesh*, translated here as "soul" means simply "life" or "personality." The verse means: we would have been submerged completely and lost our life. The phrase is condensed. Its full meaning is, the waters would have gone over our head and destroyed our life. See also Psalm 69:2, "Save me, O God; for the waters are come in even unto the soul," i. e., the waters are high enough to endanger my life.

125. A SONG OF ASCENTS.
They that trust in the Lord
Are as mount Zion, which cannot be moved, but
  abideth for ever.
2. As the mountains are round about Jerusalem,
So the Lord is round about His people,
From this time forth and for ever.
3. For the rod of wickedness shall not rest upon the
  lot of the righteous;
That the righteous put not forth their hands unto
  iniquity.
4. Do good, O Lord, unto the good,
And to them that are upright in their hearts.
5. But as for such as turn aside unto their crooked ways,
The Lord will lead them away with the workers of
  iniquity.
Peace be upon Israel.

THE psalm expresses complete confidence in God who will destroy the wicked and establish those who trust in Him.

1. THEY THAT TRUST IN THE LORD. Will be established as firmly as "mount Zion which cannot be moved."

2. AS THE MOUNTAINS . . . SO THE LORD. As the ring of mountains surround Jerusalem so God encamps about His people like a protecting army. Thus, "The angel of the Lord encampeth round about them that fear Him, and delivereth them" (Psalm 34:8).

3. THE ROD OF WICKEDNESS. The sceptre of wickedness will not permanently rule "the lot" (i. e., life) of the righteous.

THAT THE RIGHTEOUS PUT NOT FORTH THEIR HANDS UNTO INIQUITY. The commentators, Ibn Ezra and Kimchi, say that this means: God will not permit the sinful to rule over the righteous lest the righteous learn evil from them, as the Israelites learned idolatry from the Canaanites. The verse may also mean: lest the righteous in despair turn to evil ways.

PEACE BE UPON ISRAEL. The commentators say, when the workers of iniquity will be removed then there will be "peace unto Israel."

363

Psalm 126

126. A SONG OF ASCENTS.

1   When the LORD brought back those that returned to Zion,
     We were like unto them that dream.
2. Then was our mouth filled with laughter,
     And our tongue with singing;
     Then said they among the nations:
     'The LORD hath done great things with these.'
3. The LORD hath done great things with us;
     We are rejoiced.
4. Turn our captivity, O LORD,
     As the streams in the dry land.
5. They that sow in tears
     Shall reap in joy.

THE psalmist remembers the return from Babylon and the joy of the pilgrims. He now asks that God continue to bless the small community with further restoration.

1. WE WERE LIKE UNTO THEM THAT DREAM. When we were on our way back to Zion we could hardly believe it true.

2. THE LORD HATH DONE GREAT THINGS WITH THESE. The nations were compelled to admit that God had done great things in behalf of these exiles.

4. TURN OUR CAPTIVITY, O LORD. The psalmist asks that God continue the work of restoration. Although they are now in their native land they are still surrounded by enemies and are still, in a sense, captive. The psalmist asks that God complete the restoration.

AS THE STREAMS IN THE DRY LAND. The Hebrew word for "dry land" can also be translated "south." The southern part of Judea was semi-desert. The streams in summer dry up. In the rainy, wintry season the streams are suddenly restored. The psalmist asks for just such a dramatic restoration.

5. THEY THAT SOW IN TEARS SHALL REAP IN JOY. This beautiful sentence is amplified in the next sentence, "Though he goeth." Read as follows: though he that beareth the measure of seed, (i. e., the pack of seed from which he sows), goeth on his way weeping, he shall come, etc.

6. Though he goeth on his way weeping that beareth
   the measure of seed,
   He shall come home with joy, bearing his sheaves.

127. A SONG OF ASCENTS; OF SOLOMON.

Except the LORD build the house,
They labour in vain that build it;
Except the LORD keep the city,
The watchman waketh but in vain.
2. It is vain for you that ye rise early, and sit up late,
   Ye that eat the bread of toil;
   So He giveth unto His beloved in sleep.
3. Lo, children are a heritage of the LORD;
   The fruit of the womb is a reward.

THIS Song of Ascent is headed "Of Solomon." Kimchi suggests that the reason for the heading is that the psalmist here speaks of building the house, and it was Solomon, not David, that built the house of God.

The thought of the psalm is that not human strength but God alone is the ultimate source of all achievement. The psalmist then adds that one of God's most precious blessings is the gift of children.

1. EXCEPT THE LORD BUILD THE HOUSE. Unless it is God who builds, the labor of the builders is but in vain. Unless it is God who guards the city, the alertness of the watchman is wasted.

2. It is useless to rise early, etc., and to eat the bread of toil unless God aids us.

THE BREAD OF TOIL is reminiscent of the verse in Genesis 3:19, "In the sweat of thy face shalt thou eat bread."

SO HE GIVETH UNTO HIS BELOVED IN SLEEP. This verse has been given a famous mistranslation: "He giveth His beloved sleep," i. e., that God's greatest gift to His beloved is the gift of sleep. What the phrase actually means is that all human labor, without God's help, is useless, that God will give prosperity to His beloved, even while man sleeps.

3-5. God's great gift of children.

3. CHILDREN ARE A HERITAGE . . . A REWARD. Children are

4. As arrows in the hand of a mighty man,
    So are the children of one's youth.
5. Happy is the man that hath his quiver full of them;
    They shall not be put to shame,
    When they speak with their enemies in the gate.

128. A SONG OF ASCENTS.

Happy is every one that feareth the LORD,
That walketh in His ways.
2. When thou eatest the labour of thy hands,

to be looked upon as a divine blessing, a gift from God.

4. AS ARROWS . . . CHILDREN OF ONE'S YOUTH. The children of one's youth as contrasted with the children of one's older years were considered to be stronger and more vigorous. Thus, in Genesis 49:3, Jacob refers to Reuben, his first born, the child of his youth, in these terms: "Reuben, thou art my first-born, my might, and the first fruits of my strength." The vigorous children of youth are compared here to arrows in the hands of a mighty man. In verse 5 he continues the metaphor and says: "Happy is the man that hath his quivers full of them," i. e., his quivers full of such arrows, who has many children.

5. WHEN THEY SPEAK WITH THEIR ENEMIES IN THE GATE. The open place by the gates of the city was where the elders gathered to execute judgment. A man with many stalwart children will have adequate defense against any attempted injustice.

THE psalm presents a picture of a peaceful and happy home. Husband, wife, and children live together in harmony. The family lives on the fruits of its industry.

1. HAPPY IS EVERYONE THAT FEARETH THE LORD. This psalm opens with the same thought as Psalm 112, "Happy is the man that feareth the Lord." As Psalm 112 continues, "His seed shall be mighty upon earth," so does this psalm speak of the blessing of a large and harmonious family. The prophet Isaiah, in describing the blessed life of future days, gives a similar picture of the reward of industry: "And they shall build houses, and

Happy shalt thou be, and it shall be well with thee.
3. Thy wife shall be as a fruitful vine, in the innermost
   parts of thy house;
   Thy children like olive plants, round about thy table.
4. Behold, surely thus shall the man be blessed
   That feareth the LORD.
5. The LORD bless thee out of Zion;
   And see thou the good of Jerusalem all the days of thy life;
6. And see thy children's children.
   Peace be upon Israel!

inhabit them; and they shall plant vineyards, and eat the fruit of them" (Isaiah 65:21).

3. Some of the commentators endeavor to explain just how the vine can be in the "innermost parts of thy house," but such an explanation is unnecessary. The simile is not to be taken quite so strictly. The sentence should be understood as follows: thy wife, in the innermost parts of thy house, shall be fruitful like a vine. Similarly, the next sentence must be taken as follows: thy children round thy table will flourish like young olive trees.

5. BLESS THEE OUT OF ZION. From His sanctuary.

THE GOOD OF JERUSALEM. Note the similar blessing at the end of Psalm 122. This blessing: "See the good of Jerusalem all the days of thy life" can also mean: May you live to make very many pilgrimages to Jerusalem and see its prosperity.

The closing blessing, "Peace be upon Israel" is also found in Psalm 125.

THE psalmist, speaking in the name of Israel, describes all the vicissitudes which Israel endured in the past and which by God's help it has outlived. It asks that all the enemies of Israel be confounded.

The psalm could well have been written at the time when the small community of returned exiles, established amidst the ruins of Jerusalem, was surrounded by many enemies. The psalmist reminds the endangered community that such vicissi-

129. A SONG OF ASCENTS.
    'Much have they afflicted me from my youth up,'
    Let Israel now say;
2. 'Much have they afflicted me from my youth up;
    But they have not prevailed against me.
3. The plowers plowed upon my back;
    They made long their furrows.
4. The LORD is righteous;
    He hath cut asunder the cords of the wicked.'
5. Let them be ashamed and turned backward,

tudes are not new. Israel has always endured trouble and has survived. The passage in verses 1-3 is equivalent to the opening passage of Psalm 124. It uses the same phrase, "Let Israel now say," and is virtually one sentence whose meaning is: we have suffered much but God has delivered us.

1. FROM MY YOUTH UP. Israel has endured hostility from his very youth, from the beginning of his history.

LET ISRAEL NOW SAY. Let Israel now testify.

3. THE PLOWERS PLOWED UPON MY BACK. A vivid and rather harsh metaphor of the cruelty which the victorious foes have inflicted upon the vanquished.

4. THE LORD IS RIGHTEOUS. The Lord, being righteous, detests all cruelty and therefore has "cut asunder the cords of the wicked."

5. THEY THAT HATE ZION. Sanballat and all his allies who opposed the rebuilding of Jerusalem.

6-8. Asks that the enemy shall wither as the grass.

6. GRASS UPON THE HOUSETOPS. Sparse grass which springs from wind-blown seeds.

WITHERETH AFORE IT SPRINGETH UP. It withers before it attains its full growth.

7. THE REAPER FILLETH NOT HIS HAND. The reaper gathers a clump of grass in his left hand and cuts the bunch with the scythe in his right. The psalmist here means: may there not be enough of the grass to fill the right hand of the reaper (i. e., may our enemies be diminished).

All they that hate Zion.
6. Let them be as the grass upon the housetops,
   Which withereth afore it springeth up;
7. Wherewith the reaper filleth not his hand,
   Nor he that bindeth sheaves his bosom;
8. Neither do they that go by say:
   'The blessing of the LORD be upon you;
   We bless you in the name of the LORD.'

130. A SONG OF ASCENTS.

Out of the depths have I called Thee, O LORD.

NOR HE THAT BINDETH SHEAVES HIS BOSOM. The word "fill-eth" must be understood to govern this sentence also: nor he that bindeth sheaves fills his bosom. The binder of sheaves followed the reaper who had cut the grass. The binder's garment was equipped with a large pocket, a bosom or apron in which he put the grass, until he gathered enough to make up a sheaf. The psalmist means: may the binder not find enough grass to fill his bosom in order to make one sheaf.

8. NEITHER DO THEY THAT GO BY SAY: THE BLESSING OF THE LORD BE UPON YOU. The commentator, Kimchi, calls attention to the fact that it was the custom of passers-by to greet the reapers and thus bless the harvest. See Ruth 2:4, "And Boaz came from Beth-lehem, and said unto the reapers: 'the Lord be with you.'" The psalmist here means: may the harvest be so meagre (may our enemies be so diminished) that the passers-by will not have the heart to greet the harvesters with a blessing.

A PENITENTIAL psalm. The psalmist, aware of his own iniquity, prays to God for forgiveness. He is confident that God will forgive him and all of Israel. This psalm resembles, in mood and in language, the penitential passages in the prayer of Solomon (I Kings 8) and the prayer of Nehemiah (Nehemiah 9).

1. OUT OF THE DEPTHS HAVE I CALLED. Out of the depths of guilt, or out of the depths of despair. A similar mood is vividly

369

2. Lord, hearken unto my voice;
Let Thine ears be attentive
To the voice of my supplications.
3. If Thou, Lord, shouldest mark iniquities,
O Lord, who could stand?
4. For with Thee there is forgiveness,
That Thou mayest be feared.
5. I wait for the Lord, my soul doth wait,
And in His word do I hope.
6. My soul waiteth for the Lord,
More than watchmen for the morning;
Yea, more than watchmen for the morning.
7. O Israel, hope in the Lord;

expressed in Psalm 69:3 and 15. "I am come unto deep waters, and the flood overwhelmeth me; deliver me out of the mire, and let me not sink."

2. LET THINE EARS BE ATTENTIVE. The same phrase is used in the prayer of Solomon as given in II Chronicles 6:40.

3. IF THOU, LORD, SHOULDEST MARK INIQUITY. If Thou wouldst count against us all our sins, none of us "could stand" before Thee.

4. WITH THEE THERE IS FORGIVENESS, THAT THOU MAYEST BE FEARED. Since God forgives us we worship and revere Him. The commentators, Rashi and Kimchi, emphasize the word "Thee," taking the verse to mean: Since it is God alone who can forgive our sins, it is He whom we revere.

5. I WAIT FOR THE LORD. The psalmist knows that he will eventually be forgiven and, therefore, he continues to wait in patience for God's gracious mercy. The same thought is expressed in Psalm 27:14, "Wait for the Lord; be strong, and let thy heart take courage."

6. MY SOUL WAITETH . . . MORE THAN WATCHMEN FOR THE MORNING. More than the watchmen who guard the city all through the night wait eagerly for the dawn in order to rest from their weary task.

7. WITH HIM IS PLENTEOUS REDEMPTION. Nehemiah uses the same phrase in his penitential prayer (Nehemiah 9:17).

For with the Lord there is mercy,
And with Him is plenteous redemption.
8. And He will redeem Israel from all his iniquities.

31. A SONG OF ASCENTS; OF DAVID.

Lord, my heart is not haughty, nor mine eyes lofty;
Neither do I exercise myself in things too great, or in
things too wonderful for me.
2. Surely I have stilled and quieted my soul;
Like a weaned child with his mother,
My soul is with me like a weaned child.
3. O Israel, hope in the Lord
From this time forth and for ever.

THE psalmist describes his complete dependence upon God and his patient acceptance of whatever God will ordain for him.

1. MY HEART IS NOT HAUGHTY. Haughtiness and self-pride are frequently spoken of as sins which are particularly hateful to God. Thus, "Whoso is haughty of eye and proud of heart, him will I not suffer" (Psalm 101:5).

IN THINGS TOO GREAT . . . TOO WONDERFUL FOR ME. The commentator, Kimchi, says that this means: I do not claim to understand completely all the difficult philosophic problems. However, the psalmist may simply mean: I am not too ambitious, I do not expect too much of life. I wait for what God will send me.

2. I HAVE QUIETED MY SOUL; LIKE A WEANED CHILD WITH HIS MOTHER. As a child that has been weaned and has overcome his own resentment at having been weaned and is at last content to remain quietly with its mother, so have I given up my ambitious desires and all my restlessness, and now I wait patiently for the Lord.

The psalmist ends the poem by extending to all of Israel his own mood of quiet patience. Hence the exhortation: "O Israel, hope in the Lord."

The conclusion is virtually a repetition of verse 7 of the preceding psalm.

132. A SONG OF ASCENTS.

LORD, remember unto David
    All his affliction;
2. How he swore unto the LORD,
    And vowed unto the Mighty One of Jacob:
3. 'Surely I will not come into the tent of my house,
    Nor go up into the bed that is spread for me;
4. I will not give sleep to mine eyes,
    Nor slumber to mine eyelids;
5. Until I find out a place for the LORD,
    A dwelling-place for the Mighty One of Jacob.'
6. Lo, we heard of it as being in Ephrath;
    We found it in the field of the wood.*

THE psalm tells of David's eagerness to build the Temple, and recalls God's promise that He would establish the house of David that it may rule forever over Israel. The remembrance of the Divine promise served to enhearten the small post-exilic community.

A number of the verses of this psalm have been embodied in the version of King Solomon's prayer found in II Chronicles 6.

1. ALL HIS AFFLICTION. This sentence is followed by a statement of David's vow to build the Temple. The word "affliction" may, therefore, refer to the fact that David, in the midst of all his troubles and anxieties, made preparations for the building of the Temple. See I Chronicles 22:14, "Now, behold, in my straits I have prepared for the house of the Lord a hundred thousand talents of gold."

2. THE MIGHTY ONE OF JACOB. This description of God is first used in the blessing of Jacob, in Genesis 49:24, "by the hands of the Mighty One of Jacob." The phrase is used again in this psalm in verse 5.

3-5. David is introduced as speaker, making his promise to build a temple for God.

4. SLEEP TO MINE EYES . . . SLUMBER TO MINE EYELIDS. The

* Heb. *Jaar*. See 1 Chr. xiii. 5.

7. Let us go into His dwelling-place;
   Let us worship at His footstool.
8. Arise, O Lord, unto Thy resting-place;
   Thou, and the ark of Thy strength.
9. Let Thy priests be clothed with righteousness;
   And let Thy saints shout for joy.
10. For Thy servant David's sake
    Turn not away the face of Thine anointed.
11. The Lord swore unto David in truth;
    He will not turn back from it:
    'Of the fruit of thy body will I set upon thy throne.
12. If thy children keep My covenant
    And My testimony that I shall teach them,
    Their children also for ever shall sit upon thy throne.'

same sentence is found in Proverbs 6:4. It must have been a current expression.

6-10. Turns from David to the people of his time, or, more correctly, to the people of Solomon's time, who are about to bring the ark into the sanctuary. The psalmist writes as if the people were asking where the ark is to be found, and another group answering: "We have heard of it as being in Ephrath."

6. EPHRATH. Is another name for Beth-lehem. "In the way to Ephrath, the same is Beth-lehem" (Genesis 48:7).

THE FIELD OF THE WOOD. The Hebrew for "field of wood" may be a by-form of the name Kiriath-jearim (which means "the city of woods"). In I Chronicles 13:5, the ark is described as being in Kiriath-jearim. Ephrath and Kiriath-jearim were near each other.

We must now assume that the people have come to the place where the ark rests and have formed a procession to take it up to the Temple. The people in the procession shout: "Let us go into His dwelling-place" (verse 7).

7. HIS FOOTSTOOL. His Temple. See comment to Psalm 99:5.

8. ARISE, O, LORD UNTO THY RESTING-PLACE. The people turn to the ark and call upon God to accompany the ark on the march to the Temple.

THE ARK OF THY STRENGTH. The ark whose presence among

373

13. For the LORD hath chosen Zion;
    He hath desired it for His habitation:
14. 'This is My resting-place for ever;
    Here will I dwell; for I have desired it.
15. I will abundantly bless her provision;
    I will give her needy bread in plenty.

us gives us Thy strength. The ark is referred to as God's
strength in Psalm 78:61. There the psalmist apparently refers
to the fact that the ark was captured by the Philistines. He says:
"He delivered His strength into captivity."

9. PRIESTS CLOTHED WITH RIGHTEOUSNESS. The pure garments
of the priests which symbolized purity and righteousness.

THY SAINTS. Thy holy ones.

10. TURN NOT AWAY THE FACE OF THINE ANOINTED. Let not
the king's prayer be rejected. Let him not turn away unanswer-
ed. Look upon him with favor. The same phrase is used (but
in the positive sense) in Psalm 84:10, "O God our Shield, look
upon the face of Thine anointed."

11-18. God is now the speaker. He declares that David's children shall occupy the throne. The psalmist bases this passage
upon God's promise to David as described in II Samuel 7.

13. THE LORD HATH CHOSEN ZION. After repeating God's
promise to the Davidic dynasty, the psalmist speaks of God's
choice of Zion as His earthly abode. He makes use of the phraseology of the closing passages of Psalm 79.

14. THIS IS MY RESTING-PLACE FOREVER . . . I HAVE DESIRED IT.
As if to reassure the small community around Jerusalem after
the exile, God says: Zion will be My perpetual resting-place.
Here shall My glory dwell in your day as in the days of David
and Solomon. I will also "abundantly bless her provision."

16. HER PRIESTS . . . SALVATION; HER SAINTS . . . JOY. This is
virtually a repetition of verse 9.

17. WILL I MAKE A HORN TO SHOOT UP UNTO DAVID. This is a
familiar metaphor in the writings of the prophets. The ideal
king, the descendant of the house of David, who will rule in
righteousness over a peaceful earth, is described by Isaiah as a

374

16. Her priests also will I clothe with salvation;
And her saints shall shout aloud for joy.
17. There will I make a horn to shoot up unto David,
There have I ordered a lamp for Mine anointed.
18. His enemies will I clothe with shame;
But upon himself shall his crown shine.'

shoot growing forth from the roots of the tree of David, "There shall come forth a shoot out of the stock of Jesse, and a twig shall grow forth out of his roots" (Isaiah 11:1). In Jeremiah the same metaphor is used, "I will raise unto David a righteous shoot" (Jeremiah 23:5). In Ezekiel the metaphor is somewhat modified, and the prophet speaks as if the messiah is a horn (instead of a twig) which will spring up, "In that day will I cause a horn to shoot up unto the house of Israel" (Ezekiel 29:21). This phrase in Ezekiel is evidently a combination of two separate metaphors: the metaphor of the twig, as used by Isaiah and Jeremiah, and the metaphor of a horn (like the antlers of a stag), a symbol of pride and glory. The phrase here in the psalm, "I will make a horn to shoot up unto David," is based upon the expanded metaphor used in Ezekiel. It is from this passage in the psalm and in Ezekiel that the phraseology of the benediction for the messiah in the daily prayers was taken. "Blessed art thou, O God, who causes the horn of salvation to flourish" [*Authorized Daily Prayerbook* (Singer), page 49].

17. ORDERED A LAMP FOR MINE ANOINTED. To order a lamp means to put the lamp in order, to set up a lamp. The same phrase is used in Leviticus 24:4, where the priest is commanded to arrange the lamps, "He shall order the lamps upon the pure candlestick." The lamp was a symbol of life as in the verse, "The spirit of man is the lamp of the Lord" (Proverbs 20:27). The king's life was particularly precious and was looked upon as the light of Israel. Thus, when David's life had been endangered in a battle, the people swore that they would never again allow him so to risk his life. They said: "Thou shalt go no more out with us to battle, that thou quench not the lamp of Israel" (II Samuel 21:17).

375

Psalm 133
1

133. A SONG OF ASCENTS; OF DAVID.
Behold, how good and how pleasant it is
For brethren to dwell together in unity!
2. It is like the precious oil upon the head,
Coming down upon the beard;
Even Aaron's beard,
That cometh down upon the collar of his garments;
3. Like the dew of Hermon,

THE psalmist speaks of the blessed joy of brotherly concord. He compares it to the sacred oil with which Aaron was
anointed and also with the dew which descends upon the mountains of Palestine.

1. FOR BRETHREN TO DWELL TOGETHER IN UNITY. This theme
may have been suggested by the thought that groups of pilgrims
were journeying together to Jerusalem, and will be living together during the festival. The sight of these tens of thousands
of strangers living together in concord could well have evoked
the sentence: "Behold, how good it is for brethren to dwell together in unity." This pilgrim psalm fits well in this collection
of songs. It praises a simple, homely virtue as does Psalm 128
which speaks of the joys of home life, and Psalm 127 which
sings of the blessing of honest labor.

2. LIKE THE PRECIOUS OIL . . . AARON'S BEARD . . . HIS GAR-
MENTS. Fragrant oil was used to anoint welcome guests. The
guest in God's house says: "Thou hast anointed my head with
oil" (Psalm 23:5). Oil, as well as wine, is a symbol of joy. Thus,
too, "God hath anointed thee with the oil of gladness" (Psalm
45:8). The noblest of all the oils was the sacred oil with which
Aaron was anointed. This oil is described in Exodus 29:7, as
poured upon the head of Aaron. The psalmist means to say: As
blessed and as awe-inspiring as it must have been to see Aaron
anointed, so is it to see brethren living together in amity.

3. THE DEW OF HERMON. The tallest mountain in Palestine.
The commentator, Kimchi, says that the word "dew" must be
taken as belonging to both sentences, as follows: the dew of

376

That cometh down upon the mountains of Zion;
For there the LORD commanded the blessing,
Even life for ever.

134. A SONG OF ASCENTS.

Behold, bless ye the LORD, all ye servants of the LORD,
That stand in the house of the LORD in the night seasons.
2. Lift up your hands to the sanctuary,
And bless ye the LORD.

Hermon and the dew that cometh down upon mount Zion.

The dew in Palestine is plentiful and is deemed to be almost as great a blessing as the rainfall. In the synagogue service, there is a special series of prayers for rain at the end of the festival of Succoth, at the beginning of the rainy season, and an equally impressive series of prayers for dew at the beginning of Passover, the start of the summer season. The psalmist says that just as the glistening dew brings beauty and blessing, so beautiful and blessed is the sight of brothers living together in concord.

The psalm ends with the statement that God commands blessing there, namely, in Zion, His holy habitation and "life for ever." The commentator, Kimchi, explains this to mean, the blessing of long life.

$\mathcal{T}$HE last of the Psalms of Ascents. It is addressed to the Levites (and the priests in the Temple) and calls upon them to praise the Lord.

1. SERVANTS OF THE LORD, THAT STAND IN THE HOUSE . . . IN THE NIGHT SEASONS. During the day, the Levites and priests had their duties in the sanctuary in connection with the sacrificial services, and at night they stood watch. The psalmist calls upon those who are standing watch during the night to praise the Lord.

2. LIFT UP YOUR HANDS. In prayer to the sanctuary towards the Holy of Holies. The same thought is found in Psalm

3. The LORD bless thee out of Zion;
   Even He that made heaven and earth.

135. HALLELUJAH.

Praise ye the name of the LORD;
Give praise, O ye servants of the LORD,
2. Ye that stand in the house of the LORD,
   In the courts of the house of our God.
3. Praise ye the LORD, for the LORD is good;
   Sing praises unto His name, for it is pleasant.
4. For the LORD hath chosen Jacob unto Himself,
   And Israel for His own treasure.
5. For I know that the LORD is great,
   And that our Lord is above all gods.
6. Whatsoever the LORD pleased, that hath He done,
   In heaven and in earth, in the seas and in all deeps;
7. Who causeth the vapours to ascend from the ends of the earth;

28:2, "when I lift up my hands toward Thy holy Sanctuary."

3. THE LORD BLESS THEE OUT OF ZION. The same blessing is used in Psalm 128:5. The phrase, "Who made heaven and earth," is found also in Psalm 121:2, "My help cometh from the Lord, who made heaven and earth."

ALTHOUGH this psalm is not one of the pilgrim psalms, it begins with an expansion of the thought of the last of the pilgrim psalms (the preceding psalm). It also embodies a passage from one of the Hallel psalms.

1-4. Expands the thought of the preceding psalm, calling upon the "servants of the Lord," i. e., Levites and priests, to praise God.

3. SING PRAISES . . . FOR IT IS PLEASANT. The idea that it is a pleasant and a suitable task to praise God occurs a number of times in the Psalms. Thus, "To sing praises unto our God; for it is pleasant, and praise is comely" (Psalm 147:1).

4. CHOSEN JACOB . . . ISRAEL FOR HIS OWN TREASURE. This description of Israel as God's chosen treasure is reminiscent of a number of biblical passages, particularly Deuteronomy 7:6,

He maketh lightnings for the rain;
He bringeth forth the wind out of His treasuries.

8. Who smote the first-born of Egypt,
Both of man and beast.
9. He sent signs and wonders into the midst of thee, O Egypt,
Upon Pharaoh, and upon all His servants.
10. Who smote many nations,
And slew mighty kings:
11. Sihon king of the Amorites,
And Og king of Bashan,
And all the kingdoms of Canaan;
12. And gave their land for a heritage,
A heritage unto Israel His people.
13. O Lord, Thy name endureth for ever;
Thy memorial, O Lord, throughout all generations.
14. For the Lord will judge His people,
And repent Himself for His servants.

"The Lord thy God hath chosen thee to be His own treasure."

5. ABOVE ALL GODS. The psalmist does not mean that other gods are really gods. In the passage from verses 15-18, he speaks of them as helpless idols. He means that God is greater than all others who are worshipped as gods.

6. WHATSOEVER THE LORD PLEASED. This sentence is taken from Psalm 115:3, from which psalm the author quotes a lengthy passage.

IN THE SEAS AND IN ALL DEEPS. This means, in the seas and all the deep abysses, either below the earth or in the lowest depths of the sea, as in Exodus 20:4, "in the earth beneath, in the water under the earth."

7. WHO CAUSETH THE VAPOURS, etc. This verse is taken from Jeremiah 10:13. It means that the clouds arise at the far edges of the horizon where the heavens seem to touch the earth.

8-12. God's might is manifested not only in phenomena of nature but in the events of history. God defeated the Egyptians, smote many nations (verse 10), and gave Canaan as "a heritage unto Israel His people" (verse 12).

13. THY MEMORIAL, O LORD. Our memory of Thy deeds.

14. REPENT HIMSELF FOR HIS SERVANTS. The commentator,

379

Psalm 135
15

15. The idols of the nations are silver and gold,
    The work of men's hands.
16. They have mouths, but they speak not;
    Eyes have they, but they see not;
17. They have ears, but they hear not;
    Neither is there any breath in their mouths.
18. They that make them shall be like unto them;
    Yea, every one that trusteth in them.
19. O house of Israel, bless ye the LORD;
    O house of Aaron, bless ye the LORD;
20. O house of Levi, bless ye the LORD;
    Ye that fear the LORD, bless ye the LORD.
21. Blessed be the LORD out of Zion,

Kimchi, explains this as follows: God will decide that His people had suffered enough for their sins and He will afflict them no longer. He will repent, i. e., He will change the decree which He had issued against His people. The same verb is used in Genesis 6:7, when God sees the corruption of man He says, "it repenteth Me that I have made them."

15-20. THE IDOLS OF THE NATIONS, ETC. This description of the helplessness of the idols and the call to the various nations to bless the Lord, are taken, with slight variation, from Psalm 115:3-11.

The psalm ends with the blessing: "Blessed be the Lord out of Zion, who dwelleth at Jerusalem," i. e., from the sanctuary on Zion shall resound the blessings of the Lord who dwelleth at Jerusalem.

THIS psalm is known in Jewish tradition as *Hallel Hagadol,* "The Great Hallel" (b. Pesachim 118 a). It is a series of sentences praising God for having created the world and being the guide of Israel's history. While the psalm does not contain much that is original, its construction is unique in the Psalm Book. Every line is followed by the refrain: "O, give thanks unto the Lord, for He is good, for His mercy endureth for ever." This refrain has been used a number of times previously

380

136. O give thanks unto the Lord, for He is good,
For His mercy endureth for ever.
2. O give thanks unto the God of gods,
For His mercy endureth for ever.
3. O give thanks unto the Lord of lords,
For His mercy endureth for ever.
4. To Him who alone doeth great wonders,
For His mercy endureth for ever.
5. To Him that by understanding made the heavens,
For His mercy endureth for ever.

in the Psalms (e. g., in Psalm 118:1). But here it is interwoven into the structure of the entire psalm. Presumably it was a response to be chanted by the people or by the choir. The leader sang each verse, speaking of one of God's deeds, and the people responded with the refrain. That this must have been the method of recital seems fairly clear from the passage in Ezra which describes the celebration of the laying of the cornerstone of the Temple. At that occasion, some Levites sang the praises of God, while others responded with the same response used here in this psalm: "And they sang one to another in praising and giving thanks unto the Lord: 'for He is good, for His mercy endureth for ever toward Israel' " (Ezra 3:11).

The psalm is one of the Sabbath morning psalms in the synagogue service. It is also recited at the Seder Service on Passover Eve following the completion of the *Hallel* at the close of the meal.

2-3. THE GOD OF GODS . . . THE LORD OF LORDS. There is none that is greater than God. This description of God as paramount is based upon a passage in Deuteronomy 10:17, "For the Lord your God, He is God of gods, and Lord of lords." See comment to Psalm 135:5.

5. TO HIM THAT BY UNDERSTANDING MADE THE HEAVENS. The word for "understanding" is a synonym of "wisdom." By His wisdom He made the heavens.

381

6. To Him that spread forth the earth above the waters,
    For His mercy endureth for ever.
7. To Him that made great lights,
    For His mercy endureth for ever;
8. The sun to rule by day,
    For His mercy endureth for ever;
9. The moon and stars to rule by night,
    For His mercy endureth for ever.
10. To Him that smote Egypt in their first-born,
    For His mercy endureth for ever;
11. And brought out Israel from among them,
    For His mercy endureth for ever;
12. With a strong hand, and with an outstretched **arm,**
    For His mercy endureth for ever.
13. To Him who divided the Red Sea in sunder,
    For His mercy endureth for ever;
14. And made Israel to pass through the midst of it,
    For His mercy endureth for ever;
15. But overthrew Pharaoh and his hosts in the Red Sea,
    For His mercy endureth for ever.
16. To Him that led His people through the wilderness,
    For His mercy endureth for ever.
17. To Him that smote great kings;

12. WITH A STRONG HAND, AND WITH AN OUTSTRETCHED ARM. This metaphorical description of God's intervention is found in Deuteronomy 4:34, "by a mighty hand, and by an outstretched arm."

23. WHO REMEMBERED US IN OUR LOW ESTATE. The commentator, Kimchi, says that this refers to the exile. God remembered us during our exile and "hath delivered us from our adversaries" (verse 24).

26. THE GOD OF HEAVEN. This description of God is found only once in the Psalms. It occurs a number of times in Ezra, Nehemiah and Chronicles. Thus, Ezra 1:2, "All the kingdoms of the earth hath the Lord, the God of heaven, given me."

THIS psalm begins with a plaintive note and ends with a cry of indignant rage. The first part of the psalm speaks of the

For His mercy endureth for ever;
18. And slew mighty kings,
    For His mercy endureth for ever:
19. Sihon king of the Amorites,
    For His mercy endureth for ever;
20. And Og king of Bashan,
    For His mercy endureth for ever;
21. And gave their land for a heritage,
    For His mercy endureth for ever;
22. Even a heritage unto Israel His servant,
    For His mercy endureth for ever.
23. Who remembered us in our low estate,
    For His mercy endureth for ever;
24. And hath delivered us from our adversaries,
    For His mercy endureth for ever.
25. Who giveth food to all flesh,
    For His mercy endureth for ever.
26. O give thanks unto the God of heaven,
    For His mercy endureth for ever.

137. By the rivers of Babylon,
There we sat down, yea, we wept,
When we remembered Zion.

spiritual anguish of the exiles in Babylon and their longing for Zion. The second half of the psalm calls down God's punishment for the cruelty which Israel's enemies manifested during the time of Israel's defeat.

1. BY THE RIVERS OF BABYLON. Mesopotamia was criss-crossed by canals. Thus, there were many waters. The author, therefore, does not refer to *the* river, Euphrates, but to the rivers, the many streams and canals of Babylon.

THERE WE SAT DOWN. The past tense indicates that this song is a reminiscence. It was not written during the march into exile but some time after. The psalmist remembers how, by the rivers of Babylon, they had sat down and wept.

2. UPON THE WILLOWS . . . WE HANGED UP OUR HARPS. We hung them up because we would not use them. Not that it was forbidden to sing our songs in exile but for the reason given in the next sentence (verse 3): "They that led us captive . . . asked

2. Upon the willows in the midst thereof
    We hanged up our harps.
3. For there they that led us captive asked of us words of song,
    And our tormentors asked of us mirth:
    'Sing us one of the songs of Zion.'
4. How shall we sing the LORD's song
    In a foreign land?
5. If I forget thee, O Jerusalem,
    Let my right hand forget her cunning.
6. Let my tongue cleave to the roof of my mouth,
    If I remember thee not;

of us mirth: 'sing us one of the songs of Zion.'" Our captors desired of us to sing for their amusement the jubilant hymns which we chanted in the sanctuary. This we could not do and rather than "sing the Lord's song in a foreign land" (verse 4) at the command of brutal captors who would mock at them, we preferred to hang up our harps and not use them at all.

5. LET MY RIGHT HAND FORGET HER CUNNING. The Hebrew does not contain the word "cunning." The sentence ends sharply and perhaps even more effectively: "Let my right hand forget!" It may therefore also mean, let it forget how to move; let it be paralyzed.

6. LET MY TONGUE CLEAVE TO THE ROOF OF MY MOUTH. Let me lose the power of speech. The same phrase is used in Job 29:10, "The voice of the nobles was hushed, and their tongue cleaved to the roof of their mouth."

IF I SET NOT JERUSALEM ABOVE MY CHIEFEST JOY. Let my hand forget her cunning and my tongue grow dumb if I do not love Jerusalem more than my most cherished joys.

7-9. The tone of the psalm changes abruptly. The psalmist calls down God's sternest punishment against Edom and Babylon. If we assume that the psalm was written after the return (see verse 1), we can well understand this mood of bitterness on the part of the psalmist. The tiny community of returned exiles was subjected to constant vindictiveness, and, as the community began somewhat to prosper, it was subject to endless jealousy. In these discouraging circumstances the psalmist,

384

If I set not Jerusalem
Above my chiefest joy.
7. Remember, O LORD, against the children of Edom
The day of Jerusalem;
Who said: 'Rase it, rase it,
Even to the foundation thereof.'
8. O daughter of Babylon, that art to be destroyed;
Happy shall he be, that repayeth thee
As thou hast served us.
9. Happy shall he be, that taketh and dasheth thy little ones
Against the rock.

writing of the exile, remembers the bitter enemies who afflicted
Israel in those dark days. He speaks first of the children of
Edom. Edom was the hereditary enemy of Israel, and many of
the prophets have uttered words of indignation against it. Edom
is the subject of the indignant preachment of Obadiah. The
psalmist remembers how Edom rejoiced at "the day of Jerusalem" (verse 7) i. e., the day of Jerusalem's doom, and how it
urged the Babylonians to destroy it utterly, to "rase it, rase it
to the foundations" (verse 7). The Book of Lamentations also
speaks of the rejoicing of Edom at the destruction of Jerusalem.
(Lamentations 4:21.)

The psalmist then turns to Babylon which so mercilessly
crushed Judah and Jerusalem. He refers to Babylon as "the
daughter of Babylon, that art to be destroyed" (verse 8). Babylon was already captured by the armies of the victorious
Persians when the psalmist wrote. He anticipates (with satisfaction) that the army of Cyrus would soon requite Babylon for
her cruelty to Jerusalem, "Happy shall he be, that repayeth
thee as thou hast served us."

The last verse reaches the climax of indignation. The psalmist remembers the wholesale slaughter of Judean women and
children. Such slaughters often occurred in ancient warfare
when cities were captured. The prophet Hosea describes one
such sacking of a city when "the mother was dashed in pieces
with her children" (Hosea 10:14). So, also, the prophet Nahum,
describing the fall of Nineveh, says: "She went into captivity:

138. [A PSALM] OF DAVID.
I will give Thee thanks with my whole heart,
In the presence of the mighty will I sing praises unto Thee.
2. I will bow down toward Thy holy temple,
And give thanks unto Thy name for Thy mercy and for
Thy truth;
For Thou hast magnified Thy word above all Thy name.
3. In the day that I called, Thou didst answer me;
Thou didst encourage me in my soul with strength.
4. All the kings of the earth shall give Thee thanks, O LORD,
For they have heard the words of Thy mouth.

her young children also were dashed in pieces" (Nahum 3:10).
The same ruthlessness was manifested at the capture of Jerusalem by the Babylonians, and the psalmist in his bitterness asks
that Babylon be punished in like manner. "Happy shall he be,
that taketh and dasheth thy little ones" (verse 9), must be
taken as a specific instance of the general statement in verse 8,
"Happy shall he be that repayeth thee as thou has served us."

Verses 8 and 9 therefore must be understood as follows: O
city of Babylon, thou art about to be destroyed by Cyrus the
Persian; happy shall Cyrus be who will repay you what you
have done to us. You dashed our little ones against the stone.
He will treat you in the same manner.

THIS psalm, headed "A Psalm of David," expresses a
thought frequently found in the "David" psalms in Books One
and Two. The psalmist praises God for His many mercies and
says that all the earth, seeing God's help to Israel, will come
and sing the praises of the Lord.

1. IN THE PRESENCE OF THE MIGHTY WILL I SING. The Hebrew
word here translated "mighty" is *Elohim*, which means either
"God" or "angels" or "judges" or "the mighty."

2. I WILL BOW DOWN TOWARD THY HOLY TEMPLE. Wherever
the psalmist was he faced the temple in prayer. Thus, Daniel
when in Babylon prayed with face toward Jerusalem (Daniel

5. Yea, they shall sing of the ways of the Lord;
For great is the glory of the Lord.
6. For though the Lord be high, yet regardeth He the lowly,
And the haughty He knoweth from afar.
7. Though I walk in the midst of trouble, Thou
    quickenest me;
Thou stretchest forth Thy hand against the wrath
    of mine enemies,
And Thy right hand doth save me.
8. The Lord will accomplish that which concerneth me;
Thy mercy, O Lord, endureth for ever;
Forsake not the work of Thine own hands.

6:11). See also Psalm 5:8, "I will bow down toward Thy holy temple."

THOU HAST MAGNIFIED THY WORD ABOVE ALL THY NAME. This difficult verse has received many explanations. As translated here it means: Thou hast made Thy words of deliverance greater even than Thy fame. Men praise Thee as merciful, but Thy words of mercy were even greater than Thy praise.

6. THOUGH THE LORD BE HIGH, YET REGARDETH HE THE LOW-LY. Though God be Infinite yet He knows and He helps even the humblest. The same thought is expressed in Psalm 113:5, 6, 7, "Who is like unto the Lord our God, that is enthroned on high, that looketh down low upon heaven and upon the earth, who raiseth up the poor."

7. THOU STRETCHEST FORTH THY HAND. Thou sendest forth Thy might to protect me "against . . . mine enemies." Thus, Exodus 3:20, "I will put forth My hand, and smite Egypt."

8. THE LORD WILL ACCOMPLISH THAT WHICH CONCERNETH ME. He will fulfill the promises that He made with regard to me.

FORSAKE NOT THE WORK OF THINE OWN HANDS. "The work of Thy hands" may mean God's achievement, as Psalm 92:5, "I will exult in the works of Thy hands." The psalmist asks God not to leave uncompleted the work of deliverance which He has begun. Here "the work of Thine hands" may mean the psalmist himself whom God has created. The psalmist therefore means to say: "Forsake me not."

387

139. FOR THE LEADER. A PSALM OF DAVID.

O LORD, Thou hast searched me, and known me.
2. Thou knowest my downsitting and mine uprising,
   Thou understandest my thought afar off.
3. Thou measurest my going about and my lying down,
   And art acquainted with all my ways.
4. For there is not a word in my tongue,
   But, lo, O LORD, Thou knowest it altogether.
5. Thou hast hemmed me in behind and before,
   And laid Thy hand upon me.
6. Such knowledge is too wonderful for me;
   Too high, I cannot attain unto it.
7. Whither shall I go from Thy spirit?
   Or whither shall I flee from Thy presence?
8. If I ascend up into heaven, Thou art there;
   If I make my bed in the nether-world, behold, Thou art there.

ONE of the most intimate and spiritual of the psalms. The psalmist is so conscious of God's nearness, that he feels that God knows his every thought. But God, though intimate and near, is also omnipresent, filling the universe. There is no place where we can escape God's presence. It is no wonder that God knows our every thought since He is our Creator. But since God is near to us and since He is present in all the universe and has created us, how then can He permit the wicked and the false to remain so near to Him? The psalmist declares that he will depart from the presence of the wicked and asks God to help him purify his heart.

1. THOU HAST SEARCHED ME. Thou hast looked into the innermost recesses of my soul. The prophet Jeremiah states the same thought as follows: "I the Lord search the heart, I try the reins" (Jeremiah 17:10).

2. THOU KNOWEST MY DOWNSITTING AND MINE UPRISING. Thou knowest every movement of mine, or more specifically, Thou knowest all my purposes, as in Psalm 127:2, "It is vain for you that ye rise early, and sit up late."

5. HEMMED ME IN BEHIND AND BEFORE, AND LAID THY HAND UPON ME. Thou hast surrounded me as an invading army hems

9. If I take the wings of the morning,
   And dwell in the uttermost parts of the sea;
10. Even there would Thy hand lead me,
    And Thy right hand would hold me.
11. And if I say: 'Surely the darkness shall envelop me,
    And the light about me shall be night';
12. Even the darkness is not too dark for Thee,
    But the night shineth as the day;
    The darkness is even as the light.
13. For Thou hast made my reins;
    Thou hast knit me together in my mother's womb.
14. I will give thanks unto Thee, for I am fearfully and
       wonderfully made;
    Wonderful are Thy works;
    And that my soul knoweth right well.
15. My frame was not hidden from Thee,
    When I was made in secret,

in a city and hast placed Thy dominion (Thy hand) upon me.

6. SUCH KNOWLEDGE IS TOO WONDERFUL FOR ME. Knowledge such as Thine is too great for me to understand.

7-12. Not only is God very near, knowing every thought of the mind, but He is everywhere. We cannot escape from His presence.

9. THE WINGS OF THE MORNING. The rays of the morning sun spread out in all directions. Poetic fancy saw them as the wings of the dawn.

The psalmist continues to say that neither the "uttermost parts of the sea nor the deepest darkness can conceal me from God."

13-18. It is not strange that God knows man so well. He has created him and formed him even in the womb.

13. MY REINS. My kidneys, which were thought to be the seat of the emotions.

14. I AM FEARFULLY AND WONDERFULLY MADE. "Fearfully" means "astoundingly," so marvelously as to awaken awe and reverence.

15. WHEN I WAS MADE IN SECRET. When I grew in the dark womb.

389

And curiously wrought in the lowest parts of the earth.

16. Thine eyes did see mine unformed substance,
And in Thy book they were all written—
Even the days that were fashioned,
When as yet there was none of them.

17. How weighty also are Thy thoughts unto me, O God!
How great is the sum of them!

18. If I would count them, they are more in number than the sand;
Were I to come to the end of them, I would still be with Thee.

19. If Thou but wouldest slay the wicked, O God—
Depart from me therefore, ye men of blood;

20. Who utter Thy name with wicked thought,
They take it for falsehood, even Thine enemies—

CURIOUSLY WROUGHT IN THE LOWEST PARTS OF THE EARTH. This is parallel to "made in secret." The "dark womb" is here compared to the darkest depths of the earth. The sentence means: when I was mysteriously developed in the dark depths of the womb ("the lowest parts of the earth").

16. IN THY BOOK THEY WERE ALL WRITTEN. This sentence must be taken with the succeeding sentence as follows: in Thy book were written "the days that were fashioned, when as yet there was none of them" (verse 16), i. e., before I even had days of life (before my days were fashioned or created), already in Thy book was my life written out. Instead of "even the days," read "namely the days."

18. WERE I TO COME TO THE END OF THEM, I WOULD STILL BE WITH THEE. The Hebrew word here translated "come to the end of them" can also be translated "awake." Thus, many commentators translate this sentence, "when I awake I would still be with Thee." But since the psalmist does not speak of sleeping, this translation seems incongruous. As translated here the sentence means: were I to imagine that I have counted all your thoughts to the end, I would still be in the presence of an inexhaustible Mind.

19-24. Since he is ever in God's presence he resolves to avoid the wicked and asks God to test his thoughts and purify them of evil.

21. Do not I hate them, O Lord, that hate Thee?
And do not I strive with those that rise up
against Thee?
22. I hate them with utmost hatred;
I count them mine enemies.
23. Search me, O God, and know my heart,
Try me, and know my thoughts;
24. And see if there be any way in me that is grievous,
And lead me in the way everlasting.

140. FOR THE LEADER. A PSALM OF DAVID.

2. Deliver me, O Lord, from the evil man;
Preserve me from the violent man;

19. IF THOU WOULDEST SLAY. The sentence is incomplete. It means: if Thou wouldst only destroy the wicked it would be easy for me to be righteous. But since the wicked continue to exist, I must command them "to depart from me."

20. THEY TAKE IT FOR FALSEHOOD. The word "name" from the preceding sentence must be taken as part of this sentence also. They take Thy name in false oath. They take Thy name in vain.

23. The psalmist ends with the thought with which he began. The opening sentence was: "O Lord, Thou hast searched me," and now he asks again: "Search me, O God, and know my heart."

24. ANY WAY IN ME THAT IS GRIEVOUS. Any path of action which is evil.

THE WAY EVERLASTING. The opposite of the way that is grievous, i. e., the way that is righteous and enduring.

THE next four psalms belong together. They all express a thought that is prevalent in the early part of the Psalter, namely, the prayer that God deliver the psalmist from the sinful and the violent who have set their snares to entrap him.

3. EVERY DAY DO THEY STIR UP WARS. The very opposite of the righteous who bring harmony and peace.

3. Who devise evil things in their heart;
   Every day do they stir up wars.
4. They have sharpened their tongue like a serpent;
   Vipers' venom is under their lips.   Selah
5. Keep me, O Lord, from the hands of the wicked;
   Preserve me from the violent man;
   Who have purposed to make my steps slip.
6. The proud have hid a snare for me, and cords;
   They have spread a net by the wayside;
   They have set gins for me.   Selah
7. I have said unto the Lord: 'Thou art my God';
   Give ear, O Lord, unto the voice of my supplications.
8. O God the Lord, the strength of my salvation,
   Who hast screened my head in the day of battle,
9. Grant not, O Lord, the desires of the wicked;
   Further not his evil device, so that they exalt themselves.   Selah
10. As for the head of those that compass me about,

4. THEIR TONGUE LIKE A SERPENT; VIPERS' VENOM. The psalmist frequently compares evil tongues to arrows and swords. Sometimes he uses the simile of the poison of a serpent. Thus, "Their venom is like the venom of a serpent" (Psalm 58:5).

5-6. The familiar description of the snares and nets which the wicked set for the righteous.

6. THEY HAVE SET GINS FOR ME. Snares.

7. THOU ART MY GOD. This phrase is taken from Psalm 16:2.

8. WHO HAST SCREENED MY HEAD IN THE DAY OF BATTLE. As a soldier would raise his shield to protect the head of his comrade.

9. FURTHER NOT HIS EVIL DEVICE, SO THAT THEY EXALT THEM-SELVES. Lest they exalt themselves.

11. LET BURNING COALS FALL UPON THEM. This is a metaphor for God's flaming wrath. Thus, "Upon the wicked He will cause to rain coals; fire and brimstone" (Psalm 11:6). It is also a reminiscence of the destruction, by fire and brimstone, of the wicked cities of Sodom and Gomorrah.

12. A SLANDERER SHALL NOT BE ESTABLISHED. Slanderers will not endure. They will be caught in their own nets.

13. THE LORD WILL MAINTAIN THE CAUSE OF THE POOR. The needy and the fatherless and the stranger are God's special

Let the mischief of their own lips cover them.
11. Let burning coals fall upon them;
Let them be cast into the fire,
Into deep pits, that they rise not up again.
12. A slanderer shall not be established in the earth;
The violent and evil man shall be hunted with thrust
upon thrust.
13. I know that the LORD will maintain the cause of the poor,
And the right of the needy.
14. Surely the righteous shall give thanks unto Thy name;
The upright shall dwell in Thy presence.

141. A PSALM OF DAVID.

LORD, I have called Thee; make haste unto me;
Give ear unto my voice, when I call unto Thee.
2. Let my prayer be set forth as incense before Thee,
The lifting up of my hands as the evening sacrifice.

wards. He will defend them against all injustice. "To maintain
the cause" means here, to defend them in judgment when they
are unjustly accused. Thus, "For Thou hast maintained my
right and my cause; Thou sattest upon the throne as the righteous Judge" (Psalm 9:5).

THIS psalm expresses a mood common to most of the
"David" psalms in the early part of the Psalter. The psalmist
asks God to hear his prayer, to deliver him from "the snare
which they (i. e., the wicked) have laid for me" (verse 9). He
prays for the strength to keep from evil.

1. MAKE HASTE UNTO ME. The psalmist, in his despair, feels
that God's help is slow in coming. He asks God to make haste
to help him. Psalm 38 ends with the same plea: "Make haste to
help me, O Lord, my salvation."

2. MY PRAYER SET FORTH AS INCENSE. Many of the terms
originally used in the sacrificial cult were transferred to the
prayer worship of the Synagogue. Here, the psalmist asks that
just as the incense is arranged (i. e., set forth) before God, so
let his prayer be set forth.

393

Psalm 141

3

3. Set a guard, O LORD, to my mouth;
   Keep watch at the door of my lips.
4. Incline not my heart to any evil thing,
   To be occupied in deeds of wickedness
   With men that work iniquity;
   And let me not eat of their dainties.
5. Let the righteous smite me in kindness, and
      correct me;
   Oil so choice let not my head refuse;
   For still is my prayer because of their wickedness.

3-4. The psalmist asks that his mouth and his heart be guarded against temptation and evil. He prays that God may keep him from wickedness in word and in thought. The same idea is found in the closing sentence of Psalm 19: "Let the words of my mouth and the meditation of my heart be acceptable before Thee."

4. LET ME NOT EAT OF THEIR DAINTIES. The commentator, Rashi, says, let me not participate in the banquets of the wicked. The commentator, Kimchi, properly connects this sentence with the following one and understands the passage as follows: I do not desire the tasty food of the wicked. I prefer that "the righteous smite me in kindness" (verse 5).

5. LET THE RIGHTEOUS SMITE ME IN KINDNESS. I will gladly accept the stern criticism of the righteous. Such correction will be a greater kindness than the material pleasures which the wicked might provide. The same thought is found in Proverbs 27:6, "Faithful are the wounds of a friend," i. e., the criticism given by a friend.

OIL SO CHOICE. The stern correction of the righteous will be as welcome to me as choice and precious oil. Oil was put upon the head of a guest, "Thou anointest my head with oil" (Psalm 23:5).

FOR STILL IS MY PRAYER BECAUSE OF THEIR WICKEDNESS. For still I must pray to be protected against the wickedness of the violent. Therefore I must guard against the dainties which they offer me. I must strengthen myself with the correction given by the righteous.

394

6. Their judges are thrown down by the sides of the rock;
   And they shall hear my words, that they are sweet.
7. As when one cleaveth and breaketh up the earth,
   Our bones are scattered at the grave's mouth.
8. For mine eyes are unto Thee, O God the Lord;
   In Thee have I taken refuge, O pour not out my soul.
9. Keep me from the snare which they have laid for me,
   And from the gins of the workers of iniquity.
10. Let the wicked fall into their own nets,
    Whilst I withal escape.

6. THEIR JUDGES ARE THROWN DOWN. This must be taken with the preceding verse. It is still my prayer that the wicked judges be "thrown down by the sides of the rock," down "the side" of a mountain into the abyss.

THEY SHALL HEAR MY WORDS, THAT THEY ARE SWEET. Their wicked followers, seeing the destruction of their leaders (the judges) will realize that my words are sweet, that the doctrines of righteousness which I speak are "sweeter than honey" (Psalm 19:11).

7. AS WHEN ONE CLEAVETH . . . THE EARTH, OUR BONES ARE SCATTERED. Save us from the wicked; for as the earth is broken up by the spade and scattered about, so are our bones broken and scattered till we are at the point of death, "the grave's mouth."

8. O POUR NOT OUT MY SOUL. My life. The soul, or the life, was identified with the blood, as Deuteronomy 12:23, "for the blood is the life." Hence, this sentence means: pour not out my blood, let me not die.

9. AND FROM THE GINS. The traps.

10. WHILST I WITHAL ESCAPE. The word translated here as "withal" is the Hebrew word which means "together." The commentator, Ibn Ezra, quotes the interpretation which takes this word "together" with the preceding sentence: let the wicked fall into their own nets together, whilst I escape. As translated here, "whilst I withal escape" means that the wicked will be caught in their own snares while I escape with my life, or with my possessions.

395

142. MASCHIL OF DAVID, WHEN HE WAS IN
THE CAVE; A PRAYER.

2. With my voice I cry unto the LORD;
   With my voice I make supplication unto the LORD.
3. I pour out my complaint before Him,
   I declare before Him my trouble;
4. When my spirit fainteth within me—
   Thou knowest my path—
   In the way wherein I walk
   Have they hidden a snare for me.
5. Look on my right hand, and see,
   For there is no man that knoweth me;

THE psalmist declares that God alone is the source of his strength and his comfort. "I declare before Him my trouble" (verse 3). He asks God to deliver him from persecutors: "for they are too strong for me" (verse 7). The heading of the psalm contains a reference to the circumstances under which the psalm was written, "Maschil of David, when he was in the cave." This may have reference either to the cave of Adullam (I Samuel 22) or Engedi (I Samuel 24). This is the only psalm in Book Five that contains any such historical reference in its heading. It must have been influenced by the group of psalms in Book Two whose headings contain historical reference; thus, 'When he was in the wilderness of Judah" (Psalm 63) ; "When Saul sent, and they watched the house to kill him" (Psalm 59).

1. MASCHIL. For explanation of this technical term see comment on Psalm 32:1.

2. WITH MY VOICE I CRY. My prayers are not merely silent meditations but are also outcries to God. Thus: "With my voice I call unto the Lord" (Psalm 3:5).

4. WHEN MY SPIRIT FAINTETH. When I am in despair. A similar expression is found in Psalm 77:4, "When I muse thereon, my spirit fainteth."

THOU KNOWEST MY PATH. Thou knowest that my path is not the path of wickedness, yet the wicked have "hidden a snare for me."

I have no way to flee;
No man careth for my soul.
6. I have cried unto Thee, O Lord;
    I have said: 'Thou art my refuge,
    My portion in the land of the living.'
7. Attend unto my cry;
    For I am brought very low;
    Deliver me from my persecutors;
    For they are too strong for me.
8. Bring my soul out of prison,
    That I may give thanks unto Thy name;
    The righteous shall crown themselves because of me;
    For Thou wilt deal bountifully with me.

5. LOOK ON MY RIGHT HAND, AND SEE, THERE IS NO MAN THAT KNOWETH ME. At his right hand where his comrade should stand to help him in battle he finds no friend, "there is no man that knoweth me." The thought is continued in the next two lines.

NO MAN CARETH FOR MY SOUL. For my life. There is no one who cares for me, who loves me enough to try to save my life.

6-8. In this passage the psalmist says: since I have no comrade at my right hand to defend me, I turn to Thee, "Thou art my refuge." God becomes his comrade at his right hand. Thus, Psalm 110:5, "The Lord at thy right hand doth crush kings."

8. BRING MY SOUL OUT OF PRISON. The hostility of enemies is often described as the hemming in or as an imprisonment. Therefore, when the psalmist asks God to help him against his enemies he asks to be set free, or to be placed in "a wider place."

THE RIGHTEOUS SHALL CROWN THEMSELVES. When the righteous behold my deliverance they shall no longer be ashamed, they shall "crown themselves" with honor.

ƆN Psalm 143 the psalmist again speaks of his enemies from whose violence he asks for deliverance. But he prefaces his prayer with a confession of his own unworthiness. He does not

143. A PSALM OF DAVID.

O LORD, hear my prayer, give ear to my supplications;
In Thy faithfulness answer me, and in Thy righteousness.
2. And enter not into judgment with Thy servant;
For in Thy sight shall no man living be justified.
3. For the enemy hath persecuted my soul;
He hath crushed my life down to the ground;
He hath made me to dwell in dark places, as those that
have been long dead.
4. And my spirit fainteth within me;
My heart within me is appalled.
5. I remember the days of old;
I meditate on all Thy doing;
I muse on the work of Thy hands.
6. I spread forth my hands unto Thee;
My soul [thirsteth] after Thee, as a weary land.   Selah
7. Answer me speedily, O LORD,

declare that he is without sin, that his sufferings are unmerited.
He prays to God first for forgiveness and then for deliverance.

1. IN THY FAITHFULNESS. Since Thou art faithful, since Thou
fulfillest Thy promise to help me.

2. ENTER NOT INTO JUDGMENT . . . FOR IN THY SIGHT SHALL NO
MAN LIVING BE JUSTIFIED. The psalmist frequently asks God to
judge him and to see that he is innocent. But here, the psalmist, conscious of his own unworthiness, asks God *not* to act as
judge for there is no human being so sinless as to appear just
before the All-Holy. The same thought is found in Job 15:14,
"What is man, that he should be clean? He that is born of a
woman, that he should be righteous?" See also I Kings 8:46,
"For there is no man that sinneth not."

3-4. I need Thy help for the enemy hath "crushed my life
down to the ground."

3. TO DWELL IN DARK PLACES. He has brought me close to
death, "to the dark places" which are the dwelling-place of
those "that have been long dead."

5. I REMEMBER THE DAYS OF OLD. I recall how Thou hast
been our help in ages past.

My spirit faileth;
Hide not Thy face from me;
Lest I become like them that go down into the pit.

8. Cause me to hear Thy lovingkindness in the morning,
For in Thee do I trust;
Cause me to know the way wherein I should walk,
For unto Thee have I lifted up my soul.

9. Deliver me from mine enemies, O LORD;
With Thee have I hidden myself.

10. Teach me to do Thy will,
For Thou art my God;
Let Thy good spirit
Lead me in an even land.

11. For Thy name's sake, O LORD, quicken me;
In Thy righteousness bring my soul out of trouble.

12. And in Thy mercy cut off mine enemies,
And destroy all them that harass my soul;
For I am Thy servant.

6. I SPREAD FORTH MY HANDS. In prayer.

7. LIKE THEM THAT GO DOWN INTO THE PIT. To the grave, to
the nether-world, to death.

8. TO HEAR THY LOVINGKINDNESS IN THE MORNING. This
phrase occurs frequently in the Psalms. The psalmist spends the
weary night in weeping and despair but when the morning
dawns his hope returns. God's help has come. Thus, "Weeping
may tarry for the night, but joy cometh in the morning" (Psalm
30:6).

UNTO THEE HAVE I LIFTED UP MY SOUL. In prayer. Psalm 25:1,
"Unto Thee, O Lord, do I lift up my soul."

9. WITH THEE HAVE I HIDDEN MYSELF. God is our refuge. He
hides us in His tabernacle. This is the meaning of the opening
verse of Psalm 91: "O thou that dwellest in the covert (in the
hiding places) of the Most High."

10. LEAD ME IN AN EVEN LAND. To a broad and level place.
Thus, "My foot standeth in an even place" (Psalm 26:12).

12. FOR I AM THY SERVANT. In these words the psalmist sums
up his utter dependence upon God. "Deal bountifully with
Thy servant, that I may live" (Psalm 119:17).

399

144. [A PSALM] OF DAVID.

Blessed be the LORD my Rock,
Who traineth my hands for war,
And my fingers for battle;

2. My lovingkindness, and my fortress,
My high tower, and my deliverer;
My shield, and He in whom I take refuge;
Who subdueth my people under me.

3. LORD, what is man, that Thou takest knowledge of him?
Or the son of man, that Thou makest account of him?

4. Man is like unto a breath;
His days are as a shadow that passeth away.

5. O LORD, bow Thy heavens, and come down;
Touch the mountains, that they may smoke.

6. Cast forth lightning, and scatter them;
Send out Thine arrows, and discomfit them.

7. Stretch forth Thy hands from on high;

A PSALM of victory, a warrior psalm, chanting of God's aid in battle. It is dependent upon a number of previous psalms, particularly upon Psalms 8 and 18.

1-2. MY ROCK, WHO TRAINETH MY HANDS, WHO SUBDUETH MY PEOPLE UNDER ME. i. e., my rebellious subjects.

This entire passage is based upon a number of verses in Psalm 18, particularly verses 35, 47, 49.

3. LORD, WHAT IS MAN . . . THE SON OF MAN. This verse is found in Psalm 8:5.

4. Continues the thought taken from Psalm 8, that man is as nothing compared to God.

LIKE UNTO A BREATH. His life is brief.

AS A SHADOW THAT PASSETH AWAY. As insubstantial as the shadow which flits by and disappears.

5-7. This passage, describing the advent of God, coming as in a storm to aid His servant, is based upon Psalm 18:10 ff.

8. THEIR RIGHT HAND IS A RIGHT HAND OF LYING. The raising of the hand was the gesture which accompanied an oath. Thus, "For when I had brought them into the land, which I had lifted up My hand to give unto them" (i. e., which I swore to give

Rescue me, and deliver me out of many waters,
Out of the hand of strangers;
8. Whose mouth speaketh falsehood,
And their right hand is a right hand of lying.
9. O God, I will sing a new song unto Thee,
Upon a psaltery of ten strings will I sing praises
unto Thee;
10. Who givest salvation unto kings,
Who rescuest David Thy servant from the hurtful sword.
11. Rescue me, and deliver me out of the hand of strangers,
Whose mouth speaketh falsehood,
And their right hand is a right hand of lying.
12. We whose sons are as plants grown up in their youth;
Whose daughters are as corner-pillars carved after the
fashion of a palace;
13. Whose garners are full, affording all manner of store;
Whose sheep increase by thousands and ten thousands
in our fields;

unto them) Ezekiel 20:28. The psalmist here says that their promises are false promises. Their oaths are not to be relied upon. This sentence, beginning with "whose mouth speaketh," is repeated as a refrain in verse 11.

9. I WILL SING A NEW SONG. This verse is taken from Psalm 33:2 and 3.

10. WHO GIVEST SALVATION UNTO KINGS. This phrase has been taken over into the traditional Sabbath services. It is the opening sentence of a prayer for the welfare of the government. This prayer is recited after the reading of the Torah.

12 to the end. This closing paragraph envisages the blessed and peaceful life of Israel when God will have delivered them from their enemies.

12. WE WHOSE SONS ARE AS PLANTS. Similarly in Psalm 128:3, "Thy children like olive plants, round about thy table."

WHOSE DAUGHTERS ARE AS CORNER-PILLARS CARVED. The daughters will be beautiful and stately.

13. WHOSE GARNERS ARE FULL . . . WHOSE SHEEP INCREASE. Not only will our children grow up in health and beauty but the flocks and the herds will increase.

401

14. Whose oxen are well laden;
    With no breach, and no going forth,
    And no outcry in our broad places;
15. Happy is the people that is in such a case,
    Yea, happy is the people whose God is the Lord.

145. [A PSALM OF] PRAISE; OF DAVID.
I will extol Thee, my God, O King;
And I will bless Thy name for ever and ever.
2. Every day will I bless Thee;
   And I will praise Thy name for ever and ever.
3. Great is the Lord, and highly to be praised;
   And His greatness is unsearchable.
4. One generation shall laud Thy works to another,
   And shall declare Thy mighty acts.
5. The glorious splendour of Thy majesty,

14. WITH NO BREACH, AND NO GOING FORTH, AND NO OUTCRY
IN OUR BROAD PLACES. The broad place is the wide space around
the city gates where the people gather. The psalmist says there
will be no breach in our city walls, no going forth into exile
(or no need to sally forth to repel an attack), and no need for
outcry against the violence of an invading army.

15. HAPPY IS THE PEOPLE THAT IS IN SUCH A CASE. Happy the
people that will live in such circumstances. This sentence is
joined with the next Psalm when it, (Psalm 145), is recited in
the synagogue services.

AN acrostic psalm. The letter *nun* between verses 13 and
14 is missing. The Talmud says that the verse was left out because it was an ominous verse (taken from Amos 5:2) describing the complete destruction of Jerusalem: "The virgin of
Israel is fallen, she shall no more rise." This sentence begins
with the letter *nun*, the opening word being *naflah* (fallen).
The Greek translation, the Septuagint, has another verse for
the letter "n." This verse is: "Faithful is the Lord in all His
words." In Hebrew this sentence would likewise begin with an
"n," *ne'emon* ("faithful").

And Thy wondrous works, will I rehearse.
6. And men shall speak of the might of Thy tremendous acts;
And I will tell of Thy greatness.
7. They shall utter the fame of Thy great goodness,
And shall sing of Thy righteousness.
8. The LORD is gracious, and full of compassion;
Slow to anger, and of great mercy.
9. The LORD is good to all;
And His tender mercies are over all His works.
10. All Thy works shall praise Thee, O LORD;
And Thy saints shall bless Thee.
11. They shall speak of the glory of Thy kingdom,
And talk of Thy might;
12. To make known to the sons of men His mighty acts,
And the glory of the majesty of His kingdom.
13. Thy kingdom is a kingdom for all ages,

This psalm is recited three times a day in the synagogue service, twice in the morning service and once in the afternoon service. As recited in the synagogue, the psalm is prefixed by Psalm 84:5, and Psalm 144:15. In the morning service the psalm is always recited together with the next five psalms in the Psalter, Psalms 146-150. In fact, this Psalm 145, calling upon all the living to praise God, is a fitting introduction to the next five psalms, all of which are paeans of praise, beginning and ending with the word "Hallelujah," "Praise ye the Lord."

1. A PSALM OF PRAISE. The word translated here "A Psalm of praise" is *tehilloh*. The plural of this word (*tehillim*) has become the name of the Book of Psalms. Yet, strangely enough, although the Book of Psalms is called *Tehillim*, this psalm is the only one which uses the word *tehilloh* in its heading.

3. HIS GREATNESS IS UNSEARCHABLE. God's greatness is beyond the powers of man's mind to compass. The same thought is expressed in Psalm 139:6, "Such knowledge is too wonderful for me; too high, I cannot attain unto it."

8. THE LORD IS GRACIOUS . . . FULL OF COMPASSION. This description of God's mercifulness is based upon the enumeration of God's attributes given to Moses in Exodus 34:6, "The Lord, God, merciful and gracious . . ."

403

Psalm 145

13

And Thy dominion endureth throughout all generations.
14. The Lord upholdeth all that fall,
And raiseth up all those that are bowed down.
15. The eyes of all wait for Thee,
And Thou givest them their food in due season.
16. Thou openest Thy hand,
And satisfiest every living thing with favour.
17. The Lord is righteous in all His ways,
And gracious in all His works.
18. The Lord is nigh unto all them that call upon Him,
To all that call upon Him in truth.
19. He will fulfil the desire of them that fear Him;
He also will hear their cry, and will save them.
20. The Lord preserveth all them that love Him;
But all the wicked will He destroy.
21. My mouth shall speak the praise of the Lord;
And let all flesh bless His holy name for ever and ever.

14. THE LORD UPHOLDETH ALL THAT FALL. Those who are brought to the brink of despair through persecution or sickness may rely upon the help of God. Thus, "Though he fall, he shall not be utterly cast down; for the Lord upholdeth his hand" (Psalm 37:24).

15-16. THE EYES OF ALL WAIT FOR THEE . . . THOU OPENEST THY HAND. These verses, describing God's providence to all creatures, are based upon Psalm 104:27, 28.

21. LET ALL FLESH BLESS. Let all creatures bless. Genesis 6:13 also uses the word "all flesh" in the sense of all creatures, "the end of all flesh is come before Me."

PSALMS 146-150 are the closing psalms of the Psalter. They begin and close with the word "Hallelujah," "praise ye the Lord." Unlike many of the plaintive psalms in the Psalter which are the outpourings of troubled hearts, these psalms are such jubilant hymns of praise that they seem to have been written for accompaniment by instrumental music and to be chanted in the Temple.

The theme of Psalm 146 is that mortal power is merely

404

146. HALLELUJAH.
Praise the LORD, O my soul.
2. I will praise the LORD while I live;
I will sing praises unto my God while I have my being.
3. Put not your trust in princes,
Nor in the son of man, in whom there is no help.
4. His breath goeth forth, he returneth to his dust;
In that very day his thoughts perish.
5. Happy is he whose help is the God of Jacob,
Whose hope is in the LORD his God,
6. Who made heaven and earth,
The sea, and all that in them is;
Who keepeth truth for ever;
7. Who executeth justice for the oppressed;
Who giveth bread to the hungry.
The LORD looseth the prisoners;

transitory. Therefore, "Put not your trust in princes" (verse 3); God, "who made heaven and earth" is the sole source of help for the oppressed.

2. I WILL PRAISE THE LORD WHILE I LIVE. The psalmist frequently expresses the thought that the dead are not able to praise the Lord. They live "in the land of forgetfulness." Therefore, as long as he will live he will sing the praises of the Lord. This sentence, "I will praise the Lord while I live," is taken from Psalm 104:33.

3. PUT NOT YOUR TRUST IN PRINCES. The same thought is expressed in Psalm 118:9, "It is better to take refuge in the Lord than to trust in princes." Human monarchs, although they seem powerful, are as mortal as the humblest of their subjects. A king's decree may seem important but when "he returneth to his dust . . . his thoughts perish."

6. THE SEA, AND ALL THAT IN THEM IS. The sea and all the creatures that inhabit it. The same phrase is used in the Fourth Commandment (Exodus 20:11).

WHO KEEPETH TRUTH FOR EVER. The commentator, Rashi, explains this to mean, whose promises of deliverance remain true for ever.

405

$\mathcal{P}$salm 146
8

8. The LORD openeth the eyes of the blind;
    The LORD raiseth up them that are bowed down;
    The LORD loveth the righteous;
9. The LORD preserveth the strangers;
    He upholdeth the fatherless and the widow;
    But the way of the wicked He maketh crooked.
10. The LORD will reign for ever,
    Thy God, O Zion, unto all generations.
    Hallelujah.

147. HALLELUJAH;
    For it is good to sing praises unto our God;
    For it is pleasant, and praise is comely.
2. The LORD doth build up Jerusalem,
    He gathereth together the dispersed of Israel;

9. THE LORD PRESERVETH THE STRANGERS. Strangers who, among all other ancient people, were regarded with suspicion and even with hostility, are described in the Bible as the special wards of God. And Israel, obeying God's command, is asked to be especially considerate of strangers. Thus, "Love ye therefore the stranger; for ye were strangers in the land of Egypt" (Deuteronomy 10:19). Also, "The stranger that sojourneth with you shall be unto you as the home-born among you, and thou shalt love him as thyself" (Leviticus 19:34).

THE WAY OF THE WICKED HE MAKETH CROOKED. The path of the wicked becomes twisted and confused. It leads nowhere. The same thought is expressed at the end of Psalm 1: "The Lord regardeth the way of the righteous; but the way of the wicked shall perish."

10. THE LORD WILL REIGN FOR EVER, etc. This sentence is used in the synagogue services as the ending for the Sanctification (the *Kedushah*).

THE psalmist calls upon the worshippers to praise God for having rebuilt Jerusalem; and then speaks of God's mastery over nature. He "prepareth rain for the earth" (verse 8); "He

406

3. Who healeth the broken in heart,
   And bindeth up their wounds.
4. He counteth the number of the stars;
   He giveth them all their names.
5. Great is our Lord, and mighty in power;
   His understanding is infinite.
6. The LORD upholdeth the humble;
   He bringeth the wicked down to the ground.
7. Sing unto the LORD with thanksgiving,
   Sing praises upon the harp unto our God;
8. Who covereth the heaven with clouds,
   Who prepareth rain for the earth,
   Who maketh the mountains to spring with grass.
9. He giveth to the beast his food,
   And to the young ravens which cry.

hath blessed thy children within thee" (verse 13) ; "He causeth His wind to blow, and the waters flow" (verse 18).

1. TO SING PRAISES . . . IS PLEASANT . . . IS COMELY. It is a joy to us and it becometh us to praise God. The same phrase is found in the opening sentence of Psalm 33.

2. DOTH BUILD UP JERUSALEM, GATHERETH TOGETHER THE DISPERSED OF ISRAEL. This verse seems to indicate that the psalm was written in the early days of the return from Babylon when the small community was endeavoring to rebuild the ruined city of Jerusalem.

3. HEALETH THE BROKEN IN HEART, AND BINDETH UP THEIR WOUNDS. God, who has punished us, will also forgive and heal us. The prophet Hosea, comforting the people of Israel, says: "Let us return unto the Lord; for He hath torn, and He will heal us, He hath smitten, and He will bind us up" (Hosea 6:1).

4. HE COUNTETH . . . THE STARS, HE GIVETH THEM ALL THEIR NAMES. God, who has created the heavens encompasses them all with His infinite knowledge. See Isaiah 40:26, "Lift up your eyes on high, and see: who hath created these? He that bringeth out their host (i. e., the host of the stars) by number, He calleth them all by name."

9. HE GIVETH TO THE BEAST HIS FOOD. All living creatures de-

407

10. He delighteth not in the strength of the horse;
    He taketh no pleasure in the legs of a man.
11. The LORD taketh pleasure in them that fear Him,
    In those that wait for His mercy.
12. Glorify the LORD, O Jerusalem;
    Praise thy God, O Zion.
13. For He hath made strong the bars of thy gates;
    He hath blessed thy children within thee.
14. He maketh thy borders peace;
    He giveth thee in plenty the fat of wheat.
15. He sendeth out His commandment upon earth;
    His word runneth very swiftly.

pend upon God for their sustenance. The same thought is expressed in Psalm 104:27, "All of them (all creatures) wait for Thee, that Thou mayest give them their food in due season."

TO THE YOUNG RAVENS WHICH CRY. The commentator, Kimchi, says that ravens are born white; the parent birds do not recognize them as their offspring and abandon them. Therefore, God sends the young ravens their food. The psalmist means that the young and the helpless of all living creatures depend upon God for their life.

10. DELIGHTETH NOT IN THE STRENGTH OF THE HORSE . . . IN THE LEGS OF A MAN. The strength of a war horse or the fleetness of a warrior are as nothing in the eyes of God. God taketh pleasure only "in them that fear Him" (verse 11), i. e., in those who revere His name. The same description of the insignificance of the strength of warrior and war horse is found in Psalm 33:16, 17. "A mighty man is not delivered by great strength; a horse is a vain thing for safety."

13. BLESSED THY CHILDREN WITHIN THEE. Within thy walls, O Zion.

14. THE FAT OF WHEAT. The fatness or the richness of wheat. The same phrase is found in Psalm 81:17, "They should also be fed with the fat of wheat."

17. HE CASTETH FORTH HIS ICE LIKE CRUMBS. Hailstones.

19-20. HE DECLARETH . . . HIS ORDINANCES UNTO ISRAEL. That he has not dealt so with any nation. The psalmist expresses here

408

16. He giveth snow like wool;
    He scattereth the hoar-frost like ashes.
17. He casteth forth His ice like crumbs;
    Who can stand before His cold?
18. He sendeth forth His word, and melteth them;
    He causeth His wind to blow,
    And the waters flow.
19. He declareth His word unto Jacob,
    His statutes and His ordinances unto Israel.
20. He hath not dealt so with any nation;
    And as for His ordinances, they have not known them.
    Hallelujah.

a thought found frequently in the Book of Deuteronomy, that it is a joy and a privilege to obey God's statutes and ordinances; that Israel should be grateful for having been given the opportunity to obey God's commandment. Thus, "And what great nation is there, that hath statutes and ordinances so righteous as all this law, which I set before you this day?" (Deuteronomy 4:8). The rabbis explain that the privilege of possessing the law was not offered to Israel alone, that God had offered it to many nations first, but that they did not wish to bind themselves to obey its strict injunctions. (Sifre 142 b.) In fact, Israel itself hesitated to accept the burden of the law but, the rabbis say, God virtually forced them to accept it. (b. Shabbas 88 a.)

The psalmist speaks in Psalm 148 of God as the Creator of the world. He begins the psalm by calling, not upon the worshippers in the Temple, but upon the heavens and the angels to praise God who created them. Then he turns to all living creatures on earth and asks them to praise the Lord. The psalm, therefore, is a mighty antiphony, in which heaven and earth alternate in the praise of the Infinite Creator. This magnificent conception—man joining in the chorus of the heavens to praise the Lord—is found also in the *Kedushah* (the Sanctification) in the daily service in the synagogue. This prayer, built around the sentence in Isaiah 6:3, "Holy, holy, holy, is the Lord of

409

148. HALLELUJAH.

Praise ye the LORD from the heavens;
Praise Him in the heights.
2. Praise ye Him, all His angels;
Praise ye Him, all His hosts.
3. Praise ye Him, sun and moon;
Praise Him, all ye stars of light.
4. Praise Him, ye heavens of heavens,
And ye waters that are above the heavens.
5. Let them praise the name of the LORD;
For He commanded, and they were created.
6. He hath also established them for ever and ever;
He hath made a decree which shall not
be transgressed.
7. Praise the LORD from the earth,
Ye sea-monsters, and all deeps;

hosts," is introduced by this sentence: "We hallow Thy name on earth even as it is hallowed in Heaven."

2. HIS ANGELS . . . HIS HOSTS. The phrase, "Lord of Hosts," has meant, "The Lord of the heavenly hosts" as well as the Lord who aided Israel's hosts.

4. YE HEAVENS OF HEAVENS. i. e., the highest heavens. This phrase is found also in Psalm 68:34, "To Him that rideth upon the heavens of heavens."

YE WATERS THAT ARE ABOVE THE HEAVENS. According to the account in Genesis, God created heaven and earth by dividing the waters. Thus, there were waters below the heavens, i. e., the seas, and waters above the heavens. See Genesis 1:6.

6. HE HATH MADE A DECREE WHICH SHALL NOT BE TRANS-GRESSED. God established the heavens to obey His will. They follow His decree. His changeless laws govern the universe.

7-14. The psalmist turns his attention from the heavenly hosts to the earth. He speaks first of the sea, then of the winds, the mountains and the beasts, the kings, the princes and the humble, old and young, and finally, the people of Israel. All of them are called upon to praise the Lord. Thus the first half of the psalm says: "Praise ye the Lord from the heavens"

8. Fire and hail, snow and vapour,
Stormy wind, fulfilling His word;
9. Mountains and all hills,
Fruitful trees and all cedars;
10. Beasts and all cattle,
Creeping things and winged fowl;
11. Kings of the earth and all peoples,
Princes and all judges of the earth;
12. Both young men and maidens,
Old men and children;
13. Let them praise the name of the LORD,
For His name alone is exalted;
His glory is above the earth and heaven.
14. And He hath lifted up a horn for His people,
A praise for all His saints,
Even for the children of Israel, a people near unto Him.
Hallelujah.

(verse 1), and the second half: "Praise the Lord from the earth."

14. LIFTED UP A HORN FOR HIS PEOPLE. As a stag proudly raises his horn. The "lifting up of the horn" is a symbol of dignity and pride. God, delivering Israel from his sorrows, gives him pride and self-respect. Thus, "My horn hast Thou exalted like the horn of the wild-ox" (Psalm 92:11).

The closing sentences of the Psalm, beginning with "His glory is above the heaven" (verse 13), are recited in the synagogue when the Scroll is returned to the Ark.

PSALM 149 is addressed to Israel, calling upon the people to praise God with singing and dancing. The psalm ends in a stern tone, speaking of punishment to be meted out to the surrounding nations. Evidently, it was written at a time when Israel's joy was marred by the hostility of the peoples about them. The successive phrases, "The praises of God in their mouth" and "a two-edged sword in their hand" (verse 6), seem to reflect the circumstances in the early days of the return when the various nations used every means to prevent the new community from rebuilding the walls of Jerusalem. Nehemiah de-

149. HALLELUJAH.

Sing unto the LORD a new song,
And His praise in the assembly of the saints.
2. Let Israel rejoice in his Maker;
Let the children of Zion be joyful in their King.
3. Let them praise His name in the dance;
Let them sing praises unto Him with the
timbrel and harp.
4. For the LORD taketh pleasure in His people;
He adorneth the humble with salvation.
5. Let the saints exult in glory;
Let them sing for joy upon their beds.
6. Let the high praises of God be in their mouth,

scribes the hostility of the Arabians and the Ammonites and the Ashdodites. Their enmity was so great that the masons working on the walls had to carry swords: "They that builded the wall and they that bore burdens . . . every one with one of his hands wrought in the work, and with the other held his weapon" (Nehemiah 4:11).

1. A NEW SONG. Since God's mercies are renewed every day our songs to Him must spring anew from every grateful heart. (See Psalm 96:1.)

3. LET THEM PRAISE HIS NAME IN THE DANCE. Dancing was widely used among ancient peoples as a religious ceremonial. Miriam and all the women danced when they sang their hymns to God by the Red Sea. (Exodus 15:20.) David danced before the Ark. (II Samuel 6:14.) In the post-exilic community dancing was part of the celebration of at least one festival. During the festival of Succoth, at the end of the first day, a vast concourse of people gathered to see in the Temple Court the great torch-dance, i. e., the dance of the water festival. (m. Succah V, 2-4.) (See "Feast of the Water Drawing," *Jewish Encyclopedia*, Vol. XII, p. 476.)

4. HE ADORNETH THE HUMBLE WITH SALVATION. The salvation and the deliverance which God will grant to the humble will adorn them with dignity and honor.

And a two-edged sword in their hand;
7. To execute vengeance upon the nations,
   And chastisements upon the peoples;
8. To bind their kings with chains,
   And their nobles with fetters of iron;
9. To execute upon them the judgment written;
   He is the glory of all His saints.
   Hallelujah.

150. HALLELUJAH.

Praise God in His sanctuary;
Praise Him in the firmament of His power.
2. Praise Him for His mighty acts;
   Praise Him according to His abundant greatness.

6. A TWO-EDGED SWORD IN THEIR HAND. See introduction to this psalm.

TO EXECUTE VENGEANCE UPON THE NATIONS. The commentator, Ibn Ezra, says this means, "to bring them to serve God together," i. e., to punish them for their sins and thus lead them to righteousness.

9. THE JUDGMENT WRITTEN. The judgment which God has pronounced against the wicked so that they may return to Him and know that "He is the glory of all His saints," i. e., of all the righteous.

THIS psalm calls upon the worshippers in the sanctuary and all the hosts of the heavens to praise God together. He builds up a symphony of instrumental music whose tones blend in praise of God. This entire psalm can be considered the doxology for the whole Book of Psalms. After all the sufferings and sorrow, and after all the despair and heartbreak which come into human life, the conclusion of all the varied experiences, personal and social, recorded in the Psalter is: "Let everything that hath breath praise the Lord."

1. IN HIS SANCTUARY . . . IN THE FIRMAMENT. In the Temple and in the heavens.

413

𝒫salm 150

3

3. Praise Him with the blast of the horn;
   Praise Him with the psaltery and harp.
4. Praise Him with the timbrel and dance;
   Praise Him with stringed instruments and the pipe.
5. Praise Him with the loud-sounding cymbals;
   Praise Him with the clanging cymbals.
6. Let every thing that hath breath praise the LORD.
   Hallelujah.

3. THE PSALTERY. A stringed instrument.

4. TIMBREL AND DANCE. The tambourine which accompanies the dance.

6. LET EVERYTHING THAT HATH BREATH PRAISE THE LORD. Samuel Francis Smith used this line in the hymn "America":

> "Let mortal tongues awake
> Let all that breathe partake."

The verse, "Let everything that hath breath praise the Lord," is a fitting close for the Psalm Book. It sounds a noble universal tone. Not only the Levites in the Temple but all of Israel; not only Israel but all of mankind; all that breathe are asked to join in the final "Hallelujah," "Praise ye the Lord."

414